Making Use of JavaScript

Shweta Bhasin

Wiley Publishing, Inc.

Publisher: Robert Ipsen
Editor: Ben Ryan
Assistant Editor: Kathryn A. Malm
Managing Editor: Pamela Hanley
New Media Editor: Brian Snapp
Text Design & Composition: John Wiley Composition Services

Designations used by companies to distinguish their products are often claimed as trademarks. In all instances where John Wiley & Sons, Inc., is aware of a claim, the product names appear in initial capital or ALL CAPITAL LETTERS. Readers, however, should contact the appropriate companies for more complete information regarding trademarks and registration.

This book is printed on acid-free paper. ∞

Published by Wiley Publishing, Inc.

Published simultaneously in Canada.

This publication is designed to provide accurate and authoritative information in regard to the subject matter covered. It is sold with the understanding that the publisher is not engaged in professional services. If professional advice or other expert assistance is required, the services of a competent professional person should be sought.

Library of Congress Cataloging-in-Publication Data:

Bhasin, Shweta, 1977-
  Making use of JavaScript / Shweta Bhasin.
    p. cm.
"Wiley Computer Publishing."
Includes index.
  ISBN 0-471-21976-2 (paperback : acid-free paper)
  1. JavaScript (Computer program language) I. Title.
QA76.73.J39 B45 2002
005.13'3--dc21
                        2002007257

Wiley also publishes its books in a variety of electronic formats. Some content that appears in print may not be available in electronic books.

Printed in the United States of America.

10 9 8 7 6 5 4 3 2 1

Contents

Introduction

The tremendous growth of the World Wide Web has resulted in a demand for dynamic and interactive Web sites. To attract customer attention on the Web, companies need to hire experts for creating their Web sites. There is a tremendous scope for those who want to be the pillars of such companies by mastering scripting languages that give life to Web sites. One such language that is easy to master and handle is JavaScript.

This book is an attempt to bridge the ever-increasing gap between the market demand and availability of such expertise. The first step in becoming an expert involves gaining in-depth knowledge of JavaScript, and that is exactly what this book offers. The book will begin with the basics of scripting and then discusses the intricacies of scripting.

Along with conceptual information, the book will provide extensive practical exercises for the reader. This will help the reader gain valuable exposure to the procedures for designing Web sites by using JavaScript. The book content will consist of lucid examples, code sample, visuals, and demonstrations. The concepts covered will be supported adequately by case studies that will be formulated in such a way that they provide a frame of reference for the reader. Problems are presented to the reader against the backdrop of real-life scenarios. The practical approach followed will help readers understand the real-life application and usage of JavaScript in various scenarios.

The aim of this book is to make learning an enjoyable and energizing process.

Overview of JavaScript

JavaScript is a powerful scripting language that enables you to add dynamism and interactivity to your Web pages. The following are a few things that JavaScript enables you to do:

- Collect data from HTML forms and process the same on a user's computer without having to interact with a server

- Create and store data on a user's computer by using cookies
- Add interactivity to graphics
- Modify page elements dynamically based on user input

Technologies Before JavaScript

Before JavaScript came into existence, it was a tiresome and tedious job for Web developers to create interactive Web pages. Web developers used a scripting language known as Common Gateway Interface (CGI) to collect and process user input. Since a CGI script is processed on a server, it has a lot of overheads attached to it, which create unnecessary load on the processing time of a Web page. For instance, to use a CGI script, you first need to design an HTML-based user interface that will accept data from a user. Then, you need to create a CGI script, which is written in advanced languages, such as Perl or C, to process the data on the server. After this is done, each time a user accesses the Web page and submits the form, the data is sent from the Web browser to the CGI script on the server. The CGI script then processes the data and returns the processed output to the user in a new HTML-based Web document. This process is repeated each time a user makes new entries in the HTML form. This absorbs the CPU power of server and also wastes the transmission time between the client and the server.

Why Use JavaScript?

JavaScript addresses many of the problems discussed in the preceding section by collecting and processing the data in the Web browser of a user's computer. JavaScript is an interpreted language. This implies that it does not need any executable file on a specific user's computer. Instead, JavaScript code executes on a JavaScript interpreter, which is built into a user's browser. JavaScript code executes on any system with a JavaScript-capable browser, such as Netscape Navigator 2.0 or later or Microsoft Internet Explorer 3.0 or later, and on any computer platform.

History of JavaScript

Netscape Corporation initially developed a language called LiveScript that provided basic scripting capabilities to both Navigator and its Web server. Later, when support for Java Applets was added to Navigator 2, Netscape signed a contract with Sun Microsystems and in the process, named LiveScript as JavaScript. The renaming of LiveScript to JavaScript was mainly due to Java's popularity than due to any similarity between the two languages.

The original version of JavaScript, also called LiveScript, was named JavaScript 1.0. It is supported by Navigator 2.0 and Internet Explorer 3.0. Netscape later introduced JavaScript 1.1 with Navigator 3 and JavaScript 1.2 with Navigator 4. JavaScript 1.1, which is also supported by Internet Explorer 4.0, introduced features such as support for more browser objects and user-defined functions. JavaScript 1.2, which is also partially supported by Internet Explorer 4.0, added new objects, properties, and methods and support for style sheets, layers, regular expressions, and signed scripts.

Since no standards were defined for scripting languages, Netscape and Microsoft submitted their scripting languages to the European Computer Manufacturers Association (ECMA) for standardization. Taking into account the best features of JavaScript and Microsoft JScript, ECMA released the ECMA-262 Standard. This standard is also popularly known as standards for ECMAScripting. Based on ECMAScripting standards, Netscape released its new version, JavaScript 1.3, which is supported by Navigator 4.06 and 4.5.

Having discussed the history of JavaScript, let us look at some myths attached with this language.

JavaScript Myth

JavaScript is the subject of a fair bit of misinformation and confusion. Therefore, it is important that we demystify a common and unrelenting myth about the language.

JavaScript and Java

Since JavaScript and Java share a similar name, there has been a fallacy that JavaScript is a simplified version of Java, which is the programming language of Sun Microsystems. Other than an incomplete syntactic similarity and the fact that both Java and JavaScript can provide executable content in Web browsers, the two are entirely unrelated.

Table I.1 compares JavaScript and Java.

JAVASCRIPT	JAVA
Interpreted by the client-side computer.	Compiled on the server before being executed on the client-side computer.
Supports dynamic binding. Object references are checked at run time.	Supports static binding. Object references must exist at compile time.
Does not have explicit data types. Therefore, there is no need to declare variable data types.	Variable data types must be declared.
Code is integrated with and embedded in HTML.	Code is not integrated with HTML.
Is limited to browser functions.	Applications written in Java are stand-alone applications.
Can access browser objects and their functionality.	Java has no access to browser objects or their functionality.

Features of JavaScript

JavaScript supports both client-side and server-side scripting. The client- and the server-side JavaScript share same basic programming features. Here are some of the features of JavaScript:

- **Event-driven:** JavaScript can respond to events such as mouse movements and the loading of a Web page.

- **Platform-independent:** JavaScript programs are designed to run inside HTML documents. These programs are not dependent on any specific hardware platform or operating system. You can run JavaScript on Netscape Navigator 2.0 or higher or on Internet Explorer 3.0 or higher.

- **Enables quick development:** JavaScript does not require time-consuming compilation. Scripts can be developed in a relatively short time. This is enhanced by the fact that browser and HTML code handles most interface features, such as forms, frames, and Graphical User Interface (GUI) elements. JavaScript programmers do not need to create or handle these elements for their applications.

- **No complex syntax or set of rules:** Even if you do not know any programming language, it will not be difficult to learn JavaScript. A basic knowledge of HTML would be sufficient for you to learn JavaScript.

- **Object-based, not object-oriented:** An object-oriented program handles a program as a collection of individual objects that are used for specific tasks and not as a sequence of statements that perform a specific task. JavaScript is not object-oriented, as it does not allow object inheritance. JavaScript is, however, an *object-based* language because it depends on a collection of built-in objects for its functionality. Using JavaScript, you can create your own objects.

How This Book Is Organized

This book steers clear of the traditional content-based approach and uses a problem-based approach to deliver the concepts of JavaScript. The problems presented in the book relate to real-life scenarios. Each problem is followed by a task list that helps solve the given problem, in the process delivering the concepts and their implementation. This practical approach will help readers understand the real-life application of the language and its usage in various scenarios. Moreover, to provide appropriate learning experience, the concepts discussed will be supported adequately by case studies that will be formulated in such a way that they provide a frame of reference to the reader.

This book is organized into three parts. Part One is a detailed introduction to JavaScript; Part Two delves into developing basic applications by using JavaScript; and Part Three moves further into developing advanced applications by using browser objects, cookies, plug-ins, layers and server-side scripting.

Chapter 1 introduces the essential Internet concepts that a reader should be aware of before proceeding to other chapters. This chapter provides an introduction to frequently used Internet terminology and also offers a brief introduction to effective cross-browser application development.

Chapter 2 is a getting-started guide that discusses the basics of JavaScript. This chapter discusses the basic syntax of embedding JavaScript in HTML documents. Then, the chapter gives a solution for executing JavaScript applications in a JavaScript-incompatible browser. Next, the chapter discusses how you can add comments to JavaScript and details a comparison between HTML and JavaScript comments. The chapter also introduces JavaScript external files. Finally, the chapter discusses how you can create HTML tags in JavaScript scripts.

Chapter 3 introduces you to the programming basics of JavaScript. The chapter covers concepts such as data types, literals, expressions, and operators that are used in JavaScript. The chapter begins by discussing how to create variables and assign values to these variables. Then, it explores the different data types, such as Number, String, Boolean, Null, Undefined, and Arrays, supported by JavaScript. Moving ahead, the chapter guides you through the process of displaying the data stored in a variable on a Web page. Finally, the chapter gives details about various types of operators and then proceeds to explain how these operators merge with variables to form different expressions.

Chapter 4 covers concepts related to the conditional and looping statements of JavaScript. The chapter discusses each of these statements in isolation to each other. Conditional statements cover the `if` statement, the `if...else` statement, the `else...if` statement, and the `switch` statement. Looping statements cover the `while` statement, the `do...while` statement, and the `for` statement. The chapter also discusses the `break` and `continue` statements used in JavaScript.

Chapter 5 illustrates the use of functions and events in JavaScript. The chapter discusses the types of functions and the difference between user-defined functions and built-in functions. Next, the chapter discusses how functions help add and implement dynamism, readability, and efficiency in a program. Next, the chapter discusses the concept of events in JavaScript. The chapter introduces you to event-handling functions and informs you about the way you can associate events with user interface actions. Finally, the chapter delves into how you can merge user-defined functions, built-in functions, and events to provide dynamism to a Web page.

Chapter 6 introduces the concepts of objects and object-oriented programming languages. It begins with an introduction to the difference between object-oriented and object-based programming. Then, it discusses the JavaScript object model. The chapter gives details about various pre-defined object types, such as `Array`, `Object`, `Boolean`, `String`, `Date`, `Global`, `Math`, and `Number`. Finally, the chapter discusses how to create custom object types in JavaScript.

Chapter 7 delves into error handling concepts. The chapter begins with an introduction on how and why errors occur in a program. It then progresses with an explanation on how the `error` event provides the capability of handling the errors that are generated in a document. Next, the chapter introduces you to exception handling using the `Error` object and the `try...catch...finally` block. Finally, the concept of the nested `try...catch` statement is discussed that is also used with the `throw` statement.

Chapter 8 covers the concepts of controlling the features and functions of a Web browser. The chapter discusses the six main objects of the JavaScript browser hierarchy model: window, document, history, location, form, and frames. Each of these objects is discussed in the context of a separate scenario keeping in mind the practical implementation of these in real life.

Chapter 9 introduces the important concept of cookies and how they are implemented using JavaScript. The chapter begins with an introduction on how you can maintain the state information of a Web browser. Next, the chapter discusses the modus operandi of a cookie, its common features, application areas, and its limitations. Finally, the chapter discusses the built-in functions that are used to create, set, and read the cookies saved on a client's computer.

Chapter 10 gives an introduction to plug-ins and the methods used in JavaScript to interact with plug-ins. The chapter provided an overview of the development process involved in creating a plug-in.

Chapter 11 gives a detailed explanation on style sheets and the methods used in JavaScript to interact with style sheets. Next, the chapter discusses cascade style sheets and how they help Web developers create style sheets at different levels and then use them together to generate a cascade effect. The chapter also gives a brief introduction to DHTML and the layers in JavaScript.

Chapter 12 discusses developing server-side scripts with the Microsoft IIS server. The chapter assumes that the reader has basic knowledge about server-side scripting, databases, RDBMS concepts, and their implementation. The chapter begins by comparing two technologies, ASP and LiveWire and suggesting when each of them may be appropriate for use. The chapter discusses the various server-side objects of ASP, such as Request, Response, Application, and Session. The various properties, collections, and methods of each of these objects are also discussed in detail. Finally, the chapter delves into the concept of database interaction using ADO objects.

The Appendix introduces JavaScript as a server-side scripting language. Appendix is divided into three sections. The first section discusses the implementation of JavaScript as a server-side scripting language by using LiveWire. The second section details the basic concepts of databases, RDBMS concepts, and their implementation. The third section delves into discussing how you can use LiveWire to interact with databases.

Who Should Read this Book

This book would be a guide for readers with a basic knowledge of HTML and no experience in scripting. For those with intermediary knowledge, the book also covers the advanced concepts of JavaScript. In a nutshell, this will be a book that a JavaScript developer must not miss out on. The book will be of great help to people with the following job titles:

- Software engineers
- Web application developers

The book will provide the necessary skills to create GUI Web applications.

Tools You Will Need

To perform the tasks listed in this book, you will need a Pentium 200-MHz computer with a minimum of 64 -B RAM (128-MB RAM recommended).

You will also need the following software:

- **Operating system:** Windows 98 or Windows NT server
- **Web browser:** Internet Explorer 3.0 or higher and Netscape Navigator 3.0 or higher
- **Web Server:** Internet Information Server (IIS) 4.0
- **RDBMS:** MS Access 2000

While reading this book, you will notice that most of the codes are either executed in Internet Explorer 6 or in Navigator 6. The exhibits depict the same.

Installations

To view and create JavaScript-enabled Web pages, no special installations are required. All you need is a text editor, such as Notepad, and the latest version of Netscape Navigator or Internet Explorer. In fact, you should be using at least a 3.0 version of Navigator or IE.

What's on the Web Site

All the code snippets used in the book will be available on the site www.wiley.com/compbooks/makinguse.

Scenario

All the problem statements in this book are based on the scenario of Web Shoppe, the online shopping mall. The following section elaborates on the how the Web Shoppe site evolved.

Web Shoppe: Online Shopping Mall

Scott, a senior developer in the technical support team of Toy Universe, one day walked into his office and found a note on his workstation from his team leader, Victor Singer. Victor wanted Scott to go and meet Cynthia, the founder and CEO of Toy Universe Inc. one of the leading toy stores. As Scott walked down to Cynthia's cabin, he wondered what the call was all about...

During his meeting with Cynthia, he learned that because the store had been performing very well the management was considering its expansion. The store had been receiving requests from various product manufacturers and traders who wanted to explore the possibility of selling their products online to achieve an increase in sales. The requests came from a wide range of product manufacturers ranging from Book Marts to Jewelry Marts.

Considering the vast number of requests, Cynthia conducted a survey of existing customers to find out the type of products they would be interested in buying from an on-line store. Based on the results of the survey, Cynthia short-listed three products to be added to the toy store: flowers, confectionery, and books. She decided to convert the toy store into an online shopping mall named Web Shoppe.

Cynthia decided that the technical support department would be responsible for creating, deploying, and maintaining the site. The technical support department will primarily consist of developers who will write the code for the site and a system administrator who will maintain the computer systems and the servers used. Scott has been appointed as the head of the development team for creating and maintaining the Web Shoppe site.

Site Architecture

Scott and the development team of Web Shoppe have together decided that they will try that there is minimum interaction with the server to reduce the load on the server. Therefore, all validations and processing of data for the site will be performed on the client computer. To implement this, JavaScript will be used. In addition, Active Server Pages will be used for interacting with the IIS server. The back-end server would be Access that will store site-related data. The following will be the structure of the site:

The site will implement a shopping cart that will accept valid global credit cards for payment for the products bought online.

To purchase products, each user will need to create a login id in the site. After a user creates a login id, all personal details pertaining to that user will be stored in a table in a database. To send updates to the customer, this information will be used from time to time and will also be updated as and when a user purchases products.

The products available on the site will be categorized on the following basis:

Toys

Flowers

Confectionery

Books

User Interface of the Site

The user interface will primarily include the following:

A page that will accept a customer's name and take the customer to the home page.

The home page will display details about how Web Shoppe evolved. It will also display a personalized message along with the number of times the customer has visited the site. The home page will also have links to various other sections of the site.

A page that accepts the login id and password of the customer and takes the customer to the shopping cart page.

After the customer has added the items to be purchased to the cart, a page for accepting the personal details of the user will appear. Customers who have earlier made a purchase from this site, the page will display the details. The customer will be allowed to make modifications to the details.

A page displaying the video listing of all the products will also be added to the site. Customers who don't have the necessary software to view video files will be given the necessary directions to view the files.

The site will also allow the customer to change the styles applied to the various elements on the page according to the customer's preferences. Two options will be available to the customer. The first option will display the Web site in a corporate style by using varying shades of gray and black and formal fonts. The other option will use different colors and styles to present a colorful Web site.

Future Plans

As part of the future plans, the Technical Support team along with the Marketing team has decided to implement the following:

Improve the product collection available for sale by adding items to each of the following product categories:

Toys

Flowers

Confectionery

Books

Introduce a new range of clothing that would include sweatshirts, headbands, jackets, and carry bags displaying the Web Shoppe logo.

Create a page where details about products will be available in text files and will be freely downloadable.

Introduce a page that will display the new products available on the site. This page will also display discount schemes available on the product.

Introducing Web Development

Getting Started

The Internet represents a transformation and evolution of the entire information age. It has been the most common word of the last decade and is still gaining popularity. It is an amazing phenomenon that is spreading like wildfire! Before the advent of the Internet, sending or receiving data within a matter of seconds to someone located on the other side of the Pacific was unthinkable. However, in this Internet-oriented world, transferring data to anyone across the globe is just a matter of a few keystrokes. But what is the Internet? What are the services available on it? How does it facilitate access of information with such ease? If these questions have been on your mind for quite some time, then this chapter is for you!

This chapter deals with the history of the Internet, how the Internet operates, the Internet governing bodies, and its various access methods. The chapter also discusses various components of the Internet that enable you to access its various services. It also introduces you to issues like cross-browser capability and the key to effective cross-browser development.

Let's start with a definition of the Internet.

What Is the Internet?

The Internet is a collection of computers of different types that belong to diverse networks all over the world.

This definition of the Internet sounds very technical. It uses technical terms like "computers of different types" and "diverse networks." Let us therefore break this definition into parts and understand its meaning.

- **Collection of computers of different types.** Computers of different types mean that the Internet can contain computers of different configurations. For example, a Unix-based computer can interact with a Windows based-computer.

- **Diverse networks.** By definition a network contains a group of computers that are linked and that facilitate sharing of computer equipment and programs, messages, and information. Therefore, diverse network means that several different networks combine to create a large network called the Internet. Earlier, computer networks were limited to Local Area Networks (LANs) and Wide Area Networks (WANs). However, the Internet tries to connect LANs and WANs, and so on. As a result, the Internet can also be referred to as a network of networks.

- **All over the world.** This means that one can, regardless of location and time, connect to the Internet. The Internet has connected the world by linking computers located in the remotest of locations.

Now we have defined the Internet. Let us move ahead and see how the Internet has evolved over the years.

How Did the Internet Evolve?

The Internet began 30 years ago when an agency of the U.S. Department of Defense (DoD) called Defense Advanced Research Projects Agency (DARPA) initiated a project as a reaction to the Cold War (1969). That agency, realizing that the military communications network needed improvement, formed a network called Advanced

Research Projects Agency (ARPA). Before DARPA was formed, technology allowed exchange of messages in one direction only. This meant that if one computer crashed, the complete network would be immobilized. To overcome this shortcoming, DARPA envisaged a more efficient system in which information could be sent through several networks and to several destinations instantly, and if one network crashed, the information could be routed through other networks. This new network later came to be known as ARPANET and allowed more than 10,000 people to access different services at one time.

While the U.S. Department of Defense was still endeavoring to build on a secure channel for communication to counter the threat of a nuclear war, the scenario changed. The Cold War began to wane, and nuclear threats began to subside. The end of the Cold War defeated the very purpose of developing ARPANET. Since this project used very expensive supercomputers, the Defense Department did not find the cost associated with this project reasonable. However, at the same time, there were other developments taking place in universities where the supercomputers for ARPANET were installed. In these universities, the researchers working for ARPANET began using the network for exchanging messages among colleagues located in other places. Eventually, the exchange of electronic messages spread across countries, and, ultimately, all over the world. These internetworks among countries later came to be known as "internet." In a short time, thousands of universities, government agencies, and even businesses began to connect to computers globally. By the mid-1980's, the contemporary Internet began to take shape.

Having looked at the evolution of the Internet, we will introduce you to how the Internet operates.

How Does the Internet Operate?

As stated earlier, a computer network facilitates sharing of resources among computers. The important feature of a network is that it allows data transfer in the form of files between two particular computers. But how does transmission of data takes place? Transmission of data on a network requires a secure mode of transferring data in the form of electronic signals and the address of the source and the destination computer.

Before we proceed further with the explanation of the above two requirements, let's first familiarize you with some terms that are very commonly used in the Internet scenario: the client, the server, and the client/server network. These three terms will lay the foundation for understanding how data is transferred over a network.

Client

A client is a destination computer on the network that requests services from another computer on the network. This computer requires adequate access permissions to be able to request services and access resources from other computers.

Server

A server is a source computer that receives requests from the client computer, processes these requests, and serves the requested information and/or data to the client computer. The server computer has a range of services to offer to a client; for example, a server computer can offer information, software, games, music, and print services. However, the client can access these services only if it has adequate permissions. The server computer delineates these permissions for the client.

The Client/Server Network

The client/server network forms the basis of computer connectivity on a network. This network consists of several client computers that are connected to the server and also to each other. Let's discuss the request/response cycle in a client/server network.

The client computer sends a request to the server computer. The server computer accepts the request if the client has necessary permissions. Assuming that the server computer accepts the client request, the server then serves the requested information to the client computer.

Figure 1.1 illustrates how client computers interact with server computers in the client/server network.

The Internet also follows the client/server architecture where several clients and servers interoperate with each other. In the Internet scenario, a server is also termed a Web server or the host computer, which provides Web services to clients on the Internet. However, a client as well as a server can also host information to another computer, and thus act as a client and a server.

We now understand how computers are placed in a network and what role or roles they play. Let's proceed with the requirements of data transmission on a network.

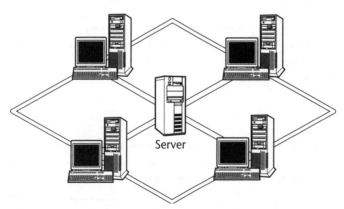

Figure 1.1   Client/server network.

Mode of Data Transmission

The Internet is an open network that is prone to a large number of network attacks, such as intrusions and hacking. As a result, to transmit data over the Internet, you need to follow certain rules and/or protocols that can help you transmit data in a secure manner. These rules are implemented in two sections on the network and are known as Transmission Control Protocol (TCP) and the Internet Protocol (IP), or collectively as TCP/IP. TCP is used to divide data into smaller data packets, also called *datagrams*, before data is transferred over a network. To ensure that packets are reassembled without any data being lost or damaged in transit, TCP also attaches special information to the packets, such as the packet location and error rectification code.

The role of IP is to attach the destination address information (client/address information) onto packets. The packets on the Internet are passed through various paths on a network to balance the load. After passing through various network paths, the packets reach the destination address and TCP reassembles the packets using the attached information.

Until now, we have discussed how data flows from one computer to another. There is another vital ingredient in data transmission, that is, the address of the source (server) and destination (client) computer. These addresses are called IP addresses. IP addresses will be discussed in detail later in this chapter. However, at this point, it is important to know that each computer has a unique IP address assigned to it. Now to facilitate communication between the client and the server on the Internet, it is essential for the client computer to know the address of the Web server from which it wishes to extract information. In the same manner, it is also essential for the server computer to know the address of the client computer to which it has to route the data packets.

Now that we have discussed the operational aspects of the Internet, we will introduce the following guidelines. We will revisit these concepts many times in the course of the chapter.

- **High-speed connections form the backbone of the Internet.** These high-speed connections are capable of transferring large volumes of data between strategic locations. Many such high-speed connections are owned and operated by different telecommunications companies.

- **Local Access Points or Points of Presence (POP).** POP is an access point that enables users to access the Internet provider's services. These POPs are run by phone companies and local Internet Service Providers (ISPs). Corporate LANs, WANs, and even individual users with dial-up modems can connect to these points. The details on how connection is made with the Internet is explained in the section *How Can I Connect to the Internet?* later in this chapter.

- **Transmission Control Protocol/ Internet Protocol (TCP/IP).** The TCP/IP acts as the common set of rules for the Internet.

- **IP addresses.** IP addresses are used to uniquely identify computers on the Internet. No two host computers connected to the Internet can have the same IP address.

Now that we have discussed the history and the basics of the Internet, did you guess who administers the Internet or who is behind managing this enormous network?

Who Administers the Internet?

The Internet has no president or chief executive officer to manage it. It is governed by a number of authorities, such as are ISOC, IAB, and IETF. The fundamental authority of the Internet remains with the Internet Society (ISOC), which is a voluntary membership organization. The main goal of this organization is to sponsor global exchange of information. Another vital authority is the Internet Architecture Board (IAB). This organization primarily consists of invited volunteers whose main function is to set standards and assign Internet addresses (IP addresses) to Web sites. The Internet Engineering Task Force (IETF) oversees the technical and operational problems of the Internet.

How Can I Connect to the Internet?

When we summarized the guiding factors of the Internet, we stated that high-speed connections are the backbone of the Internet. However, how exactly can you connect to the Internet? You can connect to the Internet by two methods: dial-up connection and leased lines.

Dial-up Connection

To connect to the Internet through dial-up connection, the essential components required are telephone lines and a modem. A *modem* is a hardware device that transmits data using telephone lines. It converts analog signals that are transmitted through telephone lines to digital signals that can be interpreted by a computer. In the case of a dial-up connection, whenever a user wishes to connect to the Internet, the user must specify a user name, a password, and a telephone number. The user name and password are a means of authenticating a user on the Internet and are provided to the user by ISPs. Internet Service Providers are companies that provide access to the Internet and other related services, such as Web site building and hosting.

Figure 1.2 illustrates a dial-up connection.

Leased Lines

In the case of leased lines, a dedicated connection is maintained with the Internet. A dedicated connection allows the client or the user computer to remain connected to the Internet 24 hours a day. Unlike a dial-up connection, with leased lines a user need not connect to the Internet through a modem. Leased lines are faster than dial-up connections because they can handle higher data transmission speed.

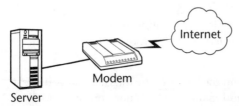

Figure 1.2   Dial-up connection.

Figure 1.3 illustrates how a corporate network is connected to the Internet using leased lines.

We have discussed various aspects of the Internet. However, there are a variety of services available on the Internet, such as electronic mail (email), group membership, and file transfer. The following section discusses the basic components of the Internet that enable us to use these different services.

Components of the Internet

The various components of the Internet are:

- World Wide Web (WWW)
- Web page
- Hypertext Markup Language (HTML)
- Web browser
- Uniform Resource Locator (URL)
- Hypertext Transfer Protocol (HTTP)
- Transmission Control Protocol/Internet Protocol (TCP/IP)

Let's look at each of these components in detail except for TCP/IP, which we have already discussed in the section *Mode of Data Transmission.*

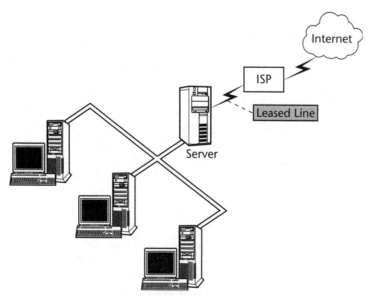

Figure 1.3   Connecting to the Internet by using leased lines.

World Wide Web

The WWW, or the World Wide Web, is a collection of Internet servers that provide an easy-to-use *point-and-click* interface. The WWW, or the Web (as it is commonly called), is the only multimedia service on the Internet. It supports an array of resources ranging from text to multimedia presentation and can be used as a marketplace, library, art gallery, news bulletin, and music center, to name a few. The World Wide Web contains documents that are called Web pages. Web pages contain hypertext that links one Web page to another Web page, video, graphics, sounds, and images. A user just needs to click the link, and the browser takes you to the linked resource.

Web Page

A Web page is a document or a single unit of information that belongs to a Web site and consists of information on that site. There are millions of Web pages spread across the Web. A Web page can contain text, video, graphics, and audio files and links to various other Web pages. To make a Web page available to everyone on the Internet, you need to host the Web page on a site that is placed on a Web server. You can choose any of the following methods for hosting Web pages, depending on the available financial resources and the size of the Web site:

- You can set up your own Web server to host the Web page. However, setting up a Web server is a costly affair.

- If you have financial constraints, you can acquire services from an Internet Service Provider to host your Web page. Most ISPs offer space on their Web server to its clients at a nominal price.

- You can request a company that provides Web-hosting services to rent you Web space at a reasonable price.

HyperText Markup Language

HyperText Markup Language (HTML) is a markup language used to create Web pages. HTML is a versatile language and can be used on any platform or desktop. This language originated from another language, which is called Standard Generalized Markup Language (SGML). Being platform-independent, HTML indicates the manner in which the Web page is to be read at a client computer (through a Web browser).

The appearance of a Web page is important, and HTML provides tags to make the document look attractive using graphics, different sizes of fonts, color, and other effects. This language allows the creation of hypertext links, as mentioned earlier.

Web Browser

In order to access information, you need a Web browser. Web browsers are client programs that fetch Web pages for you. They act as an interface between the client computer and the Web server. Web browsers allow users to perform a variety of tasks such as sending and receiving email messages, reading messages from newsgroups, and browsing the Web.

A Web browser can be text-enabled or graphical. Text-based Web browsers allow you to view only text-based information. An example of a text-based Web browser is Lynx. Examples of graphical Web browsers are Internet Explorer, Netscape Navigator, and Spry Mosaic.

Software programs can be configured to a Web browser to enhance its capabilities. When the browser encounters a sound, image, or video file, it passes the control to other programs, called plug-ins, which run and display these files, thus creating a seamless multimedia experience. Additional plug-ins can be obtained from special download sites on the Web, or from the Web sites of the companies that created these programs. Many plug-ins are available for free.

ActiveX is another technology that offers the opportunity to embed animated objects and data on Web pages and thus enhance browser capabilities. A Web browser that supports ActiveX can render most items on a Web page. For example, you can view and edit PowerPoint presentations directly within your Web browser.

There are several scripting languages available that allow you to create interactive Web pages. A scripting language is a programming language that can be embedded within HTML tags. Chapter 2 introduces you to the evolution of scripting language, in particular JavaScript. Chapter 2 will give you an insight into how JavaScript scripting language merges with HTML and display documents on the user's Web browser.

Every Web site on the Web has an IP address. An IP address is what you type into your Web browser's address bar to instruct the Web browser to load a particular Web page. This address is known as the Uniform Resource Locator (URL) of a site.

Uniform Resource Locator (URL)

A URL contains the exact location of any document. It is an addressing scheme that provides the path to an Internet resource. When a user clicks a link, the URL provides information about that link to the Web browser, which in turn displays the linked Web page. Therefore, links are always implemented by using URLs. A URL may point to a document, image, video, or graphic.

A typical URL would be of the following format:

```
protocol://host.domain-name.toplevel-domain-name/path/dataname
```

where:

- *protocol* refers to the type of protocol to be used.
- *host* refers to the server where the resource is stored.
- *domain-name* and *toplevel-domain-name* are the name and the type of the domain, respectively. The types of domains include *com* (used for commercial institutions), *edu* (educational institutions), *net* (network organizations), *org* (miscellaneous organizations), *gov* (government entities), and *mil* (U.S. military).
- *path/dataname* refers to the location on the server where the data is stored.

HyperText Transfer Protocol

HyperText Transfer Protocol (HTTP) is a protocol used to transfer hypertext documents between computers on the Internet. Before proceeding with details about HTTP, let's first look at what a protocol is. A protocol is a set of rules that governs the Internet. Protocols help the Internet to function smoothly and effectively. There are different types of protocols, for example, File Transfer Protocol (FTP), Telnet, etc. Protocols are rules that a computer uses to communicate with other computers. We have already discussed one of these protocols—TCP/IP.

HTTP works in a client/server environment, where the browser enables users to request Web pages from an HTTP (Web) server, and the server, in turn, displays the requested Web page on the computer screen.

Having looked at the basic components of the Internet, let us now discuss the different services available on the Internet.

Services on the Internet

Some of the common services on the Internet are as follows:

- Email
- FTP
- Gopher
- Newsgroups

We will now discuss each one of these services in detail.

Email

Email is the oldest service on the Internet, dating back to the 1970s. Email messages allow you to type text, attach files, and encrypt messages (so that no one else except the intended reader is able to read them). Although most of us know how to write and send an email, there are some writing guidelines that need to be kept in mind:

- Make sure that your message is not too long.
- Keep varying the length of your sentences.
- Be clear on what you write. Clarity is very important.
- Compose your message in a word processor, if possible. A word processor has more powerful features than a message editor.
- Spell-check before sending the message to avoid any grammatical mistakes and spelling errors.
- Read your message once before sending it.
- Add a signature at the end of the message.

There are many email programs available today. For example, Microsoft Internet Mail, Netscape Mail, and Eudora are some of the most commonly used email programs. You can also customize email programs. For example, you can create separate folders for official and personal mail and arrange your mail in a manner that suits you.

File Transfer Protocol

File Transfer Protocol (FTP) is used to transfer files between two computers. FTP works on the client/server principle. Files are stored on the FTP server and an FTP client program is used to access these files. An FTP client downloads files from any remote server that is connected through the Internet or a local network. Users need to establish an account with the FTP site to be able to transfer files. However, many FTP sites allow users to access their files without establishing an account with them. These sites are called *anonymous FTP sites*.

While transferring files, you might want to compress files to save time. Compressed files take up less space on the server and can be transferred in less time. In order to use a compressed file, the file needs to be decompressed using appropriate software. FTP helps you to transfer files in compressed format.

Gopher

Gopher is an Internet-based document retrieval system, which allows you to gather information from across the Internet. The information can be in the form of text, image, and sound or services in the form of telnet connections and phone book servers. Gopher is a menu-driven program and is very simple to operate.

Gopher works in a client/server environment where users running client software on their local computers interact with remote servers or computers. These servers are called Gopher servers. The information stored on nongopher servers is also accessible through special Gopher servers that act as gateways. Computers such as Mac or UNIX or larger computers can act as a Gopher server. Gopher servers not only contain databases, files, and directories, but may also contain references to other servers. You need to run a Gopher client application on your machine to access these servers. An example of a Gopher client application is TurboGopher.

Newsgroups

Newsgroups are groups of users on the Internet, which can hold discussions on a range of topics. Any Internet surfer can access some of these newsgroups for free; you will need to subscribe to others and agree not to forward the information. You can read articles and post your own articles on newsgroups. You can even post follow-up articles and check for new groups.

We have discussed how the Internet evolved and how it functions and provides services to us. We also discussed that there are several browsers available for accessing the Internet. However, at times, while trying to access a page, the browser may display a message that the page cannot be viewed properly. The primary reason for this problem is cross-browser incompatibility. Let us explore the reasons for the incompatibility of browsers.

Effective Cross Browser Web development is the process of creating Web pages for a site that will be hosted on the Internet. Initially, when there were not many languages available for developing Web pages, developers had limited options to choose from. However, the scenario has now changed. There are several languages available for developing Web pages. For example, you can use a combination of HTML and other scripting languages to develop interactive Web pages. You can use these languages to create complex Web applications that are cross-platform compatible, useful, and dynamic. In fact, Web development has become an exciting affair with the use of languages available as it can be done with incredible speed and the developers can generate rich, useful, and complex applications without using languages like C/C++, Visual Basic, or Delphi that require you to know intricate details of coding.

Since all browsers for different operating systems do not behave similarly, you should create Web sites that display content properly, regardless of the browser or platform. For example, a Web developer might create a Web page that looks striking in a specific browser but looks dull or does not display text properly under different resolution on a different operating system or browser. To ensure compatibility across varied platforms, browsers, and resolutions, you must take certain measures. Although a browser might support different development languages, it still might not display the content of the site properly. For example, a developer might create a Web site by using the latest version of a browser. However, the user viewing this site might be using an older version. As a result, the users might not be able to view the contents of a Web page properly. Some fonts and HTML tags are browser-specific and do not display content in the same format when viewed in different browsers.

Following are a few measures that a developer should take while creating a Web site:

- Developers should go through the global browser averages that will help them decide what type of an audience they want their browser to cater to. Accordingly, they should choose the language that would be most compatible with that browser.

- Knowing the limitations of the browser helps to design an appropriate site. Developers must be familiar with the differences between the browsers and platforms that they wish to use. Developers should consider the following points:

  - Avoid a feature if it's not critical and not supported by all of the targeted browsers.

  - If possible, provide two versions of the page so that one can be viewed in the most popular browsers without any difficulty. The page may be unattractive, but this is necessary as a last resort. Providing two pages would help developers keep their cutting-edge browser clients contented.

- All resolutions do not correspond to the same content in the same manner. For example, some versions of Netscape generally display fonts smaller for a given point size, and the Mac frequently displays text differently than Windows. It's not safe to assume that 800x600 in the IE 5.5 on a Windows computer will look the same on a Macintosh computer, running NS 4.08.

- Developers should consider placing optional content outside of the dimensions that they wish to support. If they wish to put ads or low-priority information on their site, it should be placed on the right side outside of the width of the place that they have decided to use for site information. Such a location should be minimally and optimally used. Studies show that users are drawn to ads and important notices on the right side more effectively than those buried on the left side.

- While testing code for execution in the development stage as well as the final upload stage of the Web site, developers should execute the Web site on different browsers and platforms to ensure that text included is displayed clearly and properly and that important information on the site is not altered when viewed on different browsers.

- Developers should avoid using HTML tags that are not supported by certain browsers.

- Developers should avoid using fonts that are not supported by certain browsers. In addition, they must avoid specifying font sizes in pixels and try using style sheets that are tailored to the specific browsers.

The preceding guidelines are tips on how Web developers can avoid the incompatibility problem. There are other issues that Web page developers will discover as they get more practice and experience.

Summary

In this chapter, you learned about various features of the Internet. The chapter began by giving a definition of the Internet and then discussing how the Internet evolved. A detailed discussion on how the Internet operates provided insight on the operability of this diverse technology. The chapter also mentioned the guiding factors behind the Internet: high-speed connections, local access points, IP, and IP addresses.

The chapter progressed by discussing some important components of the Internet, such as the World Wide Web, Web page, Hypertext Markup Language (HTML), browsers, Uniform Resource Locators, Hypertext Transfer Protocol (HTTP), and Transmission Control Protocol/Internet Protocol (TCP/IP). Next, the chapter gave you an overview of the various services available on the Internet, such as email, telnet, gopher, and newsgroups. Finally, we discussed cross-browser support in Web applications. The chapter provided some of the reasons for incompatibility across varied platforms, browsers, and resolutions and also provided measures to cope with them.

Overview of JavaScript

OBJECTIVES:

In this chapter, you will learn to:

✔ **Explore JavaScript's capabilities**

✔ **Embed JavaScript in HTML**

✔ **Hide JavaScript from JavaScript-incompatible browsers**

✔ **Add comments in JavaScript**

✔ **Include JavaScript code in external files**

✔ **Generate HTML tags in JavaScript**

Getting Started

When the World Wide Web (WWW) first became popular, Hypertext Markup Language (HTML) was the most commonly used language for creating Web pages. However, HTML has limited capabilities; it can position text and graphics on the Web pages, but it cannot validate the information entered by a user. HTML is basically used to create client-side user interfaces and is not designed to handle client-side activities required to respond to user actions. For example, a Web page might require a user to enter the phone number in a specific format. The validation for this data cannot be handled by HTML itself because it doesn't have logic or validation capabilities. Therefore, this data has to be sent to the server for processing and validation, and then the results are returned. This is a repetitive, time-consuming task that results in extensive network traffic.

The increase in user expectations has resulted in a continual improvement in HTML and also in the advent of a set of powerful languages called *scripting languages*. These languages help in providing dynamism to HTML pages. Using scripting, you can check every keystroke on the client-side without any server interaction. A scripting language is a simple programming language designed to enable users to write useful programs easily. A script is interpreted or executed by another program, the Web browser, one line at a time as against a compiled program that is readily executable. Some of the popular scripting languages are Perl, REXX (on IBM mainframes), JavaScript, VBScript, and Tcl/Tk.

This chapter begins with an overview of the basic concepts of the JavaScript language. It describes how JavaScript works with both Netscape Navigator and Microsoft browsers and Web servers. In this chapter, you'll also learn to embed JavaScript statements in HTML documents and write simple scripts.

Types of JavaScripts

JavaScript supports both client-side as well as server-side scripting. Client-side JavaScripts are used to create dynamic and interactive Web pages that can perform client-side validations in a program. These scripts are executed by a Web browser within the context of an HTML document and can be integrated with plug-ins, ActiveX components, and Java applets.

By performing most validations, client-side JavaScript has taken a lot of load off the servers. However, server-side JavaScript still has its own place. Server-side JavaScript is used with Web servers to perform validations at the server end, for example, communicating with databases to validate the data received. These scripts also provide the capability of creating advanced Web applications, such as those that access database information, support e-commerce, or perform specialized processing with the LiveWire and LiveWire database features of its Enterprise and Fast-Track Web servers.

You can either embed JavaScript code in an HTML document or save the code in an external file called a *source file*. When a user requests an HTML file that contains embedded JavaScript code, the server retrieves and returns the requested file. The execution process of client-side JavaScript begins when the browser executes the HTML file. The browser interprets and displays the elements contained in the HTML file when the elements are encountered. This means that the browser executes the JavaScript code in the sequence in which it appears in the HTML file. Figure 2.1 displays the execution process of client-side JavaScript.

The process of interpreting and displaying the elements in an HTML file by the browser is called *parsing*. During parsing, when the JavaScript code is encountered in an HTML file, the browser executes the script before continuing with further parsing. Figure 2.2 displays the parsing of HTML files that contain JavaScript.

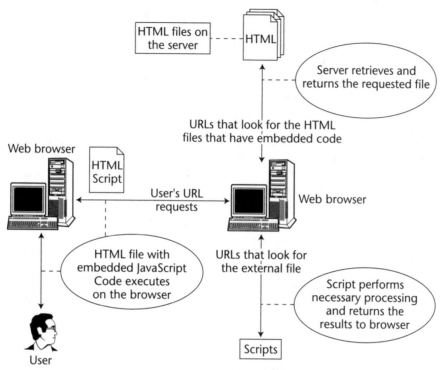

Figure 2.1 Execution process of client-side JavaScript.

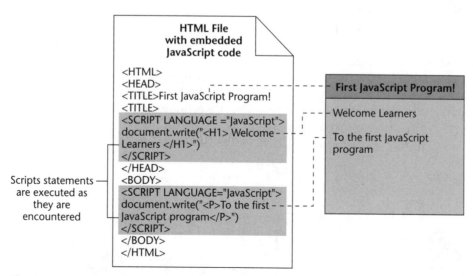

Figure 2.2 Parsing of HTML files that contain JavaScript.

The execution process of an HTML file that contains the path of an external file is slightly different. When a user requests an HTML page that contains a JavaScript external file, the HTML document is returned to the browser. Whenever the code specifying the address of an external file is encountered, the request for the external file is sent to the server. The server then returns the script file, and the code from the external file is appended to the HTML document. Thereafter, the HTML file is executed in the same manner as in the case of embedded JavaScript code.

In contrast to client-side JavaScript, in server-side JavaScript, the server invokes a script, creates objects that pass data from the browser, and makes these objects available to the script. When a request for a URL is sent by the browser, the script on the server performs its processing and returns data to the requesting browser. The server then sends the outgoing response generated by the script to the browser.

Figure 2.3 displays the execution process of server-side JavaScript.

Now that we have looked at the implementation of JavaScript at the client and the server end, let us examine the various client- and server-side features of JavaScript.

You have learned about the types of JavaScripts and their execution process at the client and server end. It is now time to discuss how you can create a simple JavaScript. Let us take the case study of Web Shoppe and see why Web Shoppe decided to use JavaScript as the scripting language and how it has implemented JavaScript in its Web page.

Creating a Simple JavaScript

Problem Statement

Web Shoppe's online mall has an HTML page that displays a list of toys along with their prices in a tabular format. The toys on this page have attained great popularity in the United States and Canada due to their quality, safety, and innovative features. Until now, the page displayed the prices of toys in U.S. dollars only. However, the general feedback showed that this was causing inconvenience to clientele in Canada. The customers in Canada had to make calculations for converting the price into Canadian dollars. In order to cater to the Canadian market, Web Shoppe has decided to give its customers the choice of viewing the prices of the toys in U.S. as well as Canadian dollars.

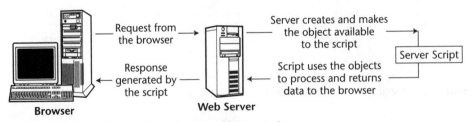

Figure 2.3 Execution process of server-side JavaScript.

However, in order to incorporate this functionality, the Web page of Web Shoppe will need to be reconstructed, and this will take some time. Therefore, Cynthia, who is responsible for the maintenance of this site, has decided that each time a customer tries to access this particular page, a message will be displayed indicating that the page is still under construction.

In addition, the page that displays details of toys has been created in HTML. Therefore, Cynthia needs to choose a mechanism so that the functionality of viewing the prices of toys in both U.S. and Canadian dollars can be incorporated in the existing HTML page in minimal time and without any major modifications to the code.

The HTML code of the page that displays the prices of toys only in U.S. dollars is given below:

```
<HTML>
<HEAD><TITLE> Toys </TITLE>
</HEAD>
<BODY bgcolor="lightgrey">
<H1 align="center"> Web Shoppe </H1>
<MARQUEE><H3 align="right"> A shop at your finger tips
!!</H3></MARQUEE>
<TABLE align="center" border=5 bgcolor="skyblue"
caption="ToyList">
<CAPTION><FONT size=+2><B>List of Toys</B></FONT></CAPTION>
<TR><TH> Toy Name </TH>
<TH>Price in $</TH>
<TH> Enter Qty Required </TH></TR>
<TR><TD>Robby the Whale</TD>
<TD align="right"><INPUT name="txtrob" type=text value=50 size=15
align="right" readonly></TD>
<TD align="right"><INPUT name="txtrobqty" type=text value=""
size=15 align="right"></TD>
</TR>
<TR><TD>Tin Drum</TD>
<TD align="right"><INPUT name="txttin" type=text value=60 size=15
align="right" readonly></TD>
<TD align="right"><input name="txttinqty" type=text value=""
size=15 align="right"></TD>
</TR>
<TR><TD>Dune Racer</TD>
<TD align="right"><INPUT name="txtdun" type=text value=50 size=15
align="right" readonly></TD>
<TD align="right"><INPUT name="txtdunqty" type=text value=""
size=15 align="right"></td>
</TR>
<TR><TD>Parachute Rocket</TD>
<TD align="right"><INPUT name="txtpar" type=text value=45 size=15
align="right" readonly></TD>
<TD align="right"><INPUT name="txtparqty" type=text value=""
size=15 align="right"></TD>
</TR>
```

```
<TR>
<TD colspan=3 align="center"><input type="button" value="Confirm"
align="center"></TD>
</TR>
</TABLE>
</BODY>
</HTML>
```

Figure 2.4 shows the page displaying details of toys available in Web Shoppe.

To display the message indicating that the page is still under construction, Cynthia has identified the following task list to implement the required functionality.

Task List

✔ **Identify the mechanism to incorporate the functionality of viewing the prices of toys in U.S. as well as Canadian dollars.**

✔ **Write the code for displaying the message that the page is still under construction.**

✔ **Execute and verify the code.**

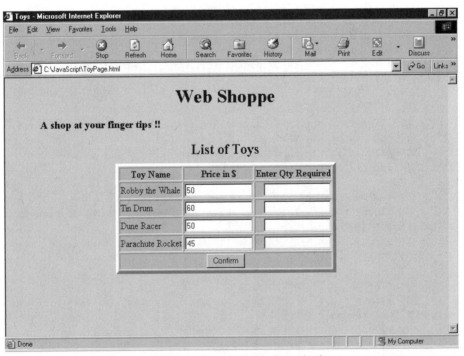

Figure 2.4   Page displaying details of toys available in Web Shoppe.

Identify the Mechanism to Incorporate the Functionality of Viewing the Prices of Toys in U.S. as well as Canadian Dollars

Result

The page that displays details of toys has already been constructed in HTML. Cynthia needs to choose a mechanism that will take the least time to be incorporated and requires fewer modifications to the existing code. To incorporate this functionality, Cynthia decides to use JavaScript. Since JavaScript can be embedded in an HTML document, Cynthia would not need to make any modifications in the existing HTML code.

Write the Code for Displaying the Message that the Page Is Still under Construction

Since the mechanism identified by Cynthia is JavaScript, let us first look at the basics of writing JavaScript code and then write the code for displaying the required message.

Embedding JavaScript in HTML

JavaScript code runs within an HTML document. The statements that structure a JavaScript code in an HTML document are enclosed between the <SCRIPT>...</SCRIPT> tag pairs. The <SCRIPT> tag notifies the Web browser that the commands following this tag need to be interpreted.

Similar to HTML tags, JavaScript tags also have attributes. The opening <SCRIPT> tag contains the LANGUAGE attribute that tells the browsers what scripting language is being used.

```
<SCRIPT LANGUAGE="JavaScript">
JavaScript statements;
</SCRIPT>
```

Most Web browsers have JavaScript as their default scripting language. Therefore, if you exclude the LANGUAGE attribute from the <SCRIPT> tag, your JavaScript program would still run. However, the Internet has been an ever-changing environment. Newer technologies, including scripting languages, are being introduced continuously. You never know when a scripting language will become dominant or when it will become the default scripting language for Internet Explorer. Therefore, it is a good practice to use the LANGUAGE attribute of the <SCRIPT> tag to indicate to the browser about a scripting language that is in use.

A <SCRIPT> tag can be placed either within the <HEAD> or <BODY> tag of an HTML document. To ensure that all JavaScript definitions are made before the body of the document is displayed, it is better to place the <SCRIPT> tag within the <HEAD> tag. You'll learn more about this later in this chapter. Let us first look at a simple example where the <SCRIPT> tag is not placed within the <HEAD> tag.

```
<HTML>
<HEAD>
<TITLE>First JavaScript Program</TITLE>
</HEAD>
<BODY>
<SCRIPT LANGUAGE="JavaScript">
document.write("My First JavaScript Program!");
</SCRIPT>
</BODY>
</HTML>
```

In the preceding example, the `<BODY>` tag contains a single script statement within the `<SCRIPT>...</SCRIPT>` tags. The browser identifies the language to be used by the LANGUAGE attribute in the `<SCRIPT>` tag. The statement "`document.write("My First JavaScript Program!");`" writes the text `My First JavaScript Program!` on the browser. In addition, observe that the statement within the `<SCRIPT>...</SCRIPT>` tag pair ends with a semicolon (`;`) to distinguish the end of one statement from the start of another statement. It is not necessary to end the statements with a semicolon (`;`), but it is good programming practice. In this book, we will follow the practice of placing a semicolon (`;`) at the end of each statement within the `<SCRIPT>...</SCRIPT>` tag pair.

Figure 2.5 displays the output of the First JavaScript Program in Netscape Navigator.

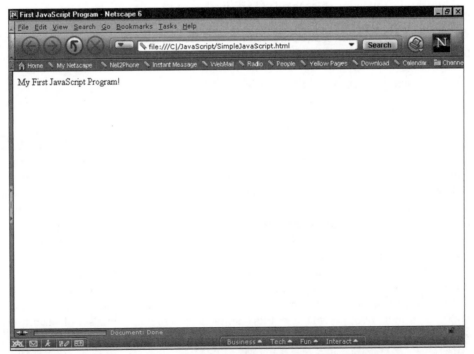

Figure 2.5 Output of the First JavaScript program in Netscape Navigator 6.

NOTE The preceding example uses the `write` **method of the** `document` **object of JavaScript. The** `write()` **method helps write text in Web pages. The** `write()` **method is prefixed with the object name** `document`**. You'll learn in detail about the document object and its methods later in this book. Readers who are already familiar with the basics of JavaScript and want to know the details of the** `write()` **method can refer to Chapter 6, "Using Objects in JavaScript."**

Figure 2.6 displays the output of the First JavaScript Program in Internet Explorer. Apart from the LANGUAGE attribute, there are some other attributes of the <SCRIPT> tag. Table 2.1 contains all the attributes of the <SCRIPT> tag with their description.

Table 2.1   Attributes of the <SCRIPT> tag

ATTRIBUTES	DESCRIPTION
SRC	Specifies the location of an external script
TYPE	Specifies the scripting language of the script and overrides the default scripting language
LANGUAGE	Specifies the scripting language of the script
DEFER	Indicates that the script is not going to generate any document content

NOTE In the preceding table, you'll notice that TYPE and LANGUAGE **attributes have a similar function. This book uses the** LANGUAGE **attribute to specify the language used in the script.**

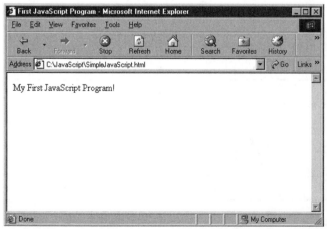

Figure 2.6   Output of the First JavaScript program in Internet Explorer 6.

Versions of JavaScript

There might be browsers that support one version of JavaScript but do not support other versions. For example, Navigator 3 only supports JavaScript 1.1 and lower. You can use the LANGUAGE attribute of the JavaScript <SCRIPT> tag to specify the version of JavaScript being used. The following code directs the browser to use JavaScript1.1:

```
<SCRIPT LANGUAGE="JavaScript1.1">
JavaScript statements;
</SCRIPT>
```

In the preceding code, you'll notice that there is no space between JavaScript and 1.1. This is because a browser will not interpret your code if there is any space between JavaScript and the version number.

You can specify the following values in the LANGUAGE attribute to specify the JavaScript capability in the browser:

- **JavaScript1.1.** If you specify JavaScript1.1, the JavaScript code can be executed only on browsers that support JavaScript 1.1. These browsers are Navigator 3 and later, Internet Explorer 4 and later, and Opera 3.5 and later.

- **JavaScript1.2.** If you specify JavaScript1.2, the JavaScript code can be executed only on browsers that support JavaScript 1.2. These browsers are Navigator 4 and later and Internet Explorer 4 and later.

- **JavaScript1.3.** If you specify JavaScript1.3, the JavaScript code can be executed only on browsers that support JavaScript 1.3. These browsers are Navigator 4.06 and later.

Table 2.2 summarizes the browser support for the LANGUAGE attribute:

Table 2.2   Browser Support for the LANGUAGE Attribute

BROWSER	JAVASCRIPT	JAVASCRIPT1.1	JAVASCRIPT1.2	JAVASCRIPT1.3
Navigator 2	X			
Navigator 3	X	X		
Navigator 4	X	X	X	
Navigator 4.06	X	X	X	X
Navigator 4.5	X	X	X	X
Internet Explorer 3	X			
Internet Explorer 4	X	X	X	
Internet Explorer 5	X	X	X	
Opera 3.21	X	X	X	X
Opera 3.5	X	X	X	X

When a browser interprets an HTML document and it encounters the JavaScript code, it checks the version number of JavaScript that is specified by the LANGUAGE attribute. If the Web browser you are using does not support the indicated version, it ignores all the statements between the <SCRIPT>...</SCRIPT> tag pair. If you want your JavaScript code to be compatible with older browsers, you need to explicitly specify the JavaScript version number that supports that browser. In this case, the syntax and elements used to structure the JavaScript program should also conform to the version of JavaScript that you have specified.

Hiding JavaScript from JavaScript Challenged Browsers

All browsers do not necessarily support JavaScript. Older browsers, such as Netscape Navigator 1, Internet Explorer 2, and the character-based Lynx browser, do not identify JavaScript code. As a result, these browsers display all the code placed between the <SCRIPT>...</SCRIPT> tag pair as normal text. Figure 2.7 displays the output of the preceding example of the First JavaScript Program in DosLynx.

As you can see, DosLynx does not display the text My First JavaScript Program!. Instead it displays the statement that we had enclosed between the <SCRIPT> tag.

To hide JavaScript statements from incompatible JavaScript browsers, HTML provides a solution. JavaScript does not provide a similar solution. HTML comment tags can be used for this purpose. HTML comments are used for inserting notes and providing description about the tags used. These cannot be viewed in the browser. The following code displays how to use the HTML comment tag to hide the code from JavaScript-challenged browsers:

```
<!--Begin hiding JavaScript
JavaScript statements;
End hiding JavaScript -->
```

Figure 2.7   Output of the First JavaScript Program in DosLynx.

The < ! -- statement indicates the beginning of the HTML comment tag and --> indicates the end of the comment tag. The comment tag will tell JavaScript-incompatible browsers to take the statements as comments. Conversely, JavaScript-compatible browsers ignore comment tags and execute the JavaScript statement in a normal manner. The following code displays the First JavaScript Program now modified to include code for JavaScript-incompatible browsers:

```
<HTML>
<HEAD>
<TITLE>First JavaScript Program</TITLE>
</HEAD>
<BODY>
<SCRIPT LANGUAGE="JavaScript">
<!--Begin hiding JavaScript
document.write("My First JavaScript Program!");
End hiding JavaScript -->
</SCRIPT>
</BODY>
</HTML>
```

The preceding code when executed on DosLynx will display no text.
Figure 2.8 displays the output of the First JavaScript Program in DosLynx.

The NOSCRIPT Tag

In the preceding section, we discussed a solution for incompatible JavaScript browsers. But how would it appear that an incompatible JavaScript browser executes an HTML file that contains JavaScript and the screen appears blank (as shown in Figure 2.8)? You would normally want to display some sort of message to indicate to a user that the browser is not compatible with the program. The <NOSCRIPT> tag enables JavaScript-incompatible browsers to display an alternative message to the user. The <NOSCRIPT> tag usually follows the <SCRIPT> tag. The following code illustrates how to use the <NOSCRIPT> tag:

```
<HTML>
<HEAD>
<TITLE>First JavaScript Program</TITLE>
</HEAD>
<BODY>
<SCRIPT LANGUAGE="JavaScript">
<!--Begin hiding JavaScript
document.write("My First JavaScript Program!");
End hiding JavaScript -->
</SCRIPT>
<NOSCRIPT>
Your program cannot be executed since the browser does not support
JavaScript
</NOSCRIPT>
</BODY>
</HTML>
```

Figure 2.8 Output of the First JavaScript Program in DosLynx.

Figure 2.9 displays the output of the First JavaScript Program in DosLynx. The message "Your program cannot be executed since the browser does not support JavaScript" is displayed.

JavaScript Comments

While writing code in any programming language, it is good practice to add comments. Comments are nonprinting notes that you add to your code to include information such as the name of the program, its date of creation, notes for yourself, or instructions for programmers who may need to modify the code at a later date. Comments do not have any effect on the appearance of a document. These are pointers for later reference. In HTML, you already know how to use the comment tags to place comments in your document.

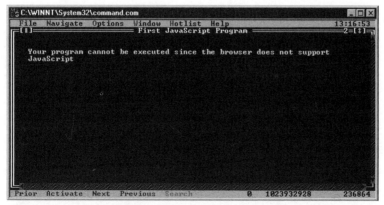

Figure 2.9 Output of the First JavaScript Program in DosLynx.

You can also use comments to prevent a section of code from executing if you need to troubleshoot your script. If you enclose a section of a suspect script within comment indicators, JavaScript will ignore that section when your script executes.

JavaScript also provides the facility to add comments to a document. JavaScript uses two types of comment indicators. The first indicator delineates a comment on a single line of script (//). The other type of comment indicator is used for multiple-line comments (/*...*/). Let us look at both of these in detail.

Single-Line Comment Indicator

You have already been using the // indicator to comment out the ending HTML comment tag. However, you can also use this method to add comments to a complete or partial line, as illustrated in the following code:

```
<HTML>
<HEAD>
<TITLE>JavaScript comments</TITLE>
</HEAD>
<BODY>
<SCRIPT LANGUAGE="JavaScript">
<!--
//document.write("My First JavaScript Program!");
document.write("My First JavaScript Program!");
-->
</SCRIPT>
</BODY>
</HTML>
```

In this example, the portion of the code from // to the end of the line will be ignored by JavaScript.

Multi-Line Comment Indicator

Eventually, you might need to use a comment that extends beyond a single line. To do this, you enclose the text to be displayed within /* and */.

The following code illustrates the use of single-line as well as multi-line comments:

```
<HTML>
<HEAD>
<TITLE>JavaScript comments</TITLE>
<BODY>
</HEAD>
<SCRIPT LANGUAGE="JavaScript">
<!--Begin hiding JavaScript
//document.write("My First JavaScript Program!");
document.write("My First JavaScript Program!");
/* document.write("My First JavaScript Program!");
document.write("My First JavaScript Program!");*/
//End hiding JavaScript-->
</SCRIPT>
</BODY>
</HTML>
```

By now, you must be quite familiar with writing simple JavaScript code. It is time to discuss a slightly advanced mode of writing JavaScript. We will look at how you can write and store JavaScript in a separate file.

The JavaScript Source File

As already discussed, JavaScript code can be embedded in an HTML document. However, you can also include JavaScript code in an external file. This external file is also known as a source file and has an extension .js. The source file contains only JavaScript statements and does not contain the HTML `<SCRIPT>...</SCRIPT>` tag pair. Instead, the `<SCRIPT>...</SCRIPT>` tag pair is positioned within the HTML document that calls the source file. The browser automatically reads the code written in the `.js` file and treats the code as if it were written between the `<SCRIPT>` tags.

The SRC Attribute

The `SRC` attribute specifies the URL or the directory location of a JavaScript source file. The following code illustrates the use of the `SRC` attribute in the `<SCRIPT>` tag:

```
<SCRIPT LANGUAGE="JavaScript1.3"
SRC="c:\JavaScript\sampleSourceFile.js">
</SCRIPT>
```

In the preceding code, `c:\JavaScript\sampleSourceFile.js` is the location of the source file `sampleSourceFile.js`. You can name a source file in any way; however, you need to include the extension `.js`. If you include any HTML tags in a source file, then the file will generate an error. In an HTML file, if you specify any JavaScript statement other than the `<SCRIPT>...</SCRIPT>` tags, then the browser ignores such statements. For example, consider the following JavaScript code. When the browser encounters the source file location, the browser reaches the file and executes the statements in it. However, it ignores the `document.write` statement:

```
    <SCRIPT LANGUAGE="JavaScript1.3"
SRC="c:\JavaScript\sampleSourceFile.js">
    document.write("The browser will ignore this statement.");
    </SCRIPT>
```

We have discussed how to include a source file into an HTML document. However, you must be wondering why you would need to create a source file if JavaScript already has the capability of embedding JavaScript code in an HTML document. Let us trace the need for creating source files.

Need for a Source File

There is no mandatory rule for creating a .js file. If the JavaScript code that you want to include in an HTML document is fairly short, then it is usually preferred to include the JavaScript code in the HTML document. However, for longer JavaScript code, it is easier to include the code in a .js file. The following are a few more reasons for using a .js source file:

To add clarity to an HTML document.   If your JavaScript code is lengthy and is embedded in the same HTML document, it gives a cluttered look and would also be difficult to understand. Therefore, if you want your document to be neat, it is preferable to use a .js file.

To share JavaScript code across multiple HTML documents.   For example, your Web site might include pages that allow customers to place orders for books from your site. For each book, the site provides a separate page but uses the same JavaScript code to collate the order information. In such a case, instead of rewriting the JavaScript code for gathering order information separately for each book, your Web site can share a common source file.

To help you hide your JavaScript code.   Usually, you can view the HTML source code for a Web page through a browser. You might spend a considerable amount of time writing JavaScript code for a file. Therefore, you would prefer that your code not be viewed and modified by others and claimed as personal copy. If you place JavaScript code in a source, or .js file, viewers can only see the location of the source file but not its contents.

There might be situations where a site has multiple HTML documents and each document requires individual JavaScript code statements, but all of these share a single JavaScript source file. For instance, a computer vendor site has multiple pages. Each page accepts orders for products that are available on the site. The site has a common source file that gathers order information, such as customer name and address, which is common to all the products sold. Besides the common order details, each product sold also has order information that is specific to the particular product. For example, a software product will have order information, such as the type of software. The type of software can include a relational database management system (RDBMS), programming language or an operating system. A hardware product can have other information such as a peripheral device, a motherboard, or an audio-video device. In such cases, it is advantageous to use a combination of embedded JavaScript code and JavaScript source files in your HTML documents.

The following code displays the combination of embedded JavaScript code and JavaScript source file in an HTML document:

```
<HTML>
<HEAD>
<TITLE>HTML document with a combination of embedded JavaScript
code and JavaScript source file </TITLE>
</HEAD>
<BODY>
<SCRIPT LANGUAGE="JavaScript1.2" SRC="c:\JavaScript\
sampleSourceFile.js ">
</SCRIPT>
<SCRIPT LANGUAGE="JavaScript1.2">
document.write("This statement is embedded in the HTML
document.");
</SCRIPT>
</BODY>
</HTML>
```

In the preceding code, notice that for each section of JavaScript code, a separate `<SCRIPT>...</SCRIPT>` tag pair is used. Each JavaScript section is executed in the order in which it appears in the HTML document.

Until now, we have placed the JavaScript code in the `<BODY>` tag of an HTML document. However, as mentioned previously, we can also place the `<SCRIPT>` tag within the `<HEAD>` tag. Let us look at the relevance of placing the `<SCRIPT>` tag in the `<HEAD>` tag and use a few examples that would substantiate the approach.

Placing the <SCRIPT> Tag in the <HEAD> Tag or the <BODY> Tag

As discussed earlier, you can place JavaScript code within either the `<HEAD>` tag or the `<BODY>` tag of an HTML document. However, the `<HEAD>` tag is a more appropriate place to include JavaScript definitions. The `<HEAD>` tag is processed before the `<BODY>` tag and, therefore, placing definitions in the `<HEAD>` tag causes them to be defined before they are used. This is important, especially in the case of variables. You'll learn about variables in the Chapter 3, "JavaScript Data Types, Variables, and Operators."

The following example illustrates how JavaScript definitions can be placed in the `<HEAD>` tag of an HTML document. `<HTML>`

```
<HEAD>
<TITLE>Using the HEAD tag for definitions</TITLE>
<SCRIPT LANGUAGE="JavaScript1.3">
<!--
newVariable="My First JavaScript Program!";
-->
</SCRIPT>
</HEAD>
<BODY>
<SCRIPT LANGUAGE="JavaScript1.3">
<!--
document.write(newVariable);
-->
</SCRIPT>
</BODY>
</HTML>
```

In the preceding code, the JavaScript code enclosed in the `<HEAD>` tag defines a variable, `newVariable`, and sets its value to the string "`My First JavaScript Program!`". The code contained in the `<BODY>` tag then displays the value of the variable, `newVariable,` in the current document.

It is essential to provide definitions for variables and functions before you can use them in a document. Otherwise, an error will appear on loading the document on the browser. The following example illustrates an HTML document that generates an error because the variable, `newVariable,` is used to display its value in the `<HEAD>` tag even before it is defined.

```
<HTML>
<HEAD>
<TITLE>Using the HEAD tag for definitions</TITLE>
```

```
<SCRIPT LANGUAGE="JavaScript1.3">
<!--
document.write(newVariable);
-->
</SCRIPT>
</HEAD>
<BODY>
<SCRIPT LANGUAGE="JavaScript1.3">
<!--
newVariable="My First JavaScript Program!";
-->
</SCRIPT>
</BODY>
</HTML>
```

Figure 2.10 displays JavaScript error since the variable is used before it is defined.
    You have learned to write a simple JavaScript code. The code used displayed text
that was simple and did not have any formatting in it. However, like HTML, JavaScript
also has the capability to enhance the appearance of text in an HTML document. In the
next section, let us see how JavaScript enables you to emphasize text that is displayed.

Creating HTML Tags

You can include HTML tags in JavaScript code to add formatting, such as boldface or
italics, to your script output. We will first take the example of a simple HTML code that
displays formatted text and then take another example that contains HTML formatting
tags in JavaScript code and display the same output as the simple HTML code.

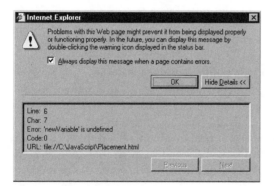

Figure 2.10   Error generated because the variable is used before it is defined.

Following is an example of a simple HTML code that displays formatted text using tags such as <B></B> and <CITE></CITE>.

```
<HTML>
<HEAD><TITLE>Creating HTML Tags</TITLE></HEAD>
<BODY>
<H1 align="center"> Creating HTML Tags </H1>
<B>We will use <CITE>HTML tags </CITE> in <CITE>JavaScript code
</CITE> to generate formatted text output. </B>
</BODY>
</HTML>
```

Following is an example that contains HTML formatting tags in JavaScript code and displays the same output as the simple HTML code.

```
<HTML>
<HEAD><TITLE>Creating HTML Tags</TITLE></HEAD>
<BODY>
<H1 align="center"> Creating HTML Tags </H1>
<SCRIPT LANGUAGE="JavaScript">
document.write("<B>" + "We will use <CITE>HTML tags " + "</CITE>"
+ "in " + "<CITE>" + "JavaScript code " + "</CITE>" + "to generate
formatted text output." + "</B>");
</SCRIPT>
</BODY>
</HTML>
```

The formatting of the output generated by the preceding code will be the same as that generated by the HTML code. The code in the preceding example includes HTML formatting tags inside JavaScript code. It also uses the string concatenation operator + to concatenate text and tags. You'll learn more about the concatenation operator in Chapter 3, "JavaScript Data Types, Variables, and Operators."

Figure 2.11 displays formatted output generated by including HTML tags in JavaScript code.

Having discussed the basic concepts that are required to write a simple JavaScript, let us now look at the code for Web Shoppe's toy page.

JavaScript Code for Web Shoppe's Toy Page

Enclose the following JavaScript code in the <HEAD> tag of the HTML code for Web Shoppe's toy page. This code will display a message to its customer indicating that the page is under construction:

```
<SCRIPT LANGUAGE="JavaScript">
<!--Begin hiding JavaScript
//The following line displays the intended message
```

```
      document.write("Sorry for inconvenience.....even though the page
displays the toys with its prices, it will be completely functional in a
week. The page is still under construction. Please visit our site again
after a week.");
      End hiding JavaScript -->
      </SCRIPT>
      <NOSCRIPT>
      Your program cannot be executed since the browser does not support
JavaScript
      </NOSCRIPT>
```

In the preceding code, the following have been used to structure JavaScript:

- The <SCRIPT>....</SCRIPT> tag pair that is placed between the <HEAD> tag has been used to embed JavaScript into the HTML document.

- The <!-- .... --> HTML comment tag has been used to hide JavaScript from the JavaScript-incompatible browser.

- The // comment tag of JavaScript has been used to write a note for later reference.

- The <NOSCRIPT> tag has been used to enable JavaScript-incompatible browsers to display an alternative message to the user.

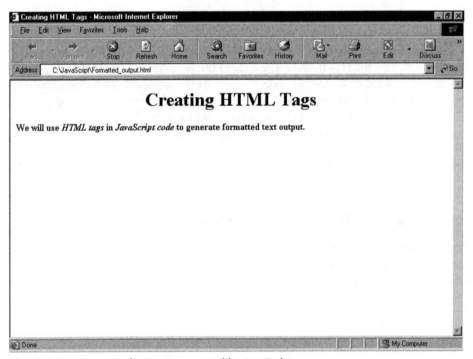

Figure 2.11 Formatted output generated by JavaScript.

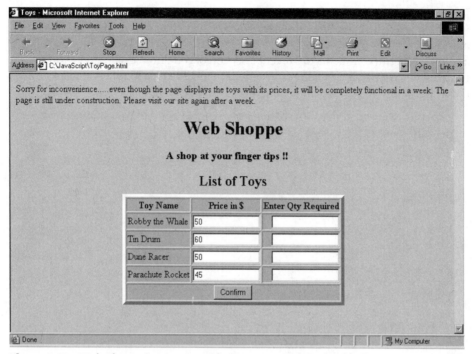

Figure 2.12   Web Shoppe's toy page with the message that page is still under construction.

Execute and Verify the Code

The method of executing an HTML file that contains JavaScript code is similar to the execution process of a normal HTML file. To execute the HTML file that contains the JavaScript code, open Internet Explorer and type the location of the HTML file as: C:\JavaScript\Name_of_the_file.html.

Assuming that you have named the HTML file of Web Shoppe's toy page as Toy-Page.html, to execute this file, type C:\JavaScript\ToyPage.html in the address bar of Internet Explorer.

Figure 2.12 displays Web Shoppe's toy page with the message that the page is still under construction in Internet Explorer.

Summary

This chapter covered a brief history and overview of the basic concepts of the JavaScript language. You learned to differentiate between JavaScript and Java. The chapter also showed how JavaScript works in the Netscape Navigator and Internet Explorer browsers. You also learned to write simple JavaScript code by embedding

JavaScript statements in HTML documents. Next, you learned to hide JavaScript code from JavaScript-incompatible browsers. In this way, you can display an alternative message by using the <NOSCRIPT> tag. In addition, you looked at the relevance of adding JavaScript comments to prevent a section of code from executing if you need to troubleshoot your script. Finally, you learned to include JavaScript code in an external file and generate HTML tags in JavaScript.

JavaScript Data Types, Variables, and Operators

Getting Started

As you know, both spoken and software languages conform to a specific structure. This structure is composed of basic building blocks specific to a language. For example, in English, letters combine to make a word and words combine to make a sentence. Sentences then combine to make a paragraph and paragraphs combine to make essays or writings, and this cycle goes on. In the same manner, JavaScript and many other programming languages use fundamental building blocks such as literal values, variables, operators, and functions that combine to make an expression. Expressions combine to create a statement, and statements combine to create programs.

In this chapter, we will begin with learning about the fundamental building blocks and work our way up from there. In the section *Variable—A StoreHouse*, you will be introduced to the concepts of literals, data types, and variables. In another section, *Expressions and Operators*, you will learn how to use expressions and operators in JavaScript. Functions will be dealt with in Chapter 5, "Functions and Events."

What is a literal value, a data type, and a variable? In our daily life, we constantly access and store information so that it can be retrieved later whenever needed. For example, let's think about the good old school days. How did you study then? While studying, most of us wrote notes so that we could refer to them quickly at the time of our exams. We were simply storing information and retrieving it later. In the same manner, while programming, we need to store values or information for later reference. We store such values in *variables*. The type of data that we store in a variable is referred to as a *data type* and the value that we assign to a variable is called a *literal value*.

Let's now discuss the methods of storing information in a variable and the relevance of expressions and operators. We will take the scenario of Web Shoppe whose Web page makes extensive uses of variables and operators. This chapter has been designed in such a manner that each task identified for the problem statement will equip you with all knowledge necessary to solve the problem statement.

Problem Statement

Along with an online shopping mall, Web Shoppe also has an outlet that sells confectionery items, flowers, and books. The name of the outlet is also Web Shoppe. For the convenience of its employees, Web Shoppe wants to create a Web page that will allow its employees to enter billing details for the outlet. Scott, a member of the development team that is developing a billing system software program for Web Shoppe, has been assigned the task of creating an application that will accept the following customer details:

- Name
- Date of birth
- Billing address
- City
- Phone number
- Total bill amount
- Amount paid

The Web page should display the amount due from a customer and also allow an employee to view the data that he or she has entered. If there is no amount due from a customer, an appropriate message should be displayed. Otherwise, the amount due should be displayed.

Task List

- ✔ **Identify the variables, data types, and operators to be used.**
- ✔ **Write the code to accept and display details.**
- ✔ **Execute the code.**

Identify the Variables, Data Types, and Operators to Be Used

Before Scott identifies the variables, data types, and operators to be used to write the code for the billing system, let's first discuss the methods to store information in a variable. The next section will discuss expressions and operators. This would enable you to understand the rationale behind the chosen variables, data types, and operators.

Variable—A StoreHouse

Like many programming languages, JavaScript also allows you to declare and use variables to store values in them. Variables are containers that store data of various types, such as ABC, 12, and 12.02. In other words, variables are names that you can associate with stored values. For example, the variable totalBill signifies a storage area that contains the total bill amount of a user's purchase.

While assigning a name to a variable, there are certain conventions that should be followed. These conventions are described below:

- Variable names can include uppercase and lowercase letters, digits from 0 through 9, the underscore (_) character, and the dollar sign ($).

- Variable names should not include spaces or punctuation characters.

- The first character of a variable must begin with an alphabetic letter or an underscore.

- Variable names are case-sensitive. For example, variable names `totalBill`, `TotalBill`, and `Totalbill` are three different variables.

Using the preceding rules, here are a few more examples of valid variable names:

```
_var40
totalBill
temp
total_Bill
```

Here are some examples of invalid variable names:

```
99temp          //Cannot begin with a number.
total&Wesson    //The ampersand (&) character is not a valid
character for a variable
```

While naming a variable, it is a common programming practice to use two words. The first word is written in lowercase letters and the first letter of the second word is capitalized, and the two words are closed up with no space in between. For example, to store someone's first name, you may use a variable called `firstName`.

NOTE The dollar sign ($) is reserved for machine-generated code and should not be used while naming variables. In particular, it should not be used in scripts that will execute in primitive browsers that are not completely ECMAScript-compatible.

There is another important point that one should keep in mind while naming a variable (or a function). You should not use certain words that have a special meaning in JavaScript. These words are called *keywords* or *reserved words*. Before we proceed with more details about variables, let's discuss JavaScript keywords and reserved words so that you don't use them as variable names or function names in your program by mistake. Using keywords and reserved words as variable names or function names in your program may result in an unidentifiable error.

JavaScript Keywords and Reserved Words

Keywords are predefined identifiers that form the foundation of JavaScript. They have special meaning. For example, the keyword var signifies that a variable is being declared. Table 3.1 lists the keywords in JavaScript that are part of the language syntax. This means that they should not be used as identifiers.

NOTE An identifier is a name assigned to some program element, such as a variable or a function.

Table 3.2 lists keywords from Java. Although JavaScript does not currently use any of these keywords, you should avoid using these in your program.

Finally, Table 3.3 lists other identifiers that you should avoid using. While these identifiers are not strictly reserved, they are the names of the data types, functions, and variables that are predefined by client-side JavaScript. Using them can cause unexpected behavior in your program.

Table 3.1   Reserved JavaScript Keywords

break	in	true
continue	int	typeof
do	labeled	var
else	new	void
false	null	while
for	return	with
function	switch	if
throw	try	catch
finally	instanceof	case

Table 3.2 Reserved Java Keywords

abstract	default	implements	private
boolean	import	protected	throws
byte	double	public	transient
extends	short	static	char
final	interface	class	float
long	super	goto	package
native	const		

Having looked at the rules for naming variables, let's now see how a variable is declared in JavaScript.

Declaring Variables

Declaring variables allocates memory to variables. Unlike in C and Java, declaring variables before they are used is not necessary in JavaScript. If you do not declare a variable in JavaScript, it is implicitly taken as declared. Although there is no compulsion to explicitly declare variables, it is considered good programming practice to declare variables before they are used. You can declare a variable in two ways: by assigning it a value (implicit declaration) or by using the keyword var (explicit declaration).

The following code is an example of implicit declaration when a variable is declared by assigning it a value:

```
firstName="Tom";
```

Here, you have declared the variable firstName and initialized it with a string value.

The following is an example of explicit declaration when a variable is declared using the keyword var:

```
var firstName;
```

Table 3.3 Other Identifiers

alert	escape	JavaPackage	onun

Here, you have defined a variable name `firstName` that does not hold any value. You can also assign an initial value to a variable while declaring it by using the `var` keyword. In the following example, a value is assigned to a variable while declaring it with the `var` keyword:

```
var firstName="Tom";
```

Since you are now comfortable with the concept of declaring variables, it is time to discuss what types of data a variable can store.

Data Types and Variables

Most programming languages require you to specify the type of data a variable will store, that is, will a variable store data containing numbers or text. JavaScript does not impose any restriction in this context. It allows the same variable to contain different types of data values, such as the text "Hi Friends!," the integer 13, the floating-point value 3.14, or the logical value true. It doesn't prevent a variable from changing the type of data while programming. JavaScript takes the responsibility of keeping track of the type of data that a variable currently contains. However, one should know the data types that JavaScript supports.

JavaScript classifies data types into three sections: *primitive, composite,* and *special*. Primitive data types are types that can be assigned a single literal value, such as a number, string, or Boolean value.

NOTE Literals are the actual data that you assign to variables. For example, if you declare a variable, newNum, which holds the value 2, then the data type of this variable is Number and its literal value is 2.

Following are the primitive data types that JavaScript supports:

- **Number.** Comprises integer and floating-point numbers.
- **Boolean.** Comprises the logical values `true` or `false`.
- **String.** Comprises a sequence of alphanumeric characters. For example, "Hello, World!", "555-1212," or "KA12V2B334."

Composite data types are types that are built from primitive data types. Following are the composite data types that JavaScript supports:

- **Object.** Is a named collection of data that has properties and can be accessed through methods.
- **Array.** Comprises objects that store a sequence of values.

Following are the special data types that JavaScript supports:

- **null.** Indicates an initial value that is different from other valid values.
- **undefined.** Indicates that a variable has been created but is not assigned a value.

Let's now look at each of these in detail.

Number Data Types

JavaScript supports both integer and floating-point values that can be represented in decimal, octal, or hexadecimal notation. Unlike other programming languages, such as C++ and Java, JavaScript does not make any distinction between integer values and floating-point values. All numbers are represented as floating-point values in JavaScript. In a numerical expression, if one value is an integer and another value is a floating-point, JavaScript automatically converts the integer value to a floating-point value. For example, you have a variable, numOne, which contains the integer value 4, and another variable, numTwo, which contains the floating-point value 2.5. The variable addNum will contain the sum of the two numbers as follows: addNum = numOne + numTwo. Here, JavaScript automatically converts the literal value of numOne to a floating-point data type. Therefore, the result in the addNum variable is 6.5.

Integer Literals

What are integers? *Integers* are numeric values that don't have a decimal or fractional part. For example, the number of whole apples in a basket is an integer value since the whole apples don't have fractional parts. However, the distance in miles between two houses is perhaps not an integer (unless the distance is an exact integer, which is very rare). It is a real number that has a fractional part.

Integer literals can be represented in decimal, hexadecimal, or octal form, in which:

- A decimal integer represents numbers to the base 10.

- A hexadecimal (base 16) integer in JavaScript begins with the characters 0x or 0X in the two left-most columns. A hexadecimal notation uses zero through nine to represent the values 0 through 9 and the letters A through F to represent the values 10 through 15.

- An octal (base 8) integer in JavaScript begins with the character 0 in the left-most column. An octal notation only uses digits 0 through 7.

Floating-Point Literals

Floating-point literals represent numbers that have a decimal or fractional part. These numbers can also be represented using an exponential notation. The example of the distance between two houses is actually an example of a floating-point literal. The following are some other examples of floating-point numbers:

```
-3.141
55.
12e2+23
1e-2
7e1
-4e-4
.57
```

As can be seen in the preceding examples, a floating-point literal may start with an integer and be followed by an optional decimal point and fraction, or followed by an optional exponent ("e" or "E") and its integer exponent value. In addition, notice that the initial integer and integer exponent value may be assigned as positive or negative (+ or -). The syntax of a floating-point literal is as follows:

```
[(+|-)] [digits] [.digits] [(E|e) [(+|-)] digits]
```

JavaScript does not specify the maximum and minimum sizes of numbers. It uses the double-precision format that has a maximum value of approximately +/- 1.79E+308 and a minimum value of approximately +/-4.94E-324.

Boolean Data Type

The Boolean data type in JavaScript symbolizes a truth value, that is, whether a condition or an expression is true or false. While performing any comparison operations by using logical operators, a Boolean value is retrieved that indicates whether the comparison has succeeded or failed. You'll learn about logical operators for performing comparisons in Chapter 4, "JavaScript Control Structures and Statements." JavaScript automatically converts the Boolean values true and false to 1 and 0, respectively, when they are used in numerical expressions. The following example illustrates the automatic conversion of Boolean values when used in a numeric expression:

```
<HTML>
<HEAD>
<TITLE>Conversion of Boolean values to numeric values</TITLE>
</HEAD>
<BODY>
<H1 align="center"> Conversion of Boolean Values in a Numeric
Expression </H1>
<SCRIPT LANGUAGE="JavaScript">
document.write("true*10 + false*7 = ");
document.write(true*10 + false*7);
</SCRIPT>
</BODY>
</HTML>
```

In the preceding code, in the statement "`document.write(true*10   + false*7);`", the expression `true*10 + false*7` converts to `1*10 + 0*7`. The code uses expressions and operators to explain automatic conversion. For a better understanding of expressions and operators, refer to the section in this chapter called *Expressions and Operators*.

Figure 3.1 demonstrates how Boolean values are automatically converted in a numeric expression.

NOTE The primitive Boolean literal values, true and false, are different from the true and false values of the `Boolean` **Object that you will learn about in Chapter 6, "Using Objects in JavaScript." If you enclose the Boolean literal values, true and false, in double quotation marks, then it becomes a string value.**

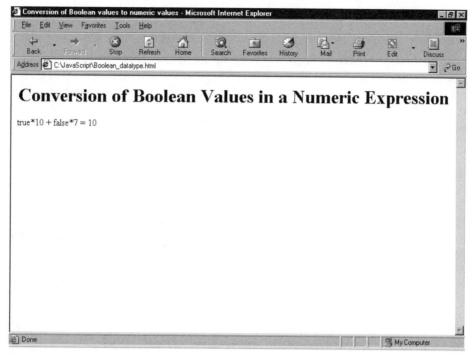

Figure 3.1   Automatic conversion of a Boolean value in a numeric expression.

String Data Type

A variable of the String type can store a sequence of alphanumeric characters, spaces, and special characters (*, &, %, and @). A string must be enclosed within quotation marks of the same type, that is, either both single quotation marks or both double quotation marks. A few examples of string literals are as follows:

```
"Hello, World!"
"555-1212"
"KA12V2B334"
"one line ends here "
```

In the preceding examples, the quotation marks explicitly tell JavaScript that the value being assigned to a variable is of the String type. Consider another example where a variable contains the string "100." Even though 100 is of the number type, JavaScript identifies it as a string since it is enclosed in quotation marks.

Special Characters in Strings

Consider a situation when you want to include a quote character (quotation mark) in a string or want to include a new line in a string. How will you do this? JavaScript provides you with some special characters that enable you to do this. Special characters are characters that cannot normally be entered into a string directly through the keyboard (such as a new line character or the Enter key) or have special meaning (reserved characters). For example, pressing the Enter key on the keyboard does not cause a new line character to be a part of a string. Instead it moves the cursor to the left of the next line on the screen. We have already taken the example of the string `'one line ends here \n second line starts from here'` that uses the special character \n. The special character \n places the string part `"second line starts from here"` in a new line.

In the same manner, to include single quotes in a string literal enclosed within double quotes or single quotes, such as `"Anna's car"`, you can use the special character `\'`. Therefore, to include an apostrophe you'll write the string `"Anna's car"` as `"Anna\'s car"`. Similarly, to include double quotes in a string enclosed within single or double quotes, you can use the special character `\"`. This technique is also called *escaping characters.* The escaping characters technique allows JavaScript to ignore the special meaning of reserved characters.

Table 3.4 lists JavaScript special characters.

The following example illustrates how JavaScript special characters are being used.

```
<HTML>
<HEAD>
<TITLE>Special Characters in Strings</TITLE>
</HEAD>
<BODY>
<H1 align="center"> Special Characters in Strings </H1>
<PRE>
<SCRIPT LANGUAGE="JavaScript">
document.write("This illustrates how the \bbackspace character
functions.\n");
document.write("This illustrates how the \ttab character
functions.\n");
document.write("This illustrates how the \rcarriage return
character functions.\n");
document.write("This illustrates how the \fform feed character
functions.\n");
document.write("This illustrates how the \nnew line character
functions.\n");
</SCRIPT>
</PRE>
</BODY>
</HTML>
```

The preceding code also uses the preformatted text tags `<PRE>...</PRE>`. The preformatted text tags prevent formatting characters from being treated as HTML white space characters. To display special characters, it is essential to use preformatted text tags. If these tags are not used, special characters don't perform their functions. In Figure 3.2, observe that the backspace character and the form feed character are ignored and the carriage return character provides the same function as the new line

Table 3.4　JavaScript Special Characters

CHARACTER	MEANING
\b	Backspace
\f	Form feed
\t	Horizontal tab
\n	New line
\r	Carriage return
\\	Backslash
\'	Single quote
\"	Double quote

character (that is, places the text following on a new line). Quite a few of the special characters, such as backspace and form feed characters, are not fully supported in the display of Web pages. However, you can still use these to insert formatting text within the code and files that JavaScript produces.

Figure 3.2 demonstrates how JavaScript special characters are being used.

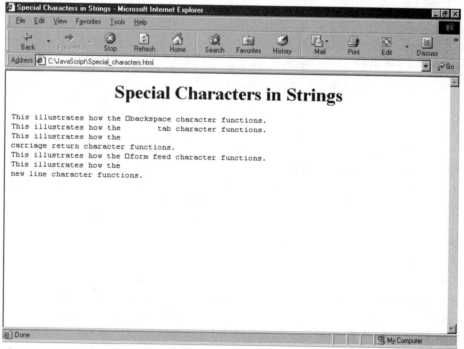

Figure 3.2　Use of JavaScript special characters.

The null Value

There might be situations when you are not certain of what value you should assign to a variable. For example, while accepting user input, you may want to store the input in a variable. But you may not be sure of the type of data that the user will enter. In such situations, you can assign a common initial value, null, to the variable. The null literal value is shared between all JavaScript data types. Using the null value avoids the occurrence of errors that may arise due to the use of variables that are not initialized or declared in a program. The data type of the variable that is assigned a null value is automatically converted to the data type of the variable with which it is used in an expression. For example, when you evaluate a null value in a numeric expression, the null value is automatically converted to 0. The following example illustrates how the variable numConvert is converted to 0 in a numeric expression:

```
var numConvert=null;
numConvert + 32 // returns 32
```

NOTE You'll see how JavaScript automatically converts data types in the section *Data Type Conversion* later in this chapter.

The undefined Value

A variable that has not been assigned a literal value has the value undefined. While evaluating an unassigned variable, which is a variable with undefined value, different results are obtained, depending on the way the variable is declared.

If an unassigned variable is declared without using the var keyword, the evaluation results in a run-time error. Consider the following example, where variable *x* is used in a function without being declared:

```
function evalSubtraction(){
      return x*32;
}
evalSubtraction() //causes runtime error
```

If an unassigned variable is declared using the var keyword, its evaluation results in the undefined value for strings, NaN (Not a Number) for the number type, and false for the Boolean type. The following example returns the NaN value when an unassigned variable, which is declared using the var keyword, is used:

```
function evalSubtraction(){
      return var x*32;
}
evalSubtraction() //returns NaN
```

The literal value, undefined, can also be used to determine whether a variable holds a value. In the following example, the variable input is not assigned any value and the if statement evaluates to true.

```
var input;
if(input==undefined){
      evalInput();
}
```

NOTE The preceding examples use functions and the conditional if statement. For details on functions refer to Chapter 5, "Functions and Events," and for conditional statements refer to Chapter 4, "JavaScript Control Structures and Statements."

Data Type Conversion

As already stated, in the case of variables of different data types, JavaScript automatically converts values from one data type to another when used in an expression. This means that in an expression, JavaScript allows you to combine variables of different data types. It performs necessary data type conversion in an expression, wherever it is required. For instance, in the expression "hello" + 100, the number type literal value 100 is converted to the string "100" and is appended to the string "hello." It therefore displays the value "hello100." JavaScript's automatic conversion also allows you to assign a data type value to a variable and later assign different data type values to the same variable.

Now, how does JavaScript determine when to perform data type conversion and what type of conversion should take place? JavaScript performs conversion between variable data types when it evaluates an expression or assigns a different value to the same variable. It performs type conversion when you assign a value to a variable to which you have already assigned a value. JavaScript parses the data type associated with the variable to the type of value that you assign later. For example, if you assign the value 100 to the variable num and later you assign the value hello to the same variable, JavaScript converts the data type of the variable num to the String type.

The conversion of data types in JavaScript expressions takes place on the basis of the order of precedence of the operators in a parse tree.

Object Data Type and Arrays

Until now we have discussed primitive data types, such as String, Boolean, and Number, and special data types, such as null and undefined. As already stated, in addition to these data types, JavaScript also supports complex data types, objects, and arrays. Complex data types are referred to as complex because they are derived from primitive data types only. We'll address objects in Chapter 6, "Using Objects in JavaScript." In this chapter, we'll only cover the array data type that is also an object.

An array is a collection of similar or dissimilar values stored in adjacent memory locations. For example, instead of defining 30 integer variables for storing the test scores of 30 students in a class, one integer array can be defined containing 30 elements to store the data. JavaScript does not put any restriction on the type of values that an array can store. The values stored can be of different types or can refer to other arrays or objects. Before progressing further with array declarations, it is essential for us to understand the need for arrays.

Let's consider a situation where information regarding 50 models of cars needs to be stored. Since a variable is capable of storing only one value at a time, defining and keeping track of 50 variables in a program is not easy. The solution is to declare one variable with 50 elements to store information about the various car models.

You can declare an array by using the following syntax:

```
arrayName = new Array(number_of_elements);
```

Based on the preceding syntax, you can declare an array for storing car models by using the following statement:

```
Car = new Array(5);
```

In the preceding statement, the size of the array is 5. When the definition of the array is executed, memory is allocated for the user-defined variable `Car`. Array elements will be positioned one after another in memory. The schematic representation of the placement of array elements in memory is shown below:

| Car[0] | Car[1] | Car[2] | Car[3] | Car[4] |

In the above example, `Car` is the name of the array variable. The elements of the array are `Car[0]`, `Car[1]`, `Car[2]`, `Car[3]`, and `Car[4]`. Here, 0, 1, 2, 3, and 4 are the subscripts or indices of the elements. Note that the index starts from 0. The subscript number or index specifies the position of an element within the array. Since the first index is 0, the last index will be 1 less than the length of an array.

To initialize this array, you need to initialize the individual elements.

```
Car[0] = "Ford";
Car[1] = "Toyota";
Car[2] = "Volkswagen";
Car[3] = "Mercedes";
Car[4] = "Honda";
```

The elements can be initialized in any order. Following is the schematic diagram of the same array after initialization:

```
Ford
Toyota
Volkswagen
Mercedes
Honda
     Car[0]         Car[1]         Car[2]         Car[3]         Car[4]
```

You can access the names of the car models in the array by using the following statements:

```
document.write(Car[0]);
document.write(Car[1]);
document.write(Car[2]);
document.write(Car[3]);
document.write(Car[4]);
```

The following example illustrates the use of arrays:

```
<HTML>
<HEAD>
<TITLE>Using Arrays</TITLE>
</HEAD>
<BODY>
<H1 ALIGN="CENTER">Displaying Names of Car Models Using
Arrays</H1>
<SCRIPT LANGUAGE="JavaScript">
Car = new Array(5);
Car[0] = "Ford";
Car[1] = "Toyota";
Car[2] = "Volkswagen";
Car[3] = "Mercedes";
Car[4] = "Honda";
document.write(Car[0] + "<BR>");
document.write(Car[1] + "<BR>");
document.write(Car[2] + "<BR>");
document.write(Car[3] + "<BR>");
document.write(Car[4] + "<BR>");
</SCRIPT>
</BODY>
</HTML>
```

Figure 3.3 illustrates how the Web page displays the content of the array Car.

Until now, you have declared arrays whose length has already been specified. You can also declare arrays whose length is not specified. This results in the declaration of an array whose length is 0. The syntax for such a declaration is as follows:

```
arrayName = new Array();
```

The following example illustrates this type of declaration:

```
Car = new Array();
```

This declaration results in an array Car of length 0. JavaScript allows the automatic extension of the length of an array when new array elements are assigned to the

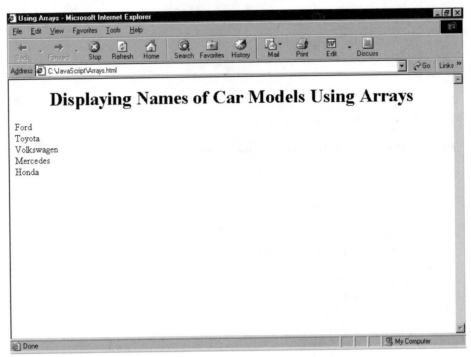

Figure 3.3 Content of the array Car.

variable. For example, the following code declares an array called Car of length 0 and consequently extends the length of the array to 10 and then 100.

```
Car = new Array();
Car[9] = "Ford";
Car[99] = "Honda";
```

In the preceding code, when JavaScript comes across the code Car[9], it extends the length of the array to 10 and initializes Car[9] to "Ford". When JavaScript comes across the code Car[99], it extends the length of the array to 100 and initializes Car[99] to "Honda".

The length of an array that has been declared with a specific length can also be extended. You can extend the length by referencing the elements that are beyond the current size of the array. This is achieved in the same manner with zero-length arrays. The following code illustrates how fixed-length arrays are expanded as new array elements are referenced.

```
<HTML>
<HEAD>
<TITLE>Using Arrays</TITLE>
```

```
</HEAD>
<BODY>
<H1 ALIGN="CENTER">Extending the length of an Array</H1>
<SCRIPT LANGUAGE="JavaScript">
Car = new Array(5);
document.write("Car.length = " + Car.length + "<BR>");
Car[9] = "Ford";
document.write("Car.length = " + Car.length + "<BR>");
Car[99] = "Honda";
document.write("Car.length = " + Car.length + "<BR>");
</SCRIPT>
</BODY>
</HTML>
```

In the preceding code, observe that the `Car.length` code is used to calculate the length of the array. As already stated, in JavaScript arrays are implemented as objects that are a collection of data that has properties and methods. A property returns a value that identifies the characteristics of an object. For example, if a pen is an object, its properties will be its length, the color of its ink, and so on. Methods are the actions that an object can be made to perform. For example, a pen can be made to write, spin, roll, and flip. In the same manner, an array object has one of its properties, length, that calculates the length of an array. The following is the syntax for accessing the property of an object:

```
objectName.propertyName
```

To access the property of the array, `Car`, the code is as follows:

```
Car.length
```

Figure 3.4 illustrates the result of extending an array.

So far, we have looked at two methods of declaring arrays. These arrays were declared first, and then each of their elements was initialized separately. JavaScript also allows us to declare arrays with the elements in them initialized at the same time. Such arrays are also called *dense arrays*. Dense arrays function in the same manner as other arrays. These arrays are the most effective in the case of a short array declaration. However, it is preferable not to define the length of an array in situations where you are not sure of the length that you want to define. The syntax of declaring a dense array is as follows:

```
arrayName = new Array(value_0, value_1, ..., value_n)
```

In the preceding syntax, since the index starts from zero, the length of the array will be n+1.

The following code declares a dense array:

```
Car = new Array("Ford", "Toyota", "Volkswagen", "Mercedes",
"Honda");
```

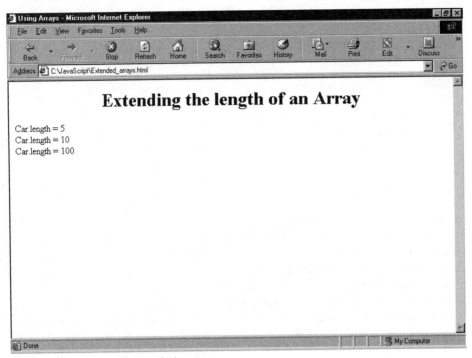

Figure 3.4   Output of extended arrays.

As stated earlier, an array can include values of similar and dissimilar types. This means that the values can be of different data types or can also include other arrays or objects. For example, you can declare an array that contains the following objects:

```
mixArray = new Array("Hello", 10.5, true, false, null, 4, new
Array(1, 2, 3));
```

In the preceding code, the array, `mixArray`, has the following seven elements:

```
mixArray[0]="Hello"
mixArray[1]=10.5
mixArray[2]=true
mixArray[3]=false
mixArray[4]=null
mixArray[5]=4
mixArray[6]=another dense array containing the values 1, 2, and 3
```

The seventh element of the array, `mixArray[6]`, consists of another array that has the value initialized at the time of declaration. To access the elements of `mixArray[6]`, you'll have to use a second set of subscripts (indices), as follows:

```
mixArray[6][0]=1;
mixArray[6][1]=2;
mixArray[6][2]=3;
```

The following example illustrates how you can use arrays for storing values of different types:

```
<HTML>
<HEAD>
<TITLE> Arrays with Different Values</TITLE>
</HEAD>
<BODY>
<H1 ALIGN="CENTER"> Arrays with Different Values </H1>
<SCRIPT LANGUAGE="JavaScript">
mixArray = new Array("Hello", 10.5, true, false, null, 4, new
Array(1, 2, 3));
    document.write("mixArray[0] = " + mixArray[0] + "<BR>");
    document.write("mixArray[1] = " + mixArray[1] + "<BR>");
    document.write("mixArray[2] = " + mixArray[2] + "<BR>");
    document.write("mixArray[3] = " + mixArray[3] + "<BR>");
    document.write("mixArray[4] = " + mixArray[4] + "<BR>");
    document.write("mixArray[5] = " + mixArray[5] + "<BR>");
    document.write("mixArray[6][0] = " + mixArray[6][0] + "<BR>");
    document.write("mixArray[6][1] = " + mixArray[6][1] + "<BR>");
    document.write("mixArray[6][2] = " + mixArray[6][2] + "<BR>");
</SCRIPT>
</BODY>
</HTML>
```

Figure 3.5 displays the values of a dense array that contains values of different types.

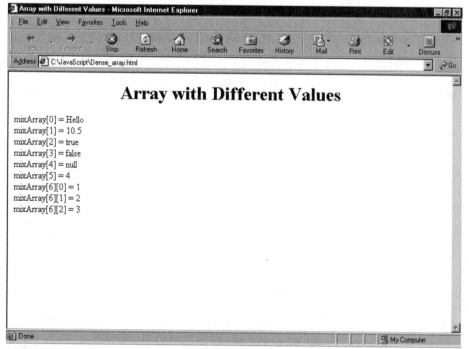

Figure 3.5   Values of a dense array that contains values of different types.

Expressions and Operators

After you have defined a variable, you can assign new values to the variable or use its existing values by using basic building blocks that are referred to as *operators* and *expressions*. We already referred to expressions earlier in this chapter. This section will explain in detail what an expression is and covers all the operators provided by JavaScript. It will help you identify how variables and literals merge with operators to form an expression.

Expressions

What are expressions? Let's again think back to our school days. Remember the first-grade math session and a simple question, "What is 2 + 2?". The statement "2 + 2" is an expression. An *expression* is a set of literals, variables, and operators that merge and evaluate to a single value. The statement "2+2" contains two literal values and the arithmetic operator plus or "+." This expression results in a single value, 4.

Most expressions take the following general form:

```
left_operand operator right_operand
```

In the preceding syntax, each operand (left_operand and right_operand) can be either a variable or a literal value, depending on the type of expression and the type of operator that controls the expression. The statement "Operator controls the expression" means that the operator directs what needs to be done with the set of operands.

Using the various operators explained later in this section, you can create four different types of Expressions in JavaScript. These types of expressions are as follows:

- **Arithmetic Expressions.** Expressions that result in a number.
- **Logical Expressions.** A special group of expressions that results in either a true or a false value.
- **String Expressions.** Expressions that evaluate to a new string. A string expression can be used to concatenate strings.
- **Conditional Expressions.** Expressions that evaluate to one of two different expressions depending on a condition. The details of this expression will be dealt with later in this chapter.

Operators

Operators are the backbone of expressions. Operators direct expressions to perform specific tasks, such as addition, subtraction, multiplication, and so on. These are used to transform one or more values into a single resultant value. We have already used some of the basic operators provided by JavaScript. We used the + operator to concatenate string and numeric types and the = assignment operator to assign values to variables.

Table 3.5 summarizes all the operators that can be used in JavaScript expressions.

Table 3.5 Operators in JavaScript

OPERATORS	DESCRIPTION
Arithmetic operators	Take numeric literals or numeric variables as their operands and return a numeric value.
Logical operators	Work with logical values, such as logical and, or, and not and return the Boolean value, true or false.
Comparison operators	Compare the values of the operands and return a Boolean value, true or false.
String operators	Take string values as their operands and return a string as their value.
Bit-wise operators	Perform operations on the bit representation (zeros and ones) of a value and return the result as a numeric value.
Assignment operators	Assign values to the left operand based on the value of the right operand.
Conditional operators	Take three operands, the condition to be evaluated, and two alternative values to be returned based on the condition.

Having looked at the types of operators that JavaScript provides, let's now discuss each one of these in detail.

Arithmetic operators are the most common operators since we use them in our daily life for performing mathematical calculations. Arithmetic operators are of two types: binary and unary. Binary operators operate on two operands (variable or literal). Let's first discuss the binary operators. Table 3.6 shows the arithmetic binary operators with examples used in JavaScript.

Table 3.6 JavaScript Arithmetic Operators

OPERATOR	NAME	DESCRIPTION	EXAMPLE	RETURN VALUE
+	Addition	Adds the operands	3 + 5	8
-	Subtraction	Subtracts the right operand from the left operand	5 - 3	2
*	Multiplication	Multiplies the operands	3 * 5	15

(continues)

Table 3.6   JavaScript Arithmetic Operators *(Continued)*

OPERATOR	NAME	DESCRIPTION	EXAMPLE	RETURN VALUE
/	Division	Divides the left operand by the right operand	20 / 5	4
%	Modulus	Divides the left operand by the right operand and calculates the remainder	20 % 5	0

In Table 3.6, the examples shown use literal values to depict the functionality of each arithmetic operator. However, you can also use variables with arithmetic operators. The following examples illustrate this:

```
var firstNum = 2;
var secondNum = 3;
add = firstNum + secondNum;//variable add contains value 5
multiply = firstNum * secondNum;//variable multiply contains value 6
```

So far, we have discussed the arithmetic binary operators that operate on two operands: variables or literals. As stated, arithmetic operators can also be of unary type. Unary operators operate on one operand, which may be a variable or a literal. Unary arithmetic operators are of two types: Increment (++) and Decrement (– –). Table 3.7 lists the unary arithmetic operator.

As can be seen in Table 3.7, the increment operator can be used in two ways: as a prefix, where the operator precedes the variable ++counter, and as a postfix, where the operator follows the variable (counter++). The following code segment differentiates the two notations:

```
counter=10;
result=++counter;
```

The equivalent of this code is:

```
counter=10;
counter=counter+1;
result=counter;
```

In this case, both the counter and the result are set to 11. However, if the code is written as:

```
counter=10;
result=counter++;
```

Table 3.7   JavaScript Unary Arithmetic Operators

NAME	EXAMPLE	RESULT
Post Incrementing operator	counter++	Returns the value of the variable counter and then adds 1 to the value.
Post Decrementing	counter--	Returns the value of the variable operator counter and then subtracts 1 from the value.
Pre Incrementing operator	++counter	Adds 1 to the value of the variable counter and then returns the new value.
Pre Decrementing operator	--counter	Subtracts 1 from the value of the variable counter and then returns the new value.

the equivalent code will be:

```
counter=10;
counter=counter++;
result=counter+1;
```

Here, the `counter` is set to 11 but the value of the result is 10.

Thus, in the prefix notation, the increment operation is performed prior to assignment whereas in the postfix notation, the assignment operation precedes the increment of the variable.

The decrement operator (--) behaves like the increment operator, except that it subtracts 1 from the variable. It can also be used in both prefix and postfix forms.

Logical operators are used to perform Boolean operations on Boolean operands. Table 3.8 shows the logical operators supported by JavaScript.

Table 3.8   JavaScript Logical Operators

OPERATOR	NAME	DESCRIPTION	EXAMPLE	RETURN VALUE
&&	Logical and	The Logical "and" evaluates to true when both operands are true	3>2 && 5<2	false
||	Logical or	The logical "or" evaluates to true when either operand is true	3>1 || 2>5	true
!	Logical not	The logical "not" evaluates to true if the operand is false, and to false if the operand is true	5!=3	true

Logical operators are best suited when you have several conditions to be tested together and there is the probability that one of the conditions may be true or false than other conditions. When JavaScript evaluates a logical expression, it only evaluates as many subexpressions as are needed to get the result. This increases the speed of execution of the script. For example, if you have an "And" expression such as ((x==100) && (y==125)), JavaScript first verifies if x is equal to 100. If x is not equal to 100, the value of y is not checked.

Comparison operators are used to compare two numerical values. Table 3.9 shows the comparison operators supported by JavaScript.

The operators strictly equal (===) and strictly not equal (!==) are part of the ECMAScript 1 standard. These operators were introduced to Navigator in JavaScript 1.3 and are only supported by Navigator 4.06 and later versions. These are also supported by Internet Explorer 4 and later versions.

Table 3.9 JavaScript Comparison Operators

OPERATOR	NAME	DESCRIPTION	EXAMPLE	RETURN VALUE
==	Equal	Performs type conversion before testing for equality	"5"==5	true
===	Strictly Equal	Performs no type conversion before testing for equality	"5"===5	false
!=	Not equal	Evaluates to true if the operands are not equal	5!=2	true
!==	Strictly not equal	Performs no type conversion before testing for nonequality	5!=="5"	true
>	Greater than	Evaluates to true if the left operand is greater than the right operand	2>5	false
<	Less than	Evaluates to true if the left operand is less than the right operand	2<5	true
>=	Greater than or equal	Evaluates to true if the left operand is greater than or equal to the right operand	5>=2	true
<=	Less than or equal	Evaluates to true if the left operand is less than or equal to the right operand	5<=2	false

Table 3.10 JavaScript String Operator

OPERATOR	NAME	DESCRIPTION	EXAMPLE	RETURN VALUE
+	String con-catenation	Joins two strings	"Hello"+"World"	HelloWorld

NOTE There is a fault in Navigator. If the `<SCRIPT>` tag's language attribute is set to "JavaScript1.2," Navigator 4 and later versions treat the equal operator (= =) as the strictly equal operator. For example, "2"= =2 evaluates to false.

The string operator performs operation on strings. JavaScript only supports one string operator, which is shown in Table 3.10 with a supporting example.

Bit manipulation operators perform operations on the bit representation of a value, such as shifting bits right or left. Bit manipulation operators supported by JavaScript are listed in Table 3.11.

Table 3.11 JavaScript Bit Manipulation Operators

OPERATOR	NAME	DESCRIPTION	EXAMPLE	RETURN VALUE
&	Bitwise AND	It examines each bit position in each of its operands. If both operands have 1 bit in a given position, then that bit will also be set to 1 in the result. In all other cases, the output bit position is zero.	If x=0x00001234 and y=0x8000ABCD then z=x&y	Z=0x00000204
|	Bitwise OR	If either bit is 1 in any bit position, then that bit will be 1 in the result.	w = x | y	w=0x8000BBFD
^	Bitwise XOR	It sets a bit in the result if either bit in the operand is set, but not both.	v =x ^ y	v=0x8000B9F9
<<	Bitwise left shift	Shifts the bits of an expression to the left.	Temp=14<<2	56

(continues)

Table 3.11 JavaScript Bit Manipulation Operators *(Continued)*

OPERATOR	NAME	DESCRIPTION	EXAMPLE	RETURN VALUE
>>	Bitwise signed right shift	Shifts the bits of an expression to the right maintaining a sign.	Temp=-14>>2	-4
>>>	Bitwise Zero-fill right shift	Shifts the bits of an expression to the right.	Temp=3>>>1	3

Assignment operators are used to assign values to variables. Table 3.12 shows the assignment operators supported by JavaScript.

JavaScript supports the conditional expression operator, ? :. This operator (also called the *ternary operator*) takes three operands: the condition to be evaluated and two alternative values to be returned based on the condition. The following is the syntax of writing a conditional operator in a conditional expression:

```
(condition) ? expression1: expression2
```

In the preceding syntax, if the condition is true, expression1 is evaluated. If the condition is false, expression2 is evaluated. The following is an example of using a conditional expression:

```
(x < y) ? a=10 : b=15
```

Table 3.12 JavaScript Assignment Operators

OPERATOR	DESCRIPTION	EXAMPLE	RETURN VALUE
=	Assigns the value of the right operand to the left operand	A=2	2
+=	Adds together the operands and assigns the result to the left operand	A+=5	7
-=	Subtracts the right operand from the left operand and assigns the result to the left operand	A-=5	2
*=	Multiplies the operands and assigns the result to the left operand	A*=5	10
/=	Divides the left operand by the right operand and assigns the result to the left operand	A/=5	2
%=	Divides the left operand by the right operand and assigns the remainder to the left operand	A%=2	0

In the preceding example, if the value of variable *x* is less than the value of variable *y*, then a=10. If the value of variable *x* is greater than the value of variable *y*, then b=15.

JavaScript also supports a number of other operators that cannot be categorized as arithmetic, logical, comparison, string, bit manipulation, assignment, or conditional operators. These operators are as follows:

The , (Comma) operator.   Evaluates two expressions and returns the value of the second expression. For example, counter = (2+3), (2*10). In this example, both the expressions (2+3) and (2*10) are evaluated and the result of the second expression, 20, is stored in counter.

The delete operator.   Deletes a property of an object or an element in the array index. For example, delete arr[10] deletes the eleventh element of the array arr.

The new operator.   Creates an instance of an object type.

The typeof operator.   Returns a string value that identifies an operand type. For example, in the statement, varStr = typeof("Hello"), assigns a value of the type String to the variable, varStr.

The void operator.   Can be used to specify an expression as a hypertext link. When used to specify as a link, the expression is evaluated but is not loaded in the place of the current document. For example, the following code creates a hypertext link with the void operator. This link does not take the user to any URL.

```
<A HREF="javascript:void(0)">Click here...No response</A>
```

NOTE The delete and new operators will be dealt with in detail in Chapter 6, "Using Objects in JavaScript."

Operator precedence determines which expressions will be evaluated before others. In the expression 4 + 6 * 2, for example, remember that multiplication takes precedence over addition and the expression would evaluate to 16. However, if we rewrite the above expression as (4 + 6) * 2, it would evaluate to 20 because parenthetical expressions take precedence over multiplication. Table 3.13 shows the precedence of JavaScript operators.

Table 3.13   Order of Precedence of Operators

PRECEDENCE	OPERATOR
1	Parentheses, function calls, or array subscripts
2	, ~, -, ++, – –, typeof, new, void, delete
3	*, /, %
4	+, -
5	<<, >>, >>>

(continues)

Table 3.13 Order of Precedence of Operators *(Continued)*

PRECEDENCE	OPERATOR
6	<, <=, >, >=
7	==, !=, ===, !==
8	&
9	^
10	|
11	&&
12	||
13	?:
14	=, +=, -=, *=, /=, %=, <<=, >>=, >>>=, &=, ^=, |=
15	The comma(,) operator

If more than one operator is listed at a level, the operators listed are of equal priority. JavaScript reads an expression from left to right. At that level of precedence, it evaluates operators as it comes across them.

For a better understanding of the concept of operator precedence, let's look at the following expression that consists of several operators.

```
Temp = (19 % 4) / 1 - 1 + !false
```

In the preceding code, since parenthetical expressions take precedence over all other operators, the expression 19 % 4 is evaluated first. It generates the following result:

```
Temp = 3 / 1 - 1 + !false
```

NOTE As discussed earlier, the % (modulus) operator divides the left operand by the right operand and calculates the remainder. For example, 19 % 4 = 3, since 19 / 4 = 4 with 3 as the remainder.

Now, the negation operator, !, has the highest precedence in the expression. After evaluating ! as false, the resultant expression is as follows:

```
Temp = 3 / 1 - 1 + true
```

The / operator is to be evaluated. Therefore, we get the following expression:

```
Temp = 3 - 1 + true
```

Between the – and the + operator, the + operator has the highest precedence. As already stated, in a numeric expression, the logical value true is converted to 1 and the expression 1 + `true`, thus evaluated to 2. The expression is now as follows :

```
Temp = 3 - 2
```

The expression is evaluated to:

```
Temp = 1
```

Finally, the = assignment operator assigns the integer value 1 to the variable `Temp`. **Now that we have looked at all the operators, it should be easy for you to identify the different types of expression statements that we had discussed earlier.** Each of the expressions below relies on an operator:

- Assignment expression:

```
a = 25
```

The value 25 has been assigned to the variable, a. Therefore, the operator used is = (Assignment).

- Arithmetic expression:

```
var a = 25
var b = 75
var c = a + b
```

This expression adds the values of variables *a* and *b*, which are 25 and 75, respectively. The resultant value 100 is assigned to variable *c*.

Operators used in the preceding expression are + (Addition) and = (Assignment).

- String expression:

```
"Hello, " + "Sandy"
```

This evaluates to a new string that says "Hello, Sandy." The operator used in this expression is + (Concatenation).

- Logical expression:

```
25 < 75
```

Since 25 is less than 75, this expression evaluates to the Boolean value, true. The operator used in this expression is < (Comparison).

```
25 >= 75
```

Since 25 is not greater than or equal to 75, this expression evaluates to the Boolean value, false. The operator used in this expression is >= (Comparison).

Result

As per the preceding discussion, Scott has identified the data types in Table 3.14 for accepting and storing details of customers.

The following are the operators that Scott identified to calculate the outstanding amounts of the customers:

The - operator.   This operator will subtract the value in the variable `custA-mountPaid` from the value in variable `custAmount` and thus store the balance amount due in the `custBalAmount` variable. The code for calculating the balance amount is as follows:

```
custBalAmount = custAmount - custAmountPaid;
```

Table 3.14   Variable Names and Data Types with Description

VARIABLE NAME	DATA TYPE	DESCRIPTION
CustName	String	Stores the name of the first/second customer
CustDob	String	Stores the date of birth of the first/second customer
CustAddress	String	Stores the address of the first/second customer
CustCity	String	Stores the city where the first/second customer stays
CustPhone	String	Stores the phone number of the first/second customer
CustAmount	Number	Stores the total bill amount of the first/second customer
CustAmountPaid	Number	Stores the amount paid by the first/second customer
CustBalAmount	Number	Stores the outstanding amount of the first/second customer
FirstCustomer	Array	Stores details such as the name, date of birth, address, city, phone, and outstanding amount of the first customer
SecondCustomer	Array	Stores details such as the name, date of birth, address, city, phone, and outstanding amount of the second customer
BillDetails	Array	Stores the details of first and second customer in the form of arrays within arrays

The conditional expression operator (? :) This operator will evaluate the condition whether or not the value in the variable custBalAmount is equal to 0. If it is 0, it displays the outstanding amount as zero or else displays the actual outstanding amount due from the customer. The code for testing the preceding condition is as follows:

```
        (custBalAmount == 0) ? document.write("Amount Outstanding:
" + custBalAmount"):document.write("No amount due")
```

The string concatenation operator +. This operator has been used to concatenate the values of variables with text while displaying details to an employee.

Write the Code to Accept and Display the Details

The following is the code for accepting and displaying the details of the customer:

```
<HTML>
<HEAD><TITLE> Billing System of Web Shoppe </TITLE></HEAD>
<BODY>
<H1 align="center"> Billing System of Web Shoppe </H1>
<SCRIPT LANGUAGE="JavaScript">
firstCustomer = new Array();
secondCustomer = new Array();
billDetails = new Array(firstCustomer, secondCustomer);
var custName;
var custDob;
var custAddress;
var custCity;
var custPhone;
var custAmount;
var custAmountPaid;
var custBalAmount;
custName=prompt("Enter the first customer's name:", "");
custDob=prompt("Enter the first customer's date of birth:", "");
custAddress=prompt("Enter the first customer's address:", "");
custCity=prompt("Enter the city:", "");
custPhone=prompt("Enter the first customer's phone number:", "");
custAmount=prompt("Enter the total bill amount of the first
customer:", "");
custAmountPaid=prompt("Enter the amount paid by the first
customer:", "");
custBalAmount = custAmount - custAmountPaid;
firstCustomer[0]=custName;
firstCustomer[1]=custDob;
firstCustomer[2]=custAddress;
firstCustomer[3]=custCity;
firstCustomer[4]=custPhone;
firstCustomer[5]=custBalAmount;
document.write("<B>" + "You have entered the following details for
first customer:" + "<BR>");
```

```
document.write("Name: " + billDetails[0][0] + "<BR>");
document.write("Date of Birth: " + billDetails[0][1] + "<BR>");
document.write("Address: " + billDetails[0][2] + "<BR>");
document.write("City: " + billDetails[0][3] + "<BR>");
document.write("Phone: " + billDetails[0][4] + "<BR>");
(custBalAmount == 0) ? document.write("Amount Outstanding: " +
custBalAmount):document.write("No amount due")
custName=prompt("Enter the second customer's name:", "");
custDob=prompt("Enter the second customer's date of birth", "");
custAddress=prompt("Enter the second customer's address", "");
custCity=prompt("Enter the city", "");
custPhone=prompt("Enter the second customer's phone number", "");
custAmount=prompt("Enter the total bill amount of the second
customer:", "");
custAmountPaid=prompt("Enter the amount paid by the second
customer:", "");
custBalAmount = custAmount - custAmountPaid;
secondCustomer[0]=custName;
secondCustomer[1]=custDob;
secondCustomer[2]=custAddress;
secondCustomer[3]=custCity;
secondCustomer[4]=custPhone;
secondCustomer[5]=custBalAmount;
document.write("<BR>");
document.write("<BR>");
document.write("You have entered the following details for second
customer:" + "<BR>");
document.write("Name: " + billDetails[1][0] + "<BR>");
document.write("Date of Birth: " + billDetails[1][1] + "<BR>");
document.write("Address: " + billDetails[1][2] + "<BR>");
document.write("City: " + billDetails[1][3] + "<BR>");
document.write("Phone: " + billDetails[1][4] + "<BR>");
(custBalAmount == 0) ? document.write("Amount Outstanding: " +
custBalAmount):document.write("No amount due ")
</SCRIPT>
</BODY>
</HTML>
```

In the preceding code, notice that the prompt() method has been used to accept user input. The prompt() method requests user input through a text field within a dialog box. It's a method of a document object. You will learn about this in detail in Chapter 8, "Working with Browser Objects."

Execute the Code

After writing the above code, execute the application and enter the following details in the corresponding dialog boxes that appear:

```
Details for the first customer:
Name: Micheal A. Long
Date of Birth: 10/8/71
Billing Address: 14, George Street, New York
City: California
Phone number: 534-177-3312
Total Bill Amount: 2000.00
Amount Paid: 1000.00
Details for the second customer:
Name: Jennifer Brown
Date of Birth: 05/2/69
Billing Address: 201, East 98th Street, Indianapolis, IN, USA
City: Indianapolis
Phone number: 456-234-659
Total Bill Amount: 2967.75
Amount Paid: 2967.75
```

Figure 3.6 illustrates the output of the code for the billing system page.

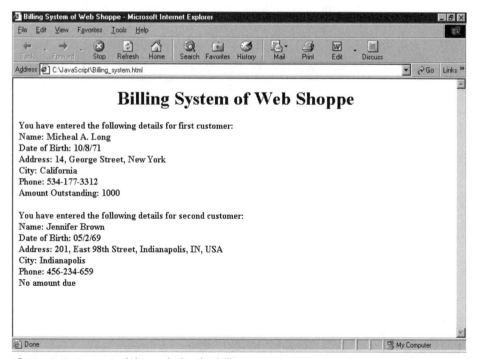

Figure 3.6   Output of the code for the billing system page.

Summary

In this chapter, we discussed variables, data types, operators, and expressions. The chapter began by discussing how to create variables and assign values to these variables. The conventions used for naming variables are also discussed.

The second section of the chapter introduced you to data types and explained how JavaScript assigns data types to variables. It also explored different data types, such as Number, String, Boolean, null, undefined, and Arrays, supported by JavaScript. The chapter guided you through the process of displaying the data stored in a variable on a Web page.

This chapter introduced you to expressions and operators. It provided details about the various types of operators and then proceeded to explain how these operators with variables form different expressions.

JavaScript Control Structures and Statements

Getting Started

So far, we have learned about the basics of writing simple JavaScript code. Therefore, by now you should be familiar with the elements of a simple JavaScript code, such as comments, expressions, data types, and variables. These scripts or code contain instructions that are straightforward. Moreover, these statements execute in the same order in which they appear in the code. Such scripts are unrealistically simple because they do not include any logic. However, in an actual problem-solving environment, you need to make decisions and branch out to a certain part of the code. These are situations where you need to determine whether certain conditions are true or false, or you need to repeatedly execute a group of statements, or make a selection of one group of statements out of several other possibilities. This is the role of programming statements. Programming statements allow you to make decisions and perform actions based on particular conditions.

In this chapter, you'll use conditional and looping statements to execute programs conditionally. To understand control statements, we will discuss the case of Web Shoppe, Inc., whose Web page makes extensive use of control statements.

Using Programming Statements

Problem Statement

The online shopping system of Web Shoppe needs a page on its site that displays the new product line of the store. Cynthia, the head of the development team, who is responsible for the maintenance of this site, already has the design of the page. She has now assigned Scott, a Web developer, to add the following functionality to the site:

- The site should ask a customer to enter the category of a product.

- Based on the choice entered by the customer, the program should then ask for the item that the customer wants to purchase. This process should continue until the customer chooses not to make any further purchases.

- Finally, the program should calculate the total purchases made by the customer and then evaluate the discount based on the following criteria:

TOTAL PURCHASE	DISCOUNT
Greater than $0 but less than or equal to $100	10%
Greater than $100 but less than or equal to $450	20%
Greater than $450	30%

Figure 4.1 displays the output of the interface that contains the new product line by category.

To incorporate the above functionality in the page that displays the new products of the store, the following task list has been identified.

NOTE For the code of the new Web Shoppe interface page, refer to www.wiley.com/compbooks/makinguse. While executing the code, remember to save the associated graphic and binary files in the same folder.

Task List

✔ Identify the conditional and looping statements to be used.

✔ Write the code.

✔ Execute and verify the code.

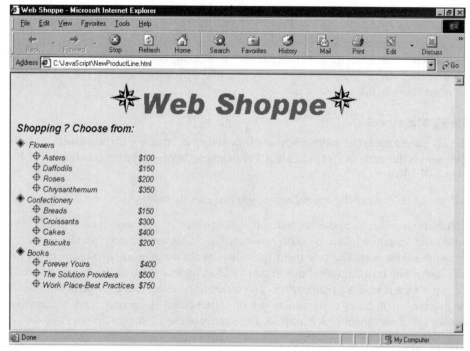

Figure 4.1   The new Web Shoppe page.

Identify the Conditional and Looping Statements to be Used

Before identifying the conditional and looping statements to be used to write the code, let's first discuss various conditional and looping statements available in JavaScript.

Programming statements can be split into two categories: conditional statements and looping statements.

Conditional Statements

The ability to make decisions is a fundamental characteristic of human beings. Just as humans have the ability to make decisions, you can also write programs that have decision-making abilities. You can incorporate decision-making ability into a program by using conditional statements. Conditional statements are constructs that help you control the flow of a program or incorporate decision-making in a program. The process of determining the order in which statements are executed in a program is called decision-making or flow control. In addition, conditional constructs allow selective execution of statements, depending on the value of expressions associated with them. Consider the following example of a Web shopping mall where a user can place online orders. You want the Web shopping mall page to function in a manner such that if a user clicks on the Add to Shopping Cart button, a set of statements that builds a list of items to be purchased is executed. However, if the user clicks a Checkout button, a different set of statements that allows a user to sign out of the site is executed. In this example, the program has the ability to make a decision based on the value associated with the buttons that are used by the user.

The if Statement

The if statement is the main conditional statement in JavaScript. The meaning of this statement is the same as that in English. For example, here is a typical conditional statement in English:

If you score 75 out of 100 in your exams, you will pass the course.

This statement is composed of two parts: a condition (*If you score 75 out of 100 in your exams*) and an action (*you will pass the course*). The if statement in JavaScript works in almost the same way. The statement provides the ability to modify the flow of a program execution based on a condition that yields a logical value. If the logical value of the expression is true, a particular set of statement(s) is executed. If the logical value of the expression is false, a particular set of statement(s) is ignored and, optionally, another set of statement(s) is executed. The syntax of the if statement is as follows:

```
if (condition) statement;
```

In the syntax above, you'll see that the if statement is composed of the following three elements:

- The keyword if that always appears in lowercase.
- The next element that appears immediately after the keyword if is a condition or expression that is enclosed within parentheses. The expression yields a logical true or false value.
- The third element is the executable statement or action that is executed if the condition enclosed within the parentheses, which is being evaluated in an if statement, yields a true value.

Here is an example of a basic if statement:

```
var chr;
chr = window.prompt("Enter a character:", "");
if(chr=='A') alert("Character is A.");
```

In the preceding example, the user is prompted to enter a character. If the user enters the character as 'A', then the message "Character is A" appears. This is because the if statement includes the condition "chr==A" that verifies the variable chr and an action statement, alert("Character is A"), which displays the message. However, if the user enters any character other than 'A', then the condition becomes false and the program executes any subsequent code that comes after the `if` statement.

Until now, the example that we have considered has only one statement to be executed. However, an `if` statement can also have multiple executable statements. The syntax of the `if` statement, where there are multiple statements, is as follows:

```
if (condition ){
    block of statements;
}
```

In the preceding syntax, the only difference is that the third element now contains a block of statements to be executed, which are enclosed within curly braces. Consider the following example that contains multiple executable statements if the condition holds true:

```
var chr = 'A';
if(chr == 'A'){
    document.writeln("The condition evaluates to true.");
    document.writeln("The variable chr is equal to A.");
    document.writeln("Each of these statements will be printed.");
}
document.writeln("This statement is always executed after the if
statement.");
```

In the preceding example, the `if` statement contains a block of statements that are executed if the condition of the statement evaluates to true. Therefore, if the variable `chr` is equal to 'A', then it displays four messages. However, if the condition does not hold true, then the statements in the command block are skipped and only the message "This statement is always executed after the if statement." is displayed.

In an `if` statement, while the instructions that need to be executed can comprise any JavaScript statements, the conditional part of the statement follows its own syntax. The conditional part generally includes two values to be compared. In the previous examples, the values were `chr` and `A`. These values can be variables, constants, or an expression. You can compare a variable and a value, two variables, or two constants. Between the two values to be compared, there is a conditional operator. Again going back to the preceding examples, we used the equality operator `==` to test whether the two values are equal. You can also use other conditional operators, such as `!=` (is not equal to), `<` (is less than), `>` (is greater than), `<=` (is less than or equal to), and `>=` (is greater than or equal to), in the `if` statement.

There might be situations where you want to test a variable for more than one possible value or test more than one variable at the same time. For example, you might want to test whether the variable `chr` holds the vowel A or O. In a normal course, you would write the `if` statements as follows:

```
if(chr == 'A') document.write("The variable contains a vowel.");
if(chr == 'O') document.write("The variable contains a vowel.");
```

However, instead of writing two if statements, you can combine the preceding two statements and write only one if statement. JavaScript provides logical operators, also called Boolean operators, for merging conditions. The following statement displays how you can merge two if statements into one by using the logical operator || (Or):

```
if(chr == 'A' || chr == 'O') document.write("The variable contains a
vowel.");
```

An additional logical operator && (And) can also be used to combine conditions in an if statement. Consider the following example:

```
if(chr == 'A' && chr1 == 'O') document.write("The variables contain
a vowel.");
```

This statement uses the && (And) operator instead of the || (Or) operator. Therefore, the message "The variables contain a vowel." will be displayed if both conditions (chr == 'A' and chr1 == 'O') hold true.

An added advantage of logical operators is that they increase the speed of your scripts. If the JavaScript interpreter discovers an answer to even one of the conditions before reaching the end of the conditional expression, then the interpreter does not evaluate the rest of the conditions. For instance, in the preceding example, if the first condition separated by the && operator evaluates to false, then the second condition is not evaluated.

The if...else Statements

To inform the JavaScript interpreter about the next action to be taken if the condition in the if statement holds a false value, you can include an else clause in an if statement. Consider the following situation where after placing an online order on the Web Shopping mall site, a user is prompted to enter credit card details. The user is asked to enter the choice of the card by which the user will make the payment. On the basis of the selection criterion, which can be MasterCard or Visa, the appropriate Web page for entering further details of the credit card is displayed to the user. In this particular example, you can use the if...else statement. This means that if the condition evaluates to true (user selects the MasterCard option), then the if statement displays a Web page for MasterCard details. If the condition evaluates to false (user selects the Visa card option), then the statement in an else clause displays the Web page for Visa card details.

The syntax for an if...else statement is as follows:

```
if (condition) statement;
else statement;
```

The syntax for an if...else statement where multiple statements are to be executed is as follows:

```
if (condition) {
  block of statements;
```

```
    }
    else {
      block of statements;
    }
```

The following code shows the use of the if...else statement:

```
    var chr;
    chr=prompt("Enter a character:", "");
    if(chr == 'A') document.write("Character is A.");
    else document.write("Character is not A.");
```

In the preceding example, if the user enters the character 'A', then the message "Character is A." is displayed. Otherwise, the message "Character is not A." is displayed.

The else if Statement

There might be situations where you want to include a condition in the else statement as well so that the statements in the else block are executed only when that condition is true. The else if statement in JavaScript allows you to test for multiple expressions for one true value and executes a particular block of code as soon as one of the conditions evaluates to true. The syntax for an else if construct is:

```
    if (condition)
  statement;
    else if (condition)
  statement;

              .
              .
              .

    else if (condition)
  statement;
    else
  statement;
```

The following example illustrates the use of the else if statement:

```
    var chr;
    chr=prompt("Enter a character in lower case:", "");
    if(chr == 'a')
       document.write("You entered the vowel a.");
    else if(chr == 'e')
       document.write("You entered the vowel e.");
    else if(chr == 'i')
       document.write("You entered the vowel i.");
    else if(chr == 'o')
       document.write("You entered the vowel o.");
    else if(chr == 'u')
       document.write("You entered the vowel u.");
    else
       document.write("The character is not a vowel.");
```

The preceding code prompts the user to enter a character in lowercase and checks whether it is a vowel. To better understand, the execution process in relation to the preceding example is explained in the following steps:

- The statement tests if the value entered by the user is a. If the condition is true, it prints the vowel a.

- However, if the condition is not true, the control moves to the first else if statement. This process continues until a true condition is found in the else if statements.

- If a true condition is found, then the statements in the else if block are executed and the control passes out of the construct.

- However, if the true condition is not found, then the control finally passes to the else statement.

NOTE An else if **statement can have several** else if **blocks but can have only one** else **statement.**

The Nested if/if...else Statement

Consider a situation where you have a program that uses an if statement to find out whether users like reading books. If the users answer positively, the program further asks the users for the type of books they like. The choice for the category of books (Fiction or Romance) is provided by using another if statement. Now, a second if statement is placed within the first if statement to incorporate this functionality. You can include any JavaScript code within the if statement or the if...else statement. Therefore, you can also include another if statement or if...else statement. An if statement that is contained within another if or if...else statement is called a nested if statement. Similarly, an if...else statement contained within another if or if...else statement is called a nested if...else statement. Nested if and if...else statements are used to execute conditional assessments, in addition to the original conditional assessments. The following example illustrates the nested if...else statement:

```
var chr;
chr=prompt("Enter a character:", "");
if(chr >= 'A'){
   if(chr <= 'Z')
      document.write("Upper Case");
   else if(chr >='a'){
      if(chr <='z')
         document.write("Lower Case");
      else
         document.write("Character entered > z");
   }
   else
      document.write("Character entered > Z but less than a");
```

```
    }
    else
        document.write("Character entered is less than A");
```

The `switch` Statement

Another conditional construct available in JavaScript is the `switch` statement. The `switch` statement is similar to the `if` and `else if` statement. Recall the example of vowel testing in the `else if` statement. Although the code in that example was formatted properly, it still looks complex due to several blocks of statements to be tested and executed. You can write the same logic with a `switch` statement. It is preferable to use the `switch` statement as compared to an `if` and `else if` statement when you use multiple conditions. This is because the program is more efficient and easier to read and understand.

The `switch` statement allows you to merge several evaluation tests of the same variable or expression into a single block of statements. The execution process of `switch` statements is similar to that shown in the preceding example of vowel testing. The syntax of the `switch` statement is as follows:

```
switch(expression) {
    case label1:
        statement(s)
        break
    case label2:
        statement(s)
        break
    ....
    ....
    ....
    ....
    ....
    ....
    case labeln:
        statement(s)
        break
    default:
        statement(s)
}
```

In the preceding syntax, you'll see that the `switch` statement comprises the following components: the keyword `switch`, an expression, an opening brace, a `case` label, the keyword `break`, a `default` label, executable statements, and a closing brace. When the switch statement is executed, its expression, which can also be a variable, is evaluated and compared with each `case` label. If one of the `case` labels is equal to the value of the expression, control is passed to the statement following the matched case label. If no case label matches the expression and there is a `default` label, the control passes to the statement with the label `default`. If no `case` matches and if there is no `default` label, then none of the statements in the `switch` is executed. A `break` statement is used to exit the `switch` statement.

Unlike other programming languages, such as Java and C++, JavaScript does not require all `case` labels within a `switch` statement to be of the same data type. This means that the data type of the `case` labels can be different from that of the `switch` expression. The following are the examples of various `case` labels:

```
case exampleVariable:      // variable name
    statement(s)
case 100:                  // integer literal
    statement(s)
case 100.5:                // floating-point literal
    statement(s)
case "test string":        // string literal
    statement(s)
```

If the value of the expression in the switch statement matches any of the case labels, then the control passes to the first statement following the end of the switch statement. The `break` statement, when used in the `switch` statement, causes the program flow to exit the body of the `switch` statement. However, if the `break` statement is not used, the control passes to the next `case` label. In this way, all `case` labels in the `switch` statement are executed one after another.

The statements associated with the default keyword are executed if the value of the switch variable or expression does not match any of the case labels.

The `else if` vowel example is converted to use the `switch` statement:

```
var chr;
chr=prompt("Enter a character in lower case:", "");
switch(chr) {
    case 'a' :
       document.write("Vowel a");
       break;      //break out of the switch statement
    case 'e' :
       document.write("Vowel e");
       break;
    case 'i' :
       document.write("Vowel i");
       break;
    case 'o' :
       document.write("Vowel o");
       break;
    case 'u' :
       document.write("Vowel u");
       break;
    default   :
       document.write("The character is not a vowel.");
}
```

Looping Statements

So far, all the conditional statements that you have worked with execute in a linear fashion. This means that these statements execute only once and stop when the condition is fulfilled. However, there might be situations when you want a set of statements to repeat a specific number of times. Consider the following example, where at the end of each month, the inventory supervisor of a company has to take a day-wise stock report for that month. Here, the program that will help achieve the functionality of generating this report needs to repeat the same set of statements 30 times. This type of task can be incorporated into programs by using looping statements. The technique of executing the same lines of codes repeatedly is called *looping*. The repetition in a loop continues while the condition set for the loop remains true. When the condition becomes false, the loop ends and the control passes to the statement following the loop.

JavaScript supports three types of loop statements: the `while` statement, the `do while` statement, and the `for` statement. JavaScript also supports the `break` and `continue` statements. Let's look at each of these statements in detail.

The `while` Statement

The `while` statement is a basic loop statement that is used to repeat the execution of a set of statements as long as a specified condition is `true`. The specified condition has to be a logical expression and must return either a `true` or a `false` value. The syntax for the `while` statement is as follows:

```
while (condition){
    statement(s);
}
```

The preceding syntax contains the keyword `while` and a condition that is enclosed within parentheses. In a program, as soon as a `while` statement is encountered, the `while` condition is evaluated. If the condition is `true`, the body of the loop is executed. The loop body comprises the statements that are enclosed within curly braces. After the execution of the body of the loop, the condition in the `while` statement is evaluated again. After the condition becomes `false`, the loop ends and the next statement following the `while` statement executes.

To end the `while` statement after the desired tasks have been executed, you track the progress of the loop and the status of the conditional expression. You can track the progress of a `while` statement by using a *counter*. A counter is nothing but a variable that is incremented or decremented with each repetition of a loop statement. You can give any name to a counter, such as count, counter, or letter 'i'. Using such names helps you remember that the variable used is a counter and also helps in tracking the variable.

The following example illustrates the use of the `while` statement. The code declares a variable `counter`, which is initialized to 1. The expression `counter <= 10` is evaluated when the program reaches the `while` statement. The loop executes the calculation 10 times and increments the value of `counter` by 1 during each iteration. The output of the code consists of numbers printed from 1 through 10.

```
var counter = 1;
while(counter <= 10) {
    document.write(counter + "<BR>");
    counter = counter + 1;
}
```

Figure 4.2 demonstrates the working of the `while` statement.

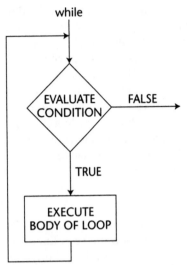

Figure 4.2   The while **statement execution process.**

Consider another example of a while statement where the code generates the Fibonacci series between 1 and 200. In a Fibonacci series, each number is a sum of its two preceding numbers. The series starts with 1.

```
var num1 = 0;
var num2 = 1;
document.write(num1 + "<BR>");
while(num2 < 200) {
        document.write(num2 + "<BR>");
        num2 = num1 + num2;
        num1 = num2 - num1;
}
```

The output of the preceding code in the browser will be as follows:

```
0
1
1
2
3
5
8
13
21
34
55
89
144
```

As you can see, each number in the series is the sum of the two preceding numbers.

The break **Statement**

You might sometimes come across situations where you need to exit a loop prematurely. The easiest way to do this is by using the break statement. The break statement in a while loop causes the program flow to exit the body of a while loop.

The following program illustrates the use of the break statement. The code used is the same code that generated the Fibonacci series. The only difference is in the insertion of the break statement inside the while statement. An if statement inside the while statement is used to test if the value of num2 is equal to 55. If the value equals 55, the break statement is executed and the script exits the while statement.

```
var num1 = 0;
var num2 = 1;
document.write(num1 + "<BR>");
while(num2 < 200){
        document.write(num2 + "<BR>");
        num2 = num1 + num2;
        num1 = num2 - num1;
        if(num2 == 55)
        break;
}
```

The output of the preceding code after the insertion of the break statement is as follows:

```
0
1
1
2
3
5
8
13
21
34
```

The continue **Statement**

The continue statement returns the control to the beginning of a while statement, skipping any statement following the continue statement in the loop body. As opposed to the break statement, the most common use of the continue statement is to conditionally skip instructions in the loop but not exit the loop (as the break statement does). The following example illustrates the use of the continue statement:

```
var reply='y';
while(reply != 'n') {
    number=window.prompt("Enter a number less than or equal to
100", "");
  if(number > 100) {
      alert("The number is greater than 100", "");
```

```
        continue;
    }
    document.write("The square of the number is " + number*number);
    reply=window.prompt("Do you want to enter another number (y/n) ", "");
    }
```

The preceding program shows a `while` loop that prompts a user to enter a number less than `100` and prints the square of that number. The `while` statement is used to execute the code as many times as the user wants to input a value. An `if` statement inside the `while` loop is used to check if the value entered by the user is less than 100. If the number entered is greater than 100, the `continue` statement is executed, and the script skips the `document.write` and `window.prompt` instructions on the next lines. However, the `while` loop doesn't stop. Instead, it continues and again asks the user to enter a number less than `100`.

The `do...while` Statement

The `do...while` statement is similar to the `while` statement because both statements iterate until the specified loop condition becomes `false`. However, the only difference is that in the `do...while` statement, the body of the loop is executed at least once, and the condition is evaluated for subsequent executions.

The syntax for the `do...while` statement is as follows:

```
do {
    statement(s);
}while(condition);
```

It can be seen that in the preceding syntax, the keyword `do` is written first and then the body of the loop. This signifies that the statements within a `do...while` loop are executed at least once before the condition is evaluated. The condition or the conditional expression is evaluated at the bottom of the loop. You'll also notice that as in other conditional or looping statements, opening and closing curly braces mark the body of the `do...while` statement. It is mandatory that the `do...while` statement have opening and closing curly braces around the body of the loop even if the body contains a single statement.

Figure 4.3 demonstrates the working of the `do...while` statement.

Consider the following simple example of the `do...while` loop where the program prints numbers from 1 through 10:

```
var number = 0;
do {
    number = number + 1;
    document.write(number + "<BR>");
}while(number < 10);
```

In the preceding example, you'll notice that the `<BR>` tag is used inside the script code. Since the specific tag is inside the quotation marks, it is justifiable to use it in the script. The output of the script including the tags is interpreted and displayed in the browser. You can use other formatting tags within quotation marks in script to include formatting attributes, such as bold and italics.

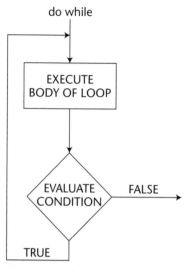

do while

EXECUTE
BODY OF LOOP

EVALUATE
CONDITION   FALSE

TRUE

Figure 4.3   The do...while statement execution process.

Consider another example of the do...while loop that also uses the switch statement. This program displays a menu to the user by using the switch statement and iterates the loop by using the do...while statement.

```
var chc, ok;
do{
    ok = "";
    chc = prompt("Please enter your choice: 1. Create a Directory 2.
Delete a Directory 3. Show a Directory 4. Exit : ", "");
    switch(chc) {
        case '1' : alert("You entered Choice 1");
            break;
            case '2' : alert("You entered Choice 2");
            break;
            case '3' : alert("You entered Choice 3");
            break;
            case '4' : alert("You entered Choice 4");
            break;
            default  : alert("Invalid Choice");
            break;
    }
    ok = prompt("Do you wish to proceed (y/n): ", "");
}while(ok == 'y');
```

In the earlier chapters, we discussed arrays. In addition, the preceding section introduced the structure of the do...while statement. Let's now merge the two to discuss array manipulation using the do...while statement.

Array Manipulation Using the `do...while` Statement

You can use the `do...while` statement to retrieve data from an array. The following example displays the use of the `do...while` statement with arrays:

```
var monthsofYear = new Array();
monthsofYear[0] = "January";
monthsofYear[1] = "February";
monthsofYear[2] = "March";
monthsofYear[3] = "April";
monthsofYear[4] = "May";
monthsofYear[5] = "June";
monthsofYear[6] = "July";
monthsofYear[7] = "August";
monthsofYear[8] = "September";
monthsofYear[9] = "October";
monthsofYear[10] = "November";
monthsofYear[11] = "December";
var counter = 0;
do {
    document.write(monthsofYear[counter] + "<BR>");
    ++counter;
}while(counter < 12);
```

In the preceding example, an array is used to store names of months of the year. A variable `counter` is initialized to 0 and is used to control the progress of the `do...while` loop. The `do...while` loop is executed once and, therefore, the instruction `document.write` displays the month `January` on the browser. In the `document.write` statement, `monthsofYear[counter]` refers to the month `January` because the array contains `January` in index 0. The variable `counter` is incremented by 1, and the condition `counter < 12` is evaluated next. Since the condition still holds true, the control goes back into the loop body and the process continues until the `counter` becomes less than 12.

The `for` Statement

The `for` statement provides a compact way of specifying the statements that control the repetition of the steps within the loop. In the `for` construct, loop control statements are not written within the body of the loop; instead, they are written at the top. This makes the program more readable and comprehensible. The `for` statement consists of the keyword `for`, followed by parentheses containing three expressions, each separated by a semicolon. These constitute the initialization expression, the test expression, and the increment or decrement expression.

The syntax of the `for` statement is as follows:

```
for(Initialization_expr;test_expr;change_expr) {
    statement(s);
}
```

In the statement,

```
for(ivar = 0; ivar <= 10; ivar++)
```

`ivar = 0` is the initialization expression, `ivar <= 10` is the test expression, and `ivar++` is the increment expression.

For more clarity, let's discuss each of the three expressions in detail:

- **The initialization expression.** Executed only once when the control is passed to the loop for the first time. It gives the loop variable an initial value, such as `counter = 0` or `i = 1`. It is often 0 or 1, but it can be any number. You can have multiple initializations or multiple reinitializations, but these have to be separated by commas.

- **The test expression (or condition).** Executed each time the control passes to the beginning of the loop. The body of the loop is executed only after the condition has been checked. If the condition evaluates to `true`, the loop is executed. Otherwise, the control passes to the statement following the body of the loop.

- **The increment/decrement expression.** Always executed when the control returns to the beginning of the loop. Just like the `counter` variable in the `while` statement, this expression helps you track the progress of the loop and the status of the conditional expression. The increment indicates how the `for` loop will increase; the decrement indicates how the `for` loop will decrease. This is an expression and usually takes the form of `counter ++`, where `counter` is the name of the variable first assigned in the initialization expression. For example, `counter ++` increases the value of the `counter` variable by 1 for each iteration.

NOTE Unlike all other constructs in JavaScript, the `for` statement uses semicolons instead of commas to separate its arguments. If you delete an expression in the `for` statement, be sure to include that segment within the body to end the `for` statement. Otherwise, the program might be caught in an infinite loop. For example, if the test expression and/or condition is omitted, the `break` statement must be provided in the body of the loop. The details of infinite loops will be discussed a little later in this chapter.

Figure 4.4 displays the sequence of execution of a complete `for` statement.

The code specified below uses the `for` statement to display the square of numbers from 1 through 10:

```
for( counter = 1; counter <= 10; counter++){
   document.write(counter * counter + " ");
}
```

The output of the program is: `1 4 9 16 25 36 49 64 81 100`.

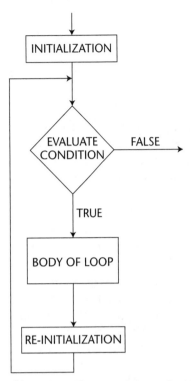

Figure 4.4 The for statement execution process.

Consider another code where the initialization expression and the test expression are omitted in the for statement. The program will accept and display 10 numbers.

```
var num, times;
times = 0;
for( ; ; times = times + 1) {
    if(times >= 10) break;
    num = prompt("Enter a number: ", "");
    document.write(num + "<BR>");
}
```

A common mistake that programmers make is to terminate the for loop with a semicolon. For example, check the following statement:

```
for( num = 0; num <= 10; num++); {
    document.write(num * num + "<BR>");
}
```

The output of the preceding statements is 121. Since the for statement is terminated with a semicolon, it becomes a self-executing for loop that moves to the next statement only when the condition in the for loop becomes false. The for loop is exited when the value of num is 11, and therefore, the output is 121 (11 × 11).

The `break` and `continue` Statements

In earlier sections of this chapter, you learned how to implement the `break` and `continue` statements in the `switch` and `while` statements. Similar to a `while` statement, you use the `break` statement to exit from a `for` statement. In addition, the `continue` statement is used to skip all the subsequent instructions and take the control back to the loop.

The following code is the same as the one we considered in the `while` statement. The code prompts the user to enter a number less than 100 and prints the square of that number.

```
for(var reply='y'; reply != 'n';) {
        number=window.prompt("Enter a number less than or equal to
100.", "");
    if(number > 100) {
        alert("The number is greater than 100.", "");
        continue;
    }
    document.write("The square of the number is " + number*number);
    reply=window.prompt("Do you want to enter another number (y/n) ",
    "");
}
```

Recall the example of months of the year that we discussed in the `do...while` statement. You can also use the `for` statement or the `while` statement to perform the same operations.

Infinite Loops

When you write `while` and `for` statements, be sure that you do not give a condition that results in never-ending or infinite loops. The following example illustrates an infinite `for` loop:

```
for( num = 1; num <= 10;) {
    document.write(num * num + "<BR>");
}
```

In the preceding example, the increment-decrement expression is missing. As a result, there is no change in the value of the variable called num, resulting in an infinite loop.

Result

Based on previous discussion, the conditional and looping statements that you'll use to add the functionality stated in the problem statement are as follows:

- According to the specifications, each time the customer opens the Web page of Web Shoppe, a dialog box should be displayed asking for the product category from which the customer wants to make purchases. Depending on the choice entered, corresponding instructions related to each category should be executed.

The conditional statements if and else if need to be used to incorporate this functionality. Therefore, by using the else if statement, if the customer chooses to make purchases from the Flowers category, a set of instructions are executed. However, if the customer chooses Confectionery or Books, another set of instructions is executed.

- Next, in each if and else if block, for each item in the three categories of products, a switch statement needs to be used. These switch statements will calculate the total amount of purchases made.

- After the purchase of each item is made, the new Web page of the site of Web Shoppe needs to confirm from the customer if he or she wants to proceed with the purchasing. Depending on the value entered, which in our case would be Y or N (Yes or No), the program would proceed further. To implement this, you'll need to use the do...while statement. The do...while statement as discussed earlier lets you execute instructions within a loop at least once and then checks for the condition. Using the do...while statement, the program can display a dialog box the moment a customer opens this page and, consequently, after each purchase, a confirmation is taken from the customer. This loop will contain the else if and switch statements discussed above.

- At the end of the purchase, in order to display the items that the customer has opted to purchase, the items first need to be stored. To store the items purchased, you can use an array. To retrieve the items stored in an array, you can use the for statement.

- Finally, the program needs to calculate the discount on the total purchases made by the customer. To implement this, you can again use an else if statement.

Write the code

Embed the following code before the closing code of the <BODY> tag (</BODY>) in the HTML program:

```
<SCRIPT LANGUAGE="JavaScript">
var chr, choice, choice1, total, counter1, counter2;
var string1 = new Array();
total = 0;
counter1 = 0;
do {
    choice = prompt("Enter the product category from which you want
to make purchases: Flowers, Confectionery, or Books", "");
    if(choice == "Flowers"){
        choice1 = prompt("Enter the flower name:", "");
        switch(choice1) {
            case 'Asters' :
            total=total + 100;
            break;
            case 'Daffodils' :
```

```
            total=total + 150;
            break;
            case 'Roses' :
            total=total + 200;
            break;
            case 'Chrysanthemum' :
            total=total + 350;
            break;
            default :
            break;
        }
    }
    else if(choice == "Confectionery"){
        choice1 = prompt("Enter the confectionery item:", "");
        switch(choice1) {
            case 'Breads' :
            total=total + 150;
            break;
            case 'Croissants' :
            total=total + 300;
            break;
            case 'Cakes' :
            total=total + 400;
            break;
            case 'Biscuits' :
            total=total + 200;
            break;
            default :
            break;
        }
    }
    else if(choice == "Books"){
        choice1 = prompt("Enter the book name:", "");
        switch(choice1) {
            case 'Forever Yours' :
            total=total + 400;
            break;
            case 'The Solution Providers' :
            total=total + 500;
            break;
            case 'Work Place-Best Practices' :
            total=total + 750;
            break;
            default :
            break;
        }
    }
    string1[counter1]=choice1;
    counter1++;
    chr=prompt("Do you want to shop more: Y/N", "");
```

```
        }while(chr == 'Y' || chr == 'y');
        if(total > 0){
            document.write("<I>You have chosen to purchase the following
item(s):</I> ");
            for(counter2 = 0; counter2 < counter1; counter2++){
                document.write("<B>" + string1[counter2] + "</B>");
                if(counter2 + 1 < counter1){
                    document.write(", ");
                }
            }
        }
        else
            document.write("<B><I>Thanks for visiting our site
!!</I></B>");
        document.write("<BR>");
        if(total > 0 && total <= 100){
            total = total * 0.9;
            document.write("<I>You receive a discount of</I> " +
"<B><I>10%</I></B> " + "<I>on the purchase and your bill amounts to
<B>$</B></I>" + "<B><I>" + total + "</I></B>");
        }
        else if(total > 100 && total <= 450){
            total = total * 0.8;
            document.write("<I>You receive a discount of</I> " +
"<B><I>20%</I></B> " + "<I>on the purchase and your bill amounts to
<B>$</B></I>" + "<B><I>" + total + "</I></B>");
        }
        else if(total > 450){
            total = total * 0.7;
            document.write("<I>You receive a discount of</I> " +
"<B><I>30%</I></B> " + "<I>on the purchase and your bill amounts to
<B>$</B></I>" + "<B><I>" + total + "</I></B>");
        }
    </SCRIPT>
```

Execute and Verify the Code

Execute the code and verify the successful running of the preceding script code by performing the following steps:

1. In the dialog box where you are prompted to enter the category of the product, type Flowers. Ensure that you write Flowers with F in uppercase and other letters in lowercase (Flowers). This is because the code is case-sensitive. Case-sensitive code will be discussed later in other chapters.

2. Another dialog box is displayed. This dialog box prompts you to enter the product name; type Roses. Type as instructed or as shown on the Web page because of case sensitivity.

3. In the third dialog box, you need to confirm whether you want to make any more purchases or not. Accordingly, you enter 'Y' or 'y'.

4. Repeat the same process, from steps 1 through 3, for two product categories: Books and Forever Yours.

5. Next, in the confirmation dialog box, enter 'n' or 'N'. At the bottom of the Web page, the following messages are displayed (also refer to Figure 4.5):

   ■ *"You have chosen to purchase the following item(s):* **Roses**, **Forever Yours**
   You receive a discount of **30%** *on the purchase and your bill amounts to* **$420"**

NOTE Ensure that the values you enter are the same as those displayed in the browser.

Figure 4.5 displays the output after steps 1 through 5.

6. Refresh the page and click on the Cancel button of the dialog boxes that you encounter. At the bottom of the Web page, the following message is displayed (also refer to Figure 4.6):

   ■ *"Thanks for visiting our site !!"*

Figure 4.6 displays the output after step 6.

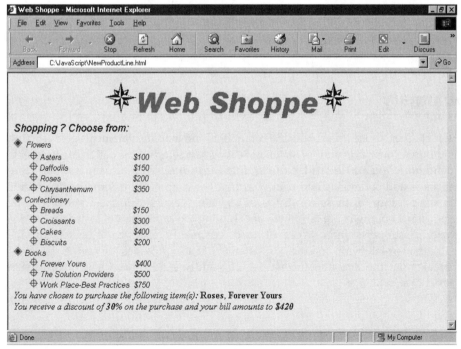

Figure 4.5 The messages on the browser after performing steps 1 through 5.

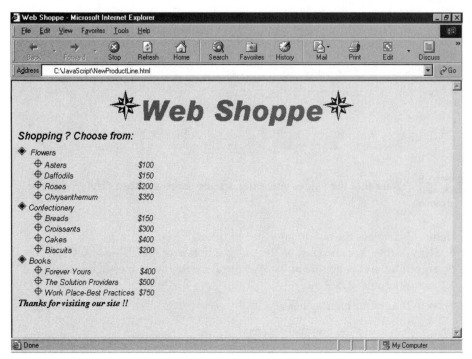

Figure 4.6 The message on the browser after performing step 6.

Summary

In this chapter, you learned about the conditional and looping statements of JavaScript. Conditional constructs and/or statements allow the selective execution of statements in a program. You also learned to use if, if...else, else...if, and switch statements and add conditions into your program. The chapter provided you with inputs about application of these constructs in real life. Next, you learned about looping statements. Looping is the technique of executing the same lines of codes repeatedly. JavaScript supports three types of loop statements: the while statement, the do...while statement, and the for statement. It also provides the break statement to break from the for and the while loop and the continue statement to skip instructions.

Functions and Events

Getting Started

In today's world, the success of a Web page can be judged by its dynamism and user interactivity. Static content in Web pages is no longer the order of the day. Web pages that offer a large amount of user interactivity are preferred to those that allow bare minimum user activity. Two tools that allow you to make your Web pages considerably dynamic and interactive in JavaScript are functions and events. Functions add readability and scalability to your Web page. They allow you to use programming code at more than one place in a program without having to retype it. Events in conjunction with functions allow interaction with a Web page and the ability to obtain the desired output.

In this chapter, you will learn about the functions and events in JavaScript and their implementation. You will also learn about the interrelationship between functions and events and how they integrate to add dynamism to your script. As in previous chapters, this chapter begins with a problem statement that discusses a situation in Web Shoppe, Inc. This problem statement projects a problem that is to be solved with the help of functions and events.

Problem Statement

Initially, when the online shopping mall of Web Shoppe had not attained great popularity among its customers, the site allowed all users to view and buy items from this site. However, now that Web Shoppe has proved its worth in the e-commerce market, Web Shoppe has changed its policy. It has assigned usernames to its regular and important customers. Per the new company policy, a customer cannot access the Web Shoppe site without providing his or her login name and password.

Scott, a Web developer, has been assigned the task of creating a login page for the Web Shoppe site that validates the login names and passwords of users. Scott has been directed to include the following elements in the login page:

- Login field
- Password field
- Submit button

Task List

To design the page, Scott needs to perform the following steps:

✔ **Identify the data that needs to be accepted.**

✔ **Design the user interface screen to accept the data.**

✔ **Identify functions and events to ensure the entry of a username and a password.**

✔ **Write the code for the Web page.**

✔ **Execute and verify the code.**

In the preceding chapters, you would have noticed that either the HTML page or the source code of the HTML page was provided to you. You were simply asked to embed JavaScript code in HTML code. However, by now you must be quite comfortable writing JavaScript code. Therefore, in this chapter you will learn how to design a Web page using HTML. Consequently, you will notice that in the preceding task list, there are tasks that are related to designing a Web page.

Identify the Data that Needs to Be Accepted

Every customer at Web Shoppe, Inc., has been assigned a unique username. This username helps Web Shoppe keep track of its customers. This username is the same as the login name that will go into the login page being created by Scott. For security reasons, each customer needs to have a password. Without entering any one of these details, a customer cannot access the Web Shoppe site. Therefore, the login name and password of a customer are the necessary data that needs to be accepted.

Design the User-Interface Screen to Accept Data

It is rightly said that the first impression is the last impression. Therefore, designing a good user-interface screen is very important because a user forms the first opinion about your application on looking at the interface. From an end user's perspective, an application with a good user interface that is easy to use is preferable. The guidelines that Scott will follow for designing the user interface are given below:

- Identify the input elements to be used.
- Identify names for input elements.
- Organize the elements on a page.

You'll see that the input elements required for the login page are text control for login, password control for the password, and button control for submitting the data.

Table 5.1 describes the controls required along with their details.

After Scott has identified the elements, he needs to organize the contents on the page, as shown in Figure 5.1.

Identify Functions and Events to Ensure the Entry of the Username and the Password

Before identifying the functions and events that will ensure the entry of a username and a password, let's begin with the basics of functions and events.

Functions

A function is a block of organized reusable code that is used to perform a single, related action. In other words, it is a set of statements that is executed when the user performs an action. Function blocks begin with the keyword `function` followed by the function name and parentheses `()`. Every function is placed within curly braces (`{}`) and contains a block of statements that is to be executed. You can pass information to a function by enclosing the information in parentheses after the name of the function. Such information that is passed to a function is called a *parameter* or an *argument*. In case there is more than one parameter to be passed to a function, the parameters passed are separated by a comma within parentheses.

JavaScript supports two types of functions: built-in and user-defined.

Table 5.1   The Input Controls for the Login Page

INPUT FOR	INPUT TYPE	INPUT NAME	CAPTION
Visitor name	text	`txtVisitorName`	Login
Password	password	`passVisitor`	Password
Submit button	button	`cmdSubmit`	Submit

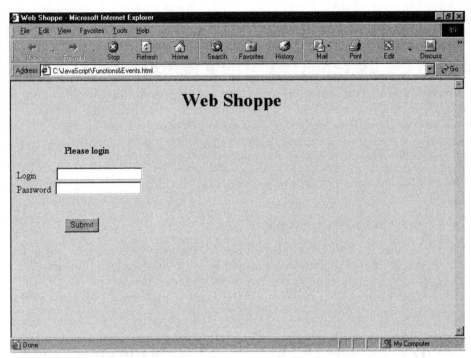

Figure 5.1 Web Shoppe login screen.

Built-In Functions

Built-in functions are provided to users by the language and have predefined functionality. There is no need to write code to use built-in functions because built-in functions are already coded to ease a programmer's task. Some of the built-in functions in JavaScript are as follows:

- `eval`
- `isFinite`
- `isNaN`
- `parseInt`
- `parseFloat`
- `ScriptEngine`
- `ScriptEngineBuildVersion`
- `ScriptEngineMajorVersion`
- `ScriptEngineMinorVersion`

Let us now discuss each one of these in detail.

The eval function evaluates a string of JavaScript code without referencing a particular object, meaning that the eval function is not associated with any object. The

eval function takes only one parameter, that is, the code to be evaluated. The syntax of the eval function is as follows:

```
eval(expr)
```

where, expr is the string to be evaluated. If the string represents an expression, eval evaluates the expression. If the string represents one or more JavaScript statements, eval evaluates the statements.

Since JavaScript automatically evaluates the arithmetic expressions, it is preferable that you do not use the eval function. However, if you want to dynamically evaluate an arithmetic expression, you can use this function. For example, suppose you have a variable *x*. You can dynamically evaluate an expression that includes *x* by assigning the string value of the expression, say "x + 2 * 5", to a variable *y* and then call eval later in the script whenever required.

The following example uses the eval function to evaluate the string str. This string contains the if...else JavaScript statement:

```
<HTML>
<HEAD><TITLE>The eval Function </TITLE>
</HEAD>
<BODY>
<H1> The eval Function </H1>
<SCRIPT LANGUAGE="JavaScript">
x=prompt("Enter a number greater than 5", "");
var str = "if(x >= 5) {document.write('You have entered number ' +
x);} else {x=prompt('Please enter a number greater than 5', ''); if(x >
5) document.write('You have entered number ' + x)}";
eval(str);
</SCRIPT>
</BODY>
</HTML>
```

In the preceding example, the string str consists of JavaScript statements that display the value of variable *x* if it is greater than 5. Otherwise, it opens a prompt dialog box that asks the user to enter a number greater than 5. If the number specified is greater than 5, the value of variable *x* is displayed.

NOTE Observe that in the preceding code, the statements within the document.write **method and the** prompt **method are enclosed within single quotation marks and not double quotation marks. Although statements can be enclosed within double quotation marks, because the variable** str **contains a string value that needs to include text in double quotation marks, any value within the quotation marks needs to be enclosed in single quotation marks.**

The isFinite function evaluates a number argument and determines if it is finite. The number argument can be any numeric value. This function returns true if the number is any value other than NaN (not a number), negative infinity, or positive infinity. The function returns false if the number is one of the above three cases.

The following code tests whether input from the client is the finite number or not:

```
<HTML>
<HEAD><TITLE>The isFinite Function </TITLE>
</HEAD>
<BODY>
<H1> The isFinite Function </H1>
<SCRIPT LANGUAGE="JavaScript">
x=prompt("Enter a finite number ", "");
if(isFinite (x)==true){
    document.write('You have entered finite number, ' + x);
}
else{
    x=prompt("You have not entered a finite number, please enter a
finite number ", "");
        if(isFinite (x)==true){
            document.write('You have entered finite number, ' + x);
        }
}
</SCRIPT>
</BODY>
</HTML>
```

In the preceding example, the user is prompted to enter a finite number. Using the `if` statement, the `isFinite()` function checks if the input number from the user is a finite number or not. If the number is a finite number, the value entered by the user is displayed on the screen. Otherwise, in the `else   if` statement, the user is again prompted to enter a finite number. Depending on the value entered, a check is made again to establish whether the number is finite or not.

The isNaN function evaluates an argument and determines if it is a reserved NaN (not a number). The syntax of this function is as follows:

```
isNaN(numberVal)
```

where, `numberVal` is the argument that is to be verified against NaN. This function returns `true` if the argument is `NaN`. Otherwise it returns `false`. You typically use this function to check the return value of the `parseInt` and `parseFloat` functions.

The parseFloat function takes a string as an argument and returns a numeric value, which is a floating-point number. The syntax of the `parseFloat` function is as follows:

```
parseFloat(str)
```

where `parseFloat` parses `str` and returns a floating-point number. While parsing, if the function encounters a character other than a sign (+ or -), a numeral (0-9), a decimal point, or an exponent, then the function returns the floating-point value up to that point only. It ignores that character and all the succeeding characters. If only the first character cannot be converted to a number, then the function returns "NaN".

The parseInt function takes a string as an argument and returns a numeric value (integer number) of the radix (base), specified by the second argument. The syntax of the parseInt function is as follows:

```
parseInt(str [, radix])
```

where the value for the radix ten indicates that the string has to be converted to a decimal number. Similarly, the value for the radix eight has to be converted to octal, for the radix sixteen to hexadecimal, and so on. While parsing in a specified radix, if the function encounters a character that is not a numeral (0-9), then the function ignores that character and all successive characters.

NOTE You'll see the implementation of parseInt and parseFloat **functions in the code of the problem statement.**

The ScriptEngine function returns a string indicating the scripting language in use. The syntax of the ScriptEngine function is:

```
ScriptEngine()
```

The ScriptEngineBuildVersion function returns the build version of the script engine in use. The return value corresponds to the version in the dynamic link library for the scripting language in use. The syntax of this function is:

```
ScriptEngineBuildVersion()
```

The ScriptEngineMajorVersion function returns the major version of the script engine in use. The return value corresponds to the version in the dynamic link library for the scripting language in use. The syntax of this function is:

```
ScriptEngineMajorVersion()
```

The ScriptEngineMinorVersion function returns the minor version of the script engine in use. The return value corresponds to the version in the dynamic link library for the scripting language in use. The syntax of this function is:

```
ScriptEngineMinorVersion()
```

User-Defined Functions

As we just discussed, built-in functions have predefined functionality. They behave in a specific manner, and you cannot change them to suit your needs. However, there may be situations that require certain functionality, which cannot be achieved using built-in functions. For example, you might need to validate some input accepted from the user (as in the case of the problem statement). For validating the user input, there is a very limited scope of checking the values if only built-in functions are used.

However, you need to create your own functions, so that they meet your requirements. These tailor-made or customized functions are referred to as user-defined functions. These functions not only best suit your needs, but also enhance the performance of your code by adding dynamism, scalability, and readability. However, before using a function in JavaScript, you need to first define it and then execute it.

You define a function by assigning it a name and structuring it in an organized way. You can use the following syntax to define a user-defined function:

```
function <function_name>(parameters){
   //block of code
}
```

In the syntax above, you'll notice that a function is composed of the following three elements:

- **The keyword function and the name of the function.** The keyword `function` is always in lowercase letters, and it tells the JavaScript interpreter that the code includes a function. A function name is, at times, also known as an identifier because it uniquely identifies a function in a program.

- **The parameter/argument.** The parameter/argument is the next element that appears immediately after a function name. A parameter is a variable that is assigned to a function. It is always enclosed within parentheses ( ). A function might or might not contain parameters.

- **A block of code.** The third element of a function is a block of code, which is a set of statements used to define the functionality of a function. It is always enclosed within curly braces { }.

The following example illustrates the various elements of a user-defined function:

```
function fnSquare(number){
   var x;
   x = number * number;
}
```

In the preceding example, the name of the function is "fnSquare" and the function has a parameter, "number." The block of code consists of the statements enclosed within curly braces { }.

After you have defined a function, you need to execute it to implement its functionality.

As discussed, defining a function only gives it a name, specifies the parameters that are to be included, and structures the block of code. After the basic structure of a function is in place, you can execute the function by calling it from another function or from an event. We will discuss events later in this chapter.

The following code calls one function from another function.

```
<HTML>
<HEAD><TITLE> Calling a Function</TITLE>
</HEAD>
<BODY>
```

```
<H1> Calling a Function </H1>
<SCRIPT Language="JavaScript">
var userName;
function showName(){
   getName();
   alert("Hello " + userName + " !");
}
function getName(){
   userName=prompt("Please enter your name:", "");
}
showName();
</SCRIPT>
</BODY>
</HTML>
```

In the preceding example, the function "showName" calls the function "getName." The getName function prompts a user to enter a username. After the user has entered the name, the showName function shows an alert message box that displays the text Hello plus the value of the variable userName. Therefore, if the user enters the name Michael, the alert message box displays a greeting message "Hello Michael!".

NOTE **The preceding example uses the** alert() **method of the** window **object of JavaScript. The** alert() **method alerts the user with a message. You'll learn in detail about the** window **object and its methods later in Chapter 6, "Using Objects in JavaScript."**

Figure 5.2 displays the greeting message "Hello Michael !".

Returning a value means that when a function calls another function, the called function returns the result of its operation to the calling function. The return value from the called function is stored in a variable, which is defined in the calling function. However, to return a value you need to make sure that the return statement is within the called function. Let us look at the following code to understand the return value of a function.

```
<HTML>
<HEAD>
<TITLE> Return Value of a Function </TITLE>
</HEAD>
<BODY>
<H1> Return Value of a Function </H1>
<SCRIPT LANGUAGE = "JavaScript">
function add(){
   var result;
   result = sum (1, 2);
   alert("The sum of 1 and 2 is: " + result);
}
function sum (num, num1){
   var addition;
```

```
      addition = num + num1;
      return addition;
}
add();
</SCRIPT>
</BODY>
</HTML>
```

In the preceding code, add() is the calling function and sum() is the called function. The return value from the sum() function is stored in variable, addition. This value is then returned to the add function.

Figure 5.3 displays the sum of two numbers that is returned by the sum() function to the add() function.

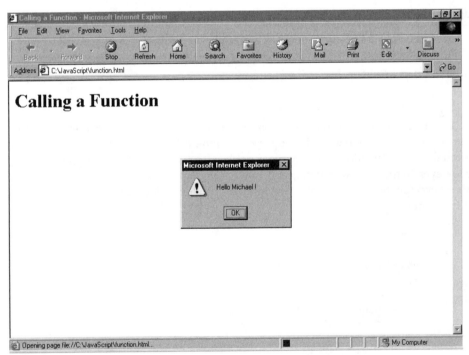

Figure 5.2   The alert message box with greeting message for the user.

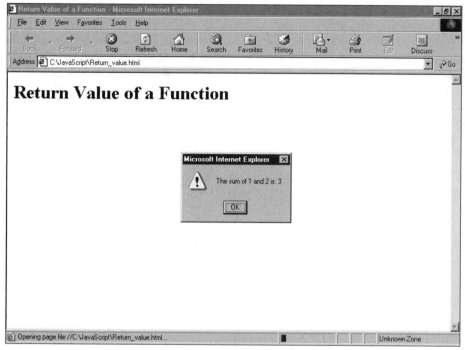

Figure 5.3 The alert message box that displays the sum of two numbers.

We discussed the procedure for calling a function from another function. Before we proceed with how we can call a function from an event, let us discuss another very important concept related to functions: the scope of variables. We did not discuss the scope of variables in Chapter 3, "JavaScript Data Types, Variables, and Operators," because in real terms a function defines the scope of a variable.

Scope of a Variable

You need to be conscious of the scope of a variable when you use a variable in a complex JavaScript program that uses functions. The scope of a variable refers to where in your program a declared variable can be used. A variable's scope can be either global or local. A global scope variable, also called a global variable, is one that is declared outside a function and is accessible to all the parts of your program. A local scope variable, also called a local variable, is declared inside a function and is accessible only in the function in which it is declared. This means that a local variable stops existing when the function ends. If you try to access a local variable outside the function in which it was declared, your program results in an error.

The following example contains two global variables and a function that contains a local variable. The global variables and the function are included in the <SCRIPT>...</SCRIPT> tags. When the function variableScope() is executed from the <BODY> of the HTML code, the values in the global variable and the local variable are displayed successfully on the screen from within the function. After a call to the function, the program again displays the value of the second global variable from the <BODY> section. However, when the program tries to display the local variable from the <BODY> section, the value is not displayed. This is because the local variable ceases to exist when the function ends.

```
<HTML>
<HEAD>
<TITLE>Scope of Variables</TITLE>
<H1>Scope of Variables</H1>
<SCRIPT LANGUAGE="JavaScript">
var firstGlobalVariable = "First global variable";
var secondGlobalVariable;
function variableScope() {
    secondGlobalVariable = "Second global variable";
    var localVariable = "Local variable";
    document.write("The value in the first global variable: " +
firstGlobalVariable + "<BR>");
    document.write("The value in the second global variable: " +
secondGlobalVariable + "<BR>");
    document.write("The value in the local variable: " +
localVariable + "<BR>");
    }
</SCRIPT>
</HEAD>
<BODY>
<SCRIPT LANGUAGE="JavaScript">
variableScope();
document.write("The value in the first global variable: " +
firstGlobalVariable + "<BR>");
document.write("The value in the second global variable: " +
secondGlobalVariable + "<BR>");
document.write("The value in the local variable: " + localVariable
+ "<BR>");
</SCRIPT>
</BODY>
</HTML>
```

Figure 5.4 displays the values of local and global variables.

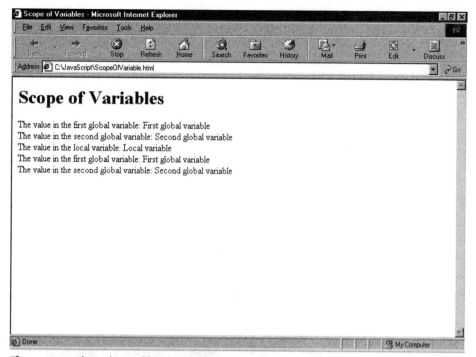

Figure 5.4   The values of local and global variables.

You should not assign the same name to a local and a global variable in a program because it may lead to confusion. Consider the following example where, in the function `sameVariableName()`, the local variable `carModel` has been given the same name as the global variable. When the function `sameVariableNames()` is called in the `<BODY>` of the `HTML` document, the function displays the value of the local variable `carModel` as `Toyota`. After the function `sameVariableNames()` is called, the `document.write` statement displays the value of the global variable `CarModel` as `Ford`. Now, the value of the global variable `carModel` is changed to `Mercedes`. Therefore, the statement `document.write` displays the value of the global variable as `Mercedes`. However, at this point when the function `sameVariableNames()` is called again, the value of the local variable `carModel` is again displayed as `Toyota`.

```
<HTML>
<HEAD>
<TITLE>Local and Global Variables with Same Name</TITLE>
<SCRIPT LANGUAGE="JavaScript">
```

```
var carModel = "Ford";
function sameVariableNames() {
   var carModel = "Toyota";
   document.write("<B>" + carModel + "<BR>"); //displays Toyota
}
</SCRIPT>
</HEAD>
<BODY>
<H1> Local and Global Variables with Same Name </H1>
<SCRIPT LANGUAGE="JavaScript">
sameVariableNames();
document.write(carModel + "<BR>"); // displays Ford
carModel="Mercedes";
document.write(carModel + "<BR>");
sameVariableNames();
</SCRIPT>
</BODY>
</HTML>
```

Figure 5.5 displays the values of local and global variables when they are assigned the same name.

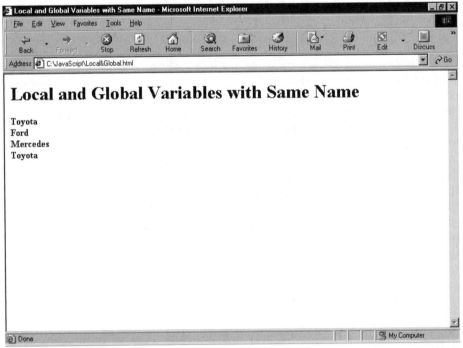

Figure 5.5 The values of local and global variables when they are assigned the same name.

Having discussed functions in detail, let us now look at how we can call a function from an event. Before we begin, it is necessary to know what an event is and how JavaScript handles events.

Events

Events are the actions that occur as a result of some browser-related activities or user interaction with Web pages. An event is generated whenever a user performs an action, such as when a user clicks a mouse button or enters data in a form. After an event occurs, the browser processes the programming code for that event. For example, when a user clicks on a button in a form, the browser executes the part of a program that has been designed to be executed in response to such an action. This process of a browser functioning according to the events generated is known as *event handling.* The function that is executed in response to an event is called an *event handler.*

Figure 5.6 depicts how events occur and are handled in JavaScript.

JavaScript allows you to change the default action associated with events. Let us consider a simple example of event processing where a user clicks a hyperlink on a page. Clicking on the hyperlink generates an event and the default-associated action, which is that the browser loads and displays the page associated with that URL. However, in JavaScript, you can change this default action and write your own event handler that will be associated with this hyperlink.

The following are a few other tasks that you can do with events using JavaScript event handlers:

- Validate the data entered by a user in a form.
- Shift the focus of controls from one field to another in a form.
- Load and display animation when a user clicks a button.
- Communicate with Java applets and browser plug-ins.
- Display a dialog box when a user moves the mouse over a link.

Having looked at how the event-handling features of JavaScript enable you to create dynamic and interactive Web pages, let us discuss how JavaScript handles events internally.

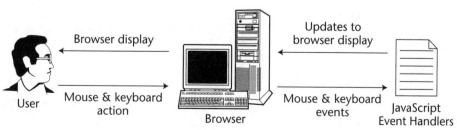

Figure 5.6 Events and event handling.

JavaScript's Approach to Event Handling

JavaScript event handling can be summarized as defining events and providing a method or event handlers that link the defined events to user-defined JavaScript code. JavaScript defines events for most of the objects found on a Web page, including links, images, form elements, and windows. To provide a standard method that links events with user-defined JavaScript code, JavaScript defines special attributes, also called event handlers, for HTML tags. These attributes allow the script to identify event-handling JavaScript code instead of the default HTML event handlers.

Table 5.2 summarizes a few events defined by JavaScript and specifies the various tags associated with HTML elements that contain the special attributes. These events are common to both Netscape Navigator and Internet Explorer.

Table 5.2 does not contain a comprehensive list of all events defined by JavaScript. There are other events besides these that are supported by Internet Explorer 4 and later. Also, some of the preceding events can be an amalgamation of other events. For example, the `click` event is a combination of `mouseDown` and `mouseUp` events.

Event Handlers

As stated earlier, JavaScript defines special attributes, also called event handlers, for the HTML tags (listed in Table 5.2) that provide a method of linking events with user-defined JavaScript code. These attributes and/or event handlers indicate what action is to be performed in response to a particular event. The syntax of writing an event handler within an HTML tag is as follows:

```
<HTMLtag eventHandler="JavaScript Code">
```

Event handler names are quite similar to the name of the events they handle. The only difference is that each event handler name consists of the prefix *on* followed by the name of the event. For example, the event handler for the `click` event is `onClick`, and the event handler for the load event is `onLoad`. HTML tags are not case-sensitive. However, JavaScript code is case-sensitive. Since event handlers form an attribute of HTML tags, you need not worry about case sensitivity. Therefore, you can write the `onClick` event handler as ONCLICK, onclick, or OnClick. However, it is considered to be good programming practice to capitalize the first letter of an event handler name.

JavaScript code for an event handler is enclosed within quotation marks following the name of the event handler. The following code uses the `<INPUT>` tag to create a command button. The tag also includes an `onClick` event handler that executes the built-in JavaScript `alert()` method, in response to the `click` event. The code executed by the `onClick` event handler, which is the `alert()` method, is contained within quotation marks.

```
<INPUT TYPE="button" onClick="alert('You clicked a button!')">
```

You can also call a user-defined function through an event handler. For example, consider the following line of code:

```
<INPUT TYPE="submit" onClick="userDefined()">
```

Table 5.2 Events Defined by JavaScript

HTML ELEMENTS	HTML TAGS	JAVASCRIPT-DEFINED EVENTS	DESCRIPTION
link	\<A\>...\</A\>	click	The mouse is clicked on a link.
		dblClick	The mouse is double-clicked on a link.
		mouseDown	The mouse button is pressed.
		mouseUp	The mouse button is released.
		mouseOver	The mouse is moved over a link.
image	\<IMG\>	load	An image is loaded into a browser.
		abort	The loading of an image is abandoned because of a user action.
		error	An error occurs during the loading of an image.
area	\<AREA\>	mouseOver	The mouse is moved over an area of an image map in the browser.
		mouseOut	The mouse is moved from within an image map to outside of that area.
		dblClick	The mouse is double-clicked on an image map.
form	\<FORM\>...\</FORM\>	submit	The user submits a form.
		reset	The user refreshes a form.
text field	\<INPUT TYPE = "text"\>	blur	The text field loses the input focus.
		focus	The text field gains the input focus.
		change	The text field is modified.
		select	The text in the text field is selected.
password field	\<INPUT TYPE = "text"\>	blur	The password field loses the input focus.
		focus	The password field gains the input focus.

(continues)

Table 5.2 Events Defined by JavaScript (*Continued*)

HTML ELEMENTS	HTML TAGS	JAVASCRIPT-DEFINED EVENTS	DESCRIPTION
button	<INPUT TYPE = "button">	click	A button is clicked.
		blur	A button loses the input focus.
		focus	A button gains the input focus.
		mouseDown	A user presses the left mouse button.
		mouseUp	A user releases the left mouse button.
submit	<INPUT TYPE = "submit">	click	A submit button is clicked.
		blur	A submit button loses the input focus.
		focus	A submit button gains the input focus.
window, frame set, frame	<BODY>...</BODY> <FRAMESET>...</FRAMESET> <FRAME>...</FRAME>	blur	A window loses the input focus.
		focus	A window gains the input focus.
		error	An error occurs when the window is loaded.
		load	The loading of a window is successful.
		unload	The user exits the window.
		move	A window is moved.
		resize	A window is resized.

The event handler attribute `onClick` triggers the function `userDefined()` when a button is clicked.

Table 5.3 lists a few event handlers with their descriptions.

Let us discuss a few examples of how event handlers process the functions associated with an event.

In order to handle link events, HTML documents contain hypertext links that are used to open files or to navigate to other documents on the Web. A hypertext link in an HTML document is underlined and often displayed in a vibrant color. Blue is the default color for unvisited links while red is the default color of previously visited links. A hypertext link can display the name and location of a file or an HTML document or some sort of descriptive text. Other types of elements, such as images, can also be hypertext links to HTML documents, images, or files. The text or image used to represent a link in an HTML document is called an anchor.

Table 5.3 Event Handlers

EVENT-HANDLING ATTRIBUTES/ EVENT HANDLERS	TRIGGERED WHEN
onChange	The value of a text field, a text area, or a drop down list is modified.
onClick	A link, an image, or a form element is clicked once.
onDblClick	A link, an image, or a form element is double-clicked.
onMouseDown	The user presses a mouse button.
onMouseUp	The user releases a mouse button.
onMouseOver	The mouse moves over a link or an image.
onMouseOut	The mouse moves out of an image area or a link.
onLoad	A document or an image is loaded.
onAbort	The loading of an image is interrupted.
onSubmit	A user submits a form.
onReset	A form resets.
onBlur	An element, such as a radio button, becomes inactive.
onFocus	Elements such as documents, windows, frame sets, or form elements become active and receive focus.
onUnLoad	A user closes a document or a frame.
onResize	A form is resized by the user.
onMove	The user moves a window or a frame.

The primary event used with links is the `click` event. Clicking a link automatically executes the `click` event and the link's associated URL opens. When a user clicks a link, the execution of the `click` event is handled automatically by the Web browser—you do not need to add the `onClick` event handler to the `<A>` tag. However, there might be situations when you want to override an automatic `click` event with your own code. For instance, you may want to warn the user about the content of the HTML document that a particular link will open. When you want to override the automatic `click` event with your own code, you add to the `<A>` tag an `onClick` event handler that executes custom code. When you override an internal event handler with your own code, you must return a value of true or false by using the return statement. A value of true indicates that you want the Web browser to open the URL referenced by the link. A value of false indicates that you do not want the Web browser to open the link.

The following example illustrates the `onClick` event handler with the custom function attached to it:

```
<HTML>
<HEAD>
<TITLE>onClick Event Example</TITLE>
<SCRIPT LANGUAGE="JavaScript1.2">
function alertUser() {
    return confirm("This link is only for people who love Ford!");
}
</SCRIPT>
</HEAD>
<BODY>
<A HREF="Ford.html" onClick="return alertUser();">Ford Club Home
Page</A>
</BODY >
</HTML>
```

Notice that there are two `return` statements. The `return` statement in the `alertUser()` function returns a value to the `onClick` event handler. The return statement in the `onClick` event handler returns the same value to the Web browser.

Figure 5.7 displays the confirm dialog box that displays the message to the user who is about to click on the link.

The following example contains two event handlers, `onMouseOver` and `onMouseOut`:

```
<HTML>
<HEAD>
<TITLE>onMouseOver and onMouseOut Event Handlers Example</TITLE>
</HEAD>
<BODY>
```

```
<H1> onMouseOver and onMouseOut Event Handlers Example </H1>
    <A HREF="Ford.html" onMouseOver="status = 'Ford Club Home Page';
return true;" onMouseOut="status = 'You almost visited the Ford Club
Home Page!';">Ford Club Home Page</A>
    </BODY >
    </HTML>
```

Notice that in the preceding code the onMouseOver and onMouseOut event handlers are enclosed in the <A> tag. These event handlers display an appropriate message on the status bar of the current window. When the user places the mouse over the link, a message is displayed on the status bar (as shown in Figure 5.8). Similarly, when the user moves the mouse pointer away from the link, another message is displayed on the status bar of the window (as shown in Figure 5.9).

Figure 5.8 displays a message on the status bar when the user places the mouse over the link.

Figure 5.9 displays a message on the status bar when the user moves the mouse away from the link.

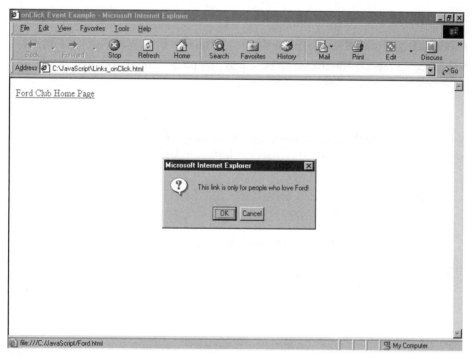

Figure 5.7   The onClick event handler.

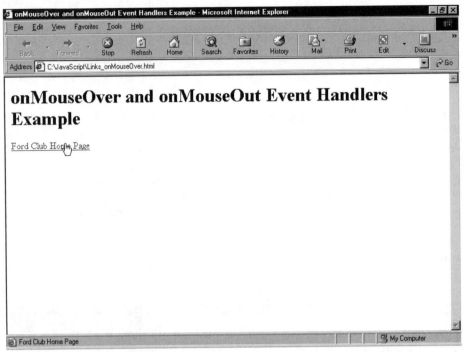

Figure 5.8   A message on the status bar when user places mouse over the link.

We have seen that there are several events that can be associated with a window. Let's take the following example where the Load and Unload events are handled.

```
<HTML>
<HEAD>
<TITLE>Load and UnLoad event In a window</TITLE>
</HEAD>
<BODY onLoad="alert('Welcome User!');" onUnload="alert('Thanks for
visiting this page');">
<H1> Load and UnLoad event in a window </H1>
<P> This is a test for load and unload event </P>
</BODY>
</HTML>
```

The preceding code displays the alert message box the moment the page is loaded into the browser. When the user exits the window, the Unload event is triggered that displays the alert message box again.

Figure 5.10 displays the onLoad message.

Figure 5.11 displays the onUnload message.

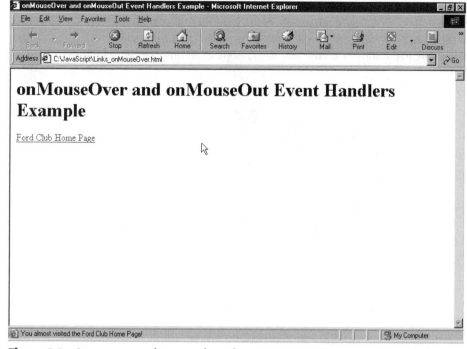

Figure 5.9   A message on the status bar when user moves mouse away from link.

Figure 5.10   The onLoad message.

Figure 5.11   The onLoad message.

Let's consider an example where a user is prompted to enter a number and when the user clicks a button, even numbers are generated less than the number specified by the user. Now, let's see how the onClick event handler handles the click event to generate even numbers. The code to generate even numbers is as follows:

```
<HTML>
<HEAD>
<SCRIPT language="JavaScript">
function generateEvenNumber(){
    //Declare variables
    var lastNumber,startNumber;
    //Assign the value
    lastNumber=parseInt(txtEvenNumber.value);
    startNumber=0;
    for(startNumber; startNumber < lastNumber; startNumber =
startNumber+2){
        alert(startNumber);
        if(startNumber < 100){
            continue;
        }
        break;
    }
}//End of the generateEvenNumber function
</SCRIPT>
</HEAD>
<BODY>
ENTER A NUMBER:
<INPUT type=text name=txtEvenNumber>
<br><br>
<INPUT type=button value=" Generate the even number " OnClick =
"generateEvenNumber();">
<br><br>
</BODY>
</HTML>
```

In the preceding code, the user is prompted to enter a number. After entering the number, the user clicks on the Generate the even number button. When the user clicks the button, the <INPUT> tag's onClick event handler starts processing the generateEvenNumber function. The following part of the code shows the onClick event handler:

```
<INPUT type=button value=" Generate the even number " OnClick =
"generateEvenNumber();">
```

As can be seen from the preceding code, as soon as the user clicks the Generate the even number button, the click event is triggered and the OnClick event handler processes the generateEvenNumber function. In other words, the click event is calling the generateEvenNumber function.

In addition, notice that in the `generateEvenNumber` function, the `input` property value is used. The value of an input element is accessed by the value property as follows:

```
txtEvenNumber.value
```

In the code, `txtEvenNumber` is the name of the input elements. The value of an input element is converted to integer by using the built-in function `parseInt()` and stored into the variable `lastNumber` as follows:

```
lastNumber=parseInt(txtEvenNumber.value);
```

Consider a situation where you have a Web page that accepts the first and last name of a user. You want the length of the first name to be calculated when the user enters the first name and shifts the focus of the control from the first name to the last name. Now, let's consider the following code and see how the `onFocus` event handler handles the `focus` event and ensures that the first name text field is not left blank.

```
<HTML>
<HEAD>
<SCRIPT language="JavaScript">
function checkFirstName(){
    //Declare variables
    var firstName;
    var firstNameLength;
    //Assign the values
    firstName=txtFirstName.value;
    firstNameLength=firstName.length;
    //Check the length of the first name
    if(firstNameLength==0){
        alert("Please Enter your First Name");
    }
}//End of the checkFirstName function
</SCRIPT>
</HEAD>
<BODY>
Enter your first name
<INPUT type="text" name=txtFirstName>
<br>
Enter your last name
<INPUT type="text" name=txtLastName onFocus="checkFirstName()">
</BODY>
</HTML>
```

In the preceding code, the user is prompted to enter the first and last names. When the user enters the first name and inserts the pointer in the `LastName` text field, the `focus` event is generated and the `onFocus` event handler processes the function `checkFirstName`. The following part of the preceding code shows you the `onFocus` event handler:

```
Enter your last name
<input type=text name=txtLastName onFocus="checkFirstName()">
```

You'll also observe the use of an `input` property, length, in the `checkFirstName` function:

```
firstNameLength=firstName.length
```

Here, the input property `length` is used to obtain the length of a variable, `first-Name`. The following code shows the input element `txtFirstName`:

```
Enter your first name
<INPUT type=text name=txtFirstName>
```

Let us now apply the concepts learned in this chapter to the problem statement of Web Shoppe.

Result

To ensure that the user enters the required details, execute the following steps:

- Create a user-defined function called `checkValues`.
- In the `checkValues` function, check the data, username, and the password entered in the input elements of the document by using the `value` property of the input element. The `value` property will return blank string if data is not entered.
- If data is not entered, display a message prompting the user to enter data.
- The username and password specified should be verified when the user clicks the `Submit` button. The `click` event is fired when the user clicks the button, and the `onClick` event handler executes the `checkValues` function.

Write the Code for the Web Page

You need to write the following code for Web Shoppe's login page.

```
<HTML>
<HEAD>
<TITLE> Web Shoppe </TITLE>
<SCRIPT language="JavaScript">
function checkValues(){
    var logName;
    var logNameLength;
    var password;
    var passwordLength;
    logName=txtVisitorName.value;
    logNameLength=logName.length;
    while(logNameLength==0){
        logName=prompt("Enter your Login Id","");
```

```
        txtVisitorName.value=logName;
        logNameLength=logName.length;
    }
    password=passVisitor.value;
    passwordLength=password.length;
    while(passwordLength==0){
        password=prompt("Enter your Password","");
        passVisitor.value=password;
        passwordLength=password.length;
    }
}
</script>
</HEAD>
<BODY bgcolor="pink">
<H1 Align="center"><Font color="blue"> Web Shoppe</Font>
</H1><BR><BR>

            
        
    <Font color="green"><B>Please login</B> </Font><BR><BR>
    Login        
    <INPUT Type="text" Name="txtVisitorName" Value=""><BR>
    Password  <INPUT Type="password" Name="passVisitor"
Value=""><BR><BR><BR>

            
        
    <INPUT Type="button" Name="cmdSubmit" onclick="checkValues()"
Value="Submit" >
</BODY>
</HTML>
```

Execute and Verify the Code

Execute the code and verify the successful running of the preceding script code by performing the following steps:

- Leave both the login id and password fields blank, click the Submit button, and observe if a message is displayed.
- Enter the login id and leave the password field blank, click the Submit button, and observe if a message is displayed.
- Enter the password and leave the login id field blank, click the Submit button, and observe if a message is displayed.
- Enter both the password and the login id field, click the Submit button, and observe if a message is displayed. If a message is not displayed, it confirms the entry of data.

Figure 5.12 displays the message shown when the user leaves the Login control blank.

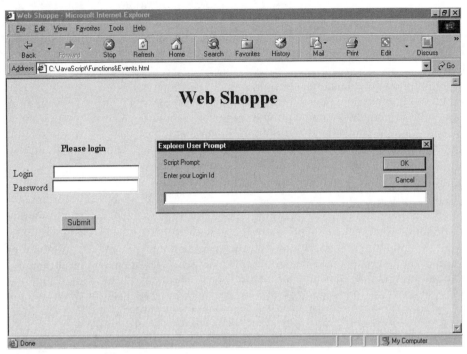

Figure 5.12   The User Prompt Message Box.

Summary

This chapter illustrated the use of functions and events in JavaScript. At each stage, the chapter provided you with real-life scenarios and case studies so that you have a clear understanding of the implementation of the concept. In the first section of the chapter, you learned to write the two types of functions that JavaScript provides, which are user-defined and built-in functions. You also learned how functions help add and implement dynamism, readability, and efficiency in a program. The second section of the chapter dealt with events. Here, you learned to write your own event-handling functions and how to associate them with user interface actions. You also learned how user-defined and built-in functions and events merge to provide dynamism to a Web page.

Using Objects in JavaScript

OBJECTIVES:

In this chapter, you will learn to:

- ✔ **Use objects and learn about object-oriented programming languages**
- ✔ **Use predefined object types**
- ✔ **Use custom object types**

Getting Started

So far, you have used built-in data types to create variables in JavaScript. However, while working on real-life projects, you may realize the need for using customized data types that represent real-life objects. This is possible by using objects and object-oriented programming. *Object-oriented* is a term that is widely used as a marketing tool for the computer or software industry. In contrast to this statement, JavaScript has a limited object model. However, this is one of the most important features of JavaScript because it enables the creation of simple, small programs that are modular and can be reused.

In this chapter, you will learn about using objects in JavaScript and their real-life implementations. You will also learn about the various predefined object types. In addition, you will also learn to create customized object types. To enable a better understanding of objects, we will discuss the case of Web Shoppe, Inc., whose Web page makes extensive use of objects.

About Objects

First, in order to understand the meaning of JavaScript as being object-based, we need to understand about objects and how they work. Objects are entities of the real world or the computer world. Two examples of real-world objects are cars and books. Whereas objects in the computer world consist of Web pages, forms, buttons, and check boxes. *Objects* store information along with the methods required for editing or using that information. Objects are a collection of properties and methods. *Properties* are the describing elements of objects while *methods* are the tasks that can be performed on objects. For example, the Ford is an instance or object of car. The Ford has certain distinctive properties, such as the body color, the body shape, the steering wheel, and radial tires. You can drive it at a specific speed, turn the lights on and off, change gears, apply brakes, and accelerate it as well. Therefore, the Ford is an object with distinctive properties and methods. Let's take an example of a computer object. A Web page is an example of a computer world object that has properties such as the title, the background color, hyperlinks, and graphics. You can perform functions such as opening or closing a Web page. Now that you know about objects, let's proceed by revisiting object-oriented programming.

Revisiting Object-Oriented Programming

In object-oriented programming, the elements of any application are modeled as objects, which are instances of a class. Don't confuse the concept of classes with that of objects. A class is an object type. It is a set of related objects that share common features. You can compare a class with a template or a user-defined data type. Objects are derived from classes as variables are derived from data types. All the objects derived from a class share similar properties and methods. For example, consider the example of an Employee class. The properties of an Employee class could be the name, the employee code, gender, the date of hire, and the office address. The methods `getProjectName()`, `durationOfProject()`, and `printSkills()` display the current project of an employee, the duration of the current project, and the skills or expertise of the employee, respectively.

The Employee class defined above is a layout or template and does not refer to any particular employee. You can further instantiate or create instances of this class that models a specific employee. You can compare the Employee class to a blank employee detail form that lists all the attributes of an employee in general. Creating an object means filling out the blank employee form for a specific employee. Creating objects from a particular class is an important feature of any object-oriented language.

Another powerful feature of object-oriented languages is its ability to reuse classes or objects. Classes are templates that are the building blocks of complex classes. The Employee class can be reused by the Financial Accounting application, the Recruitment database, or the Time logging application for a particular project. The advantage of using object-oriented languages is that it helps avoid the effort of creating the classes repeatedly. It is also useful while modifying classes. Suppose you have created separate classes for all the above-mentioned applications and you want to change the

Employee class definition. Changing the definition means that you will need to change the definition of the Employee class in all the applications. If you reuse the class definition, all you need to do is change the definition globally.

In order to reuse classes, there are certain design principles that you need to follow. One of them is *encapsulation*. The packaging technique of enclosing the properties and methods together in an object and specifying access permissions for either of these is referred to as encapsulation. The access permissions enable you to assign security rules for the data stored within a class or an object.

In order to make encapsulation successful, objects need to implement modularity and information hiding. *Modularity* refers to the objects being self-dependent and not being linked or dependent on other objects. The objects are therefore complete in themselves, and a change in them does not require changes in other objects . *Information hiding* refers to limiting access to any object feature by providing access to only the interface of the object. This is made possible by separating the internal functions of an object from its interface.

Another powerful feature of any object-oriented language is that of inheritance. *Inheritance* is defined as the technique of deriving classes from other classes. Using this approach, an abstract class is created from which more concrete classes can be defined. An abstract class is called the parent class while the derived class is called the child class. The child and/or derived class inherits all the properties and methods of the parent class; therefore, the inherited properties and methods need not be defined again. The child class can add more properties and methods to its definition and can also modify the derived properties and methods of the parent class. Therefore, by using inheritance, more detailed and advanced class definitions can be created. For example, the Automobile class is an abstract/parent class and the Car, Cab, and Bus classes are derived from it. All the three derived classes share the common methods and properties of the Automobile class, for example, they have an engine, brakes, accelerator, and wheels. However, they differ in their engine properties, seating capacities, accelerating speeds, gears, and body shape.

We will close this section by discussing the last feature of object-oriented languages, polymorphism. *Polymorphism* is defined as poly (many) and morphism (forms) of the same object. In object-oriented languages, it is referred to as a mechanism where there are many methods with the same name. The methods are differentiated at run time by the return type or the parameter list in the function call. For example, you define a Calculator object with two different methods that have a similar name: add. However, this method is different for addition. The appropriate method is selected at run time when a user enters the desired numbers either in the integer or float form. Polymorphism helps standardize and reuse software. As a result of polymorphism, you don't need to give slightly different names for methods performing the same function with different parameters and return type.

Difference between Object-Oriented and Object-Based Programming

In contrast to any object-oriented language, JavaScript is a simple object-based language. Don't be confused by the terms object-oriented and object-based. They do not represent the same concept; there is a difference between object-oriented and object-based languages. JavaScript does not support many of the object-oriented capabilities discussed in the preceding section. It does not support the features of inheritance, encapsulation, and information hiding. Remember, JavaScript is not a complete programming language; it is only a scripting language. Therefore, it supports only those features that allow you to easily generate scripts that execute in a server-side application or on a Web page. In short, JavaScript includes the features that are suitable for browser and server scripting. Here is a list of JavaScript's object-based capabilities:

- JavaScript supports both predefined and customized object types.
- JavaScript allows you to create instances of a specific object type by using the new operator.
- JavaScript does not support modular software development.
- JavaScript does not support information hiding. Therefore, encapsulation is not possible and all the properties and methods for a particular object are directly accessible.
- JavaScript does not support inheritance features.

The above features include predefined browser and server objects, and you can access related objects through the properties and methods of other objects.

JavaScript Object Model

JavaScript supports an object model consisting of a number of predefined object types. The object types under this model are described in terms of properties and methods. Properties allow you to access data contained in an object. You can read and edit these values by using the properties of an object. Remember that the properties of a few predefined JavaScript objects are read-only and cannot be edited. Methods are tasks or functions used to perform operations on any object. The properties of an object can be used by these methods. Let's learn to access the properties and methods of objects in JavaScript.

Accessing Properties

You can access the properties of an object as follows:

```
objectName.propertyName
```

For example, the current Web document is represented by the predefined object type called document. The document object contains the bgColor property that regulates the background color of the Web document. To set the background color of the document to blue, you can use the following statement:

```
document.bgColor="blue"
```

This code assigns the blue color to the bgColor property of the document object, thereby changing the background color of the document to blue.

The following example illustrates how the preceding code can be used in a script to change the background color of the document. The code creates three buttons that display different colors. When a button is clicked, the onClick event handler associated with the button object executes the statement that changes the background of the document. If the user clicks the button that has the word blue written on it, the onClick event handler executes the statement document.bgcolor="blue" and changes the document color from the default setting green to blue.

```
<HTML>
<HEAD>
<TITLE> Using JavaScript Properties </TITLE>
</HEAD>
<BODY>
<H1> Using JavaScript Properties </H1>
<SCRIPT LANGUAGE="JavaScript">
document.bgColor="Green";
</SCRIPT>
<FORM>
<P><INPUT TYPE="Button" NAME="red" VALUE="RED"
onClick='document.bgColor="red"'></P>
    <P><INPUT TYPE="Button" NAME="blue" VALUE="BLUE"
onClick='document.bgColor="blue"'></P>
    <P><INPUT TYPE="Button" NAME="red" VALUE="WHITE"
onClick='document.bgColor="WHITE"'></P>
    </FORM>
    </BODY>
    </HTML>
```

Figure 6.1 displays a page whose background color has been set to green using the bgColor property. The page also contains three buttons that are capable of changing the background color to red, blue, and white, respectively.

Accessing Methods

The syntax of accessing the methods of an object is similar to the one used to access its properties.

```
objectName.methodName(parameter list)
```

Commas separate the parameters in the list. You are already familiar with the fact that the function and method names are followed by parentheses even if the parameters are missing. For example,

```
square=Math.sqrt(x)
```

Figure 6.1   Using JavaScript properties to change background color.

The sqrt() method of the predefined Math object is called with x as the parameter. This method returns the square root of x, and this value is then assigned to the variable square.

NOTE You have already used the methods of predefined objects in earlier chapters. An example is the write() statement that you used in Chapter 2. The write() method is a method of the document object and is used to write text in the current document. You will learn more about predefined objects later in this chapter.

Creating Instances of Objects

You can create instances of objects of a particular class and/or object type by using the new operator. Recall that the new operator is also used to create array objects. The syntax of the new operator for creating objects is similar to that used for creating array objects.

```
variable = new objectType(parameters)
```

In the above syntax, the function `objectType(parameters)` is referred to as a *constructor*. A constructor has the same name as the object type and is used to construct and initialize an object of the given object type. A given program can have more than one constructor that differs in the number of parameters in the argument list.

For example, `Date` is a predefined object type. The following statement creates an instance of this object type by assigning the current date and time to a variable, `doj`.

```
doj = new Date()
```

The above example can be taken as an example of a constructor without any arguments. Consider the following code statement:

```
doj = new Date(99,14,6)
```

This statement creates an instance of the object type `Date` and assigns the date, 14 June 99, to the `doj` variable. The constructor in the above statement takes three parameters: `year`, `date`, and `month`.

NOTE The `Date` **object type has additional constructors other than the ones discussed in this section. The** `Date` **object type will be discussed later in this chapter.**

You have learned about the basic access procedures for objects and how to create them. Now, let's discuss the hierarchy of the JavaScript object model.

Overview of the Object Hierarchy Model

There are certain JavaScript objects that are created when a Web page is loaded in a Web browser. These objects are used to interact with the various HTML elements contained in the Web page. A few of these important objects along with their uses are described in Table 6.1.

Table 6.1 The Input Controls of the Login Page

OBJECTS	DESCRIPTION
navigator	Provides properties that retrieve information about the current browser to JavaScript objects.
window	Used to access a browser window or frames within the Web page.
document	Used to access a current HTML document in the browser window.

(continues)

Table 6.1   The Input Controls of the Login Page *(Continued)*

OBJECTS	DESCRIPTION
location	Used to create, access, or modify a URL.
history	Maintains a history of the URLs visited within a window.
link	Used to access a text or graphic anchor of a hypertext link. There is a links array for this object that stores all link objects within an HTML document.
image	Used to access the images embedded in an HTML document. The images array is used to access all the images in the document.
form	Used to access an HTML form. The forms array is used to store all the form objects in the document.

NOTE **A browser automatically creates the objects shown in Table 6.1 when a Web page is loaded in the browser. In addition to these, JavaScript also supports predefined object types that are independent of the Web page loaded in the browser. These predefined objects will be discussed in the next section.**

In Table 6.1, you will notice that certain objects have arrays with similar names. These arrays store the different instances of a particular object type. For example, if the loaded document contains three forms, then the forms array will contain three form objects corresponding to the three forms defined in the document.

The objects discussed above are organized in a hierarchy with respect to the sequence they follow when loaded in the browser. This hierarchy is called *instance hierarchy,* and the window object is the top-most element in the hierarchy. An example of instance hierarchy can be a window that contains a document containing forms, which further contains elements such as radio buttons or check boxes.

The navigator object is contained in the window object. Now, let's discuss the topmost object, window, in the hierarchy. We'll then discuss the navigator object.

The window Object

The window object provides methods and properties for using the actual Navigator window. The properties of the window object are used to identify the objects of HTML elements found in the window. For example, the window object contains the document property that refers to the document object contained in the browser window. The document object is one of the most heavily used objects in the instance hierarchy. This object contains objects, properties, and methods for working with document elements such as forms, links, anchors, and images. To access the properties and methods of the current window, the browser will assume the current window as the window object. Therefore, you do not need to identify the window object explicitly.

You have already learned to access objects in JavaScript. However, accessing objects in the instance hierarchy follows a different methodology. A browser organizes the objects according to the instance hierarchy. Therefore, a hierarchical naming scheme is used to access these objects. For example, consider a document containing two forms with ten elements in the first form. You need to access the name of the third element in the first form. This is possible by using the statement given below:

```
document.forms[0].elements[2].name
```

NOTE Remember that array indices start from 0.

The `navigator` Object

The `navigator` object provides properties that represent information about the current browser to JavaScript scripts. It is used to describe the browser's configuration that is used to display a window.

Predefined Object Types

In addition to the object types discussed above, JavaScript provides several objects that are not related to the current window or loaded documents. These are general-purpose object types that support common operations, such as string or mathematical operations. In this section, you will learn about a couple of such object types.

The Array Object

The Array object allows you to access arrays as objects. The two properties of the Array object are `length` and `prototype`. The length property returns the number of elements in an array. The prototype property allows you to expand the abilities of any object type by adding additional properties and methods to a particular object type.

NOTE The `prototype` property is supported by all object types.

The `Array` object contains the following methods:

- **toString().** Converts an array to a string version where array elements are separated by commas.
- **join(separator).** Similar to the `toString()` method except for the fact that the array elements are separated by a specified separator. If no separator is specified, then a comma is used.

- **reverse().** Reverses the elements of an array. The last element becomes the first element and vice versa.

- **sort(comparison function).** Sorts or arranges the elements of an array according to the comparison function defined. The comparison function takes two arguments, p1 and p2. This function returns a zero value if p1 = p2, a negative value if p2 is greater than p1, and a positive value if p2 is less than p1. If no comparison function is defined, then the elements are arranged in alphabetical order.

The following code illustrates the preceding methods. It creates an array of five integers and applies these methods to it.

```
<HTML>
<HEAD>
<TITLE>The Array Object</TITLE>
</HEAD>
<BODY>
<H1>Using Arrays</H1>
<SCRIPT LANGUAGE="JavaScript">
numArray = [3,2,4,0,5];
document.write("numArray: " + numArray + "<P>")
document.write("numArray.join(';'): " + numArray.join(';') +
"<P>")
document.write("numArray.reverse(): " + numArray.reverse() +
"<P>")
document.write("numArray.sort(): " + numArray.sort())
</SCRIPT>
</BODY>
</HTML>
```

Figure 6.2 displays the output of the above script.

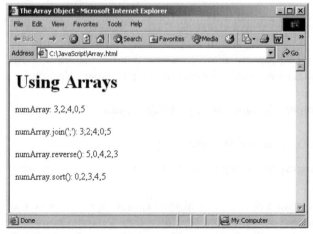

Figure 6.2 The use of `Array` object methods.

The Boolean Object

A Boolean variable can contain either true or false values. A `Boolean` object enables the use of these Boolean values (true and false) as objects. The `Boolean` object contains the `prototype` property and the `toString()` and `valueOf()` methods. The `toString()` method returns the string equivalent of a Boolean value. The `valueOf()` method returns a `true` or `false` value based on the value contained in the object. You can set the value of a `Boolean` object as true or false by passing an argument to the constructor function. For example,

```
booleanValue = new Boolean(true)
```

■ The above statement creates an object "`booleanValue`" of the `Boolean` object type with the value as true.

> **NOTE** Recall the fact that a constructor has the same name as the object type and is used to initialize and create the object.

The String Object

You can access strings as objects by using the `String` object. This object has the `length` and `prototype` properties. The `length` property returns the length of a string in characters. As discussed above, the `prototype` property is similar for all object types and allows additional properties and methods to be defined for an object type.

Table 6.2 lists the `String` object methods for manipulating strings:

Table 6.2 `String` Object Methods

METHOD	DESCRIPTION
charAt(index)	Returns a string containing the character at the specified index position of the string to which the method is applied.
fromCharCode(code)	Creates and returns a string from the comma-separated code passed as an argument to the method.
indexOf(Pattern)	Returns the index position of the first string containing the pattern specified as the parameter. The result is -1 if the pattern is not contained in the string.

(continues)

Table 6.2   String Object Methods *(Continued)*

METHOD	DESCRIPTION
lastIndexOf(Pattern)	Returns the index position of the last string containing the pattern specified as the parameter. The result is -1 if the pattern is not contained in the string.
split(separator)	Results in arrays of substrings. The separator parameter is used to separate the string into an array of substrings.
substring(startPos)	Returns the substring of a string beginning at startPos.
substring(startPos, endPos)	Returns the substring of a string beginning at startPos and ending at endPos.
toLowerCase()	Returns a copy of the string converted to lowercase.
toUpperCase()	Returns a copy of the string converted to uppercase.
valueOf()	Returns the string value of a string object.

String objects can be created in a similar manner as you create other objects by using the new operator. For example, the following statement assigns the value String1 to the variable S.

```
S = new String("String1")
```

Before providing you with an example that uses various String object methods, let's take a few of the above methods individually and see how these operate.

Searching with Strings

As stated in Table 6.2, the indexOf() and lastIndexOf() methods can be used to search for text within strings. Both of these methods start from the left. The first character starts at position zero. The methods return the position of the first character of the searched text, if the search text is found, or -1 if the text is not found. The following code returns the value 2.

```
"Buzz".indexOf("z")
```

Retrieving a Portion of a String

It is possible to retrieve a portion of a string by using `substring()` and `charAt()` methods. The `substring()` method can take one or two parameters. The `substring()` method with one parameter returns the substring of a string from the start position that you specify as the parameter. The `substring()` method with two parameters specifies the start position from where a substring has to be retrieved and the end position of the substring to be returned. Like `indexOf()` and `lastIndexOf()` methods, these methods are also zero-based. For example, the following code returns `New`:

```
"New Jersey".substring(0,3)
```

In addition, consider the following code in which the `substring()` method takes one parameter:

```
"New Jersey".substring(3)
```

The substring returned in this case is " `Jersey`".

If a single character is to be retrieved, the `charAt()` method can be used. This method returns the character at the position that is specified as the parameter. The following code returns X:

```
"XFiles".charAt(0)
```

If you specify a position that is outside the string, the method returns -1.

Case Changing Methods

The methods `toUppercase()` and `toLowerCase()` convert characters to uppercase and lowercase, respectively. These methods are useful when strings are compared without any regard to the case.

The following example illustrates the use of the various `String` object methods discussed above. The program takes a string in a variable and performs various `String` methods on the string to view the respective output.

```
<HTML>
<HEAD>
<TITLE>THE STRING OBJECT</TITLE>
</HEAD>
<BODY>
<SCRIPT LANGUAGE="JavaScript">
s = new String("Testing String Methods")
document.write('s = '+s+"<BR>")
```

```
        document.write('s.charAt(2) = '+s.charAt(2)+"<BR>")
        document.write('s.indexOf("String") =
'+s.indexOf("String")+"<BR>")
        document.write('s.lastIndexOf("ing") =
'+s.lastIndexOf("ing")+"<BR>")
        document.write('s.substring(8,15) = '+s.substring(8,15)+"<BR>")
        document.write('s.toLowerCase() = '+s.toLowerCase()+"<BR>")
        document.write('s.toUpperCase() = '+s.toUpperCase()+"<BR>")
        </SCRIPT>
        </BODY>
        </HTML>
```

Figure 6.3 displays the output of the script using `String` object methods.

The `Date` Object

You can use the `Date` object to work with date and time. This can be done through the various methods provided by the `Date` object. This object type also supports the prototype property. The following factors merit special attention:

- Following the UNIX convention, JavaScript considers January 1, 1970, as the base date. This means that JavaScript does not allow you to work with dates prior to this date.

- The date reflected on an object at the time of its creation is the date of the client's machine.

- JavaScript keeps track of date and time values in the form of milliseconds elapsed since the base date.

Encapsulated within the `Date` object is an impressive array of methods to get and set date values and convert them to various forms. Table 6.3 displays the methods of the `Date` object.

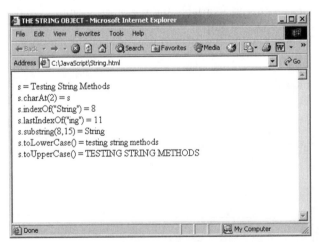

Figure 6.3 The usage of `String` object methods.

Table 6.3   Date Object Methods

METHOD	USAGE
getDate() getUTCDate()	Returns the day of the month of the date contained in the Date object.
setDate() setUTCDate()	Sets the day of the month of the date contained in the Date object.
getTime()	Returns the time of the Date object.
setTime()	Sets the time of the Date object.
getDay() getUTCDay()	Returns the day of the week of the date contained in the Date object.
getHours() getUTCHours()	Returns the hours of the date contained in the Date object.
setHours() setUTCHours()	Sets the hours of the date contained in the Date object.
getMilliseconds() getUTCMilliseconds()	Returns the milliseconds value of the Date object.
setMilliseconds () setUTCMilliseconds ()	Sets the milliseconds value of the Date object.
getMinutes() getUTCMinutes()	Returns the minutes value of the date contained in the Date object.
setMonth () setUTCMonth ()	Sets the minutes value of the date contained in the Date object.
getMonth() getUTCMonth()	Returns the month of the date contained in the Date object.
setMonth() setUTCMonth()	Sets the month of the date contained in the Date object.
getSeconds() getUTCSeconds() setSeconds() setUTCSeconds()	Returns or sets the seconds of the Date object.
getYear() getUTCYear() setYear() setUTCYear()	Returns or sets the year of the date contained in the Date object.
toString()	Returns a string value of the Date object.

NOTE The text UCT in the method names stands for Universal Coordinated Time, which is the time set by the World Time Standard.

Creating a Date Object

Creating a Date object is similar to creating a String or Array object. Using the new operator, a Date object can be defined as follows:

```
var datevar = new Date()
```

You can create instances of the Date object by using any of the constructors listed in Table 6.4.

Working with Date Values

After the Date object is created, any of the methods discussed above can be used to set or obtain the date values. For example, the following statements return the day of the current month.

```
var today = new Date()
result = today.getDate()
```

The following code changes the month for a date.

```
var somedate = new Date(1997, 07, 22)
somedate.setMonth(8)
```

Example

Having looked at the basics of creating a Date object, let us consider the following script that makes use of these methods.

```
<HTML>
<HEAD>
<TITLE>THE DATE OBJECT</TITLE>
</HEAD>
<BODY>
<SCRIPT LANGUAGE="JavaScript">
currDate = new Date()
document.write("Date:
"+currDate.getMonth()+"/"+currDate.getDate()+"/"+currDate.getYear()+"<BR
>")
document.write("Time:
"+currDate.getHours()+":"+currDate.getMinutes()+":"+currDate.getSeconds(
))
</SCRIPT>
</BODY>
</HTML>
```

Table 6.4   Date Constructor Methods

METHOD	USAGE
Date()	Creates an instance of the Date object with the current date and time.
Date(year, month, day, hours, minutes, seconds, milliseconds)	Creates a date instance with the date specified through the parameters passed in the constructor.
Date(dateString)	Creates an instance of the Date object with the date specified in the dateString parameter. The format of this parameter is "month, day, year hours:minutes:seconds".

Figure 6.4 displays the output of the script using Date object methods.

Using the above script, you can write the current date and time to the document object. Initially, the currDate variable is assigned the Date object containing the current date and time by using the new operator and the Date constructor. The date is displayed in the mm/dd/yy format with the help of the write statement and predefined getMonth(), getDate(), and getYear() methods. Similarly, the time is displayed in the hh:mm:ss format because of the write statement and getHours(), getMinutes(), and getSeconds() methods.

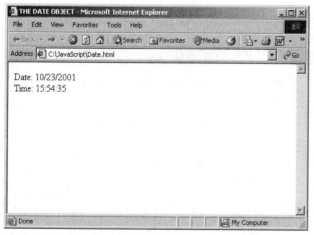

Figure 6.4   The usage of Date object methods.

The `Global` Object

The `Global` object is used to associate an object with the globally accessible variables and methods of earlier JavaScript versions. You cannot create an instance of this object type by using the `new` operator and cannot refer to it as `Global.property` or method. You may wonder how to refer to this object in JavaScript. The properties and methods of the `Global` object can be referenced directly as global variables and functions. There are two properties for this object, NaN and `Infinity`. NaN means not a number while `Infinity` refers to positive infinity.

Table 6.5 lists the various methods defined for the `Global` object.

NOTE We have already learned about a few of these methods in Chapter 5, "Functions and Events." Those built-in functions are actually the methods of the `Global` object.

The `Math` Object

The `Math` object provides a standard library of mathematical constants and functions. The constants are simply the properties of the `Math` object. Similar to the `Global` object, you cannot create instances of the `Math` object because it is not an object type but is a predefined object. Table 6.6 lists the properties of the `Math` object.

Table 6.5 `Global` Object Methods

METHOD	DESCRIPTION
escape(string)	Converts the parameter string to a string with certain characters changed to escape sequences.
unescape(string)	Converts strings affected by escape() to their original value.
isFinite(number)	If the number passed as parameter is finite, true is returned otherwise false.
isNaN(number)	NaN indicates not a number. Therefore this method returns true if the parameter is not a number and false if it is.
parseInt(string)	Parses the parameter string as a numeric value.
parseFloat(string)	Parses the parameter string as a floating-point value.
eval(x)	Evaluates the expression x and returns its value.

Table 6.6   Math Object Properties

METHOD	USAGE
E	Euler's constant
LN2	Natural logarithm of 2
LN10	Natural logarithm of 10
LOG2E	Base 2 logarithm of e
LOG10E	Base 10 logarithm of e
PI	Constant value of π
SQRT2	Square root of 2

Table 6.7 lists the various methods of the Math object.

Table 6.7   Math Object Methods

METHOD	USAGE
abs(x)	Returns the absolute value of x
acos(x)	Returns the arc cosine of x in radians
cos(x)	Returns the cosine of x
asin(x)	Returns the arc sine of x in radians
sin(x)	Returns the sine of x
atan(x)	Returns the arc tangent of x in radians
tan(x)	Returns the tangent of x
ceil(x)	Returns the smallest integer that is greater than or equal to x
floor(x)	Returns the largest integer that is less than or equal to x
exp(x)	Returns e^x
log(x)	Returns the natural logarithm of x
max(x,y)	Returns the greater one out of x and y
min(x,y)	Returns the lesser one out of x and y
pow(x,y)	Returns x^y
random()	Returns a random number between 0 and 1
round(x)	Returns x rounded to the closest integer
sqrt(x)	Returns the square root of x

The following script uses the various methods of the Math object:

```
<HTML>
<HEAD>
<TITLE>THE MATH OBJECT</TITLE>
</HEAD>
<BODY>
<H1>USING THE MATH OBJECT</H1>
<SCRIPT LANGUAGE="JavaScript">
document.write("The value of pi: "+Math.PI+"<BR>")
document.write("The value of Euler's constant: "+Math.E+"<BR>")
document.write("Math.floor(2.456): "+Math.floor(2.456)+"<BR>")
document.write("Math.round(4.68): "+Math.round(4.68)+"<BR>")
document.write("The square root of 46: "+Math.sqrt(46)+"<BR>")
document.write("48.2 to the power 4: "+Math.pow(48.2,4)+"<BR>")
document.write("The log of 13.9: "+Math.log(13.9)+"<BR>")
</SCRIPT>
</BODY>
</HTML>
```

The code displays the output using the Math object (Figure 6.5).

The Number Object

With the help of the Number object, you can treat the numbers in JavaScript as objects. Similar to other predefined objects, the Number object supports a couple of properties or methods. Table 6.8 lists the properties of the Number object. These properties are generally not used while designing scripts in JavaScript. You can use the properties of the Global object instead.

The methods of the Number object are toString(radix), which returns a string that represents the number in a radix base and NvalueOf(), which returns the numeric value of the Number object.

You can create instances of the Number object type by using the new operator and the Number constructor. Look at the following statement:

```
Num = new Number(36.85)
```

The above statement performs two operations at the same time, creating an instance of the Number object type and initializing it with the number supplied as a parameter to the constructor.

The Object object

The Object object acts like a baseline or a template for all other object types. Therefore, its properties and methods are available for all other object types. You can imagine it as being a global object from which all other object types are defined.

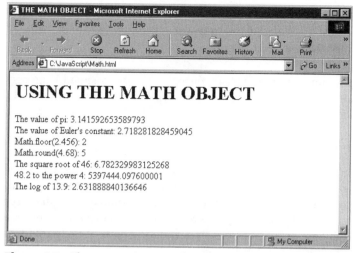

Figure 6.5 The usage of `Math` object methods.

The `Object` object contains the `prototype` and `constructor` properties. The constructor property identifies the name of the object's constructor. The methods of the `Object` object are `toString()`, which converts a given object to a string and `valueOf()`, which returns the value of the object associated with this object type. As discussed earlier, object types, such as string, number, or boolean, can be created by using the `Object` object type. Therefore, this method returns the value number, string, or boolean, depending on the object created using this object type. Otherwise, it returns the object itself.

Table 6.8 `Number` Object Properties

PROPERTY	DESCRIPTION
MAX_VALUE	This property signifies the maximum possible numeric value.
MIN_VALUE	This property signifies the minimum possible numeric value.
NaN	This signifies that the value is not a number.
NEGATIVE_INFINITY	The number is negative infinity.
POSITIVE_INFINITY	The number is positive infinity.
Prototype	As discussed earlier, all object types support this property.

NOTE Objects such as Number, Boolean, or String can be created by supplying any of these to the `Object()` constructor. However, it is better to use the built-in constructor specified for any of these types.

Now that you are acquainted with the basic concepts of object-oriented languages and have learned about the various predefined object types in JavaScript, let's implement this knowledge in a real-life scenario.

Problem Statement

You have seen in the earlier chapters that Cynthia, with the help of Scott, has improved and maintained the functionality of the Web Shoppe site. However, she wants to further improve the look and feel of the site. Every customer at Web Shoppe, Inc., has been assigned a unique username and password. You already know that for security reasons before accessing the Web Shoppe site, customers have to log on to the site by using their login name and password.

Cynthia wants the current date to appear on the Welcome page of the site. Moreover, she wants the site to have a personalized look for a customer who logs on to the site. Therefore, she decides to add the name of each customer who logs on to the site to the Welcome page. The name will appear on the page in capital letters. She has again assigned Scott the task of adding the above-mentioned functionality to the site.

To design the page, Scott needs to perform certain steps in the sequence specified in the following task list.

Task List

✔ **Identify necessary objects.**

✔ **Create object instances.**

✔ **Write the code to include the required functionality.**

✔ **Execute and verify the code.**

Identify Necessary Objects

The two requirements for the above scenario include: The current date should be displayed on the Welcome page of the site and the username should be displayed in capital letters on the Welcome page.

Scott can use the predefined object types discussed in the section above to fulfill these tasks. He will need `Date` and `String` object types to fulfill the above requirements.

Create Object Instances

Scott will need to create object instances of the predefined object types. He can then use the methods and properties of the particular object type to fulfill the required tasks. He will specifically use the `getMonth()`, `getDate()`, and `getYear()` methods of the `Date` object and the `toUpperCase()` method of the `String` object.

Write the Code to Include the Required Functionality

Next, Scott will include the functionality in JavaScript code. The code is shown below:

```
<HTML>
<HEAD>
<TITLE> Web Shoppe </TITLE>
<SCRIPT LANGUAGE="JavaScript">
function checkValues(){
    var logName;
    var logNameLength;
    var password;
    var passwordLength;
    logName=txtVisitorName.value;
    logNameLength=logName.length;
    while(logNameLength==0){
        logName=prompt("Enter your User Id","");
        txtVisitorName.value=logName;
        logNameLength=logName.length;
    }
    password=passVisitor.value;
    passwordLength=password.length;
    while(passwordLength==0){
        password=prompt("Enter your Password","");
        passVisitor.value=password;
        passwordLength=password.length;
    }
    S=new String(logName);
    document.write("<Font color = blue> <H2>Welcome to Web Shoppe: "
+S.toUpperCase()+"</H2></Font><HR color = blue>");
    currDate=new Date();
    document.write("<Font color = green>Date: " +
currDate.getMonth() + "/" +
currDate.getDate()+"/"+currDate.getYear()+"</Font><BR>");
    document.write("<BR><MARQUEE>"+"A shop at your finger
tips!!!!"+"</MARQUEE><BR>");
    document.write("<Font color = blue> <H3 align = center>TOYS
AVAILABLE "+"</H3></Font><BR>");
    document.write("Robby the Whale----$50");
    document.write("<BR>Tin Drum---------$50");
    }
</SCRIPT>
</HEAD>
<BODY bgcolor="pink">
<H1 Align="center"><Font color="blue"> Web Shoppe</Font>
</H1><BR><BR>

           
        
    <Font color="green"><B>Please login</B> </Font><BR><BR>
    Login        
```

```
        <INPUT Type="text" Name="txtVisitorName" Value=""><BR>
        Password  <INPUT Type="password" Name="passVisitor"
Value=""><BR><BR><BR>

           
       
        <INPUT Type="button" Name="cmdSubmit" onclick="checkValues();"
Value="Submit" >
        </BODY>
        </HTML>
```

Execute and Verify the Code

Execute the code and verify its successful running by performing the following steps:

- Enter the username John Pearson and the password.

- Click the Submit button.

- Observe that you are directed to the Welcome page of the site with the username being displayed in capital letters. The current date is also displayed on the Web page.

Figure 6.6 displays the Welcome page with the username and the current date.

Custom Object Types

You have learned about a couple of predefined object types and the properties and methods that they support. You must be wondering how you would create an object type to suit your own requirements. Do not worry; JavaScript provides you with this feature as well.

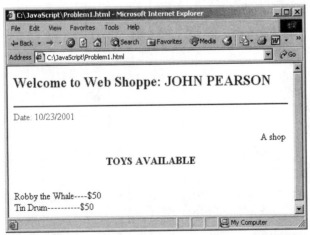

Figure 6.6 The usage of the String and Date object methods.

JavaScript allows you to create custom object types and instances of these object types. You can create varied object types. All you need to do is define a constructor function that is used to create the instances of a particular object type. The constructor function should be designed in a way that it can assign the values of the properties of a specific object type and identify the functions to be used as the methods of that object type.

Defining Properties of an Object

Before creating a new object, it is necessary to define it by specifying its properties. This can be done using the constructor function discussed above. For example, consider that you want to create an object named student with properties such as name, age, and grade. The constructor function for this object is as follows:

```
function student(name, age, grade){
    this.name = name;
    this.age = age;
    this.grade = grade;
}
```

As you can see in the code above, the student() constructor function takes the parameters name, age, and grade and assigns them to this.name, this.age, and this.grade, respectively. The this prefix is a special keyword that refers to the current object. Therefore, the this.name = name statement assigns the value stored in the name parameter to the name property of the current object. The remaining two statements work in a similar fashion.

Using this function it is now possible to create an object by using the new operator and the student constructor. For example, the following statement creates an object called student1 with three properties: name, age, and grade. This is known as an instance of the object student.

```
student1 = new student("Bob",10,75);
```

The parameters passed to the constructor function will be stored as the properties of the student1 object.

Adding Methods to Objects

You can add methods to an object definition in addition to adding properties. Methods are simply the functions associated with an object. Therefore, you first need to create a function that defines a method and then add it to the object definition.

For example, if you want to add a method to the student object to display the name, age, and grade in the document window, you will need to create a function called displayProfile() as shown below:

```
function displayProfile() {
    document.write("Name: "+this.name+"<BR>");
    document.write("Age: "+this.age+"<BR>");
    document.write("Grade: "+this.grade+"<BR>");
}
```

Updating Objects Dynamically

You can also modify or update object types after they have been created by using the new statement. JavaScript provides the capability to add properties and methods to already defined object types by using the prototype property.

Properties can be added to object definitions by setting the value of object-Name.prototype.propertyName. Here, objectName refers to the name of the constructor function, and propertyName is the name of the property or method being added to the function. For example, if you want to add an additional method called updateProfile() to the student object definition, use the following statement:

```
student.prototype.updateProfile = update;
```

Please ensure that you have already defined the update() function as shown below:

```
function update(){
    this.age = prompt("Enter the correct age for"+this.name,
this.age);
    this.grade = prompt("Enter the correct grade
for"+this.name,this.grade);
  }
```

Now all instances of student created earlier would be able to access this new method. You have created an instance of the student object, student1. The following statement can be used to update the age and grade of Bob:

```
student1.updateProfile();
```

Working with a Custom Object Type

To further demonstrate the application of objects and define your own objects, let's take an example of an employee object type. This can be used to create employee objects and display employee information. The following script asks the user for personnel information of an employee and then formats it for display on the screen.

To accomplish the above task, you need to define an employee object and methods for displaying the employee information.

```
<HTML>
<HEAD>
<TITLE>CREATING AN EMPLOYEE PROFILE</TITLE>
<SCRIPT LANGUAGE="JavaScript">
//Define Methods
function display(){
document.write("<H1>Employee Profile:
"+this.name+"</H1><HR><PRE>");
```

```
document.writeln("Employee Number: "+this.number);
document.writeln("Social Security Number: "+this.socsec);
document.writeln("Annual salary: "+this.salary);
document.write("</PRE>");
}

//Define Object
function employee(){
this.name=prompt("Enter Employee's Name","Name");
this.number=prompt("Enter Employee Number for
"+this.name,"000-000");
this.socsec=prompt("Enter Social Security Number for
"+this.name,"000-00-0000");
this.salary=prompt("Enter Annual Salary for
"+this.name,"$00,000");
this.display=display;
}
</SCRIPT>
</HEAD>
<BODY>
<SCRIPT LANGUAGE="JavaScript">
newEmployee=new employee();
newEmployee.display();
</SCRIPT>
</BODY>
</HTML>
```

Figure 6.7 shows the output of the preceding code with sample values Cynthia Anderson for Name, 234-789 for Employee Number, 234-76-0892 for Social Security Number, and $62, 068 for Annual Salary.

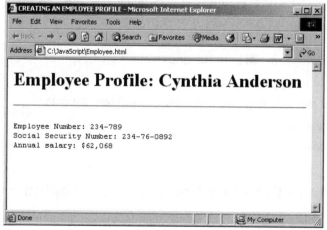

Figure 6.7   The employee details screen.

Deleting Properties and Methods

The `delete` operator can be used to delete a property or method of a user-defined object. The syntax of the `delete` operator is as follows:

```
delete objectName.propertyName
delete objectname.methodName
```

For example, if you want to remove the `grade` property from the `student` object type, you can use the following statement:

```
delete student1.grade
```

Problem Statement

The online mall of Web Shoppe now has a more personalized look for every customer. The shopping mall has organized a clearance sale for a few products that will be available at a 35 percent discount. The production of these products is being stopped because of a decline in customer demand.

The Web Shoppe online mall has a star system for its regular customers. The system rewards customers on the basis of their purchases. A sale worth $300 results in the customer being awarded 20 points. At the end of every purchase, customers are informed about their star accounts. Cynthia wants to send mailers to the first 200 customers with the highest star accounts informing them about the sale. The sale will start a week later. Therefore, the Web development team has decided to gather information from customers. The team has developed a page where customers can enter and validate their star account details and submit them to the mall. These records are maintained in a backend database.

The Web development team will then access these records and send mail messages to qualifying customers.

To design the page, the team needs to perform the steps in the following task list.

Task List

✔ Identify the customer data that needs to be accepted.

✔ Design the user interface screen to accept the data.

✔ Identify the objects and methods required to display and validate the data.

✔ Write the code for the Web page.

✔ Execute and verify the code.

Identify the Customer Data that Needs to Be Accepted

The Web development team needs to identify the customer details that they need for the mailers. They have decided on the following parameters:

- Customer name
- Customer email ID

- Star account details
- Customer age

Therefore, they will design the Web page based on the preceding parameters.

Design the User Interface Screen to Accept the Data

The customers will enter their data from system prompts. After they have entered the relevant data, the Web page containing their details will be displayed. The Web page will contain two buttons. One of them will enable customers to reenter the data. The other button will allow them to submit the data to the site.

Identify the Objects and Methods to Display and Validate the Customer Data

You have already seen the usage of predefined objects and methods in the earlier scenario. To design the page, the team will need to construct a user-defined object with customized properties and methods. The team has decided to create an object called Customer. The Customer object will have the following properties and methods:

- **custName.** Identifies the name of the customer.
- **custEmailId.** Identifies the customer email ID.
- **custStar.** Identifies the customer star account.
- **custAge.** Identifies the customer age.
- **Customer().** The constructor function that creates the Customer object with the above properties.
- **display().** Displays the customer data on the Web page.

Now that the team has decided on the design of the Customer object, they can design the Web page.

Write the Code for the Web Page

The code for the Customer data entry Web page is as follows:

```
<HTML>
<HEAD>
<TITLE>CREATING A CUSTOMER ACCOUNT</TITLE>
<SCRIPT LANGUAGE="JavaScript">
//Define Methods
function submit(){
document.write("<BR><BR><BR><BR><H1 align = center>Thanks, your data has
been submitted to the site.</H1>");
}
function display(){
document.write("<H1>Web Shoppe Customer Details:
"+this.custName+"</H1><HR><PRE>");
```

```
document.writeln("Customer Name: "+this.custName);
document.writeln("Customer E-mail id: "+this.custEmailId);
document.writeln("Customer Star Account: "+this.custStar);
document.writeln("Customer Age: "+this.custAge);
document.write("<HR></PRE>");
document.write("<BR>Please validate the data before submitting it to the
site.");
document.write('<BR><BR><INPUT Type="button" Name="cmdSubmit"
onclick="submit();" Value="Submit" >');
}
//Define Object
function Customer(){
this.custName=prompt("Enter Customer Name","Name");
this.custEmailId=prompt("Enter Email Id for "+this.custName," ");
this.custAge=prompt("Enter Age for "+this.custName," ");
this.custStar=prompt("Enter Star Account for "+this.custName," ");
this.display=display;
}
</SCRIPT>
</HEAD>
<BODY>
<SCRIPT LANGUAGE="JavaScript">
newCust=new Customer();
newCust.display();
</SCRIPT>
</BODY>
</HTML>
```

Execute and Verify the Code

Execute the code and verify the successful running of the preceding script code by performing the following steps:

- Enter the customer details.
- Click on the Submit button.
- Observe that you are directed to a page of the site informing you that your data has been submitted to the site.

Figure 6.8 displays the output of the preceding code.

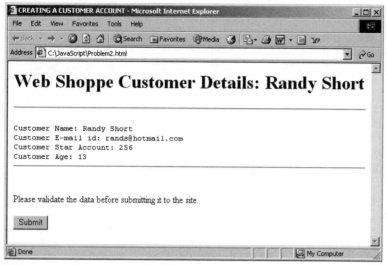

Figure 6.8 The customer details page.

Summary

In this chapter, we discussed objects and object-oriented programming languages. We listed the difference between object-oriented and object-based programming. You were introduced to JavaScript object model. You learned to access properties and methods of objects in JavaScript.

The second section of the chapter gave you an overview on the object hierarchy model. We discussed various predefined object types such as the `Array`, `Object`, `Boolean`, `String`, `Date`, `Global`, `Math`, and `Number objects`.

Next, you learned to create custom object types; you learned to define properties of a custom object. You also learned to add methods to objects and update objects dynamically. Finally, you learned to create a small application using custom object type.

Error and Exception Handling in JavaScript

OBJECTIVES:

In this chapter, you will learn to:

- ✔ Use the `onerror` event handler and the `Error` object to handle errors in JavaScript
- ✔ Identify the meaning of exception handling
- ✔ Identify how exception handling works

Getting Started

Many times, while executing your code, runtime exceptions occur and therefore a list of errors is displayed on the screen. If these errors are overlooked at this stage, they'll reappear when a user is working on the page. Imagine a situation where a user views a string of errors instead of the expected output. Wouldn't this be embarrassing for the developer who wrote the script?

As a developer, one should write scripts that are error-free and can handle runtime exceptions. Unfortunately, in JavaScript errors occur in the scripts due to incompatibilities between Netscape Navigator and Internet Explorer. We discussed browser incompatibility in Chapter 1, "Introducing Web Development." However, the situation is not as bad as it may appear. JavaScript provides the capability of handling errors that may occur during script run time. In addition to browser incompatibility issues, error handling is also important for managing situations and/or errors, such as insufficient memory or inability to find or open files. Such errors, if not trapped, can cause the program to come to an abrupt halt or produce unexpected output.

Let's begin by categorizing errors and find out why errors might occur in a program. You can categorize errors as syntax errors or exceptions. *Syntax errors* occur when statements or commands are not written in the manner accepted by the software. *Exceptions* can be defined as unexpected events that occur during program run time. These exceptions are errors that interrupt the normal flow of a program and, as a result, the interpreter (browser) reaches a point where it cannot continue with the program execution. Exceptions generally occur when a program attempts to execute an illegal command such as accessing a null object or an array element that is out of range of the array size. There is another illegal operation, the division of a number by zero, which other languages treat as an error, but JavaScript allows the execution of such an operation. In this case, JavaScript does not display any error because it assigns an infinite value to the variable that stores the result.

> **NOTE** In this chapter, you will find the terms *exception* and *error* used interchangeably. This is because exceptions are also errors, and there is actually no difference between the two.

JavaScript provides error-handling support through the `onerror` event handler, the `Error` object, the `throw` statement, and the `try...catch...finally` block. We'll first cover the `onerror` event handler and then see how the `Error` object helps in exception handling by using the `try...catch...finally` block. As is the case in other chapters, this chapter will also begin with a problem statement. You'll add exception-handling code to the discount calculation page of Web Shoppe.

Problem Statement

As a promotion strategy, the management of Web Shoppe has decided to offer a New Year discount to its premier customers. The discount is based on the total purchase made by a customer over the last year. The discount scheme is as follows:

TOTAL PURCHASE AMOUNT	DISCOUNT
Greater than $3,000 but less than or equal to $4,000	20%
Greater than $4,000 but less than or equal to $5,000	30%
Greater than $5,000	35%

Scott has written the code that accepts customer details and displays them after calculating the discount applicable to each customer. However, the code generates an error, and code execution halts. In addition, the programming logic does not add dynamism to the script.

The code for accepting and displaying customer details (after calculating the discount percentage) is given below. Scott now needs to control program execution so that the execution does not terminate abruptly and is more dynamic.

```
<HTML>
<HEAD>
<H1>Web Shoppe Customer Details:</H1>
<SCRIPT LANGUAGE="JavaScript">
function display(){
    document.write("<H1>"+this.custName+"</H1><HR><PRE>");
    document.write("Customer Name: "+this.custName + "<BR>");
    document.write("Customer E-mail id: "+this.custEmailId +
"<BR>");
    document.write("Customer Star Account: "+this.custStar +"
<BR>");
    document.write("Customer Date of Birth: "+this.custDateOfBirth+
"<BR>");
    document.write("Customer Total Purchases: " +
this.custAmount+"<BR>");
    if(this.custAmount > 3000 && this.custAmount <= 4000){
        this.custDisc=20;
    }
    if(this.custAmount > 4000 && this.custAmount <= 5000){
        this.custDisc=30;
    }
    if(this.custAmount > 5000){
        this.custDisc=35;
    }
    document.write(this.custName + " will receive a discount of " +
this.custDisc + " % on further purchases");
    document.write("<HR></PRE>");
}
//Define Object
function Customer(){
    this.custName=prompt("Enter Customer Name","Name");
    this.custEmailId=prompt("Enter Email Id for "+this.custName,"
Name@hotmail.com**");
    this.custDateOfBirth=prompt("Enter Date of Birth of
"+this.custName," mm/dd/yy ");
    this.custStar=prompt("Enter Star Account for
"+this.custName,"00-000-00");
    this.custAmount=prompt("Enter Total Purchases made by "
+this.custName+" till date", "1000");
    this.custDisc=0;
    this.display=display;
}
newCust = new Array();
newCust[0]=new Customer();
newCust[1]=new Customer();
ctr=0
while(ctr<=2){
    newCust[ctr].display();
    ctr=ctr+1;
}
</SCRIPT>
</HEAD>
</HTML>
```

Based on the problem statement and the preceding code, the following tasks have been identified.

NOTE The preceding code when executed in Internet Explorer 6 accepts and displays details of two customers and then halts abruptly. It is possible that you won't be able to view the error message. This is because of the unpredictable behavior of Internet Explorer. If you execute the above code in Netscape Navigator, the program will behave in a similar manner. However, you can view the error in Netscape Navigator 6 if you choose Tasks, Tools, JavaScript console.

Task List

✔ **Identify the errors in the preceding code.**

✔ **Identify the mechanism for trapping errors.**

✔ **Write the code for exception-handling.**

✔ **Execute the code.**

Identify the Errors in the Preceding Code

The preceding code has three errors:

- The code does not take into account the condition the total purchase amount may be less than $3, 000.

- The code has limited functionality because it accepts details of only two customers. It should be made dynamic so that it accepts details of a greater number of customers.

- In addition, the code also functions to access the third newCust array object that does not exist. This will generate an error and will bring code execution to an abrupt end.

Identify the Mechanism for Trapping Errors

Before identifying the mechanism for trapping the exception and/or error for the discount calculation page of Web Shoppe, let's first discuss exception-handling-error-trapping statements in detail.

The onerror *Event Handler*

The error event provides the capability of handling errors related to loading images and documents. These errors may occur due to syntax errors and runtime errors. To handle the error event, JavaScript provides the onerror event handler. The onerror event handler is associated with the window object.

NOTE There is a reason for attaching the `onerror` event handler with the `window` object. The `window` object is placed on top in the Object hierarchy model of JavaScript. Therefore, associating the `onerror` event handler with the `window` object can take care of all `error` events that may be generated at any subsequent levels in the hierarchy.

Now, let's see how the `onerror` event handler operates in JavaScript. The `onerror` event handler functions in a different manner than usual event handlers. Usually, event handlers (apart from the `onerror` event handler) are inserted in HTML tags as shown below:

```
<A HREF="http://cnn.com" onClick="alert('Hello user')">CNN</A>
```

The `click` event corresponds to the link that is clicked; therefore, the event handler is inserted as an attribute in the HTML tag. However, the `onerror` event handler breaks normal rules. The `error` event is related to the entire Web document, and a separate `window` tag does not exist. As a result, the `onerror` event handler cannot be inserted in any tag. Due to this constraint, developers of JavaScript invented an alternative method of declaring this event. The following syntax illustrates this method of associating the `onerror` event handler with a function:

```
<SCRIPT LANGUAGE="JavaScript">
window.onerror=//function that handles the error event
</SCRIPT>
```

In the preceding syntax, notice that the `onerror` event handler is associated directly with the `window` object and is declared in the script tags. The code on the right of the `equal to` operator contains the function that will handle the `error` event.

The following example illustrates how the `error` event is handled in a program:

```
<HTML>
<HEAD>
<TITLE>ERROR-HANDLING WITH onerror EVENT HANDLER</TITLE>
<SCRIPT LANGUAGE="JavaScript">
function errorHandler(){
    alert("An error has occurred!");
}
window.onerror=errorHandler;
</SCRIPT>
</HEAD>
<BODY>
<H1> ERROR-HANDLING WITH onerror EVENT HANDLER</H1>
<SCRIPT LANGUAGE="JavaScript">
document.write("Hello User;
</SCRIPT>
</BODY>
</HTML>
```

When the preceding code is executed, the document is loaded successfully. However, when the browser reaches the statement "`document.write(Hello User);`", an error (syntax error) occurs because a closing parenthesis is missing from this statement. At this point, the `window.onerror` event handler becomes active and passes the error information to the `errorHandler()` function. The `errorHandler()` function executes the statement "`alert("An error has occurred!")`" and displays the message "`An error has occurred!`". Notice that the event handler declaration is written as `window.onerror=errorHandler`. You can also write the same statement as `onerror=errorHandler` because the event is specified for the current window only. In addition, notice that just as with other event handlers, you cannot write `onerror` as Onerror or onError. The declaration part of the `onerror` code is case-sensitive because it is written within the `<SCRIPT>...</SCRIPT>` tags.

Figure 7.1 demonstrates the output of the preceding code.

We just looked at how the `onerror` event handler operates in JavaScript. We also mentioned that when the `window.onerror` event handler becomes active, it passes the error information to the `errorHandler()` function. Now, let's find out more about the information that is passed to the error-handling function. When an error occurs, the browsers, Netscape Navigator and Internet Explorer, automatically pass all error-related information to the function handling the error event. This information is the same as that displayed in the default browser error message box each time an error occurs. Before we continue to discuss more about the information that the browser

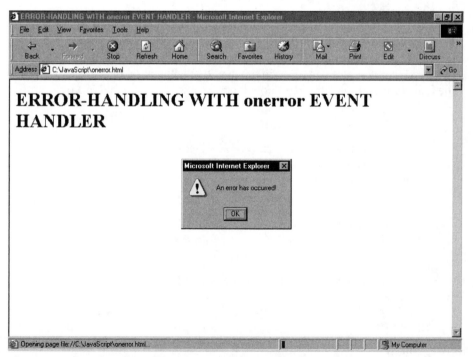

Figure 7.1 Error handling with the `onerror` event handler.

passes to the onerror event handler, let's first examine what the default error box indicates in the event of an error. The information in the message box is usually similar to that shown in Figure 7.2.

Figure 7.2 displays the error message box displayed in Internet Explorer.

The browser passes the information in the form of the following three parameters through the event handler onerror:

errorMessage: The error messages associated with the error.

url: The URL of the document where the error has occurred.

line: The line number at which the error has occurred.

The preceding parameters (information) can be used to provide customized information to the user at the time of occurrence of an event. The following example illustrates how you can use these three parameters and customize the message displayed.

```
<HTML>
<HEAD>
<TITLE>ERROR-HANDLING WITH onerror EVENT HANDLER</TITLE>
<SCRIPT LANGUAGE="JavaScript">
function errorHandler(errorMessage, url, line){
     document.write("<P><B>Error Message:</B> " + errorMessage+
"</P>");
     document.write("<P><B>URL:</B> " + url+ "</P>");
     document.write("<P><B>Line number:</B> " + line+ "</P>");
}
onerror=errorHandler
</SCRIPT>
</HEAD>
<BODY>
<H1> ERROR-HANDLING WITH onerror EVENT HANDLER</H1>
<FORM>
<INPUT TYPE="Button" onClick="nonexistentFunc()" value="If you
click on this button, an error will generate.">
</BODY>
</HTML>
```

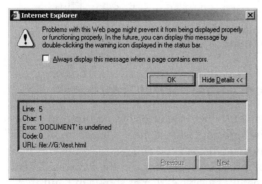

Figure 7.2 The error message box in Internet Explorer.

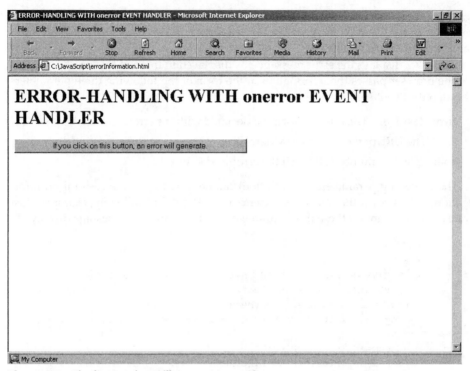

Figure 7.3   The button that will generate a runtime error.

When the above code is executed, the page as shown in Figure 7.3 is displayed in the browser. When a user clicks the If you click on this button, an error will generate. button, the onClick event handler of the button invokes the nonexistentFunc() function. This function does not exist; therefore, a runtime error occurs. The error event information (with three parameters) through the onerror event handler passes to the errorHandler() function. The runtime error as displayed in Figure 7.4 occurs in the program.

Figure 7.3 demonstrates the page that contains the button, which when clicked generates an error.

Figure 7.4 illustrates the runtime error message displayed in the browser.

Using the onerror Event to Conceal JavaScript Errors

So far, we have learned to identify when and where the error has occurred in a program. You can also suppress errors so they are not visible to users. To accomplish this task, you simply need to create a function that returns true and associate this function with the onerror event handler. The following example includes the true statement that will not display the error message that was visible earlier as shown in Figure 7.2.

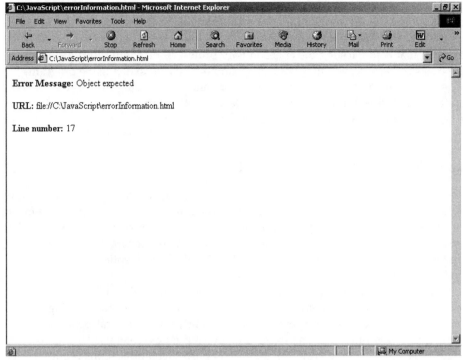

Figure 7.4   The runtime error message in the browser.

```
<HTML>
<HEAD>
<TITLE>ERROR-HANDLING WITH THE onerror EVENT HANDLER</TITLE>
<SCRIPT LANGUAGE="JavaScript">
function errorHandler(){
    return true;
    alert("An error has occurred!");
}
window.onerror=errorHandler
</SCRIPT>
</HEAD>
<BODY>
<H1> ERROR-HANDLING WITH THE onerror EVENT HANDLER</H1>
<SCRIPT LANGUAGE="JavaScript">
document.write("Hello User");
</SCRIPT>
</BODY>
</HTML>
```

The only difference in this code is that it includes a `return true` statement before the `alert()` statement. When this statement is executed in Netscape Navigator or Internet Explorer, the error message is not displayed.

However, suppressing errors in this manner only hides the errors from users but does not rectify the errors. Therefore, you should be careful while hiding errors because it is possible that later you might not be able to detect the problem in the code. It is advisable that before testing the codes in your browser, you should turn off the error suppressor; otherwise, you may have to spend hours trying to debug the program.

We just looked at the first approach to error handling by using the `onerror` event handler. Let's proceed further and see how JavaScript performs exception handling by using the `Error` object and `try catch` blocks.

Exception Handling in JavaScript

As stated earlier, an exception is simply an error that is generated by a script to draw attention to a problem that has occurred during run time of the program. Programmers provide error messages in a program to alert them that an error has occurred. In the core exception language, languages like Java say that you generate an exception by throwing it. The code that handles an exception is called an exception handler. Exception handlers are said to catch exceptions.

Figure 7.5 illustrates the exception-handling process in JavaScript.

Exception handling is superior to the `onerror` event handler in handling exceptions. Scripts that can perform exception handling provide several benefits. These scripts can respond to errors and exceptions in a structured manner. This allows the programmer to focus on algorithms that accomplish Web applications requirements rather than error capturing. Exception handlers enclose the program logic and function outside the normal flow of the scripts. Function outside the normal flow of the scripts means that exception handlers come into play only when an error occurs. If an error does not occur, the program progresses without any effect.

The only drawback to exception handling is that it is not supported by earlier versions of browsers. However, there is a solution to this problem also. You can use server-side scripts to identify the browser version and then selectively insert the exception-handling statements.

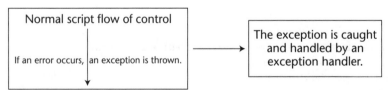

Figure 7.5   Exception-handling process in JavaScript.

Catching Exceptions

The try...catch...finally statement catches exceptions resulting from an error. The syntax of writing a try....catch...finally block is as follows:

```
try{
    //Statements that might result in an error and thus throw
exceptions
}catch(errVar){
    //Statements that execute in the event of an exception
}finally{
    //Statements that execute eitherways
}
```

The try block should contain statements from which you expect an exception (error) might arise. In other words, the try block should enclose the statements for which exception handling is to be executed. A catch block immediately follows the try block. The catch block performs exception handling and takes the errVar variable as a parameter. Whenever an error occurs in a program, an instance of the Error object is created. This instance is passed to the variable errVar in the catch block.

Let us summarize the process of catching exceptions through the following steps:

- Initially, the statements within the try block execute.

- In the try block, if an exception is thrown (an error occurs), the script's control flow instantaneously shifts to the statements in the catch block. The information regarding error is sent as a parameter to the catch block.

- In the try block, if no error occurs or if an exception is not thrown, the catch block is skipped.

- After the execution in the catch or try block is complete, the statements in the finally block are executed.

Figure 7.6 summarizes the process of a try...catch...finally statement.

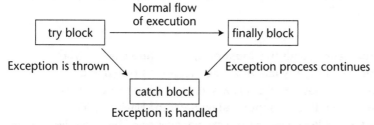

Figure 7.6   Operation of a try...catch...finally statement.

Let's try to understand how a try...catch...finally statement operates with the help of an example.

```
<HTML>
<HEAD>
<TITLE>AN EXAMPLE OF A try...catch...finally STATEMENT</TITLE>
</HEAD>
<BODY>
<SCRIPT LANGUAGE="JavaScript">
try{
    document.write("The try block begins" + "<BR>");
    document.write("No exception has occurred yet!!" + "<BR>");
    //Create a syntax error
    eval("10 + * 5");
    document.write("The try block ends here with no exception
thrown" + "<BR>");
    }catch(errVar){
    document.write("Exception caught, thus executing the catch
block" + "<BR>");
    document.write("Error name: " + errVar.name + "<BR>");
    document.write("Error message: " + errVar.message + "<BR>");
    }finally{
    document.write("Executing the finally block");
    }
</SCRIPT>
</BODY>
</HTML>
```

In the preceding code, when the script is executed, the control goes to the try block. After executing the statement, "document.write("No exception has occurred yet!!" + "<BR>");", the program generates an error as the statement "eval ("10 + * 5")" has a syntax error. As a result, the error throws an exception. Thereafter, the rest of the statements in the try block are skipped and the catch block begins executing. The errVar parameter receives the exception's Error object and thus the script shows the output as object's name and message properties. Lastly, the finally block executes.

NOTE The preceding code uses two properties, name and message, of the Error object. The name property identifies the exception's type and the message property is the message that is passed when an Error object is created. These two properties are supported by Netscape Navigator and Internet Explorer 5.5 and later versions but are not supported by its earlier version Internet Explorer 5. Internet Explorer 5 supports the number and description property.

Figure 7.7 displays the output of the preceding example.

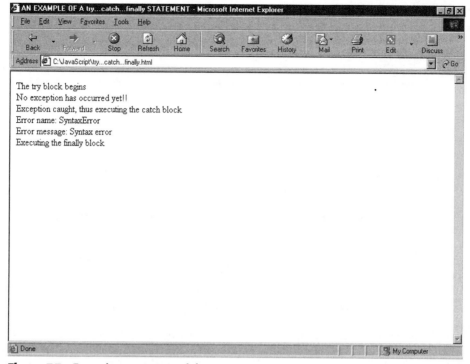

Figure 7.7   Execution sequence of the `try...catch...finally` statement.

However, you must be wondering what happens if no exception occurs. If you do not want the preceding example to generate an error, you must modify the script and comment out the statement that causes the error, as shown:

```
// eval("10 + * 5");
```

Commenting out the statement as shown will generate the output:

```
The try block begins
No exception has occurred yet!!
The try block ends here with no exception thrown
Executing the finally block
```

Different Forms of the `try...catch...finally` Statement

You can have variations of the `try...catch...finally` statement in a program. You can skip writing either the `catch` block or the `finally` block, but not both. This is because if you do not write both the blocks, the very basis of writing the `try` block will be defeated. If you don't write the `finally` block, the execution proceeds from the `try` block (if no exception is thrown) or the `catch` block (if an exception is thrown) to any statements immediately after the entire try...catch statement. The following example demonstrates the try...catch statement:

```
<HTML>
<HEAD>
<TITLE>AN EXAMPLE OF A try...catch...finally STATEMENT</TITLE>
</HEAD>
<BODY>
<SCRIPT LANGUAGE="JavaScript">
try{
    document.write("The try block begins" + "<BR>");
    document.write("No exception has occurred yet!!" + "<BR>");
    //Create a syntax error
    eval("10 + * 5");
    document.write("The try block ends here with no exception
thrown" + "<BR>");
    }catch(errVar){
    document.write("Exception caught, thus executing the catch
block" + "<BR>");
    document.write("Error name: " + errVar.name + "<BR>");
    document.write("Error message: " + errVar.message + "<BR>");
    }
document.write("Executing the finally block");
</SCRIPT>
</BODY>
</HTML>
```

You will often find try...catch statements used in a program. However, omitting the catch block will mean that the exception thrown in the try block is not captured. Therefore, you will rarely see the try...finally statement used in a program.

Creating Custom Exceptions

Now that you are comfortable with catching error exceptions, it's time to introduce you to the concept of creating your own exceptions. As stated earlier, exceptions in JavaScript exist as Error objects. This object has two properties: name and message. The ECMA 262 specification identifies six standard values for Error.name:

EvalError. Signifies that the use of the eval() function is not compatible with its definition.

RangeError. Signifies that a numeric value has exceeded its permissible range.

ReferenceError. Signifies an invalid or unrecognizable reference value.

SyntaxError. Signifies that a parsing error has occurred.

TypeError. Signifies that the actual type of an operand is different from its expected type.

URIError. Signifies that the use of a global URI handling function is not compatible with its definition.

The preceding error types cover most of the errors that are thrown while interpreting scripts. However, you can also create your exception types with the `Error` object constructor. The following code creates an exception type with the `Error` constructor:

```
customError = new Error(msg);
```

The `msg` parameter is a string that provides the new exception's (`customError`) `message` property.

You have already created custom objects in Chapter 6 "Using Objects in JavaScript." In the same manner, you can also create your own object type, which will be a subtype of the `Error` object. Following is the syntax for creating the object type `customError`.

```
function CustomError(msg){
    this.name="customError";
    this.message=msg;
}
CustomError.prototype= new Error;
```

In the preceding syntax, the object type `customError` has been created. You can now create instances of your error subtype by writing the following code:

```
customError = new CustomError("My error message");
```

Throwing Exceptions

Since you have learned to create an `Error` object, you can also use it to throw it as an exception by using the `throw` statement. The `throw` statement is generally used when you want to validate data.

Following is the syntax of writing a `throw` statement:

```
throw errObj;
```

In the preceding syntax, `errObj` is an `Error` object or its subtype similar to the one we just created (`customError`). If you throw an exception in the `try` block, then the control shifts directly to the following `catch` block. The following example displays how program execution is interrupted as soon the interpreter encounters the `throw` statement:

```
<HTML>
<HEAD>
<TITLE>Throwing exceptions</TITLE>
</HEAD>
<BODY>
<H1>Example of throwing exceptions</H1>
<SCRIPT LANGUAGE="JavaScript1.5">
var str;
try{
```

```
        str = "Hello ";
        throw new Error("Error generated");
        str += "Everybody!";
    }catch(err){
        str += err.message;
    }
    str+=" Friend!";
    alert(str);
    </SCRIPT>
    </BODY>
    </HTML>
```

When the above code is executed, an alert message box is displayed to the user. This message box shows the text "Hello Error generated Friend!"

Nested Exception Handling

JavaScript allows you to nest `try` statements within each other. Nesting `try` statements enables you to implement multiple-tier exception handling that allows exceptions to be thrown again. Figure 7.8 illustrates how nested exception handling allows exceptions to be thrown again. Notice that in Figure 7.8, there are two blocks, Outer-block and Inner-block, defined for exception handling. The Inner-block `try...catch` statement is enclosed between the Outer-block `try` statement. If an exception is thrown at the Outer-block `try` block, the control passes to the `catch` of the same block. If an exception occurs at the Inner-block `try` block, the control passes to the Inner-block `catch` block. However, if even at this stage the `catch` statement encounters an error in handling the exception, then the control passes to the `catch` statement of the Outer-block. This implies that an Inner-block `catch` block can again throw an exception to the Outer-block `catch` block.

Figure 7.8 displays nested exception handling that allows exceptions to be thrown again.

The following example illustrates nested exception handling:

```
<HTML>
<HEAD>
<TITLE>NESTED EXCEPTION HANDLING</TITLE>
</HEAD>
<BODY>
<SCRIPT LANGUAGE="JavaScript1.5">
var innerBlock;
var outerBlock;
try{
    document.writeln("Outer try block begins from here. No
exception has occurred yet");
    try{
        document.writeln("Inner try block begins from here. No
exceptions has occurred yet ");
        // Create an error
        document.writeln(undefinedVar);
```

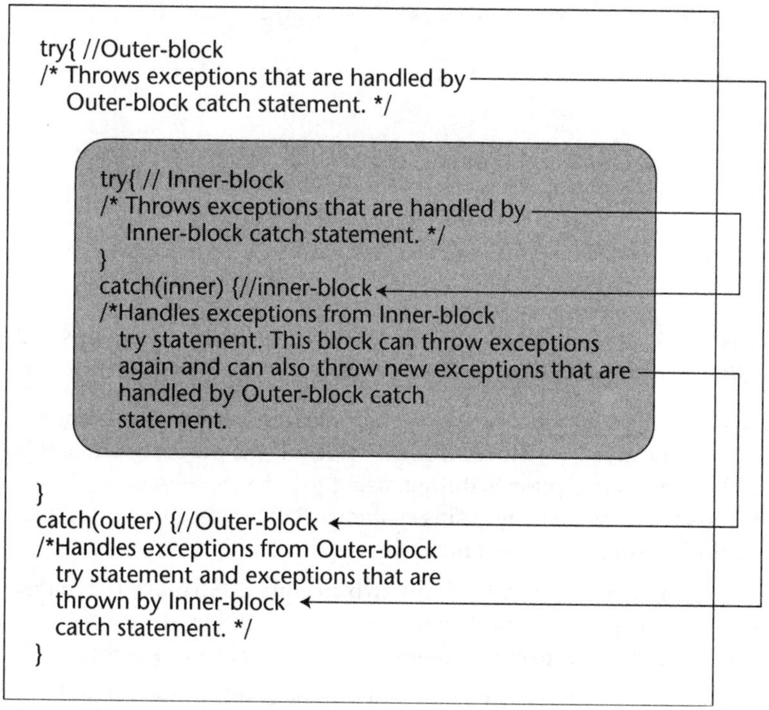

```
try{ //Outer-block
/* Throws exceptions that are handled by
   Outer-block catch statement. */

      try{ // Inner-block
      /* Throws exceptions that are handled by
         Inner-block catch statement. */
      }
      catch(inner) {//inner-block
      /*Handles exceptions from Inner-block
        try statement. This block can throw exceptions
        again and can also throw new exceptions that are
        handled by Outer-block catch
        statement.

}
catch(outer) {//Outer-block
/*Handles exceptions from Outer-block
  try statement and exceptions that are
  thrown by Inner-block
  catch statement. */
}
```

Figure 7.8 Nested exception handling.

```
        document.writeln("Inner try block finishes here. Still no
exception has occurred");
      } catch(innerBlock) {
        // Handle the exception
        document.writeln("Trying to access an undefined variable,
thus an exception has occurred. From here begins an inner catch block");
        document.writeln("Error type: " + innerBlock.name);
        document.writeln("Error message: " + innerBlock.message);
        throw inner;
        document.writeln("No exception is thrown in inner catch
block");
      } finally {
        document.writeln("Executing inner finally block");
      }
    document.writeln("Finished executing the outer try block with no
exceptions");
    } catch(outerBlock) {
      // Handle the exception
      document.writeln("Exception is caught. The outer catch block
begins from here");
      document.writeln("Error type: " + outerBlock.name);
```

```
        document.writeln("Error message: " + outerBlock.message);
    } finally {
        document.writeln("Executing the outer finally block");
    }
</SCRIPT>
</BODY>
</HTML>
```

Result

Based on the preceding discussion, Scott will do the following to trap exceptions and/or errors for the discount calculation page of Web Shoppe:

- To take into account the condition that checks if the total purchase amount is less than 3000, write an if statement in a try block. If the purchase amount is less than 3000, then an exception is thrown using the throw statement. This statement sends the error message "This customer will not receive a discount." The catch block displays the error message.

- The current page accepts the details of only two customers. To make it dynamic, a variable ctr1 is declared that will store the input entered by the user. A while loop should be used to create an instance of the object Customer.

- Another while loop should be used that will call the display method of the Customer object and thus display the details of the customer with the discount he or she will receive. This while loop should also be placed inside a try...catch block to trap any error that might occur.

- Alternatively, if dynamism is not taken into account, you can use the try...catch block to capture the error in the current code (displayed in the problem statement), as shown below:

```
<HTML>
<HEAD>
<H1>Web Shoppe Customer Details:</H1>
<SCRIPT LANGUAGE="JavaScript">
function display(){
    document.write("<H1>"+this.custName+"</H1><HR><PRE>");
    document.write("Customer Name: "+this.custName + "<BR>");
    document.write("Customer E-mail id: "+this.custEmailId +
"<BR>");
    document.write("Customer Star Account: "+this.custStar +"
<BR>");
    document.write("Customer Date of Birth:
"+this.custDateOfBirth+ "<BR>");
    document.write("Customer Total Purchases: " +
this.custAmount+"<BR>");
        if(this.custAmount > 3000 && this.custAmount <= 4000){
            this.custDisc=20;
        }
```

```
        if(this.custAmount > 4000 && this.custAmount <= 5000){
            this.custDisc=30;
        }
        if(this.custAmount > 5000){
            this.custDisc=35;
        }
        document.write(this.custName + " will receive a discount of
" + this.custDisc + " % on further purchases");
        document.write("<HR></PRE>");
    }
    //Define Object
    function Customer(){
        this.custName=prompt("Enter Customer Name","Name");
        this.custEmailId=prompt("Enter Email Id for
"+this.custName," Name@hotmail.com**");
        this.custDateOfBirth=prompt("Enter the Date of Birth of
"+this.custName,"mm/dd/yy ");
        this.custStar=prompt("Enter Star Account for
"+this.custName,"00-000-00 ");
        this.custAmount=prompt("Enter Total Purchases made by "
+this.custName+" till date", "1000");
        this.custDisc=0;
        this.display=display;
    }
    newCust = new Array();
    newCust[0]=new Customer();
    newCust[1]=new Customer();
    ctr=0
    try{
        while(ctr<=2){
            newCust[ctr].display();
            ctr=ctr+1;
        }
    }
    catch(err){
        alert("Error number: " + err.number + "Error description
" + err.description );
    }
    </SCRIPT>
    </HEAD>
    </HTML>
```

When the above code is executed, the moment the program tries to access the third instance of Customer object that does not exist, an alert message is displayed as shown in Figure 7.9.

Figure 7.9 shows the alert message displayed on the occurrence of an error in Web Shoppe's page.

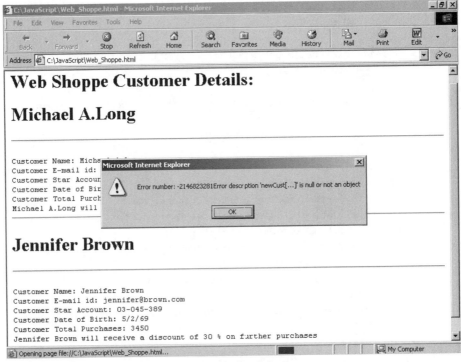

Figure 7.9   The alert message box with details of the error.

NOTE The preceding code uses the `number` **and** `description` **property of the Internet Explorer. The Internet Explorer 5.5 and later versions support the usage of the** `name` **and** `message` **properties.**

Write the Code for Exception-Handling

The following code traps exceptions and/or errors generated by the discount calculation page of Web Shoppe:

```
<HTML>
<HEAD>
<H1>Web Shoppe Customer Details:</H1>
<SCRIPT LANGUAGE="JavaScript">
function display(){
    document.write("<H1>"+this.custName+"</H1><HR><PRE>");
    document.write("Customer Name: "+this.custName + "<BR>");
    document.write("Customer Email id: "+this.custEmailId +
"<BR>");
```

```
            document.write("Customer Star Account: "+this.custStar +"
<BR>");
            document.write("Customer Date of Birth: "+this.custDateOfBirth+
"<BR>");
            document.write("Customer Total Purchases: " +
this.custAmount+"<BR>");
          try{
              if(this.custAmount<=3000){
              throw new Error("This customer will not receive a
discount");
              }
          }catch(err){
              s=err.message;
              document.write(s);
          }
           if(this.custAmount > 3000 && this.custAmount <= 4000){
              this.custDisc=20;
              document.write(this.custName + " will receive a discount of
" + this.custDisc + " % on further purchases");
          }
          if(this.custAmount > 4000 && this.custAmount <= 5000){
              this.custDisc=30;
              document.write(this.custName + " will receive a discount of
" + this.custDisc + " % on further purchases");
          }
          if(this.custAmount > 5000){
              this.custDisc=35;
              document.write(this.custName + " will receive a discount of
" + this.custDisc + " % on further purchases");
          }
                    document.write("<HR></PRE>");
      }
      //Define Object
      function Customer(){
          this.custName=prompt("Enter Customer Name","Name");
          this.custEmailId=prompt("Enter Email Id for "+this.custName,"
Name@hotmail.com**");
          this.custDateOfBirth=prompt("Enter the Date of Birth of
"+this.custName,"mm/dd/yy ");
          this.custStar=prompt("Enter Star Account for
"+this.custName,"00-000-00 ");
          this.custAmount=prompt("Enter Total Purchases made by "
+this.custName+" till date", "1000");
          this.custDisc=0;
          this.display=display;
      }
      ctr1=prompt("How many customer details do you want to enter? ",
"");
      ctr1=ctr1-1;
      newCust = new Array();
```

```
        ctr2=0;
        while(ctr2<=ctr1){
           newCust[ctr2]=new Customer();
           ctr2++;
        }
        ctr=0
        try{
           while(ctr<=ctr1){
             newCust[ctr].display();
              ctr=ctr+1;
           }
        }catch (err){
           alert("Error has occurred in the program. Error number is: " +
err.number + " Error description is: " + err.description);
        }
        </SCRIPT>
        </HEAD>
        </HTML>
```

NOTE You can also generate an exception in the preceding code and view the error message. Replace the `while` loop that executes the display method of `newCust` instance with the following code:

```
        while(ctr<=ctr1+1){
           newCust[ctr].display();
           ctr=ctr+1;
        }
```

Execute the code

Execute the code and enter the following details in the message boxes that are displayed:

- In the first message box that displays the message "How many customer details do you want to enter?", enter 2.

- Enter the following details for the two customers:

```
        Customer Name: Michael A. Long
        Email Id: michaela@mymail.com
        Date of Birth: 10/8/71
        Star Account No: 01-050-456
        Total Purchase Amount: 4500
        Customer Name: Jennifer Brown
        Email Id: jennifer@brown.com
        Date of Birth: 5/2/69
        Star Account No: 03-045-389
        Total Purchase Amount: 3450
```

Figure 7.10 displays the final output of Web Shoppe's page.

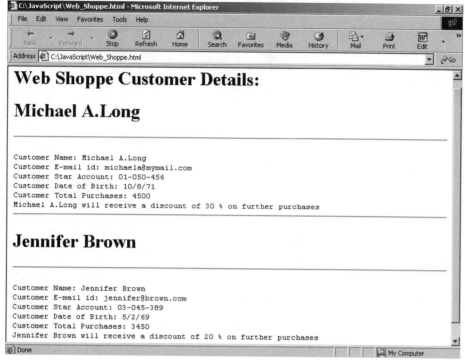

Figure 7.10   The Web Shoppe page.

Summary

In this chapter, you learned how JavaScript handles errors using the `onerror` event handler, the `Error` object, the `throw` statement, and the `try...catch...finally` block. The chapter began with an introduction on how and why errors generate in a program. It then progressed with an explanation on how the `error` event provides the capability of handling errors that are related with loading of images and documents. The chapter discussed that JavaScript provides the `onerror` event handler to handle the `error` event.

The next section of the chapter introduced you to exception handling using `Error` object and the `try...catch...finally` block. Here, you learned that an exception is nothing but an error that is generated by the script to draw attention to a problem that has occurred during run time of a program. The chapter also discussed variations of `try...catch...finally` block. Next, you were introduced to creating custom exceptions. Finally, the concept of nested `try...catch` statements was discussed that also used the `throw` statement.

Working with Browser Objects

Getting Started

In Chapter 6, "Using Objects in JavaScript," you learned about the built-in support in JavaScript for objects and object-based programming. In that chapter, you were introduced to predefined objects in JavaScript, such as `Math`, `String`, `Object`, `Boolean`, and `Date`. These objects enable you to store data in a simple way. JavaScript also provides you with objects that can control and manipulate the displays of browsers. JavaScript is designed to make Web pages more dynamic and interactive. When a browser loads a Web page, it creates a number of JavaScript objects. These JavaScript objects form part of the browser hierarchy model of JavaScript.

In this chapter, you will look at the browser hierarchy model of JavaScript. The chapter is divided into three sections, each containing a scenario of the practical implementation of objects. The first section discusses `window` and `document` objects in detail. This includes a scenario of Web Shoppe that accepts orders from customers and creates a document at run time. This document displays the total cost of a purchase by using `window` and `document` objects. The second section of the chapter introduces you to three other objects of the browser hierarchy model: `history`, `location`, and `form`. This section covers another scenario of Web Shoppe in which the `form` object is used to accept customer details after the customer has chosen the items to be purchased. The third section introduces you to `frame` objects. This section discusses another scenario of Web Shoppe in which two Web pages are merged into one document by using the `frame` object.

Before we begin to discuss the above-mentioned objects in detail, let us understand the browser hierarchy model of JavaScript. We have already given you an overview of the concept of the JavaScript Object model in Chapter 6. Here, we examine the specifics of the browser hierarchy model.

Browser Hierarchy Model

The browser hierarchy model of JavaScript allows you to control the features and functions of a Web browser window or the HTML document being displayed. The JavaScript browser object model is a hierarchy of JavaScript objects, each of which provides programmatic access to different aspects of an HTML page or a Web browser window. You can use the methods and properties of objects to manipulate the window, frames, and HTML elements displayed in a Web browser. Netscape Navigator 6.0 and Microsoft Internet Explorer 5.0 support the object model of JavaScript.

Figure 8.1 shows the JavaScript browser hierarchy model with a comprehensive listing of all the objects in it. The objects in this hierarchy are organized in a way in which each corresponds to the structure of a loaded Web document and the current state of the browser. The notation 3.0 indicates the objects that were implemented with the release of Netscape Navigator 3.0.

The hierarchy depicted in Figure 8.1 demonstrates the principle of *containership*. For example, the controls `button` and `checkbox` are contained within the `form` object. The `form` object is contained within the `document` object, which is, in turn, contained within the top-level `window` object.

Containership refers to the principle that objects cannot be used or referenced without referring to the container object, which is also known as the parent object. For example, to access a `checkbox` object, `chkTennis`, contained in a `form` object, `myForm`, which, in turn, is contained in a document, you will use the following code:

```
document.myForm.chkTennis
```

After looking at the browser hierarchy model, let's begin with the first section that covers the `window` and `document` objects. As in other chapters, we'll introduce you to concepts with the help of a scenario of Web Shoppe.

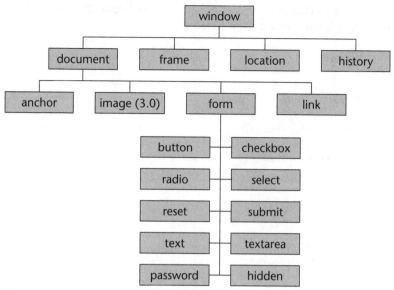

Figure 8.1   JavaScript browser hierarchy model.

Creating Documents at Run Time

Problem Statement

The online mall of Web Shoppe has a page that displays a list of toys along with their prices in a tabular format. The toys have attained great popularity in the United States and Canada due to their excellent quality and innovative features. Considering the popularity of the toys and wanting to cater to the Canadian market, Web Shoppe has offered its customers the choice of viewing the prices of toys in U.S. or Canadian dollars. Until now, the page accepted orders from the user and displayed the bill on the same page. However, the general feedback showed that this was causing inconvenience to the clientele. The customers could not view the order that they had placed because the page displaying the bill amount replaced the page with the order. Now, considering the response and inconvenience of the customers, Web Shoppe wants to generate and display the bill for the toys purchased in a separate window.

Cynthia, the head of the development team, has assigned the task of incorporating the above functionality to Scott, a Web developer. Scott will be responsible for generating a new window that will display a bill with the names of the toys and the corresponding prices in a tabular format.

To expedite Scott's task, he has been provided with code for the interface that displays the list of toys along with their prices. The table in the interface uses JavaScript to display the prices of toys in U.S. or Canadian dollars, depending on the choice of the customer. The following is the code for the interface:

```
<HTML>
<HEAD>
<TITLE> Toys </TITLE>
<SCRIPT LANGUAGE="JavaScript">
function convDollars(){
        var ch = optAmt.value;
        if(ch == 1){
                txtrob.value=txtrob.value/1.57;
                txttin.value=txttin.value/1.57;
                txtdun.value=txtdun.value/1.57;
                txtpar.value=txtpar.value/1.57;
        }
        else{
                txtrob.value=txtrob.value*1.57;
                txttin.value=txttin.value*1.57;
                txtdun.value=txtdun.value*1.57;
                txtpar.value=txtpar.value*1.57;
        }
}
</SCRIPT>
</HEAD>
<BODY bgcolor="lightgrey">
<H1 align="center"> Web Shoppe </H1>
<MARQUEE><H3 align="right"> Shopping at your finger tips
!!</H3></MARQUEE>
<TABLE align="center" border=5 bgcolor="lightblue"
caption="ToyList">
<CAPTION><FONT size=+2><B>List of Toys</B></FONT></CAPTION>
<TR><TH> Toy Name </TH>
<TH align="right"><SELECT id="optAmt" onchange="convDollars()">
<OPTION value=1>Price in US $</OPTION>
<OPTION value=2>Price in Canadian $</OPTION>
</TH>
<TH> Enter Qty Required </TH></TR>
<TR><TD>Robby the Whale</TD>
<TD align="right"><INPUT id="txtrob" type=text value=50 size=15
align="right" readonly></TD>
<TD align="right"><INPUT id="txtrobqty" type=text value="" size=15
align="right"></TD>
</TR>
<TR><TD>Tin Drum</TD>
<TD align="right"><INPUT id="txttin" type=text value=60 size=15
```

```
align="right" readonly></TD>
      <TD align="right"><input id="txttinqty" type=text value="" size=15
align="right"></TD>
      </TR>
      <TR><TD>Dune Racer</TD>
      <TD align="right"><INPUT id="txtdun" type=text value=50 size=15
align="right" readonly></TD>
      <TD align="right"><INPUT id="txtdunqty" type=text value="" size=15
align="right"></td>
      </TR>
      <TR><TD>Parachute Rocket</TD>
      <TD align="right"><INPUT id="txtpar" type=text value=45 size=15
align="right" readonly></TD>
      <TD align="right"><INPUT id="txtparqty" type=text value="" size=15
align="right"></TD>
      </TR>
      <TR>
      <TD colspan=3 align="center"><input type="button" value="Confirm"
align="center"></TD>
      </TR>
      </TABLE>
      </BODY>
      </HTML>
```

Let's discuss the preceding code. Here, optAmt is the ID of the selected element. The first option that assumes the value 1 represents the price in U.S. dollars, and the second option that assumes the value 2 represents the price in Canadian dollars. These values are obtained using the value property of the select element and stored in the variable ch as follows:

```
ch=optAmt.value
```

By default, the values are displayed in dollars. If a user selects a price in Canadian dollars, the onchange event associated with the select element triggers the convs-Dollars() function.

Figure 8.2 shows the interface that displays the toys in a table format.

NOTE The value **property is actually a property of the** options **array, which, in turn, is a property of the** select **object. The** select **object is a property of the** form **object. We'll learn about the** form **object in detail in the next section of this chapter. However, since this scenario extensively uses forms, explanation about the properties of** form **object will be provided where required.**

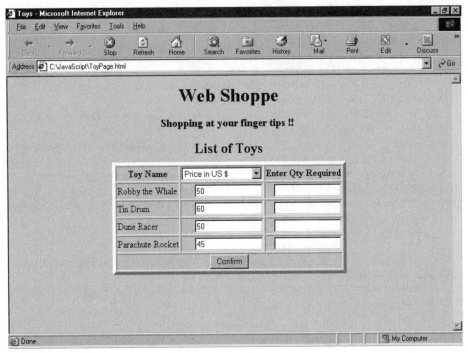

Figure 8.2 Web Shoppe's toy page.

Task List

Based on the requirements specified in the preceding scenario, Scott has identified the following tasks:

✔ **Identify data for bill details.**

✔ **Identify the events required.**

✔ **Identify a mechanism (objects) to display the bill details.**

✔ **Write a script for the creation of the bill.**

✔ **Execute and verify the page.**

Having identified the tasks, let's discuss each task individually so we can understand the concepts required for this scenario.

Identify Data for Bill Details

According to the problem statement, the data that needs to be displayed on the new bill details window is:

■ Toy name

■ Amount to be paid for each toy, which should be calculated as price × qty

■ Total amount of the bill

Identify the Events Required

The order details page of Web Shoppe contains a Confirm button. This button needs to be associated with an event that will open a new bill details window.

The onClick event can be associated with the Confirm button to confirm an order and generate the new bill window.

Identify a Mechanism (Objects) to Display Bill Details

Bill details need to be displayed in a separate window. Therefore, let us discuss the methods and properties of window and document objects. Then, we will finally list the properties and methods of these objects and see which of these will help Scott create a new window at run time.

The window Object

The window object is the highest-level object in the JavaScript browser object hierarchy. It is the default object, which implies that a window object is created automatically when a Web page is loaded in a browser. This implies that a separate window object is created for each window that is opened in the browser. You can view the number of windows opened in Netscape Navigator from the Tasks menu, as shown in Figure 8.3.

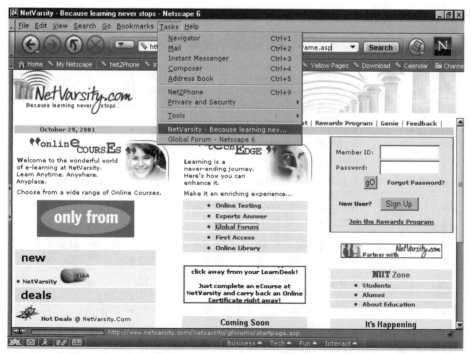

Figure 8.3   Netscape browser with windows menu listing all the windows currently opened.

NOTE Internet Explorer does not have a similar capacity for viewing the number of windows opened.

The `window` object is the default object of a browser window. Therefore, you may omit writing `window` explicitly while writing scripts. For example, consider the following statement in a script:

```
document.write("Text on the current window.")
```

In this case, JavaScript assumes that you are referring to the current `window` object and executes the following statement:

```
window.document.write("Text on the current window.")
```

The window object includes several properties that contain information about the Web browser window. For example, the `status` property contains information displayed on the status bar of a Web browser.

The window object also contains the methods that allow you to manipulate the Web browser window. For example, the `alert()` method will display a message box containing an alert message.

Tables 8.1 and 8.2 outline the properties and methods associated with the `window` object. Both Netscape Navigator and Internet Explorer support these properties and methods.

Table 8.1: Properties of the window Object

PROPERTY	DESCRIPTION
defaultStatus	A string value containing the default status bar text.
frames	An `array` object that tracks the number of frames in a window. You can target a frame in JavaScript by referencing its frame number in the frames array.
length	An integer value representing the number of frames in the parent window.
name	A string value containing the name of a window or a frame.
parent	A string value containing the name of the parent window if the document has one.
self	A string value containing the name of the current window. This property is an alternative for using a name as described above.
status	A string value representing status bar text.
top	A string value representing the topmost window in a series of nested windows.
window	An alternative that identifies the current window.

Table 8.2:   Methods of the window Object

METHOD	DESCRIPTION
alert(messageText)	Pops up a window with messageText as the message.
close()	Closes the current window.
confirm(messageText)	Pops up a message box with messageText displayed with buttons for OK and CANCEL.
open(url,name,featureList)	Opens a new window populated by a URL, the target name of the window, and the features identified in the feature list.
prompt(messageText,response)	Pops up a message box displaying messageText with a text box for the user's response. The text box contains the value response, if passed to the function prompt(). If left empty, the word "undefined" is displayed in the text box.
setTimeout(expression,time)	Executes an expression after the elapse of the interval time, an integer value representing milliseconds.
clearTimeout(timerID)	Cancels the setTimeout() method.
alert(messageText)	Pops up a window with messageText as the message.

Opening and Closing Windows

As stated earlier, a window object is created when you open your browser. Then, the browser creates and opens a window to display a default page. The question that arises now is: When is a new window object created? Generally, when you access the Internet or open a local file, a new Web document or file opens in the same browser window. In this case, the default page contained in the browser window is replaced by the new document. This implies that a new document is created and not a window object. A new window object is created only when you choose either File, New, Navigator Window in Netscape Navigator or File, New, Window in Internet Explorer.

The two methods of window object, open() and close(), are used to open and close browser windows in JavaScript.

The open() method opens a new or existing window. The invocation of this method returns a window object. You can store a window object in a variable to keep track of the windows you created. The syntax of the open() method is as follows:

```
objWindow = open("URL", "WindowName", "Attributes");
```

where,

- objWindow depicts the variable in which the object returned by the open() method is stored. You can assign any name to this variable.

- URL stands for the address of the existing window or space for an empty window.

- WindowName stands for the name of the window.

- Attributes is a list of features that can be attached with the window. You may or may not specify the attributes of a window. If you want to specify more than one attribute, a comma should separate each attribute. Table 8.3 lists the attributes that are supported by Netscape Navigator and Internet Explorer.

The following code displays the use of the open() method. This code creates a new blank window:

```
swindowName = open("","Window","scrollbars=1,status=1");
```

The following code displays the use of the open() method. This code will open an existing window.

```
sWindowName =
open("http://www.hotmail.com","Hotmail","scrollbars=1,status=1");
```

The close() method closes the current or specified window. The syntax for this method is as follows:

```
close();                    //closes the current window
objWindow.close();          //closes the specified window
```

Table 8.3: Window Attributes of the open() Method

ATTRIBUTE	DESCRIPTION
toolbar	Creates the standard toolbar
location	Creates the location entry field
directories	Creates standard directory buttons
status	Creates the status bar
menubar	Creates the menu bar at the top of a window
scrollbars	Creates scrollbars when a document exceeds the size of the current window
resizable	Enables the resizing of the window by the user
width	Specifies the window width in pixels
height	Specifies the window height in pixels

The following statement closes the window with the name `Window`:

```
sWindowName.close();
```

The following example illustrates how to work with the `open()` and `close()` methods of the `window` object. The example creates a Web page that announces a symposium on JavaScript:

```html
<HTML>
<HEAD>
<TITLE> Symposium </TITLE>
<SCRIPT LANGUAGE="JavaScript">
var sWindowName;
function fnNewWindow()
{
        sWindowName = open("Schedule.html", "Schedule");
        sWindowName.status = "You have opened JavaScript schedule
window";
}
</SCRIPT>
</HEAD>
<BODY>
<H1> Symposium on JavaScript !!!</H1>
<P><B>Date/Time:</B> January 15, 2001 10:00 AM </P>
<P><B>Venue:</B> 201 W. 103RD STREET, INDIANAPOLIS, IN 46290 </P>
<FORM>
<INPUT TYPE="Button" VALUE="Click for schedule"
onClick="fnNewWindow()">
</FORM>
<P>Send the request latest by January 10, 2001
<A HREF="mailto:sjohnson@usa.co.net">
<I>sjohnson@usa.co.net</I></A></P>
</BODY>
</HTML>
```

In the preceding code, "`sWindowName = open("Schedule.html", "Schedule");`" is the statement that opens the file "`Schedule.html`". This statement is contained within the function `fnNewWindow()`, which is called when the user clicks the "`Click for schedule`" button.

Figure 8.4 displays the JavaScript symposium Web page.

The code to generate the `Schedule.html` page is as follows:

```html
<HTML>
<HEAD>
<TITLE> Schedule </TITLE>
</HEAD>
<BODY>
<H1 ALIGN="center"> Welcome to the JavaScript Symposium !!!</H1>
<MARQUEE><H3 align="right"> Schedule for the Symposium
</H3></MARQUEE>
```

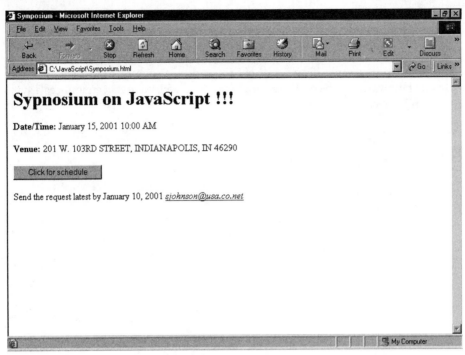

Figure 8.4 JavaScript symposium Web page.

```
        <TABLE ALIGN="CENTER" BORDER=5 BGCOLOR="SKYBLUE"
CAPTION="SCHEDULE">
      <TR>
            <TH><B> TIME </B></TH>
            <TH><B> TOPICS COVERED </B></TH>
      </TR>
      <TR>
            <TD>10:00 AM-12:00 Noon </TD>
            <TD>JavaScript Core </TD>
      </TR>
      <TR>
            <TD>12:00 Noon-2:00 PM </TD>
            <TD>Controlling Program Flow </TD>
      </TR>
      <TR>
            <TD>2:00 PM-2:30 PM </TD>
            <TD>Lunch Break ! </TD>
      </TR>
      <TR>
            <TD>2:30 PM -5:00 PM</TD>
            <TD>Object Hierarchy Model</TD>
      </TR>
```

```
        <TR>
                <TD>5:00 PM -6:00 PM</TD>
                <TD>Exception Handling </TD>
        </TR>
        <TR>
                <TD>6:00 PM -6:30 PM </TD>
                <TD>Recap </TD>
        </TR>
        </TABLE>
        <FORM>
        <p><INPUT TYPE="BUTTON" VALUE="Close the window"
onClick="window.close()">
        </FORM>
        </BODY>
        </HTML>
```

In the preceding code, notice the statement "<INPUT TYPE="BUTTON" VALUE=
"Close the window" onClick="window.close()">". When the user clicks the
Close the window button, the onClick event handler triggers the window.
close() function.

Figure 8.5 displays the Web page that contains the symposium schedule.

Figure 8.5   Symposium schedule Web page.

Interacting with the User

JavaScript provides a few methods to support interactivity. These methods display interactive dialog boxes, such as `alert` and `prompt` dialog boxes. Let us now look at each of these methods of the `window` object in detail:

The confirm() method is used to obtain a confirmation from the user to perform a specific action. This method displays a dialog box with a message and has two buttons, `OK` and `Cancel`. Based on whether the user selects `OK` or `Cancel`, it returns true or false, respectively. The syntax of the `confirm()` method is as follows:

```
val = confirm("Message to be displayed");
```

The following example illustrates the use of the `confirm()` method:

```
<HTML>
<HEAD>
<TITLE>Example of confirm() method </TITLE>
</HEAD>
<BODY>
<FORM>
<INPUT TYPE="BUTTON" VALUE="Confirm" onClick="confirm('Do you wish
to continue')">
</FORM>
</BODY>
</HTML>
```

Figure 8.6 shows the confirm dialog box that is displayed when the user clicks the `Confirm` button.

Figure 8.6 Output of the `confirm()` method.

The **prompt() method requests user input by using a text field within a dialog box.** The text that the user types in the text box is returned as the result of the `prompt()` method. The syntax of this method is as follows:

```
val=prompt("Message to the user", "Default value on the text
field");
```

The following example illustrates the use of the `prompt()` method:

```
<HTML>
<HEAD>
<TITLE>Example of prompt() method </TITLE>
</HEAD>
<BODY>
<FORM>
<INPUT TYPE="BUTTON" VALUE="Prompt" onClick="prompt('What is your
name?', '')">
</FORM>
</BODY>
</HTML>
```

Figure 8.7 shows the prompt dialog box that is displayed when the user clicks the `Prompt` button.

The **alert() method sends an alert message to a user.** The syntax of this method is as follows:

```
alert("Message to the user");
```

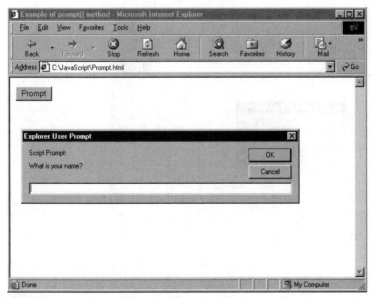

Figure 8.7 Output of the `prompt()` method.

You have seen the implementation of `alert()` and `prompt()` methods. Let us now look at how you can use the `alert()` and `prompt()` methods together to make a document interactive. For example, the following code will first ask the user to enter a name and then display the message "`Hello`", followed by the name entered.

```
<HTML>
<HEAD> <TITLE> Example that uses alert() and prompt() method
together </TITLE> </HEAD>
<BODY>
<SCRIPT LANGUAGE="JavaScript">
<!--
alert("Hello, "+prompt("What is your name?","")+".");
-->
</SCRIPT> </BODY>
</HTML>
```

Figure 8.8 shows the output of the `alert()` and `prompt()` methods.

The `setTimeout()` and `clearTimeout()` Methods

You may have come across several Web pages that automatically perform certain actions if the pages are not acted upon for the stipulated period of time. For instance, consider the case of the fictitious Earnest Bank that has a home page that displays a `Login` button. When the user clicks the `Login` button, a login page that accepts the account ID and password of the user is displayed. If the user does not click the `Login` button, the login page is displayed automatically after 5 seconds. How can this functionality be implemented in this Web page? The `setTimeout()` and `clearTimeout()` methods of the `window` object enable the above functionality. These methods

Figure 8.8 Output of `alert()` and `prompt()` methods.

adopt a methodology that enables a user to wait for a specified period of time before performing a particular action. If the action does not occur within the stipulated time period, JavaScript performs the time-out process.

The setTimeout() method is used to automatically display a message or a new window after a specified time period has elapsed. The code executed with the set-Timeout() method is executed only one time. The syntax of the setTimeout() method is as follows:

```
ID = setTimeout("expression", time in milliseconds);
```

where, expression can be any function, statement, or series of JavaScript statements. The expression must be enclosed in double quotation marks. ID is an identifier that is used with the clearTimeout() method to cancel the setTimeout() method before the expression is evaluated. The amount of time the Web browser should wait before executing the code argument of the setTimeout() method is specified in milliseconds.

The clearTimeout() method is used to cancel the setTimeout() method call. If the setTimeout() method to which the clearTimeout() method refers was given a timerID, the clearTimeout() method would clear the time-out so that the related procedure would not run again at the lapse of the specified interval. The syntax of the clearTimeout() method is:

```
clearTimeout(ID);
```

where ID is the identifier returned by the setTimeout() method.

The code for the example of the home page of Earnest bank, which will automatically display the login page after 10 seconds if the user does not click the Login... button, is as follows:

```
<HTML>
<HEAD>
<TITLE>Earnest Bank</TITLE>
<SCRIPT language="JavaScript">
function go()
{
        open("Login.html","Login");
}
</SCRIPT>
</HEAD>
<!--Once the page is loaded, the onload event handler fires the
setTimeout() method. Following a wait-period of 10 seconds, this method
executes the go() function. The setTimeout method returns an id which is
stored in variable timeout. -->
        <BODY bgcolor="LightBlue"
onLoad="timeout=setTimeout('go()',10000);">
        <H1 align="center">
        <U>Earnest Bank</U>
        </H1>
        <H2 align="center">
```

```
            Welcome to the Web Site!!
            </H2>
            <MARQUEE>
            Click on the Login button or wait for ten seconds to Login!
            </MARQUEE>
            <!-- Before the period of 10 seconds elapses, if the user clicks
on the Login... button, then the onclick event handler fires the
clearTimeout() method. The id returned by the setTimeout() method
becomes the parameter of clearTimeout() method. This method cancels the
setTimeout() method. -->
            <INPUT type=button value="Login..."
onClick="clearTimeout(timeout);go();">
            </BODY>
            </HTML>
```

The code for the Login.html page is as follows:

```
            <HTML>
            <HEAD>
            <TITLE>Earnest Bank</TITLE>
            </HEAD>
            <BODY bgcolor="LightBlue">
            <H1 Align="center">Earnest Bank</H1><BR>
            <H2 Align="center">
            <U>Banking Online</U></H2>


<BR><BR>          
                     
            <FONT color="Black" ><B>Login information:</B></FONT><BR><BR>
            Account ID      
            <INPUT Type="text" Name="txtAccountID" Value=""><BR>
            Password         
            <INPUT Type="password" Name="pass" Value="">
     
            <INPUT Type="button" Name="cmdSubmit" Value="Submit" >
            </BODY>
            </HTML>
```

Displaying a Message on the Status Bar

To display the status information on the status bar of the browser window, you can use the following properties:

- The defaultStatus property that displays a permanent message on the status bar

- The status property that displays a message that appears as a result of a user action

The following example uses the status property and the setTimeout method to scroll a message on the status bar of the window:

```
<HTML>
<HEAD>
<TITLE> Scrolling Text </TITLE>
<SCRIPT LANGUAGE="JavaScript">
var msg = "How do you find this text scrolling on the status
bar?";
var space = "...";
var i = 0;
function ScrollText(){
    window.status = msg.substring(i, msg.length) + space +
msg.substring(0, i);
    i++;
    if(i > msg.length) i = 0;
    window.setTimeout("ScrollText()", 100);
}
ScrollText();
</SCRIPT>
</HEAD>
<BODY>
<H1>Scrolling Text</H1>
Notice the status bar at the bottom of this page.
</BODY>
</HTML>
```

Figure 8.9 displays a scrolling message on the status bar of the window.

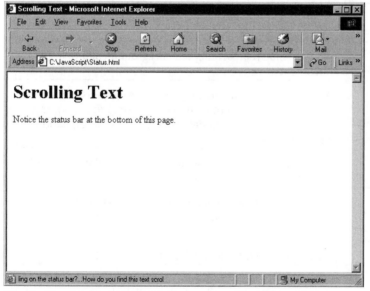

Figure 8.9 Scrolling message on the status bar of the window.

The document *Object*

The document object is one of the important objects in any window or frame. The document object is subordinate to the window object in the browser object hierarchy. This implies that the document object is the child of the window object. The document object represents a Web document or a page in a browser window. It enables you to update the document that is being uploaded and to access the HTML elements contained in a loaded document. The document object is defined when the <BODY> tag is evaluated in an HTML page. The object exists as long as the page is being loaded.

There may be situations when you access multiple sites simultaneously. In such situations, there would be multiple windows opened. Each of these windows would have a corresponding window object, and each window object would also have its own document object. Now, to use one of these document objects, you use the names of the window and the document.

The document object provides several properties and methods that allow you to work with many aspects of the current document, such as information about its anchors, forms, links, title, and current colors. Tables 8.4 and 8.5 outline the properties and methods associated with the document object.

Table 8.4: Properties of the document Object

PROPERTY	DESCRIPTION
alinkColor	A string value representing the color for active links.
anchors	An array object containing references to each anchor reference on a page.
bgColor	A string value representing the background color of a document.
cookie	A string value containing the name = value pairs of data that will persist in the client memory either until the browser is cleared (if no expiration date is present) or the expiration date is reached.
fgColor	A string value representing the foreground color or text color of a document.
forms	An array object containing references to each form in a document. Form elements are contained within the form object.
linkColor	A string value representing the color of unvisited links.
lastModified	A string value representing the date and time when a document was last modified. Notice that the appearance of this string is not consistent between browsers.
links	An array object containing references to each link on a page.

Table 8.4 *(Continued)*

PROPERTY	DESCRIPTION
location	A string value representing the current URL.
referrer	A string value representing the URL of the document from which the current document was accessed.
vlinkColor	A string value representing the color of visited links.
title	A string value representing the text between the <TITLE> and </TITLE> tags.

NOTE In Table 8.5, the term *stream* refers to a sequence of input or output characters.

Writing Content in a Document

We have already used a few document object methods to generate text in your document. For example, we have extensively used the write() method to write text to a document. There is another method, writeln(), which performs a similar function. Before discussing the details of the writeln() method, let us revise the write() method.

The write() method helps write text on Web pages. This method is prefixed with the object name document. Since the window object is the default object, specifying the name before the method is not necessary. The syntax of the write() method is as follows:

```
document.write("Text to be  displayed");
```

The following example illustrates the use of the write() method:

```
document.write("Welcome to Scripting");
```

Table 8.5: Methods of the document Object

METHOD	DESCRIPTION
clear()	Clears the document window.
close()	Closes a write() stream.
open()	Opens a document to receive data from a write() stream.
write(content)	Writes the text of content to a document.
writeln()	Writes the text of content to a document, followed by a carriage return.
clear()	Clears the document window.

Similar to the `write()` method, the `writeln` method writes the contents on a Web page. The only difference between the two is that this method includes a carriage return at the end of the text. The syntax of the `writeln()` method is as follows:

```
windowObject.document.writeln("content");
```

Here, specifying the `window` object name is not necessary.

The `document` object also provides `open()` and `close()` methods that help write content in a Web document. Unlike `open()` and `close()` methods of the `window` object, these methods don't actually open and close new documents or windows. Instead, the `open` method opens a stream of characters. This method clears the current document and allows you to write anew with the `write` or `writeln` method. Any content in the document is erased.

The content or data that you write using the `open()` method will not be displayed until you close the stream of characters in the document. You use the `document.close()` method to close the stream.

Enlisting the Content of a Document

There may be situations where a Web page has been created but it has a very poor representation. To improve the aesthetics of this page, you will need to know about the elements used in the creation of such a Web page. The `document` object provides several properties to access the elements used to create a document. These properties have been listed in Table 8.4. In many cases, document properties refer to the objects that are contained within a displayed document.

The following code illustrates the use of document properties:

```
<HTML>
<HEAD><TITLE>Enlisting Contents of the Symposium Document</TITLE>
<SCRIPT LANGUAGE="JavaScript">
function extractDetails(){
        winName = open("", "NewWindow");
        winName.document.open("text/plain");
        winName.document.writeln("Title: " + document.title);
        winName.document.writeln("Links: " + document.links.length);
        winName.document.writeln("Forms: " + document.forms.length);
        winName.document.writeln("Images: " + document.
images.length);
        winName.document.close();
}
</SCRIPT>
</HEAD>
<BODY>
<H1> Sypnosium on JavaScript !!!</H1>
<P><B>Date/Time:</B> January 15, 2001 10:00 AM </P>
<P><B>Venue:</B> #201 W. 103RD STREET, INDIANAPOLIS, IN 46290 </P>
<FORM>
<INPUT TYPE="Button" VALUE="Click for schedule">
```

```
<P>Send the request latest by January 10, 2001
<A HREF="mailto:sjohnson@usa.co.net">
<I>sjohnson@usa.co.net</I></A></P>
</FORM>
<SCRIPT LANGUAGE="JavaScript">
setTimeout("extractDetails()", 2000);
</SCRIPT>
</BODY>
</HTML>
```

The preceding code is very similar to the one we discussed in the `open()` and `close()` methods of the `window` object. The only difference is that we have included a function, `extractDetails()`, which will extract the elements that have been used to create this document. When you execute this code, a document, as shown in Figure 8.4, is generated. Now, the primary contents of this Web page are a form with a button, an anchor that is not visible, and a link element. Notice that the body tag contains a script that executes the `extractDetails()` method after 2 seconds. This causes a new window to open as shown in Figure 8.10, which displays all the contents of this document. To open a new window, the function includes the `document.open()` method that with `document.writeln` statements helps write the contents of the document to the new window. The `document.close()` method has been used to close the stream that you opened using the `document.open()` method.

Figure 8.10 displays the new window that lists the elements used to create the symposium page.

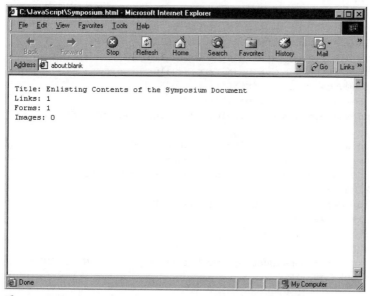

Figure 8.10 A new window with the elements of the symposium page listed.

Result

Based on the previous discussion, the properties and objects that Scott will use to add the functionality stated in the problem statement are as follows:

- According to the specifications provided to Scott, a new window should be opened to display bill details. Therefore, the `open()` method of the `window` object will be used to generate a separate window.

- The `open()` method of the `document` object will also be used so that each time a new window is created, the document is written afresh. If these methods are not used, the document in the new window is appended to the original bill details. To enable each user to view a fresh document in the new window, it is necessary to use the `open()` method of the `document` object.

- Now, since the `open()` method of the `document` object will be used, it becomes essential to use the `close()` method if you want to view the contents written in the document.

- To display bill details in a table format, the `writeln` method of the `document` object will be used.

Write a Script for the Creation of the Bill

Add the following script to generate a bill:

```
function bill(){
        var sum=0;
        iRobval=txtrobqty.value * txtrob.value;
        iTinval=txttinqty.value * txttin.value;
        iDunval=txtdunqty.value * txtdun.value;
        iParval=txtparqty.value * txtpar.value;
        windowName=open("", "Bill");
        windowName.document.open("");
        windowName.document.writeln("<H1 align='center'> Web Shoppe
</H1>");
        windowName.document.writeln("<MARQUEE><H3 align='right'>
Shopping at your finger tips !! </H3></MARQUEE>");
        windowName.document.writeln("<TABLE align='center' border=5
bgcolor='lightblue'>");
        windowName.document.writeln("<CAPTION><FONT size=+2 ><B>Bill
Details</B></FONT></CAPTION>");
        var ch=optAmt.value;
        if(ch=="1"){
                windowName.document.writeln("<TR><TH>Toy Name</TH>
<TH>Amount in $<TH></TR>");
        }
        else{
```

```
                         windowName.document.writeln("<TR><TH>Toy Name</TH>
     <TH>Amount in Canadian $</TH></TR>");
                }
          if(iRobval > 0){
                     windowName.document.writeln("<TR><TD>Robby the
     Whale</TD>");
                         windowName.document.writeln("<TD align='right'>");
                         windowName.document.writeln(iRobval);
                         windowName.document.writeln("</TD></TR>");
                         sum=sum+iRobval;
                }
          if(iTinval > 0){
                     windowName.document.writeln("<TR><TD>Tin drum</TD>");
                     windowName.document.writeln("<TD align='right'>");
                     windowName.document.writeln(iTinval);
                     windowName.document.writeln("</TD></TR>");
                     sum=sum+iTinval;
                }
          if(iDunval > 0){
                     windowName.document.writeln("<TR><TD>Dune
     Racer</TD>");
                     windowName.document.writeln("<TD align='right'>");
                     windowName.document.writeln(iDunval);
                     windowName.document.writeln("</TD></TR>");
                     sum=sum+iDunval;
                }
          if(iParval > 0){
                     windowName.document.writeln("<TR><TD>Parachute
     Rocket</TD>");
                     windowName.document.writeln("<TD align='right'>");
                     windowName.document.writeln(iParval);
                     windowName.document.writeln("</TD></TR>");
                     sum=sum+iParval;
                }
          windowName.document.writeln("<TR><TH>Total</TH><TH
     align='right'>");
                windowName.document.writeln(sum);
                windowName.document.writeln("</TH></TR>");
                windowName.document.writeln("</TABLE>");
                windowName.document.bgColor="lightgrey";
                windowName.document.close();
          }
```

NOTE Make sure that you associate the onClick **event handler with the** Confirm **button. In addition, associate the function** bill() **with the event handler** onClick **by using the following code:**

```
          <TD colspan=3 align="center"><INPUT type="button"
     value="Confirm" onclick="bill()" align="center"></TD>
```

Scott has decided to write the following code to calculate the total amount to be paid for each toy. The total amount (quantity * price) is calculated for each toy and stored in program variables. Let's discuss this code.

```
function bill(){
        var sum=0;
        //Calculating quantity * price and storing in respective
values
        iRobval=txtrobqty.value * txtrob.value;
        iTinval=txttinqty.value * txttin.value;
        iDunval=txtdunqty.value * txtdun.value;
        iParval=txtparqty.value * txtpar.value;
}
```

The variables will contain the value 0 if the quantity is not entered for a specific toy. Notice that txtrobqty, txttinqty, txtrob, and so on are all IDs of the input types in the table displayed on the toy page of Web Shoppe. Refer to the code specified for the toy page in the beginning of the chapter.

A table is created to display bill details. This table is created in the document opened in a new window. The detail for each selected toy is added as a new row to the table.

The background color of the document is changed to gray by the bgColor property of the document as follows:

```
windowName.document.bgColor='Grey';
```

> **NOTE** The code also uses the value **property of** text **object to extract details from the text fields. The** text **object is a property of** form **object. The details of** form **object will be covered in the next section.**

Execute and Verify the Page

Before you execute the preceding code, be sure that you have associated the function bill() with the event handler onClick.

Execute the code and verify its successful operation by performing the following steps:

- On the toy page of Web Shoppe, enter the quantities Robby the Whale 1, Tin Drum 1, Dune Racer 2, and Parachute Rocket 1 for each toy.

- Now, click the Confirm button. A window, as shown in Figure 8.11, is displayed.

- Again, on the toy page of Web Shoppe, enter the quantities Robby the Whale 1, Tin Drum 1, Dune Racer 0, Parachute Rocket 1 for each toy.

- Now, click the Confirm button. In the bill details window that was created in step 2, verify that the document is refreshed. The table contains the prices of three toys; Dune Racer is not there. The document is refreshed because Scott used the open() method of the document object.

Figure 8.11 displays the bill details window of Web Shoppe.

We just now looked at how the bill details page of Web Shoppe was generated in a separate window at run time by using the properties and methods of the window and document object. Let us proceed by discussing the other two objects of the browser hierarchy model: history and location.

The *history* Object

The history object is another child object of the window object. It is placed below the window object in the browser object hierarchy. You have been using the information used by the history object. Each time you visit a Web page and click on the Back or Forward arrow buttons on your browser toolbar, you access the history list. If you want to enable the same type of functionality on your own page, you can add similar buttons or links that allow the user to move backward or forward through the stored history.

Tables 8.6 and 8.7 outline the properties and methods associated with the history object.

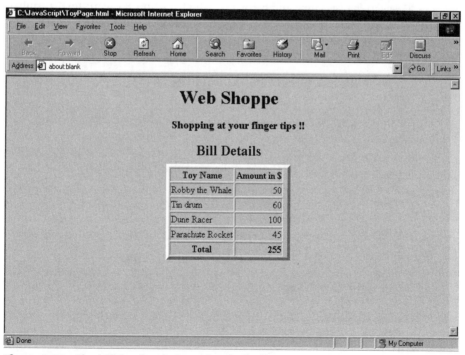

Figure 8.11   The bill details window of Web Shoppe.

Table 8.6 Properties of the `history` Object

PROPERTY	DESCRIPTION
length	Is an integer value representing the number of links currently referenced by the history object.
current	Contains the URL of the current page that the user is accessing.
next	Contains the URL of the next entry in the history list to which the user will be sent if the user clicks the `Forward` button.
previous	Contains the URL of the previous entry in the history list to which the user will be sent if the user clicks the `Back` button.

NOTE The `history` **object does not have events associated with it.**

NOTE The **methods** `history.back` **and** `history.forward` **do not work well with all versions of Netscape Navigator. Therefore, it is best to use** `history.go()`.

The following example creates a script that displays the Back and Forward text that navigates a user to the previous and next sites. The Back and Forward text is equivalent to the back and forward arrow buttons on the toolbar of the browser.

```
<HTML>
<HEAD>
<TITLE> Back and Forward Functionality </TITLE>
</HEAD>
<BODY>
<H1> Back and Forward Functionality</H1>
<HR>
This page lets you go back or forward to pages in the history
list. These should be equivalent to the back and forward arrow buttons
in the browser's toolbar.
<HR>
<A HREF="javascript:history.go(-1);">
<B>BACK</B>
</A>
<br>
<A HREF="javascript:history.go(1);">
<B>FORWARD</B>
</A>
<HR>
</BODY>
</HTML>
```

Table 8.7 Methods of the `history` Object

METHOD	DESCRIPTION
back()	Sends the user to the previous page in the history list.
forward()	Sends the user to the next page in the history list.
go(x)	The user will be sent back or forward by x number of pages in the history list if x is an integer. If x is a string value, the user will be sent back to the page in the history list that has a URL matching x.

In the above code, the part of the script that sends the user to the previous page in the history list is as follows:

```
<A HREF="javascript:history.go(-1);">
<B>BACK</B>
</A>
```

The part of the script that sends the user to the next page in the history list is as follows:

```
<A HREF="javascript:history.go(1);">
<B>FORWARD</B>
</A>
```

You must have noticed that the above script does not use JavaScript tags. It only uses two commands to move the user backward and forward in the history list.

The *location* Object

Instead of using text or graphic links that allows users to move to different targets, you can create buttons to take users to different targets. The `location` object enables you to provide this type of functionality to a button. The `location` object is subordinate to the window object in the browser object hierarchy. It allows you to specify URLs in a script.

The key property of the `location` object is `href`. You'll use this property frequently to specify the hypertext reference for the current or required URL. For example, adding the line

```
location.href="http://www.whitehouse.gov"
```

would take the user to the White House Web site, when the statement is processed. To include such a statement in a `<Button>` tag, the code will be as follows:

```
<FORM>
<INPUT TYPE="button" VALUE="Click Here"
onClick="location.href='http://www.whitehouse.gov';">
</FORM>
```

In the preceding code, note how the script from the beginning of location to the end of the tag is enclosed in double quote marks while the URL is enclosed in single quotes. Make sure that you do not use double quote marks within double quote marks. This will cause errors.

The properties of the location object relate to the various pieces of information that constitute a complete URL. The parts are identified as follows:

```
protocol://hostname:port/pathname/search#hash
```

Each element of this can be extracted from the location object as indicated in Table 8.8.

Combining the `location` Object with the Conditional Assignment Operator

You had earlier learned about the conditional assignment operator, which returns one value if the specified condition is true and a different value if the condition is false. You can combine this operator with the location object by writing the following statement:

```
location.href=(condition)? true : false
```

This combination will result in the user being taken to one of two locations, depending on the answer to the condition specified.

Table 8.8 Properties of the `location` Object

PROPERTY	DESCRIPTION
hash	Internal link anchor name, which follows # in the URL.
host	The `hostname:port` portion of the URL.
hostname	Only the host name of the URL.
href	The partial or full URL of a file or a site. The value can be http://www.cnn.com, page2.htm, or page2.htm#Section2.
pathname	The part of the URL that indicates the path.
port	The port number if port is provided.
protocol	http:, ftp:, or whatever represents the protocol currently in use.
search	If a search string is present, this returns the text following the ? character.

Consider the following code:

```
<HTML>
<HEAD>
<SCRIPT LANGUAGE="JavaScript">
function loctn(){
     var ans,x;
     ans=txtname.value;
     x=(ans=='yes')?'C:\temp.html':'C:\temp2.html';
     location.href = x;
}
</SCRIPT>
</HEAD>
<BODY>
Enter the name of page you want to open:
<INPUT TYPE="text" Id="txtname">
<INPUT TYPE="button" VALUE="Click Here" onClick="loctn()">
</BODY>
</HTML>
```

The preceding code displays a page with an input box and the button `Click Here`. The user is prompted to enter the name of the page that the user wants to open. When the user enters the page name and clicks the button, the function `loctn()` is executed. The `loctn()` function contains the statement "`x=(ans=='yes')?'C:\\temp. html':'C:\\temp2.html';`". This statement merges the `location` object with the conditional assignment operator to check the value of the variable `ans` and open a page.

You have learned about the four main objects of JavaScript: `window`, `document`, `history`, and `location`. Let us now discuss how the `form` object helps retrieve the values from a form. We have already used a basic-level form in the scenario of the preceding section. You learned how to retrieve data from a text input field and use it for validation purposes. However, there are many more `form` elements and details about the `form` object that we have not yet discussed. The next section covers the details of data retrieval by using the `form` object.

Retrieving Values from a Form by Using a `form` Object

Forms enable you to obtain user input by using a range of interface tools, including text fields, check boxes, radio buttons, and drop-down lists. However, the level of user interactivity in forms is restricted because, eventually, the data in the forms has to be submitted to the server for processing. Using JavaScript at the client side, you can extend user interactivity in forms without requiring the data from the form to be submitted to the server. The first step in creating an interactive form is to create an HTML form.

Before discussing how data is retrieved from forms by using JavaScript, we will create a form for Web Shoppe .

Problem Statement

Web Shoppe has decided to add a page to its site, which accepts details from the customer after the customer has selected items for purchase. Web Shoppe wants this page to contain a form that accepts the customer details. It also wants to retrieve the information entered by the customer in the form and display the details to the customer. This is done so that the customer can confirm the details entered. The task for creating the customer details form is assigned to the development team at Web Shoppe.

Task List

Based on the requirements mentioned above, the development team will need to perform the following tasks:

✔ **Identify the components of user interface.**

✔ **Identify the form elements for the customer details form.**

✔ **Identify the objects to retrieve data from the form.**

✔ **Write the code to create the customer details form and to retrieve values from the form.**

✔ **Execute the code.**

Identify the Components of User Interface

Per the problem statement, the form should be designed as a user interface to gather information about the customer. Ideally, information from forms is validated at the client side for correct format entries and at the server side before it is transferred to the database. In order to gather user-specific information, the form should contain the following categories of input and controls:

- Personal details
  - The customer name that can be split into three parts for the title, the first name, and the last name
  - The address consisting of the home address and region where the customer is placed
  - The home phone number
  - The email ID
- Payment details
  - The credit card or payment after delivery details
  - The card type and card number in case the customer chooses to pay through a credit card
  - Items updating details in order to receive updates on new additions on items such as flowers, confectionery, books, toys

Identify the HTML Form Elements for the User Interface

The components of the user interface that will be part of the customer details form have been identified. Therefore, let us now discuss HTML tags and elements for the display of various controls of the customer details form. Table 8.9 describes the tags and elements for the controls of the page.

Table 8.9 Controls of Customer Details Form

INPUT	TYPE OF CONTROL	TAG TO BE USED
Title (Mr., Mrs., Ms., or Dr.)	Radio buttons	\<INPUT TYPE="radio" NAME="Title" VALUE=" ">
First Name	Text Field	\<INPUT TYPE="text" NAME=" " VALUE=" ">
Last Name	Text Field	\<INPUT TYPE="text" NAME=" " VALUE=" ">
Address	Text Field	\<INPUT TYPE="text" NAME=" " VALUE=" ">
Region	Combo box	\<select name= "Region"> \<option value= "Appalachia">Appalachia \</option> \</select>
Home Phone	Text Field	\<INPUT TYPE="text" NAME=" " VALUE=" ">
Email	Text Field	\<INPUT TYPE="text" NAME=" " VALUE=" ">
Mode of Payment (Credit card or Payment after delivery)	Radio buttons	\<INPUT TYPE="radio" NAME="ModeOfPayment" VALUE=" ">
Card Type	Radio buttons	\<INPUT TYPE="radio" NAME="CardTypes" VALUE=" ">
Card Number	Text Field	\<INPUT TYPE="text" NAME=" " VALUE=" ">
Item categories (flowers, confectionery, books, and toys) for receiving updates	Check box	\<INPUT TYPE="checkbox" NAME="Items" VALUE=" " checked>

Identify the Objects to Retrieve Data from the Form

Having laid the foundation of creation of the customer details form of Web Shoppe, let us discuss how the form object of JavaScript helps retrieve information from an HTML document. Before we begin with the concepts that will help retrieve the data from forms, let us quickly recap the concept of the <FORM> tag used to create an HTML form.

The <FORM> Tag

You create an HTML form by enclosing all form elements in the <FORM>....</FORM> tag. The opening form tag <FORM> indicates that a form is beginning and the closing form tag </FORM> marks the end of the form element.

The <FORM> tag includes five attributes and the onSubmit event handler associated with it. Let us look at the five attributes in detail.

The ACTION Attribute

The ACTION attribute specifies the URL that indicates the location to which the contents of the form are submitted to elicit a response. Typically, the target location is a CGI script on the server that handles the processing of the form. If this attribute is missing, the URL of the document itself is assumed.

The METHOD Attribute

The METHOD attribute specifies the format in which the form data has to be transmitted to the server for processing. This attribute assumes two values: GET or POST. These values are actually methods of submitting data. Before we delve into the details of the GET and POST methods, let's look at the following syntax for the METHOD and ACTION attributes:

```
<FORM METHOD="GET/POST" ACTION="URL_Of_the_target_file">
```

The GET Method

The GET method appends the information entered by a user to the URL specified in the ACTION attribute in the form of a query string. The following statement shows what a GET-type submission looks like:

```
URL_Of_the_target_file?element_name_1=element_value_1&element_name_2=ele
ment_value_2
```

In the preceding statement, the data after the ? sign is the query string. The data entered by the user in the form is separated by the & symbol.

There are a few constraints of using the GET method. The GET method is not appropriate for sending huge volumes of data. This is because certain browsers limit the size of a URL that can be specified. This method is not suitable for transmitting confidential information. This is because the form data is appended as a query string to the URL, which is visible on the address bar or the status bar of the browser window.

The POST Method

The POST method stores the form in the POST method, unlike the GET method in which the data is appended as a query string. Form data is stored within the body of the request. This method is used to send unlimited volumes of data to the server. This method is ideal for transmitting confidential information of a user because the information is not visible while it is being transmitted.

The TARGET and the NAME Attributes

The TARGET attribute indicates the window or frame where the result of processing the form data is to be displayed. The NAME attribute is used to specify the name of the form. It is not mandatory to specify the name of the form. However, to easily access forms in JavaScript, it is recommended to assign a name to the form.

The ENCYPT Attribute

The ENCYPT attribute specifies the format (MIME type) of submitting the data if the protocol does not impose a format itself. MIME type refers to Multipurpose Internet Mail Extension Type, which identifies the type of content in a file.

We have discussed the basic <FORM> tag and its five attributes. Let us now learn about the form object and see how it helps retrieve the data from a form.

The form Object

In JavaScript, forms are defined with the form object. The form object is accessed as a property of the document object and bears the same name as the NAME attribute in the FORM tag. Each form element in a form, such as text input fields and radio buttons, is further defined by other objects. How are these objects created? As stated earlier, depending on the content of a Web page, JavaScript automatically creates the browser objects when the page is loaded into the browser. Therefore, if a Web page contains a form that contains text input fields, drop-down lists, and radio buttons, the form object and objects that correspond to the elements of the form are automatically created.

Now, consider a situation where you have more than one form in your document. How do you access these forms? As stated earlier, the form object is accessed as a property of the document object. The browser creates a unique form object for each form that is contained in a document. These objects can be accessed through the document. forms[] array. For example, if your document contains two forms, using the forms[] array you can access the forms by writing the following two statements:

```
document.forms[0]      //access the first form
document.forms[1]      //access the second form
```

Alternatively, you can also access the form by addressing the form name. For example, if the first form in a document has the name form1, you can refer to it by the following statement:

```
document.form1
```

Properties of the `form` Object

The `form` object has several properties that can be divided into two categories. As mentioned earlier, each form element in a form, such as text input fields and radio buttons, is further defined by other objects. Therefore, the first category of properties comprises element-based objects. The second category contains six other properties. Before we discuss the objects defined by elements of a form, let us discuss the six properties in the second category. These include:

1. **The `action` property.** This property returns a string that indicates the ACTION attribute of the `<FORM>` tag. Assigning a new string to the property can dynamically change this property. Dynamically changing the property overrides any ACTION value specified in the `<FORM>` tag. For example, if the ACTION attribute of a form named `form1` contains the URL `www.SCRIPT_URL` in the `<FORM>` tag, the statement `document.form1.action = "www.New_SCRIPT_URL";` would change the value of ACTION attribute to `www.New_SCRIPT_URL`. Any subsequent attempt to submit the form would direct the form content to `www.New_SCRIPT_URL` instead of `www.SCRIPT_URL`.

2. **The `elements` array.** This is an array of objects for referencing each element in the form. This array stores the elements in the order in which the elements appear in the HTML form. For example, if the text field is the first element defined in the form, you can refer to this element by the following statement:

    `document.form1.elements[0]`

    Alternatively, you can refer to it as `document.form[0].elements[0]`. An alternative method of referring to form elements is by name. The statement `document.form[0].fieldName` refers to the element that bears the name `fieldName`.

    You can determine the number of elements defined in a form by using the length property of the elements array. The statement `document.form[0].elements.length` extracts the number of elements in the form.

3. **The `encoding` property.** This property returns a string that indicates the value of the ENCYPT attribute of the `<FORM>` tag. Similar to the `action` property, a new value assigned to this property overrides the value specified in the ENCYPT attribute of the `<FORM>` tag.

4. **The `length` property.** Similar to the `length` property of the `elements` array, the `length` property of the `form` object determines the number of elements in the form. Therefore, while the statements `document.form[0].elements.length` extracts the number of elements in the form, so does the statement `document.form[0].length`.

5. **The `method` property.** This property returns a string that indicates the value of the METHOD attribute of the `<FORM>` tag. This property assumes the value `get` or `post`. Similar to the `action` and `encoding` properties, a new value assigned to this property overrides the value specified in the METHOD attribute of the `<FORM>` tag.

6. **The `target` property.** This property returns a string that indicates the value of the `TARGET` attribute of the `<FORM>` tag. Again, a new value assigned to this property overrides the value specified in the `TARGET` attribute of the `<FORM>` tag.

Methods of the `form` Object

The `form` object has three methods: `handleEvent()`, `submit()`, and `reset()`. The `handleEvent()` method is used to invoke the event handler of the form, the `submit()` method is used to submit a form, and the `reset()` method resets the entries to their default values in the form.

Event Handlers of the `form` Object

The `form` object has two event handlers, `onSubmit()` and `onReset()`. Similar to the other HTML elements, you can either specify a group of JavaScript statements or call a function for these events within the `<FORM>` tag. If you either specify a group of statements or call a function for the `onSubmit` event, the statements or the function are called before the form is submitted to the CGI script on the server. You can prevent a form from being submitted to the server by returning a `false` value from the `onSubmit` event handler. If you return the `true` value, the data is submitted to the form. Similarly, you can prevent a `Reset` button from triggering the `onReset` event handler.

The following example illustrates the use of the `form` object and the properties and event handlers discussed up to this point:

```
<HTML>
<HEAD>
<TITLE>Extracting form elements example</TITLE>
<SCRIPT LANGUAGE ="JavaScript">
function displayFormDetails(){
    newWin=open("", "New_window");
    newWin.document.open("text/plain");
    newWin.document.writeln("This document has " +
document.forms.length + " forms.")
    for(i=0; i<document.forms.length; ++i){
        newWin.document.writeln("Form " + i + " has " +
document.forms[i].elements.length + " elements.");
        for(j=0;j<document.forms[i].elements.length; ++j){
            newWin.document.writeln((j+1) + " A " +
document.forms[i].elements[j].type + " element.");
        }
    }
    newWin.document.close();
    return false;
}
</SCRIPT>
</HEAD>
<BODY>
<H1> Multiform Document Example </H1>
```

```
<FORM ACTION="nothing" onSubmit="return displayFormDetails()">
<H2>Form 1 </H2>
<P>Name: <INPUT TYPE="TEXT" NAME="Name" VALUE="Sample text"></P>
<P>Password: <INPUT TYPE="Password" NAME="Password" VALUE="Sample
text"></P>
<P>Address: <TEXTAREA ROWS="4" COLS="30"  NAME="Address">Write your
address here.</TEXTAREA></P>
<P><INPUT TYPE="SUBMIT" NAME="f1-4" VALUE="Submit">
<INPUT TYPE="RESET" NAME="f1-5" VALUE="RESET"></P>
</FORM>
<HR>
<FORM>
<H2>Form 2</H2>
Check your hobbies:
<INPUT TYPE="CHECKBOX" NAME="Music" VALUE="Music" CHECKED> Music
  
<INPUT TYPE="CHECKBOX" NAME="Games" VALUE="Games">Games
  
<INPUT TYPE="CHECKBOX" NAME="Reading" VALUE="Reading">Reading
  
<P>Select your gender:
<INPUT TYPE="RADIO" NAME="Male" VALUE="Male"
CHECKED>Male     <INPUT TYPE="RADIO" NAME="Female"
VALUE="Female">Female
<P><INPUT TYPE="FILE" NAME="File">
</FORM>
<HR>
<FORM>
<H2>Form 3 </H2>
<INPUT TYPE="HIDDEN" NAME="f3-1">
Select the shirt size:
<SELECT NAME="Shirt" SIZE="4">
<OPTION VALUE=""> Small (S)</OPTION>
<OPTION VALUE="">Medium (M)</OPTION>
<OPTION VALUE="" SELECTED>Large (L)</OPTION>
<OPTION VALUE=""> Extra Large (XL)</OPTION>
</SELECT>
</FORM>
</BODY>
</HTML>
```

The preceding code creates three forms in a document. When the user clicks the Submit button of the first form, the onSubmit() handler invokes the displayFormDetails() function. Notice that the onSubmit() handler returns the displayFormDetails() function. This results in the form submission to be abandoned when the displayFormDetails() function returns a false value. The displayFormDetails() function creates and opens a separate window and assigns the new window object to the variable newWin. The new window object opens the document in the window with a text or plain MIME type. The function uses the forms array of the document object of the current window to determine the number of forms in the document. It uses the length property of the form's elements array to determine the number of elements in a form. The function also uses the type property of the elements array to determine the type of element displayed in each form.

Figure 8.12 illustrates the document with multiple forms.

Figure 8.13 illustrates the new window that displays the content of the document that contains multiple forms.

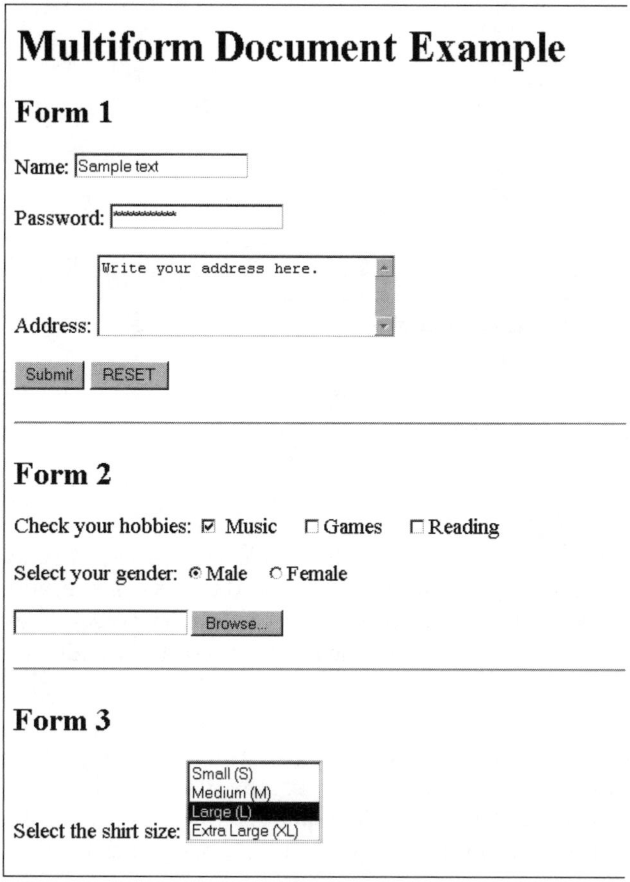

Multiform Document Example

Form 1

Name: | Sample text |

Password: | ********** |

Address: | Write your address here. |

| Submit | RESET |

Form 2

Check your hobbies: ☑ Music ☐ Games ☐ Reading

Select your gender: ⦿ Male ◯ Female

| | Browse... |

Form 3

Select the shirt size: | Small (S) / Medium (M) / Large (L) / Extra Large (XL) |

Figure 8.12 Document with multiple forms.

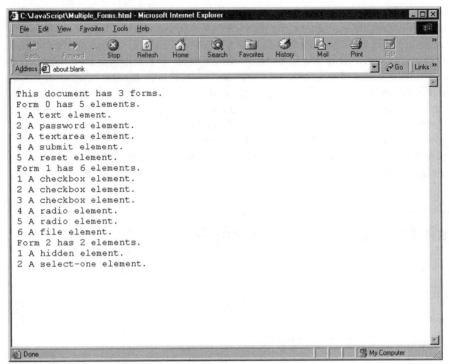

Figure 8.13 New window displaying the content of the document that contains multiple forms.

Element-Based Objects

HTML forms can include eight types of input elements: text fields, textarea fields, radio buttons, check box buttons, hidden fields, password fields, combo box select menu, and list select menu. Each of these elements is defined by objects in JavaScript. All these objects are properties of the `form` object. Let's discuss each of these objects individually.

The `text` Object

The `text` object defines the text fields in forms. The `text` object has several properties, methods, and event handlers associated with it. We have already discussed the event handlers of the text field element in Chapter 5, "Functions and Events." Let's begin with the properties of the `text` object. The three properties of the `text` object are as follows:

1. **The `defaultValue` property.** This property returns a string that identifies the default initial value to be displayed in the text field as defined by the VALUE attribute of the INPUT tag. You can change the value of `defaultValue` property. However, this does not cause the displayed value of the text field to be updated. The statement `document.testForm.firstName.default-Value="Michael";` assigns the default value `Michael` to the text field `firstName` of the form `testForm`.

2. **The `name` property.** This property returns a string that provides access to the NAME attribute of the INPUT tag. Modifying the value in the name property overrides the value specified in the NAME attribute of the INPUT tag. The statement `document.testForm.elements[0].name="firstName";` assigns the first element the name `firstName`.

3. **The `value` property.** This property returns a string that provides access to the current value in the text field. Modifying the `value` property results in a change in the current value of the text field.

Having looked at the properties of the `text` object, let's discuss the three methods of the `text` object: `focus`, `blur`, and `select`.

1. The `focus()` method places the input focus to be directed to the text field, in other words, the `text` object. The following code snippet uses the `focus()` method in the `onSubmit()` event handler to ensure that the `firstName` field is not left blank by the user. If the `firstName` field is left blank, the user is prompted with a message and the focus returns to the `firstName` field.

```
<FORM METHOD=POST ACTION="NOTHING" NAME="testForm"
onSubmit="if(document.testForm.firstName.value==""){
    alert("The first name field cannot be left blank.");
    document.testForm.firstName.focus();
    return false;
}">
<INPUT TYPE="text" NAME="firstName" VALUE="">
<INPUT TYPE="submit">
</FORM>
```

2. The `blur()` method in the `onFocus` event handler ensures that the focus is never given to a text field. This method is most appropriate for the fields that display the output of a field and where you don't want the user to modify the value of this type of field. For instance, the following code snippet ensures that the value of the field `displayField` is never given focus.

```
<INPUT TYPE="text" NAME="displayField" VALUE=""
onFocus="this.blur();">
```

3. The `select()` method selects and highlights the content in the text field. The following code snippet first directs the focus to the field `firstName` and then highlights it:

```
document.testForm.firstName.focus();
document.testForm.firstName.select();
```

The `textarea` Object

The `textarea` object defines the text area field of the form. This object has properties and methods similar to the `text` object. We'll list these with a brief explanation:

1. **The `defaultValue` property.** This property returns a string that identifies the default initial value to be displayed in the text field as defined by the VALUE attribute of the INPUT tag.

2. **The name property.** This property provides access to the NAME attribute of the INPUT tag.

3. **The value property.** This property provides access to the current value in the text field.

4. **The focus() method.** This method causes the input focus to be directed to the text area field or the textarea object.

5. **The blur() method.** This method removes focus from the text area field.

6. **The select() method.** This method selects and highlights the content in the text area field.

The radio Object

The radio object is used to define a radio button in a form. The individual radio button in a group of radio buttons is referenced by the index numbers. For example, the HTML code for defining a group of radio buttons might be as follows:

```
        <INPUT TYPE="radio" NAME="radioButton" VALUE="MASTER CARD"
checked> MASTER CARD <br>
        <INPUT TYPE="radio" NAME="radioButton" VALUE="VISA CARD"> VISA
CARD <br>
```

To refer to the second radio button, the statement will be document.testForm.radioButton[1]. To refer to the properties of this radio button, the statement will be document.testForm.radioButton[1].propertyName.

The radio object has five properties, a method, and an event handler. Since we have already discussed event handlers in earlier chapters, let us discuss the method and properties of the radio object:

1. **The checked property.** This property returns a Boolean value that indicates if a radio button is selected or deselected. This property returns a true value if the radio button is selected. To select a new radio button dynamically, the value checked can be set any time by using this property. For example, the statement document.testForm.radioButton[1].checked=true; causes the second radio button with the value VISA CARD to be selected. As a result, the first radio button is deselected.

2. **The defaultChecked property.** This property identifies if the radio button is selected by default.

3. **The length property.** This property returns an integer value specifying the number of radio buttons in a radio object. For instance, the statement document.testForm.radioButton.length will return 2 because there are two radio buttons defined with the name radioButton.

4. **The name property.** This property returns a string that indicates the NAME attribute defined in the INPUT tag. Modifying the name property overrides the value specified in the NAME attribute in the INPUT tag.

5. **The value property.** This property indicates the VALUE attribute of the INPUT tag. The value of the value property overrides the value specified in the VALUE attribute in the INPUT tag.

6. **The click() method.** This method is used to select a radio button, such as the checked property. This method simulates a mouse click on the button. The statement document.testForm.radioButton[0].click() selects the first radio button that has the value MASTER CARD.

The checkbox Object

The checkbox object defines a check box in a form. Unlike radio buttons that function in a group, check boxes are individual toggle switches that allow multiple selection. Therefore, for each check box in a form, a separate object is created as against the radio object that exists as an array that contains several radio buttons.

Similar to the radio object, the checkbox object has four properties, one method, and an event handler. Since the properties and methods are similar to those of radio object properties, we'll list these with brief explanations:

1. **The checked property.** This property returns a Boolean value that indicates if a check box is checked or unchecked. This property returns a true value if the check box is checked.

2. **The defaultChecked property.** This property identifies if the check box is selected by default.

3. **The name property.** This property returns a string that indicates the NAME attribute defined in the INPUT tag. Modifying the name property overrides the value specified in the NAME attribute in the INPUT tag.

4. **The value property.** This property indicates the VALUE attribute of the INPUT tag. The value of the value property overrides the value specified in the VALUE attribute in the INPUT tag.

5. **The click() method.** This method is used to select a check box as the checked property selects a check box. This method simulates a mouse click on the button.

The hidden Object

A hidden object indicates a text field that is not displayed in a form. The hidden object can be used to send values to the CGI scripts that are not intended for display. A hidden object has two properties, name and value. These properties function the same way as the name and value properties of text object. Both properties are string values that indicate the NAME and VALUE attributes of the <INPUT> tag. As in a text object, these properties can be assigned new values to override the values in the <INPUT> tag.

The hidden object has no methods or event handlers associated with it.

The password **Object**

The password object corresponds to the password field of a form. This object has three properties and methods associated with it. However, it has no event handlers associated with it. Let's begin discussing the properties and methods of the password object:

1. **The defaultValue property.** This property functions differently from the defaultValue property of the text object. For security reasons, instead of taking the value specified in the VALUE attribute of the <INPUT> tag, this property is assigned a null value. Similar to the defaultValue property of the text object, you can assign a new value to the defaultValue property and override the initial null value.

2. **The name property.** This property returns a string that indicates the value of the NAME attribute of the <INPUT> tag. You can modify the name property to override the value in the NAME attribute.

3. **The value property.** This property returns the same value as that of the VALUE attribute of the <INPUT> tag. You can modify the value of this property as in the case of the defaultValue property. Until now, the value property functions in the way in which the value property of the text object functions. However, the value property functions differently, if the user changes the content of the password field in the form. In this case, for security reasons the value property returns the null value.

4. **The focus() method.** This method causes the focus to be directed to the password object.

5. **The blur() method.** This method removes the focus from the password object.

6. **The select() method.** This method selects and highlights the contents of the password field. However, this method does not bring the focus back to the password field.

The select **Object**

The select object defines the select menus, both combo box and list box, in a form. The select object has four properties, two methods, and three event handlers associated with it. One of the properties of the select object, the options array, provides access to each of the options on the select menu. Let's begin by discussing the three other properties of the select object. We'll discuss the options array in detail a bit later:

1. **The length property.** This property contains the number of options in the select object.

2. **The name property.** This property returns a string that indicates the value specified in the NAME attribute of the <SELECT> tag. You can change the name of the select menu by changing the name property of the select object.

3. **The selectIndexed property.** This property returns an integer value, which indicates the index in the options array of the currently selected options. The

value of the `selectedIndex` property can be changed dynamically, which updates the menu display. However, the `selectedIndex` property is not helpful with lists that allow multiple selections. This is because the `selected-Index` property evaluates to the index of the first selected option. If a new value is assigned to the property, all the selected options are cleared and the new option is selected.

The `options` Array

The `options` array indicates the options on the select menu in the order in which they are specified in the HTML code. The options array has eight properties: `default-Selected`, `index`, `length`, `name`, `selected`, `selectedIndex`, `text`, and `value`. Let us look at each of these in detail now:

1. **The `length` property.** This property returns an integer value indicating the number of options on the select menu. The `length` property is the same as the `length` property of the `select` object.

2. **The `defaultSelected` property.** This property returns a Boolean value that indicates the state of the SELECTED attribute.

3. **The `selected` property.** This property indicates the current state of the option. Setting this property to `true` selects the option on the menu. You can use this property to select multiple options if the MULTIPLE attribute is included in the `<SELECT>` tag.

4. **The `selectedIndex` property.** This property returns the index value of the currently selected option.

5. **The `name` property.** This property returns a string indicating the name of the select options.

6. **The `text` property.** This property returns a string indicating the text displayed in the select menu for a specified option.

7. **The `value` property.** This property indicates the value of the VALUE attribute of the `<OPTION>` tag.

8. **The `index` property.** This property returns the index of the option in question.

You can dynamically update the select lists by using the `text` and `value` properties of the `option` array. Dynamically updating the select lists means that the values and text displayed on the menu are updated to reflect the new values. Consider the following code for creating a combo box in the form that is named testForm:

```
<SELECT NAME="Cuisine" SIZE=4 MULTIPLE>
<OPTION VALUE="Chinese" SELECTED> Chinese </OPTION>
<OPTION VALUE="Taiwanese"> Taiwanese </OPTION>
<OPTION VALUE="Mexican" SELECTED> Mexican </OPTION>
<OPTION VALUE="Lebanese"> Lebanese </OPTION>
</SELECT>
```

The preceding code creates a combo box that allows multiple selections from the select menu. You can change the displayed text and the value of the second option by the following statements:

```
document.testForm.Cuisine.options[1].text = "Continental";
document.testForm.Cuisine.options[1].value = "Continental";
```

Similarly, to read the value of a selected item, first use the `selectedIndex` property to determine the index of the selected option. Then, use the `value` property to determine the value of the selected choice. For instance, the following statement first evaluates the index and then extracts the value of the selected option:

```
x=document.testForm.Cuisine.selectedIndex;
val=document.testForm.Cuisine.options[x].value;
```

Result

Based on the previous discussion, the development team has identified the objects and properties needed to retrieve the values entered by the user in the customer details form as follows:

1. The following statements create the radio buttons for the title category:

```
Mr.<input type="radio" value="Mr." checked name="Title">
Mrs.
    <input type="radio" value="Mrs." name="Title">  Ms. <input
type="radio" value="Ms." name="Title">
    Dr. <input type="radio" value="Dr." name="Title">
```

2. To retrieve the value from the `Title` group radio buttons, the radio buttons have been referenced by the index number. To verify the radio button selected by the user, the `checked` property of the `radio` object has been used. The following code displays how you can verify the radio button that has been selected:

```
    if(document.customerDetailsForm.Title[0].checked==true){
    savedData+="Mr. ";
    }
    else
if(document.customerDetailsForm.Title[1].checked==true){
    savedData+="Mrs. ";
    }
    else
if(document.customerDetailsForm.Title[2].checked==true){
    savedData+="Ms. ";
    }
    else
if(document.customerDetailsForm.Title[3].checked==true){
    savedData+="Dr. ";
    }
```

3. The following code will be used to create the text fields for accepting the first name, the last name, the home address, the home phone number, and the email address from the user:

```
First Name: <input type="text" name="First_Name" size="20">
Last Name: <input type="text" name="Last_Name" size="20">
Home Address: <input type="text" name="Address" size="20">
Home Phone: <input type="text" name="Phone" size="20">
E-mail: <input type="text" name="Email" size="20">
```

4. To retrieve the value from these text fields, the `value` property of the `text` object will be used. The following code retrieves values from the first name, last name, home address, home phone, and email text fields:

```
savedData += document.customerDetailsForm.First_Name.value;
savedData += document.customerDetailsForm.Last_Name.value;
savedData += document.customerDetailsForm.Address.value;
savedData += document.customerDetailsForm.Phone.value;
savedData += document.customerDetailsForm.Email.value;
```

5. The following code will be used to create a combo box for various regions in the United States:

```
Region:<select name="Region">
<option value="Appalachia">Appalachia</option>
<option value="Atlantic Coast">Atlantic Coast</option>
<option value="Great Plains">Great Plains</option>
<option value="Midwest">Midwest</option>
<option value="New England">New England</option>
<option value="Pacific">Pacific</option>
<option selected value="Northwest">Northwest</option>
<option value="Rocky Mountains">Rocky Mountains</option>
<option value="South">South </option>
<option value="Southwest">Southwest</option>
<option value="Western States">Western States</option>
</select>
```

6. To retrieve the value selected from the `Region` combo box, the `length` and `selectIndex` properties of the `select` object and the `value` property of the `options` array will be used. The following code will help retrieve the value from the `Region` combo box:

```
i=document.customerDetailsForm.Region.length;
for(j=0;j<i+1; j++){
 if(document.customerDetailsForm.Region.selectedIndex==j){

savedData+=document.customerDetailsForm.Region.options[j].value;
   }
```

7. To retrieve the value from the `mode of payment` and `card type` group of radio buttons, the same procedure as stated in the `Title` group radio buttons will be followed.

8. To retrieve the value from the card number text field, the procedure as stated in the first name text field will be followed.

9. The customer details form also needs to include a set of check boxes for items such as flowers, confectionery, books, and toys for sending updates on these items. The following is the code for creating check boxes:

```
        Flowers <input type="checkbox" name="Flowers"
value="Flowers" checked>
        Confectionery <input type="checkbox" name="Confec"
value="Confectionery">
        Books <input type="checkbox" name="Books" value="Books">
Toys <input type="checkbox" name="Toys" value="Toys">
```

10. To retrieve the value from the preceding check boxes, the checked property of the check box object will be used. The following code verifies the check box selected by the user and then traps its value:

```
        if(document.customerDetailsForm.Flowers.checked==true){
           savedData+="Flowers ";
        }
        if(document.customerDetailsForm.Confec.checked==true){
           savedData+="Confectionery ";
        }
        if(document.customerDetailsForm.Books.checked==true){
           savedData+="Books ";
        }
        if(document.customerDetailsForm.Toys.checked==true){
           savedData+="Toys ";
        }
```

Write the Code to Create the Customer Details Form and to Retrieve Values from the Form

The code to create the customer details form that will retrieve values from the form is as follows:

```
        <HTML>
        <HEAD>
        <TITLE>Web Shoppe</TITLE>
        <SCRIPT LANGUAGE="JavaScript">
        var savedData="Name: ";
        var creditCard;
        var comp;
        function dispV(){
           newWin=open("", "window2");
           newWin.document.open(" ");
           newWin.document.bgColor='#C4FBF5';
           newWin.document.fgColor='#cc3300';
```

```
        newWin.document.write("<HTML><HEAD><p align=center><font
size=6><b>Web Shoppe</b></font></p>");
        newWin.document.write("<p align=center><b><font size=6>Customer
Details Confirmation Form</font></b></p></HEAD>");
        newWin.document.write("<body><font color=black size=4>")
        newWin.document.write("You have entered the following details:
<BR>");
        if(document.customerDetailsForm.Title[0].checked==true){
            savedData+="Mr. ";
        }
        else if(document.customerDetailsForm.Title[1].checked==true){
            savedData+="Mrs. ";
        }
        else if(document.customerDetailsForm.Title[2].checked==true){
            savedData+="Ms. ";
        }
        else if(document.customerDetailsForm.Title[3].checked==true){
            savedData+="Dr. ";
        }
        savedData+=document.customerDetailsForm.First_Name.value + " ";
        savedData+=document.customerDetailsForm.Last_Name.value ;
        newWin.document.write(savedData + "<BR>");
        savedData ="Address: " +
document.customerDetailsForm.Address.value ;
        newWin.document.write(savedData + "<BR>");
        savedData="Region: ";
        i=document.customerDetailsForm.Region.length;
        for(j=0;j<i+1; j++){
            if(document.customerDetailsForm.Region.selectedIndex==j){

savedData+=document.customerDetailsForm.Region.options[j].value;
            }
        }
        newWin.document.write(savedData + "<BR>");
        savedData="Home Phone: " +
document.customerDetailsForm.Phone.value;
        newWin.document.write(savedData + "<BR>");
        savedData="E-mail: " +
document.customerDetailsForm.Email.value;
        newWin.document.write(savedData + "<BR>");
        savedData="Mode of Payment: ";

if(document.customerDetailsForm.ModeOfPayment[0].checked==true){
            savedData+="Credit Card ";
        }
        else{
            savedData+="Payment on Delivery ";
            creditCard="Payment on Delivery";
        }
        newWin.document.write(savedData + "<BR>");
        if(creditCard != "Payment on Delivery"){
```

```
                    savedData="Card Type: ";
              if(document.customerDetailsForm.CardType[0].checked==true){
                  savedData+="Master Card ";
              }
              else
if(document.customerDetailsForm.CardType[1].checked==true){
                  savedData+="Visa Card ";
              }
              newWin.document.write(savedData + "<BR>");
              savedData="Card Number: " +
document.customerDetailsForm.CardNo.value;
              newWin.document.write(savedData + "<BR>");
          }
          savedData="Item Category: ";
          if(document.customerDetailsForm.Flowers.checked==true){
              savedData+="Flowers ";
          }
          if(document.customerDetailsForm.Confec.checked==true){
              savedData+="Confectionery ";
          }
          if(document.customerDetailsForm.Books.checked==true){
              savedData+="Books ";
          }
          if(document.customerDetailsForm.Toys.checked==true){
              savedData+="Toys ";
          }
          newWin.document.write(savedData + "<BR>");
          newWin.document.write("</font>");
          newWin.document.write("<p align=left><b><font size=3
color=#cc3300>To confirm that the details are correct, click the button
below:</font></b></p>");
          newWin.document.write("<FORM>");
          var strMsg="'Thanks for your esteemed visit on our site you will
receive your items at your door step'";
          newWin.document.write('<input type=button value=Confirm
onClick="alert('+strMsg+')";></form></body></HTML>');
          }
          </SCRIPT>
          </head>
          <body bgcolor="#C4FBF5">
          <p align="center"><font color="#cc3300" size="6"><b>Web
Shoppe</b></font></p>
          <p align="center"><b><font size="6" color="#cc3300">Customer
Details Form</font></b></p>
          <FORM NAME="customerDetailsForm">
          <p align="left"><font size="3"><b>Title:
(Optional):</b>:::::::::::::::::::::::::::::::::::::::::::::::::<b>Mr.
          <input type="radio" value="Mr." checked name="Title">  Mrs.
          <input type="radio" value="Mrs." name="Title">  Ms. <input
type="radio" value="Ms." name="Title">
            Dr. <input type="radio" value="Dr." name="Title"></b></font></p>
```

```
      <p align="left"><font size="3"><b>First Name</b></font><font
size="3"><b>:</b>::::::::::::::::::::::::::::::::::::::::::::::::::::::::</f
ont><input type="text" name="First_Name" size="20"></p>
      <p align="left"><font size="3"><b>Last Name</b></font><font
size="3"><b>:</b>::::::::::::::::::::::::::::::::::::::::::::::::::::::::</f
ont><input type="text" name="Last_Name" size="20"></p>
      <p align="left"><font size="3"><b>Home
Address:</b>:::::::::::::::::::::::::::::::::::::::::::::::</font><input
type="text" name="Address" size="20"></p>
      <p align="left"><font
size="3"><b>Region:</b></font>:::::::::::::::::::::::::::::::::::::::
:::::::::::::::::::<select name="Region">
      <option value="Appalachia">Appalachia</option>
      <option value="Atlantic Coast">Atlantic Coast</option>
      <option value="Great Plains">Great Plains</option>
      <option value="Midwest">Midwest</option>
      <option value="New England">New England</option>
      <option value="Pacific">Pacific</option>
      <option selected value="Northwest">Northwest</option>
      <option value="Rocky Mountains">Rocky Mountains</option>
      <option value="South">South </option>
      <option value="Southwest">Southwest</option>
      <option value="Western States">Western States</option>
      </select></p>
      <p align="left"><font size="3"><b>Home
Phone:</b>::::::::::::::::::::::::::::::::::::::::::::::::</font><input
type="text" name="Phone" size="20"></p>
      <p align="left"><font size="3"><b>E-
mail:</b>:::::::::::::::::::::::::::::::::::::::::::::::::::::::::
<b><input type="text" name="Email" size="20"></b></font></p>
      <p align="left"><font size="3"><b>Mode of
Payment:</b>:::::::::::::::::::::::::::::::::::::<b>Credit
      Card</b></font> <input type="radio" value="Credit Card" checked
name="ModeOfPayment">  <font size="3"><b>Payment
      on Delivery</b></font> <input type="radio" value="Payment on
Delivery" name="ModeOfPayment"> </p>
      <p align="left"><font color="#cc3300" size="3"><b>If mode of
payment selected is
      Credit Card, please provide us with Credit Card
details:</b></font></p>
      <p align="left"><b><font size="3">Card
Type</font>:</b>:::::::::::::::::::::::::::::::::::::::::::::::::::::::
:<font size="3"><b>Master
      Card</b></font> <input type="radio" value="Master Card"
name="CardType"> <font size="3"><b>Visa
      Card</b></font>  <input type="radio" value="Visa Card"
name="CardType"></p>
      <p align="left"><b>Card
Number:</b>:::::::::::::::::::::::::::::::::::::::::::::::::::<font
size="3"><b><input type="text" name="CardNo" size="20"></b></font></p>
      <p align="left"><b><font size="3" color="#cc3300">To
```

```
        receive updates on new additions, please check the item categories
:</font></b></p>
        <p align="left"><b><font size="3">Flowers </font></b><input
type="checkbox" name="Flowers" value="Flowers" checked>
        <b><font size="3">Confectionery <input type="checkbox"
name="Confec" value="Confectionery">
        Books <input type="checkbox" name="Books" value="Books"> Toys
<input type="checkbox" name="Toys" value="Toys"></font></b></p>
        <p align="left"> </p>
        <p
align="left">          
;            
;            
;            
;   
        <input type="submit" value="Submit" name="Submit"
onClick="dispV()">
        <input type="reset" value="Reset" name="Reset"></p>
        <p align="left"> </p>
        <p align="left"> </p>
        <p align="left"> </p>
        </FORM>
        </body>
        </html>
```

Execute the code

Execute the code and verify its successful operation by performing the following steps:

1. Enter the following details in the form:

```
Title: Mr.
First Name: Blake
Last Name: Stevenson
Home Address: 9966, 211th Street, Kingston Washington 98346
Region: Northwest
Home Phone: 2123273423
E mail: blakesteve@xyz.com
Mode of Payment: Credit Card
Card Type: Visa Card
Card Number: 23-457-773
Item Category: Flowers and Confectionery
```

2. Click the Submit button.

3. A new window is opened, which displays the details entered by the user.

Figure 8.14 illustrates the customer details form of Web Shoppe.

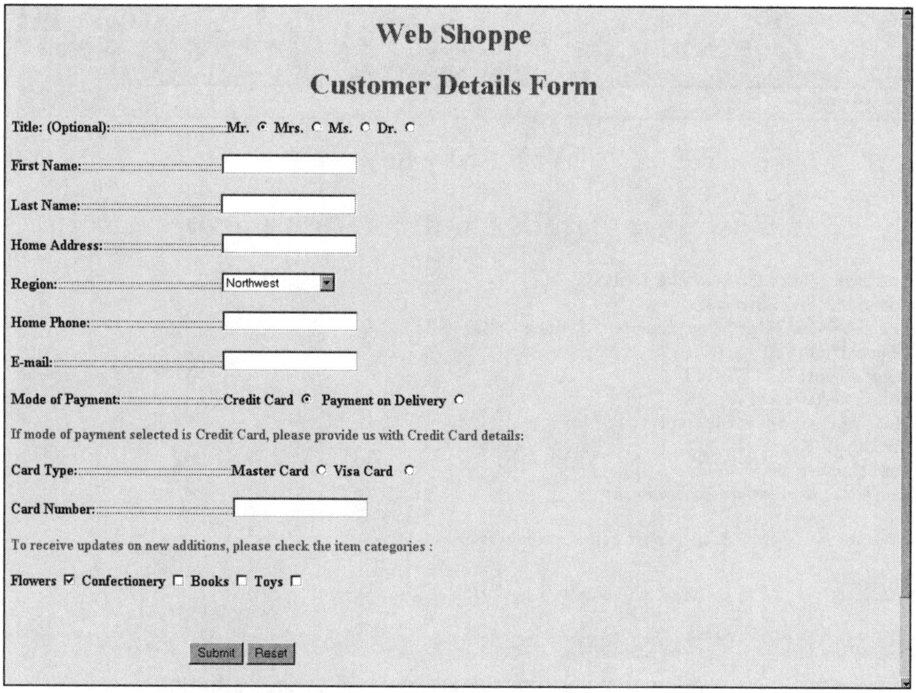

Figure 8.14 Customer details form of Web Shoppe.

Figure 8.15 illustrates the new window that displays the details entered by the customer.

We have looked at the four objects of the browser hierarchy model. Let us now see how you can use the frames in JavaScript to display several pages in one document window.

Using Frames with JavaScript to Display Several Pages in a Window

In the past, traditional Web browsers could only display an HTML document in a single-document window. When a user clicked a link on a page for new information, the complete browser window was cleared and updated with a new document.

Netscape Navigator 2 introduced an extension for HTML known as frames. Frames allow visible client area in a Web browser to be divided into more than one subregion, each containing a separate document. You can combine frames with JavaScript to create sophisticated Web-based interfaces and applications. This section of the chapter describes how Web Shoppe takes advantage of the frames on its site. You'll see how merging frames with JavaScript can enhance the Web site of Web Shoppe.

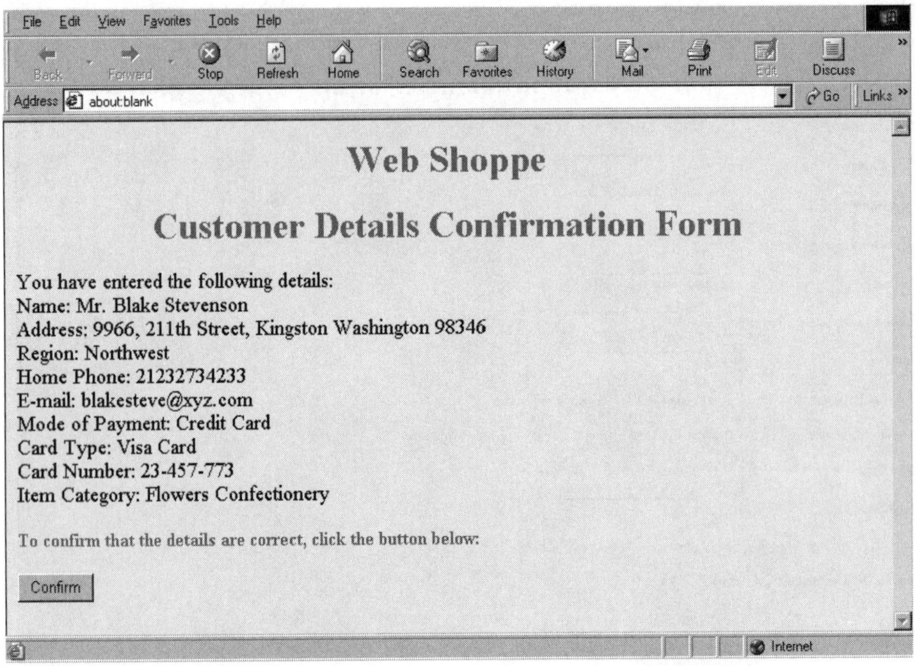

Figure 8.15   New window that illustrates details entered by the customer.

Problem Statement

The online shopping mall of Web Shoppe has a page on its Web site that displays the new product line of its store. The page prompts a customer to enter the category of a product from which he or she wants to purchase the product. Based on the choice of the customer, the page prompts for the corresponding item that the customer wants to purchase. This process continues until the customer chooses to make no further purchases. Finally, the selections made by a user on this page are used to calculate the total purchases made by the customer.

However, the market trend has now changed. The sites are now more sophisticated. The current trend is to present several related Web documents in the visible client area of a Web browser. To ensure that its site does not look outdated, Web Shoppe, Inc., has also decided to merge two related pages of its site into a Web document. The first page displays the new product line of the store. The second page displays the items chosen by the customer and the total price of toys selected.

To incorporate the above functionality in the page, the following task list has been identified.

Task List

- ✔ Identify the frames required to incorporate the preceding functionality.
- ✔ Write the code.
- ✔ Execute and verify the code.

Identify the Frames Required to Incorporate the Preceding Functionality

Before identifying the frames that will be required to create the new page of Web Shoppe according to the new trend, let's start with a quick recap of HTML frame basics and proceed with the JavaScript frame object.

The layout of the Web page can be customized using frames. Information such as messages, title, graphics, and the table of contents that the page designer wants to keep unchanged and visible can be stored on a separate frame. As the user moves through the site in one frame, the other frames are always visible and unchanged. For example, in the table of contents, one frame could contain a set of links, each of which, when clicked, targets its result in another frame. Frames can also reduce bandwidth demands by enabling common components, such as menus and logos, to be loaded once in their own frames instead of loading repeatedly with each document request by the user.

Tags for Creating Frames

The basic structure of a frame document resembles an HTML document. The only difference is that the `<FRAMESET>` tag that describes the sub-HTML documents or the frames that constitute the page replace the `<BODY>` tag. The syntax of a frame document is as follows:

```
<HTML>
<HEAD>
</HEAD>
<FRAMESET>
.
.
.
</FRAMESET>
</HTML>
```

THE `<FRAMESET>` Tag

The `<FRAMESET>` tag defines how to split a window into rows or columns. It accepts the following two attributes: ROWS and COLS. The ROWS attribute specifies the number of rows into which you may want to divide the visible client area in a browser. The COLS attribute specifies the number of columns into which you may want to divide the visible client area in a browser.

Both ROWS and COLS attributes assume a list of values that are separated by commas. These values can be pixel values, percentage values ranging from 1 through 100, or relative scaling values. Let us now discuss each of these values in detail:

Pixel value.   If pixel values are used, they should be used in conjunction with one or more relative size values explained below. Otherwise, in the case of resizing a window, the browser overrides the specified pixel value to ensure that the total proportions of the frames are 100 percent of the width and height of the user's window.

Percentage values between 1 and 100 or value%.   If the total of the percentages specified is greater than 100, all the percentages are scaled down. If the total of the percentages specified is less than 100 and the relative-sized frames exist, extra space is allocated to the relative-sized frames. If there are no relative-sized frames, all remaining space is scaled up to match a total of 100 percent.

Relative scaling values or value*.   The value in this field is optional. A single * character is a relative-sized frame and is interpreted as a request to allot the frame the remaining space. If there are multiple relative-sized frames, the remaining space is divided evenly among them. If there is a value in front of the *, that frame gets that much more relative space. For example, "2, *" would allot two-thirds of the space to the first frame and one-third to the second.

The <FRAME> Tag

The <FRAME> tag defines a single frame in a frame set. This implies that it is used to specify the document that will be loaded in a frame of a frameset. The <FRAME> tag has six attributes. Table 8.10 lists these attributes.

We have listed two main tags in our preceding discussion. However, it is still not clear how many HTML files are needed to create frames in a document. Let us take a simple example where you need to divide the visible screen area of the Web browser into four parts, each containing an HTML document. This means that at least four files are required. However, you will need another main document that will contain these four files. This means that in this case, you will need five HTML files. You will need main.html to contain the other four HTML documents, which are firstFrame.html, secondFrame.html, thirdFrame.html, and fourthFrame.html.

The code for the main.html file is as follows:

```
<HTML>
<FRAMESET ROWS="*, *" COLS="*, *">
<FRAME NAME="firstFrame" SRC="firstFrame.html">
<FRAME NAME="secondFrame" SRC="secondFrame.html">
<FRAME NAME="thirdFrame" SRC="thirdFrame.html">
<FRAME NAME="fourthFrame" SRC="fourthFrame.html">
</FRAMESET>
</HTML>
```

Table 8.10   Attributes of the `<FRAME>` Tag

ATTRIBUTE	DESCRIPTION
SRC	Indicates the URL of the document to be displayed in the frame.
NAME	Assigns a name to a frame so that it can be targeted by the links in other documents. This attribute is optional. By default, all frames are unnamed. However, naming a frame facilitates cross-frame interaction in JavaScript.
NORESIZE	Indicates that a frame is not resizable by the user. This attribute has no value. It is just a flag.
SCROLLING	Indicates whether a frame is scrollable. If the value of this field is "yes," scrollbars are visible on the frame. If the value is "no," scrollbars are not visible. "Auto" instructs the browser to decide whether scrollbars are required and place them where they are needed. The scrolling attribute is optional and, by default, the value is "auto."
MARGINHEIGHT	Indicates the width of the top and bottom margins of a frame in pixels.
MARGINWIDTH	Indicates the width of the left and right margins of a frame in pixels.

The code for the `firstFrame.html` file is as follows:

```
<HTML>
<BODY>
<H1>1st Frame</H1>
</BODY>
</HTML>
```

Replace the text 1st Frame with 2nd Frame, 3rd Frame, and 4th Frame for each file, respectively.

Figure 8.16 illustrates the `main.html` file that displays the other four HTML files in the visible client area of the browser.

Having discussed the basic frame tags and files required to create frames in a document, let us see how JavaScript supports frames by using the `frame` object.

The `frame` Object

The `frame` object in JavaScript represents the frames defined in an HTML file. The browser automatically creates the `frame` objects when a document containing frames is loaded. These `frame` objects are stored in the `frames` array of the `window` object in

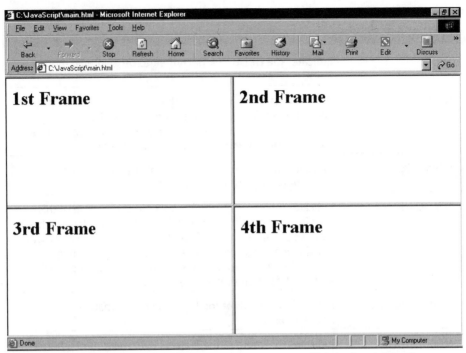

Figure 8.16 The `main.html` file that displays four HTML files in the visible client area of the browser.

the order specified in the frameset document. You can access each frame defined in a window by using an index number in the array. For example, in the case of the preceding frameset document, the HTML file `firstFrame.html` can be referenced by the statement `parent.frames[0]`. Here, since each `frame` object in a window is a child of the parent `window` object, the keywords `window` and `self` refer to the current `frame` object and the keyword `parent` refers to the main window. Remember you have already used the keyword `window` to refer to the current window that did not have frames. Similarly, you can refer to the `secondFrame.html` file with the statement `parent.frames[1]`.

Frame object names are the same as the names that you specify in the NAME attribute in the `<FRAME>` tag. Therefore, continuing with the example where four frames were created, the `firstFrame.html` file can also refer to other documents such as `parent.secondFrame` and `parent.thirdFrame`. The keywords `window` and `self` will refer to the `firstFrame` frame.

As mentioned earlier, a common use of a frame is to create a navigation frame that controls a document in another frame. While creating a navigation frame, the screen is usually divided into two parts. The left frame, which is a navigation frame, contains links to several Web documents. The right frame displays the Web document whose link is clicked in the left frame or the navigation frame. Using the `frame` object, you can create such a navigation frame.

Let's create a common navigation frame, `Table of Content`, which contains links to each chapter of a book. To begin, let's create the main HTML document that will contain the two frames: navigation frame and other documents frame.

```
<HTML>
<HEAD>
<TITLE>Frame Navigation Example</TITLE>
</HEAD>
<FRAMESET COLS="*, *">
<FRAME NAME="TableOfContent" SRC="TableOfContent.html">
<FRAME NAME="Chapters" SRC="about:blank">
</FRAMESET>
</HTML>
```

In the preceding code, notice that the second frame source is written as `about:blank`. This is because the files in the `Chapters` frame will be loaded dynamically depending on the link clicked by the user.

The following is the code for the `TableOfContent` (navigation) frame:

```
<HTML>
<HEAD>
<TITLE>Navigation Frames</TITLE>
<BODY>
<H1>Making Use of JavaScript</H1>
</P>
<UL>
<LI><A HREF="#"
onClick="parent.TableOfContent.location='chapter1.html';
window.location='chap1Details.html';">Introducing Web Development </A>
    <LI><A HREF="#"
onClick="parent.TableOfContent.location='chapter2.html';
window.location='chap2Details.html';">Overview of JavaScript </A>
    <LI><A HREF="#"
onClick="parent.TableOfContent.location='chapter3.html';
window.location='chap3Details.html';"> JavaScript Data Types, Variables,
and Operators </A>
    <LI><A HREF="#"
onClick="parent.TableOfContent.location='chapter4.html'
window.location='chap4Details;"> JavaScript Control Structures and
Statements </A>
    <LI><A HREF="#" onClick="parent.right.location='chapter5.html';
window.location='chap5Details.html';"> Functions and Events</A>
    <LI><A HREF="#" onClick="parent.right.location='chapter6.html';
window.location='chap6Details.html';"> Using Objects in JavaScript </A>
    <LI><A HREF="#" onClick="parent.right.location='chapter7.html';
window.location='chap7Details.html';"> Error and Exception Handling in
JavaScript</A>
    </UL>
    </BODY>
    </HTML>
```

The preceding JavaScript code looks quite complex. However, its main functionality is based on only two statements that are repeated for each of the links with a slight modification. Let's pick the following statement and see what it means:

```
onClick="parent.right.location='chapter1.html';
window.location='chap1Details.html';"
```

As you are aware, `onClick` is also the event handler for links. Therefore, here, the `onClick` event handler executes two statements, `parent.TableOfContent.location='chapter1.html';` and `window.location='chap1Details.html';`. The first statement loads the content to the right side of the frame. In addition, notice that the first statement uses the keyword `parent`. This is because the current frame, which is the `TableOfContent` frame, is referring to the `Chapters` frame. The second statement is used to update the `TableOfContent` frame. Since the frame is referring to itself, it uses the keyword `window`.

NOTE The preceding code can also use the `TARGET` attribute of the `<A>` tag to open a link in another frame. However, it is preferable to use the `TARGET` attribute if you want to load only one document when the user clicks a link. You should use JavaScript when you want to update two frames simultaneously. Therefore, in the preceding code, since the current frame that is the `TableOfContent` frame and the `Chapters` frame are both being updated, JavaScript is used.

In the preceding example, we have updated one frame from another frame. Now, consider a situation where you have two forms that are placed in two different frames. When you enter a value in one form, it affects the values in the other form. Let us take an example where you have two forms A and B. Form A is contained in frame A1 and form B in frame B1. When you enter any value in form A, it affects the values in form B. In a situation where you have two different forms that are contained in two different frames, you need to first retrieve the values contained in one form and then make these values accessible to the other form. To do so, you use the following syntax:

```
parent.Name_of_Frame.Name_of_Form.fieldName.value
```

The preceding syntax consists of the following:

1. **parent.** As mentioned earlier, each `frame` object in a window is a child of the `parent window` object. Therefore, the keyword `parent` refers to the main window. Since we are trying to access a frame that is contained in a window, we'll first give reference of the parent window in which the frame is contained.

2. **Name_of_Frame.** This is the name of the frame that contains the form from which you want to extract values.

3. **Name_of_Form.** This is the name of the form that you want to access.

4. **fieldName.** This can be the name of any field such as text box, text area, select box, or radio box.

5. **value.** This is the property of the corresponding object that will extract the value contained in the field.

Result

Coming back to the scenario of Web Shoppe, where we need to merge two pages into a document, cross form interaction takes place. These forms are contained in two different frames. The left frame will display the new product line of the store and the right frame will display the items selected and the total cost of the items. The following methodology and objects have been identified:

1. A file named Web Shoppe.html needs to be created. This file will contain two files NewProductLine.html and AddToCart.html in two frames. The following code will create the frames in this document:

   ```
   <FRAMESET cols="50%,*">
   <FRAME SRC="NewProductLine.html">
   <FRAME SRC="AddToCart.html" NAME="output">
   </FRAMESET>
   ```

2. In the preceding code, notice that the frame that will be placed in the other half of the document area is named as output. It is imperative to name the second frame because the values from the NewProductLine.html file frame have to be transferred to the AddToCart.html file frame. If you remember the syntax for accessing values across forms that are contained in different frames, we had mentioned that the form names should be qualified by the respective frame names. [MW1]. Therefore in our case, we'll mention the output frame.

3. To trap the values entered by the customer in the NewProductLine.html file, hidden fields will be used. Since there are 11 items and each item has a corresponding price, 22 hidden fields have been used to trap these values. For example, the following statements indicate the hidden fields for items Asters, Daffodils, Roses, and Tulips and their prices:

   ```
   <INPUT TYPE="hidden" NAME="priceAsters" VALUE="100">
   <INPUT TYPE="hidden" NAME="Asters" VALUE="Asters">
   <INPUT TYPE="hidden" NAME="priceDaffodils" VALUE="150">
   <INPUT TYPE="hidden" NAME="Daffodils" VALUE="Daffodils">
   <INPUT TYPE="hidden" NAME="Roses" VALUE="Roses">
   <INPUT TYPE="hidden" NAME="priceRoses" VALUE="200">
   <INPUT TYPE="hidden" NAME="Tulips" VALUE="Tulips">
   ```

4. In the file NewProductLine.html, the function nextItem() is declared. This function is called whenever the customer clicks the AddToCart button.

The following statement displays an example of how the nextItem() function is written in the event handler onClick:

```
<INPUT TYPE="submit" VALUE="Add to Cart"
onClick="nextItem(Asters.value, priceAsters.value)">
```

5. When the user clicks on the Add to Cart button The function nextItem() traps the value from the hidden form fields and assigns these values to the fields in the Add to Cart form.

```
function nextItem(item, price){
    parent.output.document.displayForm.hiddenPrice.value =
price;
    var toDo =
parent.output.document.displayForm.hiddenPrice.value+parent.output.do
cument.displayForm.hiddenAction.value+parent.output.document.displayF
orm.total.value;
    parent.output.document.displayForm.cartItems.value +=
item + " \n";
    parent.output.document.displayForm.cartPrices.value +=
price + " \n";
    parent.output.document.displayForm.total.value =
eval(toDo);
    }
```

Write the Code

The following is the code for the main page of Web Shoppe, which will contain the two frames NewProductLine.html and AddToCart.html. Save this code as Web-Shoppe.html file.

```
<HTML>
<FRAMESET cols="50%,*">
<FRAME SRC="NewProductLine.html">
<FRAME SRC="AddToCart.html" NAME="output">
</FRAMESET>
</HTML>
```

The following is the code for NewProductLine.html:

```
<HTML>
<HEAD>
<TITLE>Web Shoppe</TITLE>
<SCRIPT LANGUAGE="JavaScript">
    function nextItem(item, price){
    parent.output.document.displayForm.hiddenPrice.value = price;
    var toDo =
parent.output.document.displayForm.hiddenPrice.value+parent.output.docum
ent.displayForm.hiddenAction.value+parent.output.document.displayForm.to
tal.value;
```

```
            parent.output.document.displayForm.cartItems.value += item + "
\n";
            parent.output.document.displayForm.cartPrices.value += price +
" \n";
            parent.output.document.displayForm.total.value = eval(toDo);
        }
    </SCRIPT>
    </HEAD>
    <BODY bgcolor="#C4FBF5">
        <P align="center" style="margin-top: 0; margin-bottom: 0"><I><FONT
color="#CC3300" face="Arial Black" size="5">Web Shoppe</font></I></P>
        <P align="left" style="margin-top: 0; margin-bottom: 0"><I>
        <FONT face="Arial" color="#000000" size="3">
        Shopping ? Choose from:</FONT></I></P>
        <P align="left" style="margin-top: 0; margin-bottom: 0"> </P>
        <P align="left" style="margin-top: 0; margin-bottom: 0"><I><FONT
size="5" face="Arial" color="#000000"><img border="0" src="Bullet1.gif"
width="15" height="15"></FONT><FONT face="Arial" color="#000000"><FONT
size="2">Flowers</FONT>        &
nbsp;           &
nbsp;           &
nbsp;           &
nbsp;           &
nbsp;           &
nbsp;      </FONT></I></P>
        <P align="left" style="margin-top: 0; margin-bottom: 0"><I><FONT
size="2"><font face="Arial" color="#000000">   
        <IMG border="0" src="Bullet2.gif" width="15" height="15">
Asters           
   
        $100     </FONT></FONT></I><INPUT TYPE="submit"
VALUE="Add to Cart" onClick="nextItem(Asters.value,
priceAsters.value)"><I><FONT face="Arial" color="#000000">

            
            
     
        </FONT></I>
         </P>
        <P ALIGN="left" STYLE="margin-top: 0; margin-bottom: 0"><FONT
FACE="Arial" COLOR="#000000" SIZE="2"><i>   
        </I></FONT><FONT SIZE="2"><I><FONT FACE="Arial" COLOR="#000000">
        <IMG BORDER="0" SRC="Bullet2.gif" WIDTH="15"
HEIGHT="15"></FONT></I> <FONT FACE="Arial" COLOR="#000000"><I>

Daffodils          &nb
sp; $150
            </I></FONT></FONT><INPUT TYPE="submit"
VALUE="Add to Cart" onClick="nextItem(Daffodils.value,
priceDaffodils.value)"><FONT FACE="Arial" COLOR="#000000"
SIZE="2"><I>      
```

```
    </I></FONT>
     </P>
    <P ALIGN="left" STYLE="margin-top: 0; margin-bottom: 0"> </P>
    <P ALIGN="left" STYLE="margin-top: 0; margin-bottom: 0"><I><FONT
FACE="Arial" COLOR="#000000" SIZE="2">   
    <IMG BORDER="0" SRC="Bullet2.gif" width="15" height="15">
Roses           &
nbsp;  
    $200     </FONT></I><INPUT TYPE="submit"
VALUE="Add to Cart" onClick="nextItem(Roses.value,
priceRoses.value)"></P>
    <P ALIGN="left" STYLE="margin-top: 0; margin-bottom: 0"> </P>
    <P ALIGN="left" STYLE="margin-top: 0; margin-bottom: 0"><I><FONT
FACE="Arial" COLOR="#000000" SIZE="2">   
    <IMG BORDER="0" SRC="Bullet2.gif" WIDTH="15" HEIGHT="15">
Tulips           
   
    $350     </FONT></I><INPUT TYPE="submit"
VALUE="Add to Cart" onClick="nextItem(Tulips.value,
priceTulips.value)"></P>
    <P ALIGN="left" STYLE="margin-top: 0; margin-bottom: 0"> </P>
    <P ALIGN="left" STYLE="margin-top: 0; margin-bottom: 0"><I><FONT
FACE="Arial" COLOR="#000000" SIZE="2"><IMG BORDER="0" SRC="Bullet1.gif"
WIDTH="15" HEIGHT="15">
    Confectionery</FONT></I></P>
    <P ALIGN="left" STYLE="margin-top: 0; margin-bottom: 0"><I><FONT
FACE="Arial" COLOR="#000000" SIZE="2">    
    <IMG BORDER="0" SRC="Bullet2.gif" WIDTH="15" HEIGHT="15">
Breads           
   
    $150 </FONT></I>  
    <INPUT TYPE="submit" VALUE="Add to Cart"
onClick="nextItem(Breads.value, priceBreads.value)"></P>
    <P ALIGN="left" STYLE="margin-top: 0; margin-bottom: 0"> </P>
    <P ALIGN="left" STYLE="margin-top: 0; margin-bottom: 0"><I><FONT
FACE="Arial" COLOR="#000000" SIZE="2">    
    <IMG BORDER="0" SRC="Bullet2.gif" WIDTH="15" HEIGHT="15">
Croissants         
    $300    </FONT></I><INPUT TYPE="submit" VALUE="Add
to Cart" onClick="nextItem(Croissants.value,
priceCroissants.value)"></P>
    <P ALIGN="left" STYLE="margin-top: 0; margin-bottom: 0"> </P>
    <P ALIGN="left" STYLE="margin-top: 0; margin-bottom: 0"><I><FONT
FACE="Arial" COLOR="#000000" SIZE="2">    
    <IMG BORDER="0" SRC="Bullet2.gif" WIDTH="15" HEIGHT="15">
Cakes           &
nbsp;   
    $400    </FONT></I><INPUT TYPE="submit" VALUE="Add
to Cart" onClick="nextItem(Cakes.value, priceCakes.value)"></P>
    <P ALIGN="left" STYLE="margin-top: 0; margin-bottom: 0"> </P>
```

```
        <P ALIGN="left" STYLE="margin-top: 0; margin-bottom: 0"><FONT
FACE="Arial" COLOR="#000000" SIZE="2"><I>    
        <IMG BORDER="0" SRC="Bullet2.gif" WIDTH="15" HEIGHT="15">
Biscuits          &nbs
p; 
        $200    </I></FONT> <INPUT TYPE="submit" VALUE="Add to
Cart" onClick="nextItem(Biscuits.value, priceBiscuits.value)"></P>
        <P ALIGN="left" STYLE="margin-top: 0; margin-bottom: 0"> </P>
        <P ALIGN="left" STYLE="margin-top: 0; margin-bottom: 0"><I><FONT
FACE="Arial" COLOR="#000000" SIZE="2"><IMG BORDER="0" SRC="Bullet1.gif"
WIDTH="15" HEIGHT="15">
        Books</FONT></I></P>
        <P ALIGN="left" STYLE="margin-top: 0; margin-bottom: 0"><I><FONT
FACE="Arial" COLOR="#000000" SIZE="2">   
        <IMG BORDER="0" SRC="Bullet2.gif" WIDTH="15" HEIGHT="15">  Forever
Yours   
        $400    </FONT></I> 
        <INPUT TYPE="submit" VALUE="Add to Cart"
onClick="nextItem(ForeverYours.value, priceForeverYours.value)"></P>
        <P ALIGN="left" STYLE="margin-top: 0; margin-bottom: 0"> </P>
        <P ALIGN="left" STYLE="margin-top: 0; margin-bottom: 0"><I><FONT
FACE="Arial" COLOR="#000000" SIZE="2">    
        <IMG BORDER="0" SRC="Bullet2.gif" WIDTH="15" HEIGHT="15">  The
        Horizons     $500
    </FONT></I><INPUT TYPE="submit" VALUE="Add to
Cart" onClick="nextItem(TheHorizons.value, priceTheHorizons.value)"></P>
        <P ALIGN="left" STYLE="margin-top: 0; margin-bottom: 0"> </P>
        <P ALIGN="left" STYLE="margin-top: 0; margin-bottom: 0"><I><FONT
FACE="Arial" COLOR="#000000" SIZE="2"> 
         
        <IMG BORDER="0" SRC="Bullet2.gif" WIDTH="15" HEIGHT="15"> Double
Trouble  $750   </FONT></I>  
        <INPUT TYPE="submit" VALUE="Add to Cart"
onClick="nextItem(DoubleTrouble.value, priceDoubleTrouble.value)"></P>
        <INPUT TYPE="hidden" NAME="priceAsters" VALUE="100">
        <INPUT TYPE="hidden" NAME="Asters" VALUE="Asters">
        <INPUT TYPE="hidden" NAME="priceDaffodils" VALUE="150">
        <INPUT TYPE="hidden" NAME="Daffodils" VALUE="Daffodils">
        <INPUT TYPE="hidden" NAME="Roses" VALUE="Roses">
        <INPUT TYPE="hidden" NAME="priceRoses" VALUE="200">
        <INPUT TYPE="hidden" NAME="Tulips" VALUE="Tulips">
        <INPUT TYPE="hidden" NAME="priceTulips" VALUE="350">
        <INPUT TYPE="hidden" NAME="Breads" VALUE="Breads">
        <INPUT TYPE="hidden" NAME="priceBreads" VALUE="150">
        <INPUT TYPE="hidden" NAME="Croissants" VALUE="Croissants">
        <INPUT TYPE="hidden" NAME="priceCroissants" VALUE="300">
        <INPUT TYPE="hidden" NAME="Cakes" VALUE="Cakes">
        <INPUT TYPE="hidden" NAME="priceCakes" VALUE="400">
        <INPUT TYPE="hidden" NAME="Biscuits" VALUE="Biscuits">
        <INPUT TYPE="hidden" NAME="priceBiscuits" VALUE="200">
```

```
<INPUT TYPE="hidden" NAME="ForeverYours" VALUE="Forever Yours">
<INPUT TYPE="hidden" NAME="priceForeverYours" VALUE="400">
<INPUT TYPE="hidden" NAME="TheHorizons" VALUE="The Horizons">
<INPUT TYPE="hidden" NAME="priceTheHorizons" VALUE="500">
<INPUT TYPE="hidden" NAME="DoubleTrouble" VALUE="Double Trouble">
<INPUT TYPE="hidden" NAME="priceDoubleTrouble" VALUE="750">
</body>
</html>
```

The following is the code for the `AddToCart.html` page:

```
<HTML>
<BODY bgcolor="#C4FBF5">
<p align="center"><b><i><font color="#CC3300" face="Arial Black"
size="5">Cart of Selected Items</font></i> </b></p>
<p>    <font size="3"><b><i><font face="Times New
Roman, Times, serif">List
of Items</font></i></b>
            
     
    <font face="Times New Roman, Times, serif"><i><b>Price
($)</b></i></font>        </font
></p>
<FORM NAME="displayForm">
<p>
<textarea name="cartItems" cols="15"
rows="15"></textarea>     
<textarea name="cartPrices" cols="10" rows="15"></textarea></p>
<p><b><font face="Times New Roman, Times, serif"><i><font
size="3">Total ($):</font></i></font></b>  
<input type="text" name="total" value="0" size="15"> <BR>
<input type="hidden" name="hiddenPrice">
<input type="hidden" name="hiddenAction" value="+">
</p>
</form>
<p> </p>
</BODY>
</HTML>
```

Execute and Verify the Code

Execute the main page of Web Shoppe, `WebShoppe.html`, which contains the two frames `NewProductLine.html` and `AddToCart.html`. The page as shown in Figure 8.17 is displayed on the screen. The left frame contains the file `NewProduct-Line.html` and the right frame contains the file `AddToCart.html`.

To verify whether the names and values of the selected products and the corresponding total are reflected in the left frame, perform the following steps:

1. Click the `Add to Cart` button for `Asters` and `Roses` in the `Flowers` category.

2. Click the `Add to Cart` button for `Breads` and `Cakes` in the `Confectionery` category.

3. Click the `Add to Cart` button for `The Horizons` in the `Books` category.

Notice that when you click the `Add to Cart` button in each of the preceding steps, the corresponding names of the items selected are reflected in the text area named `List of Items` and the value of each item is reflected in the text area named `Prices` (`$`). Similarly, each time you click the `Add to Cart` button, the total is also calculated and displayed in the text field `Total` (`$`).

Figure 8.17 illustrates the `WebShoppe.html` file that contains two frames, `NewProductLine.html` and `AddToCart.html`.

Figure 8.18 illustrates the `WebShoppe.html` file after steps 1 to 3.

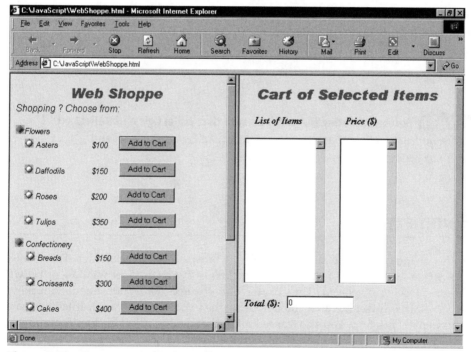

Figure 8.17   The `WebShoppe.html` file.

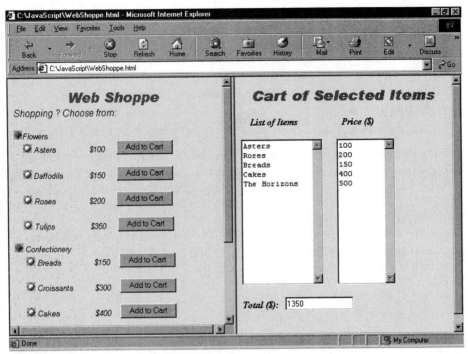

Figure 8.18 The WebShoppe.html file after steps 1 to 3.

NOTE Before executing the code, be sure that **Bullet1.gif and Bullet2.gif are in the same folder as** WebShoppe.html, AddToCart.html, **and** NewProductLine.html.

Summary

In this chapter, we discussed the JavaScript browser hierarchy model. This model allows you to control the features and functions of a Web browser window or HTML document being displayed. The chapter also covered the window and document objects of the browser hierarchy model. Using the window object, you learned to create documents at run time. You also learned to use the window object for specifying a message on the status bar and interacting with the user. The document object helps write content in a document and views the elements of an HTML document.

The next section covered the history, location, and form objects of the browser hierarchy model. You learned how the location object allows users to move to different targets by clicking a button. Next, we discussed how the history object allows the user to move backward or forward through the stored history. Finally, we created a form and accessed the values entered in the form by using the `form` object.

In the third section, we discussed how to merge frames with JavaScript to create sophisticated interfaces and Web applications.

Creating Cookies in JavaScript

OBJECTIVES:

In this chapter, you will learn to:

- ✔ Identify the relevance of cookies
- ✔ Identify how cookies work
- ✔ Identify the application area and limitations of cookies
- ✔ Use the cookie property to set and retrieve cookies

Getting Started

Before we discuss cookies, we will revisit the concept of how communication takes place on the Internet. We will also discuss how to maintain state information on the Internet. The Web server and the client communicate on the Internet by using the HyperText Transfer Protocol (HTTP). During this communication, when a client sends a request to the server, an HTTP request object is sent to the server that contains information about the request. The server then responds to the client and sends the information in an HTTP response object. Initially, Internet communication was designed to operate in a stateless mode. This meant that once the request-response cycle between the client and the server was complete, the session was closed and no information was stored about that session. If the client sent a request to the server again, a new session was created between the client and the server and, thus, information from the previous session was lost.

The stateless design of the Internet allowed early Web servers to process requests for Web pages swiftly and efficiently because the servers did not need to maintain any unique requirements for different clients. Similarly, Web browsers did not need to store any special information to load a particular Web page from a server. Although this stateless design was swift and proficient, it also had some disadvantages. In this design, a Web server could not maintain user information. Web browsers treated every visit to a Web page as an entirely new session, regardless of whether users had opened a different Web page on the same server, navigated to a different site, or closed their Web browsers entirely.

However, when the Internet became a widespread phenomenon, the state of the sessions needed to be maintained. When the Internet was used for commercial purposes, situations arose where the processing of one Web page became dependent on the processing of the previous pages visited by the customers. The sites needed to be more interactive and give a personal look and feel to each user visiting the site. For example, for a user to complete a series of forms, a customer's response to one form determines which form is to be provided next to the customer. Here, storing the customer information requires that state information be maintained. How is this information maintained? In the stateful session, when a server returns an HTTP object to a client, it sends the state information of the session that is stored on the client computer. Any future requests made by the client to the server uses the state information on the client computer for further processing.

A number of mechanisms have been introduced to enable Web applications to store state information of a session. We already used and implemented one of these mechanism, hidden form fields, in Chapter 8, "Working with Browser Objects." You may not have realized that while one form was interacting with the other, the form was actually storing the information state in the hidden form fields. The other mechanism for storing state information is the HTTP cookies.

In this chapter, you'll learn to use cookies to maintain browser state information. You will also learn to use this information to create useful and powerful Web applications.

Creating Cookies

Problem Statement

Most of the Web sites nowadays display personalized messages and the number of times a user has visited the Web sites. Messages are also displayed in a personalized format that contains the date of the user's last visit.

Considering the current trend, Web Shoppe has also decided to display personalized messages to the customer by using the customer's first name as a greeting. Web Shoppe has also decided that it would display the number of visits that a customer has made to their sites along with the date when the customer last visited the site. To incorporate this functionality, the development team has been assigned the task of creating the home page that would display the personalized message and the hit count to the customer.

However, the home page of Web Shoppe is still under construction. To display the personalized message and the hit count, the development team has been asked to use the semiconstructed page to display the message and the hit count.

Task List

Based on the requirements specified in the preceding scenario, the development team has identified the following tasks:

- ✔ **Identify the objects and properties of JavaScript to add the personalized message and the hit count to the site.**
- ✔ **Write the code.**
- ✔ **Execute and verify the successful running of the code.**

Having identified the tasks, let us now discuss each task in isolation to understand how the development team adds the personalized message and the hit count information to Web Shoppe's home page by using JavaScript.

Identify the Objects and Properties of JavaScript to Add Personalized Message and Hit Count to the Site

As stated earlier, a Web site needs to be interactive, and it should give a personal look and feel to each user visiting the site. To incorporate the functionality stated in the problem statement, where a user is greeted each time he or she visits the home page of Web Shoppe, the development team of Web Shoppe identified that they need to maintain the state information of the previous browser session when the user visited the site. To maintain the state information, the development team has identified cookies in JavaScript to be the best option since these don't need any server interaction.

Before we delve into discussing the details of how Web Shoppe would incorporate such functionality, let us look at some basic concepts of cookies that would help you to understand how cookies are used in JavaScript.

Cookie Basics

Hidden form fields enable Common Gateway Interface (CGI) programs to maintain state information about Web browsers. These fields are used in situations where the state information is to be maintained for a short time period. Let's go back to the example where a user fills out a series of forms. In such a situation, form information is maintained only for that browser session. When a user closes the browser, the information contained in a hidden form field is not available.

Now, let's examine how a cookie is different from hidden form fields in maintaining the state information about browsers. Although a cookie mechanism is not a distinctive feature of Netscape, Internet Explorer, or JavaScript, it is a universal concept that enables the browser state-related information to be stored in a persistent manner. (In a persistent manner implies that the information in a cookie is maintained across browser sessions. In other words, the information is stored on the user's computer even when the user switches off his or her computer.)

Before we proceed further, let's be aware of some myths about cookies. A common myth about Web cookies is that a cookie is a program that searches the hard disk of a personal computer and accumulates critical information, such as passwords and credit card numbers. Another myth about cookies is that it is a piece of code. In reality, a cookie is data that is sent from a Web server to a Web browser when the user visits a site on a server. In other words, a cookie is information stored on a user's computer in a .txt file. Although a cookie is stored in the user's computer, it is not code or an executable program that can damage the user's computer.

Having discussed what cookies are, let's look at how cookies operate, their common features, usage areas, and limitations.

Modus Operandi of a Cookie

Even after reading what a cookie is and why it is created, you still might question how a cookie operates. The following steps summarize the modus operandi of a cookie:

1. In response to the request of a client, the Web server sends the information requested in the HTTP response object. In addition to this information, the server also attaches an entry in the HTTP header that instructs the browser to store data in a cookie.

2. The browser stores the data in the cookie and saves it in the user's computer.

3. When a user visits the site again, the cookie information or the cookies associated with the site is also sent along with the HTTP request object.

In other words, whenever a client requests information from the Web server that had sent it a cookie, the browser sends a copy of that cookie back to the server along with the request.

Now that you know how a cookie operates and the fact that it is stored in your computer, you will want to know where a cookie is saved and how you can view the cookies that are already stored on your computer. Based on which browser and browser version you are using, cookies are stored in different folders on your computer. If you are using a Netscape browser, then all the cookies are stored in a file named cookies.txt in Windows and in a file named magiccookie on a Macintosh. Both these files are stored in the Netscape directory. You can open and edit these files in any text editor. You can also delete any cookie that you don't wish to retain. In fact, you can delete the complete cookie file itself and delete all your cookies.

In Internet Explorer, cookies are stored in separate files with the user's name and the domain name of the site that sent the cookie. An example of such a cookie file would be yourname@www.msn.co.txt. Cookie files for Internet Explorer are stored in the /Windows/cookies directory in Windows 98 and in the /Windows/profiles/ user_name/cookies directory in Win NT, where user_name is your login name.

As already stated, you can open, edit, or delete these cookie files. You can open these files to see where they came from and check out their contents. The following example displays the contents of an Internet cookie file:

```
counterCookie_1
7
www.games.com/msn.co/
```

```
0
5246546657
6456656
3647675745
53435435
*
```

Let us suppose that the preceding code is saved with the name jerry@msn.co.txt. This filename is made up of the user name (jerry) and the domain name (msn.co). The text counterCookie_1 is the name of the cookie and 7 is its value. The URL www.games.com/msn.co/ is the domain attribute, and the numbers contain the date and other attributes. This particular cookie deploys a page counter that keeps track of how many times Jerry has visited this site. Whenever Jerry visits this page again, this cookie is sent back to the server along with the request for this page. Since the value of the cookie is set to 7, the server, on receiving the cookie, knows that it is the eighth (7+1) time this user has visited the page and thus displays the hit count 8 on the site. Responding to the request, the server increments the value 7 by 1 and sends number 8 as value back to the browser along with the requested page. In the user's computer, the old cookie file is replaced by a new cookie file.

Features of Cookies

Listed below are some of the features of cookies:

- A cookie can be associated with one or more documents on the Web server. As a consequence, when a user requests one of these documents, the browser sends the information stored in the cookie to the server.

- More than one cookie can be associated with a document on the Web server. This implies that when a user requests this document, all the information stored in the cookies associated with this document is sent to the server.

- Every cookie has a NAME-VALUE pair associated with it. This means that a cookie is identified with this NAME-VALUE pair. You'll understand this better when we create and access a cookie.

- Cookies have an expiration date associated with them. This implies that you can control a cookie's life using certain functions.

Application Areas of Cookies

Listed below are some of the common uses for cookies:

- Web page customization based on user preferences. For example, when a user visits a site, the customer is asked about his or her name and favorite color. On future visits to the site, the site greets the customer with his or her name and automatically displays that background color earlier selected by the customer.

- Storage of information when navigating across a series of forms. Even though the information stored in such situations is not persistent across multiple browser sessions, you will find many sites using cookies for such purposes.

- Bookmarks for marking locations within a site.

- Shopping carts that store order information for commercial Web sites.
- Store user ID and password so that the user does not need to retype this information on every visit to the site.
- Track how many times a user has visited a site.
- Create a To Do list.
- Track a repeat customer's name, address, and payment information so that the customer does not need to retype this information for every order.
- Maintain a user's past scores on a test or game to track progress or regress.

Limitations of Cookies

As stated earlier, cookies have a lot of uses, but they also have some limitations:

- The file that stores the cookie in the user's computer can contain a maximum of 300 cookies.
- If the limit of 300 cookies is reached and a new cookie is to be saved to a file, then the least recently accessed cookie is deleted automatically.
- A site cannot send more than 20 cookies to any client's computer.
- A cookie cannot be larger than 4 KB in size.

Having looked at the basics of cookies, we need to understand how a cookie is constructed. You can create and manipulate cookies either explicitly with a CGI program or programmatically with JavaScript at the client side only. However, before we delve into understanding and implementing cookies in JavaScript, it is important to understand the basic components of standard cookies and how they are created in a CGI script.

Constructing a Standard Cookie

In response to a request, whenever the server sends a document to the browser with whom a cookie needs to be associated, the server adds a Set-Cookie header entry to the HTTP response header sent with the document. The following is the syntax of the Set-Cookie HTTP response header that is generally used by a CGI script:

```
        Set-Cookie: NAME=VALUE; EXPIRES=Date; PATH=Path;
Domain=DOMAIN_NAME; Secure
```

The preceding syntax has several attributes. Let's take each one of these attributes in isolation and understand its relevance in cookie creation.

NAME=VALUE. The NAME=VALUE pair is used to assign a name and a value to the cookie. This pair is a string that should not include any semicolon, comma, or white space.

EXPIRES=Date. The EXPIRES=Date specifies the date when the cookie should expire. EXPIRES is an optional attribute. This implies that if no date is specified, the cookie's life is only for the current browser session. In other words, the cookie will expire as soon as the user closes the browser. The date specified in the EXPIRES attribute must be specified in the Greenwich Mean Time format, which is Wdy, DD-MM-YYYY HH:MM:SS GMT. Fortunately, the date.toGMT-String() method of JavaScript will return the date in the Greenwich Mean Time format.

PATH=Path. The PATH=Path specifies the URL of the document that placed the cookie in the user's computer. The path information in the cookie file protects the privacy of the client. This implies that a cookie placed in the client computer can be read only from a document whose path matches the path specified in the PATH attribute. Consequently, by using the PATH attribute a cookie can be set by one document but can be retrieved by one or more documents. But how is this possible? You can enable this by specifying the other document's path name.

The PATH attribute is an optional attribute. If no path is specified in this attribute, then by default, the path is assumed to be the URL of the document that placed the cookie. A forward slash (/) can be used if you want any document with a matching URL, but without a document name, to retrieve the file. Let's suppose that a cookie is placed by a document whose URL is www.geocities.com/new.html and the path name specified is /; then all documents with the URL root www.geocities.com/ can retrieve that cookie.

DOMAIN=Domain_NAME. The DOMAIN=Domain_NAME specifies the full domain name of the server that placed the cookie in the user's computer. If no domain is specified, then the default value for the domain attribute is the domain of the document that set the cookie. The DOMAIN attribute enables you to make cookies accessible to all servers within the same domain. Only servers within a specified domain can set a cookie for a domain. However, to enable this, the domain names need to have at least two or three periods to inhibit cookie setting for domains of the form .com, .edu, .org, and so on.

Secure. The Secure attribute indicates whether a cookie can be passed over an insecure communications channel. This attribute is an optional attribute. This implies that if this attribute is present, a cookie cannot be transmitted over an insecure channel. If the Secure attribute is not specified, a cookie is considered safe to be passed over insecure channels.

NOTE An HTTP response header can have multiple Set-Cookie entries. The cookies with the same path, domain, and name attributes overwrite cookies created earlier. The ability to overwrite previously created cookies provides a technique for deleting cookies. You just need to specify an expiration date that has already passed.

Interacting with a Standard Cookie

Whenever a browser requests the document with the associated cookie, a cookie string is sent in the HTTP request header along with the URL of the page. Therefore, to communicate with a cookie that has already been set in a user's computer, the HTTP request header takes the form of a list of NAME=Value pairs of cookies associated with the document being requested. The following is the syntax of the Set-Cookie HTTP request header that is generally used by a CGI script:

```
Cookie: Name1=Value1; Name2=Value2; Name3=Value3 . . . .
```

Creating a Cookie in JavaScript

Even though cookies created using CGI scripting have a mechanism to store the state information, server-side processing still needs to take place. You can also create and store cookies using JavaScript. JavaScript allows you to create and store cookies at the client side itself without any need of server-side scripting or server processing and interaction. JavaScript uses a method similar to CGI to create cookies. It uses the same client cookie files and the NAME=Value pairs that CGI uses to create and store a cookie. Instead of using the Set-Cookie header, the JavaScript code (the cookie object) creates and stores similar values.

The cookie Property

The cookie property of the document object enables you to create and store cookies in JavaScript. This property is a string that represents all the attributes of the cookies associated with a document in a script.

To set cookies in JavaScript, you need to assign values to document.cookies. The values assigned to document.cookies should be a string of the same format as is sent in the Set-Cookie field in the HTTP response header. The following statement displays an example of how you can create a new cookie in JavaScript:

```
document.cookie="firstName=Don";
```

The preceding statement creates a cookie with the name firstName and has a value Don. Since there is no expiration date specified in the preceding statement, the cookie expires as soon as the user closes its browser. In other words, it lasts only for the current browser session.

Now, consider the following statement:

```
document.cookie="lastName=Thomson; expires=Wed, 14-Aug-02 12:00:00
GMT; path=/";
```

The preceding statement creates another cookie that expires on August 14, 2002. This cookie is accessible by all documents that exist in the same domain as the current document.

Let's suppose that the preceding two cookies were set in the same document. Then the statement document.write(document.cookie) would provide the following results:

```
firstName=Don; lastName=Thomson;
```

You can also create a list of cookies in one `document.cookie` statement by separating the `name=value` pairs with semicolons. If you create a list of cookies in this
manner, be sure that the semicolons that separate the `name=value` pairs are placed
inside the text string, or the semicolons will be interpreted as the end of a JavaScript
statement. Consider the following statement:

```
document.cookie="firstName=Don;" + "lastName=Thomson;";
```

At first glance it may appear that the statement creates two cookies in one statement
and that it is correct. However, the preceding statement may generate an error. This is
because the values that can be stored in a cookie cannot contain spaces, semicolons,
commas, or any other special characters. In the next section, let us look at how
JavaScript deals with this.

Encoding and Decoding Values for Cookies

As you already know, the transmission of any data between Web browsers and Web
servers uses HTTP. During transmission, HTTP does not allow certain nonalphanu-
meric characters to be transmitted in their native format. Therefore, it is good practice
to encode text before assigning it to the `cookie` property. Encoding includes converting special characters in a text string to their corresponding hexadecimal ASCII values.
These hexadecimal values are to be preceded by a (%) percent sign. Consider the following statement:

```
Thanks=Thanks for visiting our site !
```

After encoding the characters in this string, the preceding statement would read as
follows:

```
Thanks= Thanks%20for%20visiting%20our%20site%20%21
```

In the preceding statement, 20 is the hexadecimal ASCII equivalent of a space character and 21 is the hexadecimal ASCII equivalent of an exclamation mark (!).
The `escape()` method is used to encode strings in JavaScript. The following is the
syntax of writing the `escape()` method:

```
escape(text);
```

The following statements create multiple cookies in a variable named `multiple-
Cookies`. The variable is then encoded with the `escape()` method and assigned to
the `cookie` property of the `document` object.

```
multipleCookies="firstName=Don;" + "lastName=Thomson;";
document.cookie=escape(multipleCookie);
```

Similarly, while reading a cookie, the `unescape()` method is used to decode the
information stored in the cookie file. The syntax of the `unescape()` method is
`unescape(text);`.

Using Date Object for Specifying Expiration Dates

Until now, the examples that we cited for creating cookies explicitly specified the date in the format Wdy, DD-MM-YYYY HH:MM:SS GMT. However, there can be situations where you want the cookie to expire after a stipulated period of time from the date the user accesses your site. For instance, you may want your cookie to expire after 1 year from the date the user first accesses your site. You can use the Date object to manipulate date and time in such situations. Creating a new Date object gives access to the current date and time of the user's computer in a variable. You can then manipulate the date and time in the variable by using various methods of the Date object.

The following statements create an expiration date 1 year ahead of the current date and then set a cookie with that expiration date.

```
var expiryDate = new Date();
expiryDate.setTime(expiryDate.getTime() + 24*60*60*365*1000);
multipleCookies="firstName=Don;" + "lastName=Thomson;" +
document.cookie=escape(multipleCookie) + ";expires=" +
expiryDate.toGMTString();
```

In the statement expiryDate.getTime() + 24 * 60 * 60 * 365 * 1000, the date is calculated based on the following: 365 days in a year, 24 hours in a day, 60 minutes in an hour, 60 seconds in a minute, and 1000 milliseconds in a second.

Until now, we have just gained a theoretical insight into setting and retrieving cookies in JavaScript. Now is the time to put theory into practice. This chapter provides you with the standard code that you can use to set and retrieve cookies from any application. This code has been developed by Bill Dortch, who has put in a considerable amount of effort in developing it. This code is freely available in the public domain and has been used extensively by a number of Web sites.

Due to its comprehensive nature, the code developed by Bill Dortch has more or less become a standard in the industry for creating and retrieving cookies. We'll cover the SetCookie(), GetCookie(), and getCookieVal() functions developed by Bill Dortch in the next section. The SetCookie() function helps you set a cookie. The GetCookie() and getCookieVal() functions help you retrieve cookies.

The SetCookie() Function

To use Bill Dortch's SetCookie() function, you just need to copy the code into your scripts. When the function is in place, simply pass arguments needed to create the cookie to set the cookie. For clarity, we'll break the code into small code fragments and then give an explanation for each statement. However, we will first consider the complete SetCookie() function.

```
function SetCookie (name, value) {
var argv = SetCookie.arguments;
var argc = SetCookie.arguments.length;
var expires = (argc > 2) ? argv[2] : null;
var path = (argc > 3) ? argv[3] : null;
var domain = (argc > 4) ? argv[4] : null;
var secure = (argc > 5) ? argv[5] : false;
```

```
document.cookie = name + "=" + escape (value) +
((expires == null) ? "" : ("; expires=" + expires.toGMTString())) +
((path == null) ? "" : ("; path=" + path)) +
((domain == null) ? "" : ("; domain=" + domain)) + ((secure == true) ?
"; secure" : ""));
}
```

Here is the explanation of the preceding code:

1. While setting a cookie, it is essential to pass the name and value of that cookie. Passing all the other attributes is optional. This is because the SetCookie() function assumes that:

The expires attribute takes a null value. This implies that the cookie is supposed to expire at the end of the current browser session.

The path attribute takes a null value. This implies that only the current document can interact with the cookie.

The domain attribute also takes a null value. This implies that only the server from where the site is accessed can communicate with the cookie.

2. When the SetCookie() function is called, the function resolves the number of arguments that have been passed. Although there is no restriction on the number of arguments that are passed to the SetCookie() function, the function can take as many as six arguments.

3. Since a user-defined function will pass the arguments to the SetCookie() function, any string passed to this function becomes an argument property. The SetCookie() function first assigns the value of the argument string (arguments passed by a user-defined function) into the variable argv. The following statement assigns the value of the argument string into the variable argv.

```
var argv = SetCookie.arguments;
```

4. Next, the function calculates the length of the arguments passed by using the length property of the String object. The calculated value is assigned to the variable argc by the following statement:

```
var argc = SetCookie.arguments.length;
```

5. After determining the number of arguments that have been passed to the Set-Cookie() function, these values are assigned to the variables. However, since the name and value of the cookies are always passed, there is no need to create separate variables for these arguments.

6. The argv variable is an array that contains the argument string. The code now checks whether the total values passed as argument are more than 2. If this is true, then the function assigns the third argument in the argv array to the expires variable. But otherwise, the function assigns the value null to the expires variable. The following statement assigns value to the variable argv:

```
var expires = (argc > 2) ? argv[2] : null;
```

7. Similarly, the `SetCookie()` function checks whether the `argv` variable contains values more than 3. It then checks whether it is greater than 4 and lastly checks if the value is greater than 5. The following statements assign respective values to the array `argv`.

```
var path = (argc > 3) ? argv[3] : null;
var domain = (argc > 4) ? argv[4] : null;
var secure = (argc > 5) ? argv[5] : false;
```

8. After all the values are assigned in the `SetCookie()` function, the function concatenates the values into a cookie string and then sets these values into the `cookie` property of the `document` object. The following statement concatenates and assigns the values to the `cookie` property:

```
document.cookie = name + "=" + escape (value) +
((expires == null) ? "" : ("; expires=" + expires.toGMTString())) +
((path == null) ? "" : ("; path=" + path)) + ((domain == null) ? "" :
("; domain=" + domain)) + ((secure == true) ? "; secure" : ""));
```

In this section, we mentioned that to set a cookie, all you need to do is to copy the `SetCookie()` function into your scripts. Although this statement is correct, it is also deceptive. This is because your code will generate errors because the `SetCookie()` function may not have any other function that would pass arguments to it.

In order to discuss the user-defined function that will pass values to the `SetCookie()` function, let's go back to our scenario of Web Shoppe. One of the requirements of this scenario was to display a welcome message that greets the user by his or her name. The moment that the home page of Web Shoppe loads in a Web browser, it prompts the customer to enter his or her name. When the user enters his or her name, the page displays a personalized message. The following function passes the values to the `SetCookie()` function.

```
function Who(info){
    var VisitorName = GetCookie('VisitorName')
    if (VisitorName == null) {
        VisitorName = prompt("Who are you?");
        SetCookie ('VisitorName', VisitorName, exp);
    }
    return VisitorName;
}
```

NOTE You'll notice that the preceding code also calls the `GetCookie()` function. For now, let us assume that since no cookie has been set until now, the `GetCookie()` function returns `null`. We'll discuss the `GetCookie()` function in detail a little later. Also, this is not the only user-defined function that will be used for Web Shoppe. The details of other functions and how exactly the program flows will also be discussed after we are finished with the `GetCookie()` function.

There is no point in setting a cookie if it cannot be retrieved. Bill Dortch has provided two methods, GetCookie() and getCookieVal(), to retrieve value from a cookie.

The GetCookie() Function

The GetCookie() function takes the name of the cookie that you wish to retrieve as an argument. When you call the GetCookie() function, be sure that you pass the correct name of the cookie that you wish to retrieve. The GetCookie() function then requests the cookie property of the document to return the contents of the cookie file. The GetCookie() function identifies the location of the cookie that corresponds to the argument passed to this function. It then passes this location to the getCookieVal() function that ultimately returns the value saved in the cookie requested. Before we delve into more details of the GetCookie() function, let's display the complete code of this function. For better understanding, we'll then break the code into small code snippets and give an explanation for each statement.

```
function GetCookie (name) {
   var arg = name + "=";
   var alen = arg.length;
   var clen = document.cookie.length;
   var i = 0;
   while (i < clen) {
      var j = i + alen;
      if (document.cookie.substring(i, j) == arg)
         return getCookieVal (j);
      i = document.cookie.indexOf(" ", i) + 1;
      if (i == 0) break;
   }
   return null;
}
function getCookieVal (offset) {
   var endstr = document.cookie.indexOf (";", offset);
   if (endstr == -1)
      endstr = document.cookie.length;
   return unescape(document.cookie.substring(offset, endstr));
}
```

Here is the explanation of the preceding code:

1. The GetCookie() function assigns values to a list of variables in the following manner:

The function assigns the value that you passed as the name of the cookie plus =(equal sign) to the arg variable.

```
var arg = name + "=";
```

It then assigns the length of the string created by arg variable (name=) to the alen variable.

```
var alen = arg.length;
```

Next, the function stores the length of the `cookie` property in `clen` variable.

2. The `GetCookie()` function then repeats the `while` statement on condition that the variable `i` which was initialized to 0 is less than the length of the cookie file which is stored in variable `clen`.

3. Inside the `while` statement, a new variable `j` is assigned the value `i + alen`.

If the cookie property of the document object contains a substring, which is equivalent to `arg`, the `getCookieVal()` function is called. This function is passed to the char position contained in variable `j`. This location identifies the location of the first char appearing after `name=`.

Write the Code

The following is the code for the home page of Web Shoppe. This page displays a personalized message and the number of times a customer visited the site along with the date when the customer last visited the site:

```
<HTML>
<HEAD>
<TITLE>Web Shoppe</TITLE>
<SCRIPT LANGUAGE="JavaScript">
var WWHCount;
var expDays = 30;
var exp = new Date();
exp.setTime(exp.getTime() + (expDays*24*60*60*1000));
function Who(info){
    var VisitorName = GetCookie('VisitorName')
    if (VisitorName == null) {
       VisitorName = prompt("Who are you?");
       SetCookie ('VisitorName', VisitorName, exp);
    }
    return VisitorName;
}
function When(){
    var rightNow = new Date();
    var WWHTime = 0;
    WWHTime = GetCookie('WWhenH');
    var a=WWHTime;
    WWHTime = WWHTime * 1
    var lastHereFormatting = new Date(WWHTime);
    var lastHereInDateFormat = "" + lastHereFormatting;
    var dayOfWeek = lastHereInDateFormat.substring(0,3);
    var dateMonth = lastHereInDateFormat.substring(4,11);
    var timeOfDay = lastHereInDateFormat.substring(11,16);
    var year = lastHereInDateFormat.substring(23,25);
    var WWHText = dayOfWeek + ", " + dateMonth + " at " + timeOfDay
    SetCookie ("WWhenH", rightNow.getTime(), exp);
    if(a==null){
       var space=" ";
       return space;
```

```
      }
      else{
         return WWHText;
      }
   }
function Count(info){
   WWHCount = GetCookie('WWHCount')
   if (WWHCount == null) {
      WWHCount = 1;
   }
   else{
      WWHCount++;
   }
   SetCookie ('WWHCount', WWHCount, exp);
      return WWHCount;
}
function set(){
   VisitorName = prompt("Who are you?");
   SetCookie ('VisitorName', VisitorName, exp);
   SetCookie ('WWHCount', 0, exp);
   SetCookie ('WWhenH', 0, exp);
}
function getCookieVal (offset) {
   var endstr = document.cookie.indexOf (";", offset);
   if (endstr == -1)
      endstr = document.cookie.length;
      return unescape(document.cookie.substring(offset, endstr));
}
function GetCookie (name) {
   var arg = name + "=";
   var alen = arg.length;
   var clen = document.cookie.length;
   var i = 0;
   while (i < clen) {
      var j = i + alen;
      if (document.cookie.substring(i, j) == arg)
         return getCookieVal (j);
      i = document.cookie.indexOf(" ", i) + 1;
      if (i == 0) break;
   }
   return null;
}
function SetCookie (name, value) {
   var argv = SetCookie.arguments;
   var argc = SetCookie.arguments.length;
   var expires = (argc > 2) ? argv[2] : null;
   var path = (argc > 3) ? argv[3] : null;
   var domain = (argc > 4) ? argv[4] : null;
   var secure = (argc > 5) ? argv[5] : false;
   document.cookie = name + "=" + escape (value) +
   ((expires == null) ? "" : ("; expires=" +
```

```
            expires.toGMTString())) +
                ((path == null) ? "" : ("; path=" + path)) +
                ((domain == null) ? "" : ("; domain=" + domain)) +
                ((secure == true) ? "; secure" : "");
        }
        function DeleteCookie (name) {
            var exp = new Date();
            exp.setTime (exp.getTime() - 1);
            var cval = GetCookie (name);
            document.cookie = name + "=" + cval + "; expires=" +
    exp.toGMTString();
        }
        </SCRIPT>
        </HEAD>
        <BODY>
        <TABLE BORDER="1" WIDTH="101%" HEIGHT="234" BORDERCOLOR="#FFFFFF">
        <TR>
        <TD WIDTH="26%" BGCOLOR="#CCCCFF" HEIGHT="56"> </TD>
        <TD WIDTH="73%" BGCOLOR="#9F81C0" HEIGHT="56"><STRONG><U><FONT
    FACE="Arial" COLOR="#CCCCFF" size="6">Web
        Shoppe</FONT></U></STRONG></TD>
        <TD WIDTH="26%" HEIGHT="56" BGCOLOR="#9F81C0"> </TD>
        </TR>
        <TR>
        <TD WIDTH="26%" BGCOLOR="#CCCCFF" HEIGHT="166"> </TD>
        <TD WIDTH="73%" HEIGHT="166"><FONT COLOR="#5E00BB" SIZE="3"
    FACE="Arial">Experience the world's largest shopping and entertainment
    center at the mall of Web Shoppe Inc. Web Shoppe has over 350 stores and
    services, over 110 eatery joints, plus seven Superb Attractions. It's
    the only Web shopping mall of its kind - both a shopper's dream and a
    world of excitement and adventure. Open round the clock, millions of
    visitors from around the world visit this outstanding mall, which
    features sale of flowers, books, confectionery, cards, computers, and
    much more.
     </FONT></TD>
        <TD WIDTH="26%" HEIGHT="166"><IMG BORDER="0" SRC="Product.png"
    WIDTH="217" HEIGHT="230"></TD>
        </TR>
        </TABLE>
        <HR color="#9F81C0" style="border-style: dotted">
        <SCRIPT LANGUAGE="JavaScript">
        document.write("<FONT SIZE='3' COLOR='#5E00BB'> Hello <B>" + Who()
    + ". </B></FONT>");
        document.write("<FONT SIZE='3' COLOR='#5E00BB'> You've been on our
    site " + Count() + " time(s). "+  "</FONT>");
        if(WWHCount >1){
            document.write("<FONT SIZE='3' COLOR='#5E00BB'> Last time you
    were on our site on " + When() + ". </FONT>");
        }
         else{
            document.write(When());
```

```
}
</SCRIPT>
<HR STYLE="border-style: dotted" COLOR="#9F81C0">
</BODY>
  </HTML>
```

Execute and Verify the Successful Running of the Code

To verify the successful running of the code, execute the code in Internet Explorer and perform the following steps:

- Enter your name in the message box that prompts you to enter your name. The moment you click OK button of this message box you should see a welcome message that greets you with your name in the message. It also displays the message that this is the first time you have visited the site. Now, close the home page.

- Load the home page of Web Shoppe again after 5 minutes. Notice that this time the personalized welcome message appears without prompting you to enter your name. In addition, the Web page displays that this is your second visit to the site. The page also displays the date and time when you last visited the site.

Figure 9.1 displays the home page of Web Shoppe after the customer's first visit to the site.

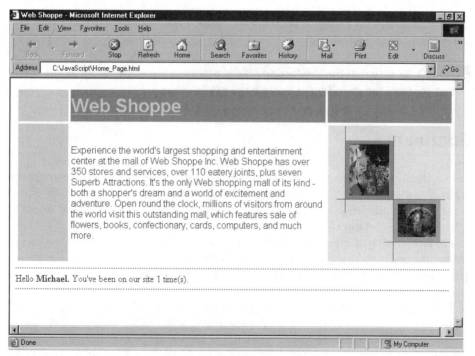

Figure 9.1   The home page of Web Shoppe after first visit.

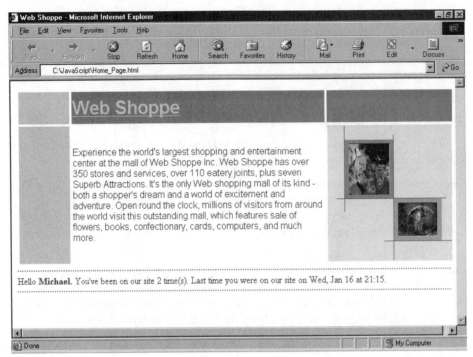

Figure 9.2 The home page of Web Shoppe after second visit.

Figure 9.2 displays the home page of Web Shoppe after the customer's second visit to the site.

> **NOTE** Be sure that the Product.png file is placed in the same folder as the file that contains the code for the home page of Web Shoppe.

Summary

In this chapter, you learned to maintain the state information of a Web browser. You learned that even though the stateless design of the Internet was fast and efficient, it also had some problems. This chapter gave you an insight on why and how the stateful design of the Internet evolved.

The next section of the chapter introduced you to cookies. Here, you learned about the modus operandi of a cookie, its common features, application areas, and its limitations. This section also introduced you to constructing and interacting with a standard cookie using CGI.

The chapter then introduced you to creating cookies in JavaScript. You learned how to use the `cookie` property of the `document` object to save and retrieve values from a cookie. Next, you also learned the importance of encoding and decoding data of cookies while transmitting them over HTTP. You learned to use the date object for specifying expiration dates of cookies. Finally, you learned about Bill Dortch's `SetCookie()` and `GetCookie()` functions.

CHAPTER 10

JavaScript and Plug-ins

Getting Started

With the ever-increasing use of the Internet, Web applications are becoming more and more important to the corporate world. In addition, the expectations from Web applications have also changed considerably. Users want Web applications to be as interactive as possible. For example, nowadays it is not enough for commercial music Web sites to display static catalogs of audio and video files. Today, commercial music Web sites need to include embedded video files that display all the products in the catalog. Other music sites also have the technical specifications of the products available in the portable document format (PDF). This helps music lovers listen to their favorite music online. Many music Web sites also feature the latest movie releases and play clips.

Commercial Web sites provide such functionality, but they use different file formats. However, users may not be able to open a particular file in their Web browser because their Web browser may not support the file format. By default, browsers can handle a few file formats only. However, there are many file formats that are available as proprietary formats from third parties. In such cases, the Web browser requires additional help in the form of plug-ins to recognize the file formats. If the browser cannot process some data in a file on its own, a plug-in is downloaded and installed.

In this chapter, you will examine plug-ins and understand how JavaScript works with plug-ins. To understand how plug-ins work, we will consider the case of Web Shoppe, Inc. The pages of the Web Shoppe site apply plug-ins.

Using Plug-ins

Problem Statement

The top management of Web Shoppe has decided to place a video file displaying the new product line of the store. Cynthia, the designer of this page, has assigned Scott, a Web developer, to add this functionality in the page.

Task List

To incorporate the functionality mentioned in the problem statement, the following task list has been identified:

✔ **Identify the objects that are used to work with plug-ins by using JavaScript.**

✔ **Write the code.**

✔ **Execute and verify the code.**

Identify the Objects that Are Used to Work with Plug-Ins by Using JavaScript

Before identifying the methods to use plug-ins with JavaScript, let us first understand what plug-ins are and how they function.

About Plug-ins

As mentioned earlier, a plug-in is required if a Web browser does not support data formats. Therefore, before we try to get an insight into plug-ins, let us first consider the type of information that a browser can support.

Consider a typical Web communication scenario. A browser requests information from the server. In response to the request, the server sends information to the browser. The information or the data received can be in different formats. The commonly used Web browsers support common data formats, such as text files and images. However, there are many other data formats that a browser does not support natively. A browser that can support data formats natively has a built-in capability to work with a specific data format or type. Each data type has a Multipart Internet Mail Extension type

(MIME type) associated with it. Plug-ins are code modules developed to work with MIME types that are not supported natively by Web browsers. When a browser receives an unknown data type from a server, the browser searches for the plug-in that is associated with the MIME type. Then, the browser loads the specific plug-in. This enables the user to view the data.

Plug-ins are available for almost all types of data. Some of the commonly used plug-ins are Adobe Acrobat viewer, RealPlayer, QuickTime, and Macromedia Flash. The Acrobat viewer of Adobe is used to view PDF documents. This can be used to display any PDF document on a site. RealPlayer is used to play audio and video files. Quick-Time is another plug-in used to display video files.

In Netscape Navigator 4.77, it is possible to determine the existing plug-ins installed on a computer. To determine the existing plug-ins, click the About Plug-ins option on the Help menu. This will display the details of the plug-ins installed on the user's computer. The details include the MIME types to which a plug-in is related. The About Plug-ins page also indicates whether the plug-ins are enabled. This feature is useful if you need to obtain information about the plug-ins already installed.

Figure 10.1 displays the About Plug-ins page in Netscape 4.77.

In Netscape Navigator 6, the About Plug-ins option is not present. The details of the plug-ins installed and MIME types supported are briefly stated in the About Netscape option on the Help menu. However, with the release of Netscape version 6.2, the About Plug-ins option is present under the same Help menu.

Figure 10.2 displays the About Plug-ins page in Netscape 6.2.

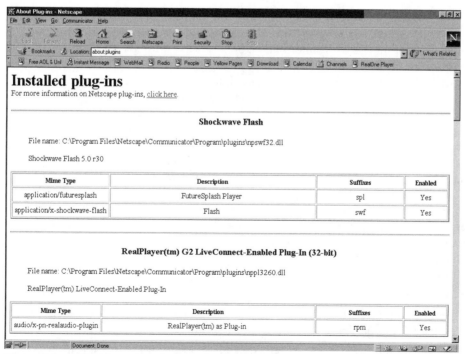

Figure 10.1 The About Plug-ins page in Netscape 4.77.

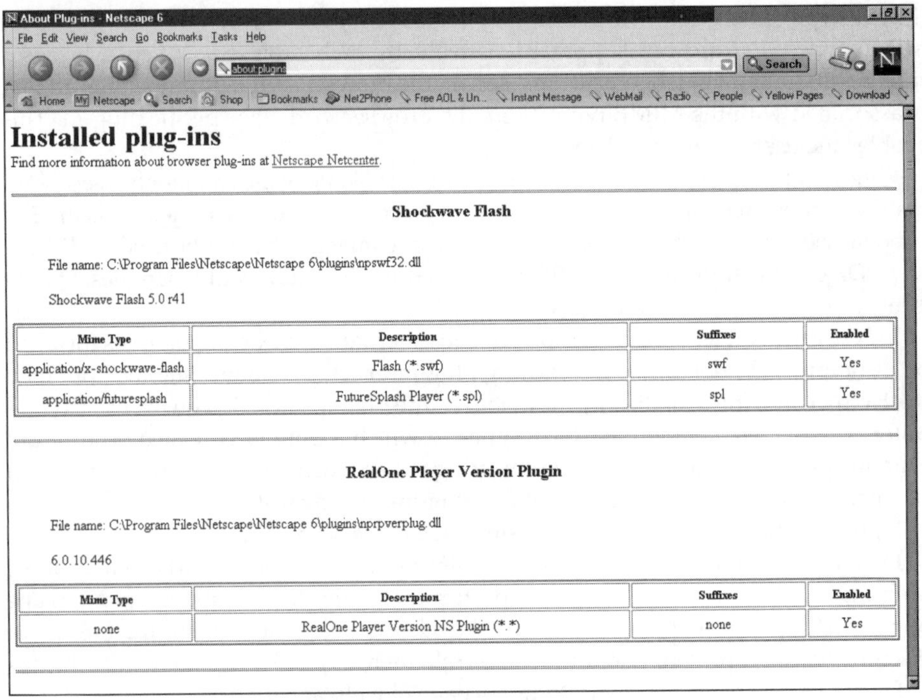

Figure 10.2 The About Plug-ins page in Netscape 6.2.

We have given you an overview of plug-ins and why plug-ins are required by a browser. To summarize this information, browsers use MIME types to detect the data type and then display the files accordingly. Plug-ins are developed to support specific MIME types. One plug-in can support multiple MIME types. For example, the Quick-Time plug-in can be used with TIFF images and MPEG audio files. There are many more MIME types that can be managed by the QuickTime plug-in.

How does a browser detect the MIME types it can support? Even though Netscape Navigator gives us the Help option to view the default plug-ins installed, how can we extract more detailed information about the plug-ins supported by a browser? The navigator object of JavaScript enables us to view detailed information about MIME types supported by a browser and the plug-ins installed.

The navigator object has a built-in object that contains information related to a browser. It has properties called mimeTypes and plugins. Let us now consider the property called mimeTypes in detail. The mimeTypes property is an array that contains mimeTypes objects. A mimeTypes object in turn has four properties that provide information related to the MIME types that are supported by a browser. The following are the properties of a mimeTypes object:

description. This property returns the description of the data type contained by the MimeType object.

enabledPlugin. This property finds the plug-in associated with a specific MIME type. If there is no plug-in associated with the MIME types, then this property returns null.

suffixes. This property returns a list of file extensions for the specific MIME type.

type. This property specifies the name of the MIME type.

NOTE Only the Netscape browser supports the `mimeTypes` **property of the** `navigator` **object. In Internet Explorer 5.x and 6.0, this property does not give the correct results. The** `navigator.mimeTypes` **shows an undefined value and the** `length` **property,** `navigator.mimeTypes.length`, **contains the value 0. Therefore,** `navigator.mimeTypes` **cannot be used with Internet Explorer browsers.**

The `mimeTypes` object has no methods and events associated with it.

Now that you are familiar with the properties of the `mimeTypes` object, let us consider the following example that will help explain how these properties are used to extract information about MIME types supported by the Netscape browser.

```
<HTML>
<HEAD>
<TITLE> Example of how to extract the information related to
supported MIME types </TITLE>
</HEAD>
<BODY>
<P>
<B>This page describes all the MIME types currently supported by
this browser.</B>
<SCRIPT LANGUAGE = "JavaScript">
    document.writeln("<HR>");
    var navmime = navigator.mimeTypes;
    var navmimelength = navigator.mimeTypes.length
    for (var mimeobj=0; mimeobj<navmimelength; ++mimeobj) {
       with(document) {
          writeln("<B> MIME Type is: </B>" + navmime[mimeobj].type +
"<BR>");
          writeln("<B> Description is: </B>" +
navmime[mimeobj].description + "<BR>");
          writeln("<B>Suffixes are: </B>" +
navmime[mimeobj].suffixes + "<BR>");
          writeln("<HR>");
       }
    }
</SCRIPT>
</BODY>
</HTML>
```

The preceding code uses the properties of the `mimeTypes` object. The code declares the variable `navmime` that is assigned the array of `mimeTypes` objects. This variable is further used in the code to refer to the properties of `mimeTypes` objects. A variable, `navmimelength`, is used to capture the number of MIME types that are supported by the browser. The code uses a `for` statement to go through all the MIME types and displays the type, description, and suffix properties for that MIME type. When the value of `mimeobj` exceeds the number of MIME types, the code exits the `for` state-ment. In this way, all the MIME types and related information are made available on a Web page. This code executes successfully in the Netscape browser but not in Internet Explorer.

The preceding code uses the `with` statement. The `with` statement provides expedi-ency to programmers as it eliminates retyping the name of an object that is to be refer-enced repeatedly in a set of statements. The following is the syntax of the `with` statement:

```
with(Object_name){
    statements
}
```

The following example illustrates the use of the `with` statement:

```
with(document){
    write("This is an example to test the with statement.");
    write("These statements will be printed on the document.");
}
```

In the preceding example, the need to attach the `document` object to the statement `document.write("This is an example to test the with statement.")` is eliminated because the object document is identified in the `with` statement. The pre-ceding code can also be written as:

```
document.write("This is an example to test the with statement.");
document.write("These statements will be printed on the
document.");
```

Figure 10.3 displays the MIME Types supported by the Netscape browser.

NOTE The preceding code will also execute in the Netscape 6.2 browser.

The `plugins` Property

The `navigator` object has a property called `plugins`. While working with plug-ins, you may want to know what plug-ins are already installed on a user's computer. This property returns the details of the plug-ins installed on a browser. These details are returned through an array. Each element in this array is a `plugins` object. The `plug-ins` object provides information about all the installed plug-ins through five proper-ties. These properties are:

description.   This property provides a description of the plug-in.

filename.   This property provides the name of the file (with the full path) for a plug-in.

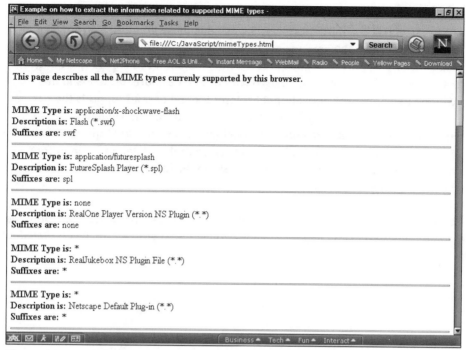

Figure 10.3 MIME types supported by the Netscape 6 browser.

length. This property returns the number of the MIME types supported by the plug-in.

name. This property specifies the name of the plug-in.

mimeTypes. Each `plugins` object has a property that specifies the MIME type that the `plugins` object supports. This contains an array of the MIME types supported by a particular plug-in. All the elements in this array are `mimeTypes` objects. This is confusing because `mimeTypes` exist as a property of the `navigator` object and as a property of the `plugins` object, which in turn is a property of the `navigator` object. There is not much difference between the information returned by the `mimeTypes` object and the `mimeTypes` object as a property of the `plugins` object. The only difference is that the information provided by the `plugins` object is more comprehensive than that provided by the `mimeTypes` object.

Using the index, information can be extracted from a `plugins` array. For example, to obtain the name of the first plug-in in the array, write the following statement:

```
document.write (navigator.plugins[0].name);
```

NOTE Only the Netscape browser supports the preceding properties of the `plugins` **object. In Internet Explorer 5.x and 6.0, these properties do not give the correct results. The** `navigator.plugins` **shows an undefined value and the** `length` **property;** `navigator.plugins.length`, **contains the value 0. The** `navigator.plugins` **cannot be used with Internet Explorer browsers in the Windows environment. The Internet Explorer 5.x and beyond supports the** `navigator.plugins` **array in the Mac environment. For the Windows environment, VBScript is required to detect plug-ins in Internet Explorer 5.x and 6.0. The plug-ins are implemented as ActiveX controls in Internet Explorer for the Windows environment. You can use VBScript inside the JavaScript functions to detect the ActiveX controls.**

Using the preceding properties, the following example will demonstrate how the information related to the plug-ins already installed for a browser can be presented to the user:

```
<HTML>
<HEAD>
<TITLE> Example on how to extract the information related to
installed plug-ins </TITLE>
</HEAD>
<BODY>
<P>
<B>This page describes all the plug-ins currently installed for
this browser. It also displays the MIME types supported by each plug-in.
</B>
<P>
<SCRIPT LANGUAGE = "JavaScript">
  document.writeln("<HR>");
  var CurrPlugins = navigator.plugins;
  var CurrLength = navigator.plugins.length
  for (var plugobj=0;plugobj<CurrLength;++plugobj) {
    with(document) {
        writeln('<P><B> Plug-in Name is: </B>' + CurrPlugins
[plugobj].name + '<BR>');
        writeln('<B> Description is: </B>' + CurrPlugins
[plugobj].description + '<BR>');
        writeln('<B> File Name is: </B>' + CurrPlugins
[plugobj].filename + '<BR>');
        writeln('<B> Supported MIME Types are: </B>');
        for (var mimeobj=0;mimeobj< CurrPlugins
[plugobj].length;++mimeobj) {
            writeln(CurrPlugins [plugobj][mimeobj].type + '<BR>');
        }
        writeln("<HR>");
    }
  }
```

```
</SCRIPT>
</BODY>
</HTML>
```

The preceding code sample uses the properties of the `plugins` object. This code also refers to these properties through proper inheritance. A variable, `CurrPlugins`, is assigned the array of the `plugins` objects. This variable is further used in the code to refer to the properties of the `plugins` object. Another variable, `CurrLength`, is used to capture the number of plug-ins that are currently installed for the browser. The code uses a `for` statement to go through all the plug-ins and outputs the name, description, and filename properties for the plug-in. In addition, it outputs the different MIME types that are supported by the plug-in. This is achieved by creating another `for` statement within the first `for` statement. The second `for` statement executes for every plug-in until all the MIME types for the plug-ins are listed. When the value of `mimeobj` exceeds the number of MIME types supported by the plug-in, the code exits the inner `for` statement. As you may have noticed, the length used in the inner `for` statement specifies the number of MIME types supported by the plug-in. When all the details for all the plug-ins are listed, the outer loop is terminated. In this way, all the installed plug-ins and related information are made available on a Web page. This code executes successfully in the Netscape browser, but not in Internet Explorer.

Figure 10.4 displays the plug-ins supported by the Netscape 6.0 browser.

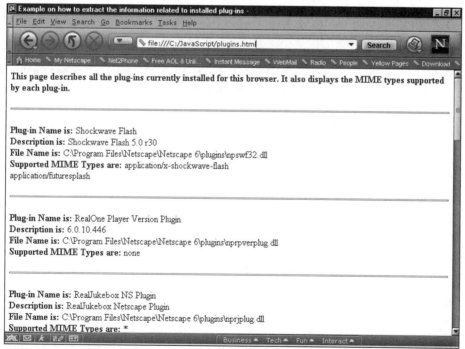

Figure 10.4 Plug-ins supported by the Netscape 6.0 browser.

NOTE The preceding code will also execute in the Netscape 6.2 browser.

You have now learned how to view MIME types and the plug-in information that a browser supports. You will now learn how to insert plug-ins in a document.

Inserting Plug-in Documents

Plug-ins are software modules that execute in the periphery of a browser window. Executing in the periphery of a browser window implies that plug-ins are compiled in the native executable code format of the operating system in which they are executed. In addition, we also know that plug-ins are used to view different MIME type documents in a browser. Now the question arises, how are plug-ins inserted in a document? Before we discuss this, however, there is another related concept that you need to know. How are plug-in documents viewed in a window? Plug-in documents can be viewed in two modes, embedded and full-page. In the embedded mode, a dedicated area of the HTML document is assigned to the plug-in document or else the plug-in document will overwrite the complete HTML document. This implies that the plug-in is displayed as part of the currently loaded document in the same browser window. In the full-page mode, the plug-in document is displayed in a separate browser window.

The manner in which you insert a plug-in document determines the appearance of the plug-in document. For example, a plug-in document that is inserted in an embedded mode appears different from a plug-in document that is inserted in a full-page mode. When you use the <EMBED> tag to insert a plug-in document in a window, the plug-in is displayed in the embedded mode. When you use a URL to reference a plug-in document in a window, the document is displayed in the full-page mode. The <A> tag is used when plug-ins are referenced.

The section below covers both methods. Let us begin by discussing the first method of inserting a plug-in in a document, that is, using the <EMBED> tag.

Using the <EMBED> tag

The <EMBED> tag is used to refer to a plug-in document. It has many attributes. Some of these attributes are processed by the <EMBED> tag for processing. The other attributes are passed on to the plug-in associated with the MIME type of the data object used in the <EMBED> tag. The syntax for the <EMBED> tag is:

```
<EMBED Attribute1 Attribute 2.....>
```

It is imperative for an <EMBED> tag to contain either an SRC or a TYPE attribute. Let us first discuss the SRC attribute. The SRC attribute is used to specify the data object, which is the plug-in document in this case. The following statement illustrates how a plug-in document is inserted using the SRC attribute.

```
<EMBED SRC="document.pdf">
```

In the preceding statement, the document specified in the SRC attribute can also be a video or audio file.

While processing the <EMBED> tag, the browser uses the value in the SRC attribute to determine the MIME type of the document. The browser receives this information from the Web server. After the MIME type is identified, the browser tries to locate the plug-in for that MIME type. A mimeTypes object array is used to find the plug-in for the MIME type returned by the Web server. If the browser finds a plug-in, it creates an instance of that plug-in. The document in the SRC attribute is then loaded in that instance. The content of the document is passed on to the plug-in in the data stream. The plug-in reads the data and displays the content based on the MIME type. When the page containing the plug-in document is no longer displayed in the browser window, the plug-in instance associated with the document is deleted. When all the instances are deleted, the plug-in is unloaded from the memory.

You can also use the TYPE attribute instead of the SRC attribute. The TYPE attribute is used by plug-ins that are not intended to be used as viewers to display documents. Instead, the TYPE attribute is used to create browser-based applications that may not necessarily be document-specific. This implies that the TYPE attribute is used to create embedded applications that may not display a specific document. The TYPE attribute specifies the MIME type without referring to a specific document. The main purpose of such embedded applications is to perform a service that is independent of a particular document. An example of an embedded application is SCIENCE.ORG's transferRNA plug-in. This plug-in is used to transfer files from one user to another.

How do plug-ins work if they are not associated with a document of a specific MIME type? Embedded application plug-ins are associated with a MIME type, but not with a specific document of that MIME type. The following statement includes the transferRNA plug-in within a document.

```
<EMBED TYPE="application/x-transferRNA">
```

When the browser loads the document with the preceding statement and encounters the preceding statement, it uses the TYPE attribute to determine the MIME type that needs to be associated with the plug-in. It then locates the plug-in registered for that MIME type in its MIME type table.

The other attributes of the <EMBED> tag that are generally used are mentioned below:

- **NAME.** This attribute identifies the embedded object uniquely so that it can be referenced by the other elements in the document. It can accept character string values.

- **HEIGHT, WIDTH.** These attributes control the displayed region for the document. You should specify these attributes in pixels.

- **HIDDEN.** This attribute is used to make the object invisible to the user. This can be used to generate background music. However, while working with the documents, this attribute is not very useful.

- **PALETTE.** This attribute is used to specify the foreground and background colors that the plug-in will use. This attribute is handled differently by Netscape Communicator and Internet Explorer. Therefore, while using this attribute, you need to refer to the documentation of the specific browser.

- **PLUGINSPAGE.** This attribute is used when the plug-in is not available on a user's computer. It specifies the address of a Web page where the usage and the download instructions related to the missing plug-in are provided. Only Netscape Communicator supports this attribute.

- **UNITS.** This attribute allows the user to specify the unit of measure for the height and width of the display area. The default unit of measure is pixels. It can also be set to en. When using en units, the size of the plug-in display can change in proportion to the other text on the same page.

Different plug-ins may need more attributes based on their functioning, but it is not possible to explain all the attributes here. A better way to know about all the required attributes is to consult the documentation of the specific plug-in.

Using the `<A>` tag

To display a plug-in document in a separate browser window, use the `<A>` tag. The plug-in document will be called from the `<A>` tag by using the attributes of this tag. Consider the following example:

```
<A HREF = "document.pdf"> This is your plug-in document.</A>
```

This is a sample syntax for an `<A>` tag. The HREF attribute contains the name of the document to be displayed. This document can also be any video or audio file. The process of document display begins when you click the link. As a first step, the browser will request the MIME type of the document from the Web server. It will then search for the MIME type in the `mimeTypes` object array. If it finds a match, it will try to obtain the name of the corresponding plug-in. If the required plug-in is available, it will be loaded and an instance of that plug-in will be initiated. The user will see the document in full view in the new browser window. The user can now interact with the plug-in document. The plug-in instance will be deleted when the window is closed.

In this section, you learned how plug-ins are embedded in an HTML document. The `<EMBED>` tag is used to insert plug-ins in the HTML documents. However, using JavaScript, you can also control the plug-ins inserted in a document. The following section covers controlling plug-ins.

Using JavaScript to Control Plug-ins

To control plug-ins in JavaScript, the `embeds` object is used. The `embeds` object refers to any embedded object in the HTML document. A collection of all these objects is referred to as an `embeds` array. This object is a property of the `document` object. You can reference each object in the `embeds` array by using the index of the `embeds` object array. The ability to reference the `embeds` object helps you control the plug-in document. There is another method by which you can control the plug-in. You can use the value specified in the NAME attribute of the `<EMBED>` tag. Before we consider an example of the `embeds` object, let us first examine how you specify the NAME attribute in the `<EMBED>` tag.

When an `<EMBED>` tag is used in a page, you can add an attribute NAME to that tag. This attribute is used to identify the embedded elements on the page. The other tags can use this attribute to interact with `<EMBED>` tags. The following statement illustrates how you specify the NAME attribute in the `<EMBED>` tag:

```
<EMBED NAME = "TheName" SRC = "TheMovie.avi">
```

Using LiveConnect, it is possible to refer to the object TheName in JavaScript. It can be referred to as the following:

```
function PlayTheMovie() {
   document.TheMovie.play()
}
```

The following example shows how to play and stop an embedded .au file by using JavaScript functions. This code will use the embeds array.

```html
<HTML>
<HEAD>
<TITLE> Example for controlling the behavior of Plug-ins by using
embeds array</TITLE>
</HEAD>
<BODY>
<SCRIPT LANGUAGE = "JavaScript">
   // This function will play the embedded audio file.
   function playthefile() {
      document.embeds[0].play();
   }
   function stopthefile() {
      document.embeds[0].stop();
   }
</SCRIPT>
<EMBED SRC = "yourmusic.au" NAME = "yourmusic" WIDTH = "300"
HEIGHT = "300" AUTOSTART="FALSE">
<FORM>
Use the Play and Stop buttons to control the au file.
<INPUT TYPE="Button" value="play" onClick="playthefile()">
<INPUT TYPE="Button" VALUE="stop" onClick="stopthefile()">
</FORM>
</BODY>
</HTML>
```

The preceding code provides an example of how the plug-ins are controlled by JavaScript by using the embeds array. When the document containing this code is opened in the Internet Explorer 6 browser, it will try and load the plug-in that is associated to its MIME type. The yourmusic file will normally start to play as soon as the plug-in loads the .au file. However, in this case, it will not work in the same way. A close look at the code will show that the AUTOSTART attribute is set to FALSE. The file will play only when the Play button is clicked. You can stop playing the audio by clicking the Stop button. There can be other methods, such as rewind and forward, depending on the plug-in used. In Internet Explorer, the default plug-in is Windows Media Player.

NOTE The default plug-in for Internet Explorer is Windows Media Player. The functions play() and stop() used in the preceding code are functions related to the Windows Media Player plug-in. In Netscape 6, there is no default plug-in installed to play a .au file. When you load this page, the Netscape 6 browser prompts you to download the appropriate plug-in for the file that you want to play. Netscape Navigator suggests QuickTime 5 as the plug-in to be used for the MIME type of this file. After installing the proper plug-in, you need to check for the corresponding functions to control the plug-in. The way in which JavaScript controls the plug-ins in Netscape differs from Internet Explorer.

The following example shows how to play and stop an embedded .avi file in Netscape Navigator 6:

```
<HTML>
<HEAD>
<TITLE> Video for Product Catalog  </TITLE>
</HEAD>
<BODY>
<SCRIPT LANGUAGE = "JavaScript">
function playtheClock() {
    document.embeds[0].DoPlay();
 }
function stoptheClock() {
    document.embeds[0].DoStop();
}
function pausetheClock() {
    document.embeds[0].DoPause();
}
</SCRIPT>
<EMBED Name="clock" HEIGHT="300" WIDTH="300"
CONTROLS="ImageWindow" SRC="clock.avi" TYPE="audio/x-pn-realaudio-
plugin">
    <FORM>
    <P>Use the Play, Pause, and Stop buttons to control the clock
display. Click 'Play' to start the clock, 'Pause' to pause the clock,
and click 'Stop' to stop the clock.
    <P>
    <INPUT TYPE="Button" VALUE="Play" OnClick='playtheClock()'>
    <INPUT TYPE="Button" value="Pause" OnClick='pausetheClock()'>
    <INPUT TYPE="Button" value="Stop" OnClick='stoptheClock()'>
    </FORM>
    </BODY>
    </HTML>
```

In the preceding code, you will notice that instead of using the play() or stop() functions, the code is using the DoPlay() or DoStop() methods, respectively. These methods help in controlling the plug-in documents in Real Player 8.

We have just examined one of the methods that can be used to control the plug-ins using JavaScript. In the preceding example, the index for the embeds array was referred to as a numeric value, such as [0]. There may be cases where the index number for the required plug-in is either not known or is cumbersome to figure out. In such situations, you can use the name of the embedded object as the index. This name is the value that you specify in the NAME attribute of <EMBED> tag. The following statement illustrates how you can use the name of an embedded object to control a plug-in:

```
function playthefile() {
    document.embeds['yourmusic'].play();
}
```

According to the second method, you can call a JavaScript function. This function takes an object that is referenced by name as the argument. If you refer to the example given below and observe the `playthefile()` function that was used in the first method, you will notice that now the plug-in object is referenced by its name.

```
function playthefile(anObject) {
    anObject.play();
}
```

Examine the following statement as well:

```
<A HREF="javascript:playthefile(document.yourmusic);">Play your
Music</A>
```

In the preceding statement, the embedded object is passed as a reference to the JavaScript function, which plays the music. The statement `javascript:playthefile(document.yourmusic)` passes an object to the function `playthefile()` described above.

A third method is also available in which you can call the method of an object by directly referring to the object name. This name is the same as the value that you will specify in the NAME attribute of the `<EMBED>` tag. The following statement illustrates how you can call the methods of an object by directly referring to the object name:

```
<A HREF="javascript:document.yourmusic.play();">Play your Music
directly</a>
```

In this method, writing a different JavaScript function is not required. Here, the object method is directly called as a JavaScript statement.

In addition, you can know the properties and methods of the plug-ins embedded in a page. In the example given above where the embedded object is passed as a reference to the function `playthefile()`, the code given below can be added to know the properties and methods.

```
function writeprop(CurrObj) {
  document.writeln ("Properties And Methods of Embedded Object")
  for (var prop in CurrObj)
  document.writeln(prop + "<BR>")
}
```

To activate this function, you include the following button on the page:

```
<input type="button" value="properties"
onClick='writeprop(document.embeds[0])'>
```

When the user clicks the button with the value `properties`, the properties of the embedded plug-in are listed in a new browser window. This is helpful if the user is trying to find the properties of an embedded object, which, in this case, is a plug-in. All the plug-ins may not respond to the properties function favorably. LiveVideo and LiveAudio plug-ins in Netscape do respond to this function.

A few plug-ins can create callback functions. For example, the following function can be called when the movie is played:

```
function PluginCallBack( ) {
}
```

This function should be included with the other pieces of JavaScript code on the page. The plug-in will execute this function if the function is defined. Different plug-ins contain different sets of methods, properties, and callback functions that are defined when the plug-ins are developed.

Netscape has introduced an environment in Netscape 3.x where the Web developers can create live content by using plug-ins, Java, and JavaScript. The newest technology, LiveConnect, allows plug-ins Java and JavaScript to interact with each other. LiveConnect provides new capabilities for developing dynamic Web pages. It is now possible for the plug-ins to communicate with the JavaScript code on the same page. As we know, even Java applets and the JavaScript code on the same page can interact with each other. This helps create Web applications that appear more real and powerful. Web developers can coordinate the actions among Java Applets, plug-ins, and JavaScript. For example, on a Web site that offers low airfares, it would be ideal if the user could be sent an audio alert when the required fares are found. This can be done by calling an audio alert plug-in from JavaScript.

The latest version of Netscape 6.2 provides different plug-ins. Nullsoft Winamp enhances audio playback capability. RealPlayer 8 is used as a plug-in for streaming media. Macromedia Flash is used for Web content packed with high graphics. It also provides an add-on application, Print Plus, from Hewlett-Packard for easy handling of printing services.

Coordinating Multiple Plug-ins

In the previous section, we examined how plug-ins are controlled from within JavaScript. There can be situations in real life where you may need to coordinate among different plug-ins. In other words, two plug-ins may need to be played together. You may have a video file that does not have sound in it. In that case, you may have to support the video display with a separate audio file. In this section, you will examine the code to coordinate between the plug-ins. The plug-ins generally do not provide any synchronization methods. These features can be provided using JavaScript. In a document, JavaScript functions are created to perform the required coordination among the plug-ins.

The following example coordinates the video .avi file with an audio .au file.

```
<HTML>
<HEAD>
<TITLE>Co-ordinating the plug-ins</TITLE>
<SCRIPT LANGUAGE = "JavaScript">
function playthefiles() {
   document.embeds['yourvideo'].play();
   document.embeds['yourmusic'].play();
}
function stopthefiles() {
```

```
      document.embeds['yourvideo'].stop();
      document.embeds['yourmusic'].stop();
   }
   </SCRIPT>
   </HEAD>
   <BODY>
   This is an example that shows the co-ordination between the
yourmusic.au file and the yourvideo.avi file. Click Play All to play
both files together, and click Stop All to stop playing both files.
   <EMBED SRC = "yourvideo.avi" NAME = "yourvideo" WIDTH = "300"
HEIGHT = "300" AUTOSTART="false">
   <EMBED SRC = "yourmusic.au" NAME = "yourmusic" WIDTH = "300"
HEIGHT = "300" AUTOSTART="false">
   <FORM>
   <INPUT TYPE="button" VALUE="Play All" onclick='playthefiles()'>
   <INPUT TYPE="button" VALUE="Stop All" onclick='stopthefiles()'>
   </FORM>
   </BODY>
   </HTML>
```

When this document is loaded in a browser, both files are loaded with the appropriate plug-ins. Because the AUTOSTART attribute is set to false, the file does not start playing when it is loaded in the browser window. The user will see two buttons marked Play All and Stop All. To play both files together, the user has to click Play All. Clicking the Play All button calls the function playthefiles(). This function has two statements. The first statement executes the play() method for the video file. The second statement executes the play() method for the audio file.

References to the embeds array are made using the name that was assigned to the embedded object. The video object is assigned a name, yourvideo, and the audio object is assigned a name, yourmusic. To stop playing the files, the user has to click the Stop button. Clicking the Stop All button calls the function stopthefiles(). This function has two statements. The first statement executes the stop method for the video file. The second statement executes the stop method for the audio file.

The preceding example demonstrates a simple coordinating exercise where two plug-ins are involved. A similar exercise can also be done using multiple plug-ins. To control the plug-ins, you need to know the properties and methods of the plug-ins that are supported in JavaScript. This information is available in the plug-in documentation. It is an important piece of information because all plug-ins are not supported equally in Netscape Navigator and Internet Explorer.

User-Friendly Plug-in Installation

You have seen how plug-ins work on an HTML page. In this section, you will examine how the plug-in installations should be supported when the user works with the pages containing plug-ins. When a browser loads a page containing a plug-in and if the plug-in is not currently installed on the user's computer, the browser should provide relevant assistance to the user to load the required plug-in.

In Netscape, if a needed plug-in is not currently installed on a user's computer, the browser deals with it efficiently. If the plug-in is not available, the browser shows an icon instead of the plug-in. Netscape then displays a dialog box, which gives the user two options. The first option is to load the required plug-in, and the second option is to cancel the operation. If the user decides to load the required plug-in, the Netscape browser obtains the value of the PLUGINSPAGE attribute specified in the plug-ins <EMBED> tag. If this operation returns a valid URL, Netscape loads that page.

The Help page should contain proper instructions for downloading the plug-in and then install it on the user's computer. If PLUGINSPAGE is not specified in the <EMBED> tag, Netscape loads the default plug-ins page from the Netscape site. This page suggests the latest plug-ins that are available for the MIME type of the file that is specified in the SRC attribute of the <EMBED> tag. If the user clicks the Cancel option during the plug-in install process, the user can click the icon that appears on the page and invoke the install help process again.

The following example will explain how developers should support the plug-in pages:

```
<HTML>
<HEAD>
<TITLE> Plug-ins Installation Help</title>
</HEAD>
<BODY>
 <EMBED SRC = "yourvideo.avi" TYPE="audio/x-pn-realaudio-plugin"
NAME = "yourvideo" WIDTH = "300" HEIGHT = "300" AUTOSTART="true"
PLUGINSPAGE = "plughelp.html">
 </BODY>
 </HTML>
```

The code sample given above shows the syntax for including the PLUGINSPAGE attribute in the <EMBED> tag. When this page is loaded in the Netscape browser, the Help dialog box is displayed if a plug-in supporting this MIME type is not found on the user's computer. The plughelp.html page will be opened in the form of a Help page to the user. On this page, you should provide proper instructions to download the plug-in and then install it. However, remember that only Netscape supports the PLUGINSPAGE attribute in the <EMBED> tag.

Creating a New Plug-in

Many plug-ins are currently available. They can be used for various MIME types. These plug-ins are available on various sites, for example, www.plugins.com or http://browserwatch.internet.com/plug-in.html. You may be working with a MIME type for which the required plug-in is not available. After you decide to create a plug-in, you have to follow a few steps to develop it. In this section, you will be introduced to the steps, and proper resources will be specified.

Creating plug-ins is a lengthy process. Therefore, only an overview is provided in this section. For details, you are advised to refer to the resources (sites) specified. The Netscape site http://developer.netscape.com provides information regarding the creation of plug-ins. In this section, the coverage will be limited to the Netscape plug-in software development kit (SDK).

To create a plug-in, you first need to select a MIME type for which the plug-in is to be written. If the MIME type does not exist, you need to register the MIME type. A

MIME type consists of two parts: major and minor. An example of a MIME type is image (major) /jpeg (minor). If you want to define a new MIME type for your plug-in, you will have to register the MIME type with the Internet Engineering Task Force (IETF). If the MIME type is not registered, it is prefixed with x-. An example of specifying the MIME type that is not registered is image/x-yourmime.

After selecting and registering the MIME type, download and install the plug-in software development kit on your computer. SDK is written in C++ and provides templates and examples for assisting the user. SDK is available for download from http://home.netscape.com/comprod/development_partners/plugin_api/index.html. It has different versions based on the operating system (OS) being used.

The next step in the process is to build the plug-in. The steps to build the plug-in are specific to the operating system. Go to http://developer.netscape.com/docs/manuals/communicator/plugin/index.htm to refer to the Plug-in Guide, which includes a section on building plug-ins.

After building the plug-in, you need to work on plug-in installation. If your plug-in is easy to install, it will be used often. The most efficient way to install the plug-in is to use the JAR installation manager in Netscape. The JAR installation manager can be configured to open as soon as the HTML page containing the embedded data for which the plug-in is not installed is loaded in the browser. Details of how the JAR installation manager works are available in the Netscape Plug-in Guide. The other options for the installation, such as manual installation or automatic installation, are also covered in the Netscape Plug-in Guide.

The last step is to test and debug the plug-in as required.

To include the LiveConnect capability in your plug-in, you will have to refer to the LiveConnect Plug-ins with Java Guide, which is also available on the developer Web site of Netscape.

Result

According to the specifications given in the problem statement, Scott has decided to provide two buttons on the All Products video file page. The first button will be labeled Play the Video. Clicking this button will play the video file. The other button on this page will be labeled Stop the Video. Clicking this button will stop the video. Create two JavaScript functions. One of the functions should play the file by using the play() method. The other function should stop the video by using the stop() method. These functions should be called from the onClick event of the buttons.

Write the Code

The site should display all the products in a video file format, which users can view on demand. This file is called Allproducts.avi.

Following is the code for the catalog.html file:

```
<HTML>
<HEAD>
<TITLE> Video for Product Catalog  </TITLE>
</HEAD>
<BODY bgcolor="#C4FBF5">
```

```
        <P align="center" style="margin-top: 0; margin-bottom: 0"><I><FONT
color="#CC3300" face="Arial Black" size="10">Web Shoppe</font></I></P>
        <P align="left" style="margin-top: 0; margin-bottom: 0"><I>
        <FONT face="Arial" color="#000000" size="3">
         <SCRIPT LANGUAGE = "JavaScript">
         function playtheCatalog() {
            document.embeds[0].Play();
         }
         function stoptheCatalog() {
            document.embeds[0].Stop();
         }
         </SCRIPT>
          <EMBED SRC = "Catalog.avi" NAME = "catalog" WIDTH = "300" HEIGHT
= "300" AUTOSTART="false" ENABLEJAVASCRIPT="true">
         <FORM>
         Use the Play and Stop buttons to control the Catalog display. You
can click on 'Play' to start the Product Catalog display. If you want to
stop the video display and look at a Product, click 'Stop'.
         </p>
         <input type="button" value="Play" OnClick='playtheCatalog()'>
         <input type="button" value="Stop" OnClick='stoptheCatalog()'>
         </form>
         </body>
         </html>
```

Execute and Verify the Code

Execute the code and verify the successful running of the preceding HTML files with the embedded JavaScript code. Open the catalog.html file in the Internet Explorer browser window. When the file is completely loaded, you should see an embedded plug-in video file and two buttons, Play and Stop. Clicking the Play button should start the video file and clicking the Stop button should stop the playing of the catalog file.

Summary

In this chapter, you learned about plug-ins and the methods used in JavaScript to interact with plug-ins. Plug-ins allow you to use the existing documents on your site. For example, you use the .pdf document on a Web site for technical reference. Plug-ins can be controlled using JavaScript. Multiple plug-ins on a Web page can be made to work together by writing appropriate JavaScript functions as required for a specific situation. When the plug-ins are used on Web pages, care should be taken to assist the users if the plug-ins are not available on the user's computer. Finally, the chapter provided an overview of the development process involved in creating a plug-in.

Styles and Layers

In this lesson, you will learn to:

- ✔ **Create dynamic Web pages**
- ✔ **Work with Cascading Style Sheets**
- ✔ **Work with layers**
- ✔ **Work with divisions**
- ✔ **Create animation effects by using JavaScript**
- ✔ **Create multimedia effects**

Getting Started

Web developers are always looking for ways to make their Web pages more interactive and appealing to targeted users. The standard HTML tags provide only limited control to the developers over how to present the Web pages. For instance, HTML has constraints in relation to dynamically changing the font color, font size, and position of the elements on the Web pages even after the Web page is loaded in a Web browser.

HTML 3.2 introduced style sheets, which provides flexibility and control to Web programmers in the presentation of Web pages. Style sheets enable you to control the color, font, margins, and many other aspects of HTML elements. This helps make Web pages lively and tailor-made for the needs of the target audience. For instance, using style sheets, you can present information in a formal style to the corporate user and in a trendy style to young professionals.

To design a Web page that is attractive and interactive, you can use DHTML, which is more popularly known as Dynamic HTML. DHTML is a combination of HTML, style sheets, and scripting languages. The word Dynamic here does not imply ever-changing. It implies that by using DHTML, Web pages can be made to respond to users' actions.

One of the features of an appealing and interactive Web page is multimedia. The features of DHTML, such as layers and divisions on a Web page, help control the positioning of elements on a Web page. This enables creation of animations and multimedia.

In this chapter, you will examine the components of DHTML. You'll also learn about some features of DHTML. This chapter will also cover the working of style sheets. The difference between JavaScript Style Sheets and Cascading Style Sheets (CSS) will also be covered in this chapter. You will also learn about the methods for using style sheets with HTML Web pages. You'll learn about the implementation of styles in the Netscape Navigator and Internet Explorer environments. After learning the topics covered in this chapter, you will be able to effectively use layers and divisions to control the placement and movement of elements on a Web page. We will also discuss how to combine all the dynamic methods and technologies to create animations and multimedia.

Before examining the details of style sheets and layers, let us explore DHTML. DHTML is the base technology, and its features include Cascading Style Sheets and layers.

Introducing DHTML

After being loaded in a browser window, HTML documents by themselves do not respond to user requests. However, Dynamic HTML enables the Web pages to be more interactive. DHTML is a combination of Document Object Model (DOM), the event model, and the Cascading Style Sheet. As per the W3 Consortium (W3C), "*DOM* is a platform-independent and language-neutral interface that allows programs and scripts to dynamically access and update the content, structure, and style of documents." To understand this and the role of DHTML in creating interactive Web pages, let us first consider the features of DHTML.

NOTE DHTML standards are controlled by W3C. W3C accepts ideas from the member companies on various issues related to markup languages. The member companies of W3C, such as Netscape and Microsoft, contribute suggestions for defining DHTML standards.

A few basic features of DHTML decided by the W3C consortium are listed:

Changing content and tags. DOM makes it possible to manipulate the styles and attributes of all the elements on a Web page. In Internet Explorer, it is possible to change the contents inside a tag by using properties such as innerHTML. For example, based on the user profile or category, the content on the Web page can be changed. When the user logs on to the site, the category of the user is stored in a variable. Then, using JavaScript functions, the user can be shown different content when the user clicks the hyperlinks on the Web page.

Dynamic positioning. This feature allows you to control the positioning of elements on a Web page after the page has been loaded in a browser. This feature is implemented differently in Netscape and Microsoft browsers. Netscape uses layers to provide control over positioning. Microsoft uses the <DIV> tag for this purpose. Layers will be discussed in detail later in the chapter.

Data binding. In the traditional interaction between a database and a Web page, after the browser receives the data, the data becomes static. If data has to be manipulated, another Web server request is required. Even if the user wants to view the same data in a different way, such as data being sorted on a different field, a request needs to be made again to the Web server. This is very time-consuming. Internet Explorer provides a feature called data binding. Using this feature, the Web page can be attached to database records—thus allowing the data to be changed dynamically without any further Web server requests.

NOTE For DHTML to work predictably, it is very important that HTML pages be created by following HTML 4.01 Document Type Definition (DTD). If all the elements are defined properly, the browsers will display the resulting pages in the proper way. However, if the parent and child tags are not defined correctly, it will be very difficult for DOM to maintain correct information about both tags. As a result, DOM will act differently in different browsers, depending on the DOM implementation in that browser. DOM might also disable the affected elements. In addition, if those elements are used in providing a DHTML effect, the effects might not be reflected correctly. In some cases, DOM might generate an error message indicating to the user that there is some problem with the page and DHTML effects might not work as expected. Owing to the difference in the DOM that a browser supports, it is important while working with DHTML to choose either Netscape or Internet Explorer as the working environment. If you work with both of these browsers, a common set of DHTML features should be used.

After having looked at the features of DHTML, let us now look at the scenario of Web Shoppe. As we move along in this chapter, we'll discuss Cascading Style Sheets and layers and find a solution to Web Shoppe's problem statement.

Using Styles and Layers

Problem Statement

New pages need to be included in the Web site of the online shopping system of Web Shoppe, Inc. The pages will display the new product line of the store. Cynthia, the head of the development team, is responsible for the maintenance of this site. Cynthia has designed the page and has assigned Scott, a Web developer, to add the following functionality to the site:

■ Create a feature on the Home Web page where the styles applied to various elements on the page can be changed as per the option selected by the user. Two options should be available. One option is to display the Web site in corporate style by using varying shades of gray and black and formal fonts. The other option should use different colors and styles to present a colorful Web site. Use two different Cascading Style Sheet style definitions on the Web site.

■ The top management at Web Shoppe has decided to apply a standard style throughout the Web site. Create a style sheet according to the style specifications provided in the style definition document. Link this style sheet to all the Web pages on the site. Certain differences in style need to exist from section to section. This should be achieved using embedded style statements. Some inline style may also be required at places. Use the inline `style` attribute or the `<SPAN>` tag to render these styles. The inline change feature should be used as little as possible.

■ Create a Web page that presents information related to a different link in the navigation scheme followed in the site. The Help page should display the purpose of each link when the customer clicks that link. This should be achieved in such a way that it should not be time-consuming or use too many resources. All the information should be presented on the same Help page.

In the products section, there are Web pages that display the images of the products sold in that section. Currently, there is a static display of product descriptions on these pages. These Web pages should be changed to display the description of products dynamically. When the customer points to a product image, the product description should display an animated slide-out layer. The description should not appear after the pointer is moved away from the image. This should happen for all images.

To incorporate the above functionality in the page that displays the new product of the store, the following task list has been identified.

Task List

✓ **Identify the methods to use styles and implement DHTML features with JavaScript.**

✓ **Write the code.**

✓ **Execute and verify the code.**

Identify the Methods to Use Styles and Implement DHTML features with JavaScript

Before identifying the methods to use styles and implement DHTML features with JavaScript, let's first understand style sheets and their functions.

Style Sheets

Styles sheets provide a way for the Web page developers to format pages differently on a Web site. Style sheets provide greater control over how to present the elements on a Web page. Before style sheets were introduced, developers used standard formatting techniques, such as using different levels of headings, paragraphs, and different font sizes and alignments for individual elements. With the introduction of style sheets, you can specify style-related attributes for an entire Web page instead of individual elements.

Generally, you format the text displayed on a Web page by using HTML tags. For example, while working with a level 2 <H2> tag, you might want to make the content of all the level 2 headings on a Web page appear in blue and the Arial font. Generally, you format level 2 headings by writing the following statement:

```
<H2><FONT face ="Arial" color="Blue"> My Level 2 Heading
</FONT></H2>
```

The preceding statement will produce the required effect on the Web page. However, this technique is not preferred. There are two reasons for this. First, HTML should ideally be used to define the document structure and not for styling information. Assume that you have to change the color of <H2> from blue to green. You'll have to change the color attribute in the <FONT> tag at all the places separately. This is time-consuming, increases the file size, and this exercise is also highly error-prone. Second, there are some formatting effects, such as line spacing, margins, and text shadows, that are not available with HTML. In the above example, to change the style of all the headings, you should use style sheets.

Now let us consider how to implement the same styling using style sheets. The following statement defines a style for <H2> headings:

```
H2{font-family:Arial;color:blue};
```

Now, if you need to change the color from blue to green, you simply need to replace the value for the attribute color from blue to green. The following statement defines the style for H2 headings with the color as green:

```
H2{font-family:Arial;color:green};
```

The preceding statement will change the formatting for all the instances of the <H2> tag in the entire page.

Style sheets also help maintain consistency across a site or even multiple sites of the same organization. A company may decide to use one background color in all its sites. There could be different development teams working for the sites. In this case, it would be very difficult to control the appearance of all the sites. Here, if a master style sheet template is created and all the teams follow this template to develop the pages, the task of a consistent look will be simplified. This will also save time for the development team, and chances of errors will be tremendously reduced.

To summarize, the advantages of using style sheets include:

- Using style sheets, content can be separated from formatting. In this way, the same content can be displayed in different styles by using a different style sheet.

- Style sheets help reduce the downloading time. When style sheets are used, the same formatting information need not be repeated. This results in smaller files and reduced downloading time.

- Style sheets provide more formatting control over the individual elements on a Web page.

- Style sheets can be used to make templates and ensure consistent appearance across the Web site.

Cascading Style Sheets

Cascading Style Sheets (CSS), which is a feature of DHTML, is a standard used to define style sheets. Cascading Style Sheets allows styles to be defined in different ways. Cascading effect and inheritance are two main features that make Cascading Style Sheets different from other style sheets. The cascading effect enables you to apply more than one style on a Web page. Cascading Style Sheets can be used with HTML documents in different ways. The details related to CSS will be discussed later. Inheritance is a feature that allows child elements to inherit the styles applied to the parent element if no style is defined for the child element. If a style is defined for the child element, it will override the style specified for the parent element.

The styles defined using CSS are saved in .css files. A .css file contains style statements that follow certain syntax. A typical style statement consists of a declaration and selectors. Each declaration is a pair consisting of a style property and the value for that property. A single style declaration statement can have multiple pairs of properties and values. For example, if you want to specify the font and color for the content appearing in paragraphs, the syntax will be:

```
P {font-family: Arial; color: Red};
```

In the preceding syntax, font-family is the property defined. This property is followed by a colon (:) and then its value. To specify more than one style for an element, use semicolons (;) as separators.

You can associate style declarations with element(s) by placing the declaration within curly braces {} and preceding it with a selector. For example, to associate style declaration `font-style:  italic` with all H2 heading elements, the statement would be:

```
H2 {font-style: italic};
```

Selectors can be of different types. The preceding statements use the simplest selector `type`. A `type` selector is used when a style has to be specified for an HTML element. For example, if you have to specify a style for the `<BODY>` tag, the style statement will be as follows:

```
BODY {font-family: Arial};
```

Using the `type` selector, you can apply the same style for all the occurrences of a specific tag or an element. However, you might want to apply different styles for the same element. This can be done using `class` selectors. For example, on a page that contains Frequently Asked Questions, you might want to display the questions in red and the answers in green. Let us assume that the element used for questions and answers is the `<P>` tag. In the style sheet, this can be applied by placing a period (`.`) after the tag followed by the class name. The questions can be displayed in the `question` style, and the answers can be displayed in the `answer` style. The style sheet would appear in the following way:

```
P.question {color: Red};
P.answer {color: Green};
```

The preceding statements are actually defining styles by using the `class` attribute. Here, question and answer are the `class` attributes. To apply the preceding style, you will use the following statement:

```
<P class ="question"> This is a question </P>
```

Now, you can also write the statement,

```
P.question {color: Red}; as:
.question {color: Red};
```

This style will be applied to all the elements having the `class` attribute as question.

While naming a `class` selector, it is a good practice to use class names to describe the content of the element. For example, to specify that all questions should be in red, instead of defining a class for questions as class="Red" we should define it as class="question". This approach will allow your style sheets to be self-documenting.

Remember the following when using the `class` selector:

- Class names should not start with a hyphen or a number.
- Class names should be in lowercase letters because most browsers do not distinguish between lowercase and uppercase letters.
- Class names should not contain spaces between the characters in their names.

Another type of selector is the ID selector. ID selectors are used in the same way as class selectors. In this case, instead of the class attribute, the ID attribute is used. One important point to remember while using ID selectors is that the IDs assigned to the elements on a Web page should be unique. In addition, the ID name should be preceded by #. The following statement defines a style by using the ID selector:

```
#mystyle {font-size: 10pt};
```

An ID selector can be used either to apply style to any element or defined specifically for an element. The following statement applies style to paragraphs:

```
P#mystyle {background-color: gray};
```

Another type of selector is the contextual selector, which can be used to have a fine control over the appearance of HTML elements. While applying style to Web pages, there could be scenarios where it would be better if the style of one element can be defined in association with another HTML element. When an element is contained within another element, you might want to change its appearance. For example, if the <STRONG> tag appears within a <P> tag and you want to change the paragraph color to blue, you can define a style statement as follows:

```
H2 strong {color: blue};
```

The link pseudo class selectors are used to apply different styles to different states of links. Links can be the usual state of an unvisited link, a visited link, and the active link that indicates that the link is being clicked. There could be another state for the links, the hover state, when the cursor is moved over a link.

NOTE The hover state is not supported by Netscape Navigator 4.x.

There are a few differences in the way link pseudo class selectors are used in style statements. They are attached to a tag name by using a colon and not a period. They have predefined names, and these names cannot be changed.

The selectors for each of the link pseudo classes have the following forms:

- For normal links: a:link
- For visited links: a:visited
- For hover links: a:hover
- For active links: a:active

Using this type of selector, the links in different states will appear in different colors. A different color effect can also be achieved using the <BODY> tag in the HTML document. However, with a link pseudo class selector, the other properties that can be assigned to an element can also be assigned to a link in any state. For example, the background color and font of a link that has been visited can be changed.

The link pseudo class selectors can be used in conjunction with class selectors to create different styles for the links being used for different purposes. For example, you might create a class of basic-level topics links and a class of advanced-level topics links on a Web site providing tutorials. The style statements will appear in the following way:

```
a.basic:link {color: red};
a.advance:link {color: blue};
```

Cascading Style Sheets Level 2 (CSS2) also specifies a few `pseudo element` selectors. All the browsers do not yet support these selectors. A brief description of these selectors is given below:

- The `:first-line` selector selects the first line of a specific type of element. This selector can be used to indicate the beginning of each paragraph.

- The `:first-letter` selector selects the first letter of an element.

- CSS2 also introduced two new `pseudo element` selectors, `:before` and `:after`. The `:before pseudo` selector selects an element and allows content such as text and images to be inserted before the selected element. The `:after pseudo` selector selects an element and allows the insertion of content after the selected element.

Other types of selectors are defined in CSS2 specifications. For more details on other types of selectors, refer to the CSS2 documentation on the W3C Web site.

Now that we are familiar with the types of Cascading Style Sheets, let us move on to discuss its two important features—cascading and inheritance—in detail.

Cascading Effects

When working with large Web sites, a single style sheet associated with the Web site is not quite adequate. A single style sheet provides the advantages of CSS but in a limited way. Large Web sites are generally maintained by a number of teams, and, at times, these teams can be at different physical locations. In this case, a single style sheet cannot be used to share common styles. Adding new styles and extending the style sheets are a limitation.

By using Cascading Style Sheets, a number of related style sheets can be linked together to create a hierarchy. This process of linking is called *cascading.* To understand this concept, we will examine the working of a large Web site. A large Web site contains many sections. If it is a Web site for a big corporation, it might have different divisions. Each division might have its own development team. However, the appearance of the Web site should be consistent. Cascading Style Sheets can help in this situation. Cascading Style Sheets do not have to work alone. They can import style from other style sheets. Style sheets that import style from other style sheets are said to cascade from those style sheets.

In the case of a large corporate site, a company-level core style sheet can be defined. This style sheet will have style statements related to the basic appearance of the site, such as fonts, color, and background colors. There may also be a style sheet defined for each section, although these style sheets may not define the styles already covered in the company-level style sheet. In these style sheets, section-specific style instruction should be included.

To ensure that company-level styles are also included in the section-specific style sheets, you should import the core style sheet by using the @import rule. Each section might also have many subsections. Separate style sheets can be defined for each subsection and import the section-level style sheet in that style sheet. Importing a section-level style sheet in the subsection style sheet will also import the company-level style sheet in it because it was imported by the section-level style sheet. Using this process, you can create a cascade of style sheets. By changing a style sheet above another in the cascade, the changes cascade automatically into the lower-level style sheets and the Web pages that are linked to the lower-level style sheets.

Inheritance

There could be many elements present in any HTML document. A tag consisting of content is called an element. For example, a paragraph is presented by a <P> tag but a paragraph element would be the statement <P> This is my paragraph </P>. Each element on a Web page is contained by another element. The element itself might contain more elements inside its container. This is known as the containment hierarchy of a Web page. In each page, the <HTML> tag is at the top. All the other elements are contained within this element. As specified in the example, the paragraph element might contain some elements and the paragraph element is contained within the <BODY> element. With CSS2 specifications, the elements are made to inherit the properties of the elements, which contain them, also known as the parent element. For example, if you define a style for the body of the Web page, such as font and color, and the <BODY> contains a few <P> tags, you do not need to define the style for the <P> element contained in the <BODY> element. You can override the inheritance by specifying a style for the contained element. There are some properties, such as the background color, which are not inherited by the child element.

Before we move on to using style sheets, let us compare JavaScript Style Sheets with Cascading Style Sheets.

Comparing JavaScript Style Sheets with Cascading Style Sheets

In the previous section, we discussed how Cascading Style sheets are defined. In this section, we will examine how JavaScript Style Sheets (JSS) work. JavaScript-based style sheets are supported by Netscape Navigator only. JavaScript Style Sheets support CSS1 specifications and provide these styles as JavaScript properties. JavaScript Style Sheets use the document object model to define styles. While defining the styles, the hierarchy of the document object model is very helpful and is used to its full capacity. For example, the following code can be used to set a style for the <P> tag:

```
document.tags.P.color = "green";
```

In the preceding statement, the color property of the <P> element is set to green. The <P> element acts as an object for the property color, but the <P> element, in turn, specifies one of the tags available in the tags array, which is a property of the document object. You can remove the document from the above code expression because the tags property always applies to the document object for the current document.

We will now examine a sample style sheet using JavaScript and the `document` object model. This style sheet has three style definitions. The first style definition specifies that the background color of the body region should be white. The second style definition specifies that the font size for all <P> elements is 20, and the third style definition specifies that the color of the <H1> tag or elements should be set to blue.

```
<STYLE TYPE = "text/javascript">
  tags.BODY.backgroundColor = "white";
  tags.P.fontSize = "20pt";
  tags.H1.color = "blue";
</STYLE>
```

You can also use the `with` notation to avoid repetition of the `tags.tagname` statement in the style specification for the elements that have many style settings. The following example specifies that all the <H2> elements should be displayed in blue. The font is specified as Arial.

```
with (tags.H2) {
  color="blue";
  font-style="italic";
  font-family="arial";
};
```

The following code example will show a similar style sheet in CSS syntax and then in JSS syntax. Using this example, you will learn about the differences in both types of style sheets. The following style sheet specifies that the <BODY> of the document should have a gray background and the Times New Roman font should be in 12 point. The text in all the <P> elements should be centered. The right margin should be 15 percent of the overall width of the document page size. All the <H3> elements should be blue and underlined. All the <H4> elements should be in lowercase letters. A 3-point-thick cyan border should be used. The padding between the text and the border should be 2 points. The text color is green, and the background color is yellow.

The CSS syntax for the above-described style sheet would be:

```
<STYLE TYPE="text/css">
BODY {
    background-color: "gray";
    font-family: "Times New Roman";
    font-size: "12pt"; };
P {
    textAlign:center; margin-right:15%;};
H3 {
    color: blue; text-decoration:underline;};
H4 {
    text-transform:lowercase;
    border-color:cyan; border-width:3pt;
    padding: 2pt;
    color: green; background-color:yellow;
};
</STYLE>
```

The same style sheet written in JavaScript is as follows:

```
<STYLE TYPE="text/javascript">
    tags.BODY.backgroundColor = "gray";
    tags.BODY.fontFamily = "Times New Roman";
    tags.BODY.fontSize = "12pt";
    with (tags.P) {
        textAlign = "center"; margin-right="15%";}
    with (tags.H3) {
        textDecoration = "underline"; color = "blue";
        }
    with (tags.H4) {
        textTransform = "lowercase";
        borderColor="cyan";
        borderWidths="3pt";
        paddings("2pt");
         color = "green";
         backgroundColor="yellow";
         }
</STYLE>
```

When these style tags are included in an HTML document, the style tags will render the styles to the elements as described in the style statements within the <STYLE> tag. JSS will apply only in Netscape Navigator, but CSS-based style will work in both Netscape and Internet Explorer. There are some other differences between JSS and CSS as listed below:

- In the case of CSS, in the <STYLE> tag, the TYPE attribute has the value text/css. In the case of JSS, the TYPE attribute contains the value text/javascript.

- The way in which the style statements are written in CSS is different from the way the style statements are written in JSS. JSS refers to elements and properties through the document object model.

- The style properties are stated as properties of the elements in JSS, but in CSS, that is not the case.

- In JSS, the elements can be referred using the with notation. This is not the convention when CSS syntax is used.

In the previous section, you learned how CSS uses different selectors, such as id and class, to provide a finer control over the appearance of the elements in HTML documents. Equivalent methods are also available in JSS, but the syntax to use id or class is different. The tags property is used to refer to the elements on an HTML document. The ids property is used to define a specific instance of an HTML element. The syntax is as follows:

```
ids.ID.property = value;
```

Here, ID is the name of the ID that needs to be defined. While using this style in the HTML document, this ID can be assigned as the ID value for the element whose style needs be modified or changed.

JavaScript Style Sheets can also be used to define classes of styles. Classes can be applied to different elements where the same style is required. Classes are defined in JavaScript Style Sheets by using the `classes` property. The classes are defined in the style sheets by using the following syntax:

```
classes.classname.tag.property = value;
```

In the preceding syntax, `classname` is the name of the class that you want to define. We have used `tag` to specify the tag or element for which this class of style is being defined. The following statement defines a style class, `myclass`, for element P.

```
classes.myclass.P.fontSize = "10pt";
```

If you want to define a class style that can be used by all elements, use `all` instead of `tag` in the above syntax. The properties can be any definable property, such as `fontSize`, and `fontStyle`. The following statement defines a style class, `myclass`, for all elements:

```
classes.myclass.all.color = "blue";
```

Now that we have discussed the basic concepts about style sheets, let us discuss how to use style sheets.

Assigning Style Sheets to HTML Documents

In some of the previous examples, you have seen the use of the `<STYLE>` tag. Here, we will examine the tag in more detail.

Using the `<STYLE>` Tag

The style information can be included in an HTML document by using the `<STYLE>` tag. The `<STYLE>` and `</STYLE>` tags are specified in the header section of an HTML document. The `<STYLE>` tags should be used before the `<BODY>` tag. The `TYPE` attribute specifies whether it is CSS or JSS. By default, the value of `TYPE` attribute is `text/css`. If a JavaScript Style Sheet is to be used, the `TYPE` attribute should be `text/javascript`.

The following example defines a style sheet that specifies that all `<H2>` elements be in red and underlined. It also specifies that all the `<P>` elements should be displayed in blue and the font style should be italic.

If CSS is used, the code for the Web page will be:

```
<HEAD>
<STYLE TYPE="text/css">
    H2 {color: red; text-decoration: underline;};
    P {color: blue; font-style: italic;};
</STYLE>
</HEAD>
<BODY>
```

```
<H2> This is sample level 2 heading </H2>
<P> This a sample paragraph. </P>
</BODY>
</HTML>
```

The same style sheet can be defined using the JavaScript syntax as follows:

```
<HEAD>
<STYLE TYPE="text/javascript">
        tags.H2.textDecoration = "underline";
        tags.H2.color = "red";
        tags.P.color = "blue";
        tags.P.fontStyle: "italic";
</STYLE>
</HEAD>
<BODY>
<H2> This is sample level 2 heading </H2>
<P> This a sample paragraph. </P>
</BODY>
</HTML>
```

Inline Style Information

The style information can be specified within the HTML tags by using the STYLE attribute of the tag. When the style is defined inline, the TYPE attribute is not used. The syntax for using the STYLE attribute is as follows:

```
<HTML>
<BODY>
This is a sample to demonstrate the usage of inline style.
<P STYLE = "font-size: 14pt; font-weight: bold"> This is test paragraph.
</P>
</BODY>
</HTML>
```

The STYLE attribute should be used only if the other style methods cannot achieve the preferred style effects. The inline use of style only affects the associated tag. Therefore, it is not an optimal method to be used.

There is another way to use inline styling by using the <SPAN> tag. This tag is used to apply style to selected portions of content in a tag. Consider that you want to develop a style that will highlight and underline important text on a Web page. You can use the <SPAN> tag to perform this task. The opening and closing <SPAN> tags enclose the text to which the style needs to be applied. The CLASS or ID attribute of the <SPAN> tag is set to the name of a class style name or ID style name. The sample presented below uses the <SPAN> tag to change the style of important text on the Web page. The background color should be changed to yellow, and the selected text should be underlined. The example shows both CSS and JSS code syntax.

The following code sample shows definition in CSS:

```
<HTML>
<HEAD>
<TITLE> Styles applied by using SPAN tag </TITLE>
<STYLE TYPE="text/css">
P.important {background-color: yellow; text-decoration: underline}
</STYLE>
</HEAD>
<BODY>
<P> This is a test Paragraph. <SPAN CLASS="important"> It contains
important text. </SPAN> </P>
</BODY>
</HTML>
```

The following code sample shows definition in JSS:

```
<HTML>
<HEAD>
<TITLE> Styles applied by using SPAN tag </TITLE>
<STYLE TYPE="text/javascript">
classes.P.important.backgroundColor =  "yellow";
classes.P.important.textDecoration = "underline";
</STYLE>
</HEAD>
<BODY>
<P> This is a test Paragraph. <SPAN CLASS="important"> It contains
important text. </SPAN> </P>
</BODY>
</HTML>
```

The above example uses the CLASS attribute in the <SPAN> tag. You can also specify the styles as IDs. The ID attribute of the <SPAN> tag can be used to apply style to the selected portion of the text.

Using External Files for Style Information

The examples used in the previous section have used style sheets that are embedded in the HTML documents. Style sheets can also be defined in a separate file and then linked to the HTML document. Style sheets used as external files are advantageous in cases where many HTML documents would be using the same style information. This means that the style sheet can be defined once and then reused. This can also help create a template that can be used by multiple HTML documents. If the style is updated, only one file needs to be changed. This saves time and avoids occurrence of errors. The external style sheets can use tags, classes, and ids properties. The syntax of CSS and JSS style sheets are also valid for defining an external file for style sheets. The <STYLE> tag is not included in the external files. The following is an example of an external style sheet file:

The following code sample uses the CSS syntax:

```
/* External style sheet yourstyle.css */
H1 {text-align: right;}
P {font-style: italic;}
/* end of the external file */
```

The following code uses the JSS syntax:

```
/* external style sheet yourJSSstyle */
tags.H1.TextAlign="right";
tags.P.fontStyle="italic";
/* end of the external file */
```

You can use external style sheets with your HTML documents in two ways. One way is to link the external file, and the other way is to import the external file. To link the external style sheet file to the HTML document, you use the <link> tag. The <link> tag creates a relationship between the HTML document and the external style sheet. The following example provides more details about the definition of the relationship between the two files. The example uses the CSS external style sheet file yourstyle.css.

```
<HTML>
<HEAD>
<TITLE> Using link tag </TITLE>
<LINK  REL=STYLESHEET TYPE="text/css" HREF="yourstyle.css">
</HEAD>
<BODY>
<H1> This is heading level 1 which is right aligned. </H1>
<P> I am an italic style Paragraph. </P>
</BODY>
</HTML>
```

The information supplied in the <LINK> tag specifies that the file mentioned in the HREF attribute is a style sheet by specifying REL=STYLESHEET. The styles in the external file are specified using CSS2 standards. This information is provided through the TYPE attribute. The <LINK> tag must be used within the <HEAD> opening and closing tag. If the JavaScript Style Sheet is used, the TYPE attribute will be changed to text/javascript.

Another way to use external style sheets is to use the @import rule within the <STYLE> tag. The @import rule uses a single parameter URL, which is used to specify the path and name of the external style sheet. Using a string enclosed in double quotes and ending with a semicolon specifies the value of the URL. The @import rule should be used before specifying any other style statements in the <STYLE> tag on an HTML document. This is because, according to CSS2 standards, the @import will be ignored and will generate an error. The following example shows the usage of the @import rule:

```
<HTML>
<HEAD>
<STYLE>
      @import "http://www.mysite.com/stylesheets/yourstyle.css";
</STYLE>
</HEAD>
<BODY>
<H1> This is heading level 1 which is right aligned. </H1>
<P> I am an italic style Paragraph. </P>
</BODY>
</HTML>
```

Now that we know how to apply styles, we will consider the rules that help resolve conflicts in situations where more than one style may be applicable.

Style Precedence

In real-life situations, you may use more than one imported style sheet and combine them with document-level styles and use inline styling. This combination will lead to confusion regarding the style to be eventually applied to a specific element. It is possible that the same property is defined in two different style sheets and the value specified for the property could be different. The text of an element cannot be displayed in two colors. This can be sorted to an extent by understanding the style precedence, which is not very clearly defined in CSS2 standards. The incomplete implementations of CSS2 standards by the browsers add to complexity in this issue. According to the CSS2 standards, this issue is called *specificity*.

The style precedence can be determined by the following rules in the order specified:

- The inline style takes precedence over the document-level style, which, in turn, takes precedence over the external style sheet.

- The styles defined with ID selectors are more specific than other styles. Therefore, they take precedence over the other selectors.

- If there is more than one applicable style:

    1. The style that is defined as a class of a tag takes precedence.

    2. If multiple styles are applicable, even after applying the rule in Step 1, the style that is more specific or contextual is applied.

    3. If multiple styles are applicable, even after applying the rule in Step 2, the last specified style is applied.

These rules apply to most situations, but you may come across situations where these rules might not work as specified. The problem may persist because W3C has not specified any clear pattern for resolving these conflicts. All the style-aware browsers also do not follow a specific order for resolving the precedence issue.

Next we will discuss implementation of styles in Netscape Navigator and Internet Explorer.

Implementing Styles in Navigator

Netscape Navigator provides support for CSS1 specifications and is working on providing support for CSS2 specifications. Navigator also provides a mapping between the CSS syntax and JavaScript syntax. Using the `document` object model, Navigator defines `tags`, `classes`, and `ids` properties for the `document` object. DOM provides access to the style properties of the HTML tags. Although the style properties of the HTML tag correspond to the CSS properties, they can be written in a different way. Most of the CSS properties contain the hyphen character in their names. The hyphen character is not valid in JavaScript. In JavaScript Style Sheets, these properties are written in a different way. For example, text-decoration is referred to as textDecoration. The styles specified using JavaScript should be included in the `<HEAD>` section. If styles are included in the `<BODY>` section, the styles are not affected immediately. If any user action causes the reformatting of the document, these styles are applied to the document.

Netscape Navigator 4 does not allow inline styling through JavaScript Style Sheets. This is mainly because Navigator 4 DOM does not provide access to the `STYLE` attribute in most of the HTML tags. In the previous sections, we have examined how JavaScript Style Sheets are defined and used.

Implementing Styles in Internet Explorer

Internet Explorer provides a different set of application programming interface for JavaScript to work with style sheets. In the Internet Explorer model, the property names are changed so that the hyphens are eliminated. Internet Explorer allows JavaScript access to styles and style sheets. In Internet Explorer, the style sheets are stored in a `styleSheets[]` array of the document. This array contains `StyleSheet` objects. Each `StyleSheet` object further contains a `rules[]` array. A `StyleSheet` object also has an `addRule()` method. The `rules[]` array contains CSS rules. Using the `addRule()` method, new styles can be defined. Netscape provides a better alternative to CSS by allowing JavaScript Style Sheets. However, in Internet Explorer, you can only access the existing style sheets. Alternatively, Internet Explorer provides access to inline styles through its Application Programming Interface (API). Navigator does not allow this. Internet Explorer DOM makes all the elements available to the scripting language. All the elements have a `style` attribute. You can use this property to set any style. The Internet Explorer model also affects the changes made to inline styles immediately. This allows the style of the elements to be changed by providing inline style information.

Dynamic Positioning

To create complex effects, Web developers need more control over the elements on a Web page. For example, the functionality on a Web page might demand that a few elements be displayed and a few hidden. CSS2 has several formatting properties to support these formatting requirements. The most commonly used property is the `position` property. The default value of this property is `static`. There are three other values possible for this property: `absolute`, `relative`, and `fixed`.

There are other properties, such as `left`, `top`, `bottom`, and `right`, which support formatting requirements. These properties help determine the position and size of an element on a Web page There are other properties, such as `clip`, `overflow`, and `visibility`, which decide how the element is displayed. If the elements are stacked one over the other on a Web page, the `z-index` property can be used to determine the stacking order of the elements.

Now, let us see how you can implement these properties in your code. The declaration `position: absolute` defines an element whose position is defined relative to the upper-left corner of the Web page. In other words, the element will take a position in the upper-left corner of the body element. The `top` property defines the distance from the top of the browser window to the top of the positioned element. The `left` property indicates the distance from the left of the browser window to the left side of the positioned element.

With absolute positioning, the element does not have a relationship with the regular flow of the content on the page. The other content ignores the absolutely positioned element. Similarly, the absolutely positioned element ignores the surrounding text. The following example shows how absolute positioning works:

```
<HTML>
<HEAD>
<TITLE> How Absolute Positioning Works </TITLE>
<STYLE TYPE = "text/css">
.yourstyle {
    color: Red;
    position: absolute;
    left: 150px;
    top: 200px;
}
</STYLE>
</HEAD>
<BODY>
This text is not positioned.
<P CLASS = "yourstyle"> This is an absolutely positioned text. </P>
Again this is not a positioned text
</BODY>
</HTML>
```

When this page is loaded in a Web browser, the page will show the nonpositioned text on the top of the page. In addition, the absolute positioned text will be displayed at the position specified by the `left` and `top` properties. Even if the page is resized, the absolute position of the element will not change.

If the value of the `position` property is set to `relative`, the positioned elements continue to maintain their relationship with the other non-positioned elements. In the case of relatively positioned elements, the `top` and `left` properties place the element relative to its normal position in the content flow. This does not affect the normal flow of content, and if the elements are moved the space that it should have occupied in normal circumstances is left empty in the content flow. The following example shows how relative positioning works:

```
<HTML>
<HEAD>
<TITLE> How Relative Positioning Works </TITLE>
</HEAD>
<STYLE TYPE = "text/css">
.yourstyle {
      color: Red;
      position: relative;
      left: 40px;
      top: 20px;
}
</STYLE>
<BODY>
This text is not positioned.
<P CLASS = "yourstyle"> This is a relatively positioned text. </P>
Again this is not a positioned text
</BODY>
</HTML>
```

When this Web page loads in a browser, the paragraph with style applied to it will be visible in red and its position will be changed. The paragraph appears with the left and top properties acting like offsets. Using this style, you can move an element in relation to its position on a Web page. You can also place absolutely positioned elements within a relatively positioned element. In such a case, the origin for the absolutely positioned elements will be the upper-left corner of the parent element. The other properties of the absolutely positioned elements will work in the same way.

The third value for the position property is fixed. The other properties of the fixed positioned elements are the same as the absolutely positioned elements. The only difference is that it is fixed on the display and does not move if the content of the browser window are scrolled using the scroll bars. Neither Netscape Navigator nor Internet Explorer successfully support fixed positioning. Therefore, the documents using fixed position can produce unpredictable results.

As stated earlier, properties such as z-index are used to control the stacking order of elements on a Web page. Positioned elements are always at the top of the non-positioned content on the page. It is not possible to hide a positioned element by positioning it below the regular, nonpositioned content on a page. Using the clip property, the browsers can display the elements with a transition effect by gradually revealing the content of the positioned element.

Another useful property is the **overflow** property. This property specifies how the browser handles a condition when the content does not fit inside the specified region. There are three possible values for this property: visible, hidden, and scroll. When the value is set to visible, the overflowing content is displayed and the element also increases in dimensions. If you want the size of the element to be fixed, use the value hidden that clips the content at the bottom and right edge of the element. The third value scroll will display the content, but the user will have to use the scroll bar because the size of the element will not change.

Cross-Browser Implementation

Developing Web pages for a worldwide audience is not a very easy task. The users around the world use different browsers. If you are using DHTML effects on a Web page, it becomes important that all the commonly used browsers and their versions support your Web site. A wrong implementation of a feature can drastically reduce your audience. You can make your Web pages compatible with most browsers and versions, but it will be highly impossible to be compatible with all Web browsers. In this section, you will learn about the common cross-browser implementation issues. Our focus will remain on Internet Explorer and Netscape Navigator versions. Common cross-browser implementation issues are as follows:

Font Size related issues.   You must have observed that the same font size appears smaller in Netscape Navigator 4.x than in Internet Explorer. There could be many reasons for this discrepancy. It may be due to the operating system, the monitor resolution, or the browser. To avoid this problem, use style sheets that are made for a specific browser. You can dynamically build the styles by using JavaScript. A browser-detecting code can be used to identify the browser, and then the correct method can be applied. The browser-detecting code will be discussed toward the end of this section.

Implementing DOM.   The document object model is implemented in many ways. Different browsers use different approaches to refer to the elements in a DOM structure. W3C is working on developing a common standard for DOM, but differences in the implementation of DOM by browsers remain. Internet Explorer 5.x uses a proprietary method to refer to the elements in DOM. It uses the `docu-ment.all` method. Netscape Navigator versions 4.x and 6.x. do not support this method. Netscape Navigator 4.x supports the `document.layers` method, which is not supported by IE5.x. Netscape versions 6.x and IE5.x support `docu-ment.getElementsByTagName` and `document.getElementByID` calls. These calls are specified in W3C DOM API and is the recommended method.

Positioning Content.   Positioning content on the page involves the issue of CSS support provided by a specific browser. The division tag and layers are also used to implement positioning. There are a few properties such as visibility and stacking that browsers support differently. Internet Explorer 5.x supports divisions but does not support layers. IE5.x also supports the `visible` and `z-index` properties. Netscape Navigator 4.x supports layers. Layers can be made visible or kept hidden by using the `visible` property. There is no support for the `z-index` property. Netscape Navigator 6.x supports divisions. The individual elements on the page can be hidden or displayed. The items can be stacked on a Web page by using the `z-index` property. If Netscape Navigator is to be supported, the capabilities related to dynamic positioning are reduced to a large extent.

Scripting Language.   The support for scripting languages provided by different browsers is not consistent. Currently, the standard specification is ECMAscript. Internet Explorer supports Jscript 5.5, which is inherited from JavaScript 1.5. It also supports VBScript. Whereas, Netscape Navigator 4.x supports JavaScript 1.3 / ECMA, Netscape Navigator 6.x supports JavaScript 1.5/ECMA. It is recommended that you use JavaScript for your Web pages because the majority of browsers support it.

Browser-Detection Code. To work successfully with different browsers, it is important that the Web page know what browser it is working with. This problem can be solved by using the browser-detecting code. This code can identify the browser for the Web page, and then the rest of the programming can be performed as per the browser support. The following code example shows a sample browser-detecting code snippet:

```
<HTML>
<HEAD>
<TITLE>Browser Detection</TITLE>
<SCRIPT>
   function detectBrowser() {
     if(document.layers) {
       // Write code for Netscape Navigator 4.x in this section
     }
     if(document.all) {
       // Write code for Internet Explorer 4.x and 5.x in this section
     }
         if(!document.all && document.getElementById){
         // Write code for Netscape Navigator 6.x in this section
     }
     }
</SCRIPT>
</HEAD>
<BODY onload="detectBrowser()">
//Page structure resides in this section
</BODY>
</HTML>
```

This is a commonly used browser-detection code. In this detection method, the way in which each browser refers to the DOM structure is accepted as the basis for differentiation. Netscape Navigator refers to the elements in the DOM structure by using the document.layers method. If this returns a true value, the browser is detected as Navigator 4.x because Navigator 6.x and IE do not support this method. Internet Explorer browsers use the document.all method to refer to the elements in a document. Netscape Navigator 6.x uses the getElementById method to refer to the elements in DOM. Internet Explorer 5.x also uses the getElementById method. Therefore, to test for a unique condition to isolate Netscape Navigator 6.x, the code tests if document.all returns null and document.getElementById is true. This combination of conditions will be true only for Netscape Navigator 6.x. This browser-detection code will work successfully for Netscape Navigator 4.x/6.x and Internet Explorer 4.x/5.x. The other browsers available are Opera, HotJava, and Web TV. You can use the properties of navigator object and build a more comprehensive browser-detection code. There are many browser-detection codes available as freeware, and they can be used with the JavaScript code on your Web page. Generally, these browser detectors are available in the form of .js files, which you have to include in the script section of your code. After these .js files become part of your code, you can use the methods provided by that function for browser detection.

Layer Object

Layers were introduced with the introduction of Netscape Navigator 4. Using layers, you can design your Web page as multiple sections that are opaque or transparent. These layers can be displayed selectively based on user response. You can also move these layers. In addition, the layers can overlap each other. While implementing layers, you can use the concepts of dynamic positioning, which was discussed in several earlier sections. Layers can be stacked one over the other, and various effects can be generated. Layers can also be used to create multimedia effects, such as making a presentation from different layers.

Layers are created on Web pages by using the <LAYER> and <ILAYER> tags. The <LAYER> tag is used to create an absolutely positioned layer, and <ILAYER> is used to create a relatively positioned layer. <LAYER> and <ILAYER> tags are not standard tags but proprietary tags developed by Netscape. These are created for use with the Netscape 4.x version of browsers. Netscape 6.x and Internet Explorer 4.x/5.x do not support these tags. The application of the <LAYER> tag can reduce the target audience. Therefore, it should only be used after analyzing the browsers used by the targeted audience. The syntax for using the <LAYER> tag is:

```
<LAYER attributes>
     Put the HTML elements here
</LAYER>
```

The <ILAYER> tag syntax is:

```
<ILAYER attributes>
     Put the HTML elements here
</ILAYER>
```

The attributes used by <LAYER> and <ILAYER> tags are the same. Some of the attributes are:

ABOVE.   Using this attribute, you can stack a layer directly on the top of another layer. The name of the other layer is specified in the `attribute` value. For example, `ABOVE="toplayer"` places the current layer above the `toplayer` layer.

BACKGROUND.   This attribute specifies the image to be used as the background with the layer.

BELOW.   This attribute allows the user to place the current layer below the layer specified as the value for this attribute.

CLIP.   This attribute helps in showing a portion of the layer. It accepts the coordinates for the upper-left and lower-right corners.

ID.   This attribute identifies the layer by a unique ID. This ID can be used by JavaScript to dynamically control the layer object under code control.

PAGEX.   This attribute specifies the *x* coordinate value of the position of the layer object in relation to the browser window.

PAGEY.   This attribute specifies the *y* coordinate value of the position of the layer object in relation to the browser window.

SRC.   This attribute helps import layer contents from an external file. It accepts a valid URL as its value.

VISIBILITY.   This attribute controls the visibility of the layer on a document. It can accept three values: SHOW, HIDE, and INHERIT. If the value is set to inherit, the visibility of the layer will be the same as the visibility of its parent.

The following example shows a layer object in an HTML document:

```
<HTML>
<HEAD>
<TITLE> Displaying layers </TITLE>
</HEAD>
<BODY>
     <LAYER ID = "testlayer" BGCOLOR =  "Magenta" LEFT = 225 TOP = 150
WIDTH = 400 HEIGHT = 150>
     <H1> This is level one heading on a layer </H1>
     <P> This is a paragraph on a layer </P>
</LAYER>
</BODY>
</HTML>
```

A `layer` object is created for each defined layer. This `layer` object can be accessed by JavaScript to create dynamic effects. JavaScript also has access to a `layers` array. The `layers` array is a property of the `document` object. Each element in the `layers` array corresponds to a layer that is defined on the document. The `layers` array does not have entries for those layers that are defined within layers. These layers can be accessed through a second-level `layers` array. For example, the second layer of a document can be accessed as `document.layers[1]`, and the third layer within this layer can be accessed as `document.layers[1].layers[2]`. The name of the layer can also be used as an index while working with a `layers` array.

The `layer` object is used to identify an individual layer. A `layer` object has several properties. Each property corresponds to the attributes of the `<LAYER>` tag. It has other properties, such as `parentLayer`, `siblingAbove`, and `siblingBelow`. The `parentLayer` property specifies the name of the parent layer. The `sibling` properties identify the layers that have the same parent. `siblingAbove` identifies the layers above the current layer, and `siblingBelow` identifies the layers below the current layer.

The methods of the `layer` object are listed below:

captureEvents(event Type).   This method can be used to allow the layer to capture all the events of the specified type.

handleEvent(event).   This method is used to invoke the event handler for an event. The name of the event is passed as a value to this method.

load(source, width).   This method can be used to load the layer with contents from an external file. The file is specified in the source parameter. The width is specified for wrapping the text at that width.

moveToAbsolute(x, y).   This method is used to move the layer to a specified position in the document.

moveTo(x, y).   This method can be used to move the layer to a specified position within a layer or a document.

moveBy(x, y).   This method can be used to move the layer by specified pixels.

moveAbove(layer).   This method is used to move the layer above the specified layer.

moveBelow(layer).   This method is used to move the layer below the specified layer.

resizeBy(width, height).   This method changes the dimensions of the layer relative to the original values.

resizeTo(width, height).   This method is used to resize the layer according to the specified dimension.

Using JavaScript functions, you can use these methods to produce dynamic effects, such as changing the content in the layers. This will be discussed in detail in the following sections.

Working with Layers

In the last section, we discussed layers and their properties. You also examined the methods related to a `layer` object. In this section, you will examine code samples to learn how JavaScript and layers can work together to produce interesting effects. JavaScript and layers can be used to produce dynamic content and more presentable Web pages.

Layers can be very useful in situations where the content of a Web page has to be changed dynamically. New content can be displayed in a layer by manipulating the SRC attribute of the layer. In the following example, the content of a layer is changed when a user clicks a link on the page. The content of the layer will be changed to changeit.html when the user decides to load new content in the layer. Examine the code below:

```
<HTML>
<HEAD>
<TITLE> Changing content dynamically </TITLE>
<SCRIPT LANGUAGE ="JavaScript">
     function changeContent () {
            document.dynamiclayer.src= ="changeit.html";
              }
</SCRIPT>
</HEAD>
<BODY>
<P> <A HREF =" javascript:changeContent()"> Change the Content in the
Layer </A></P>
<LAYER
ID = "dynamiclayer"
PAGEX = 180
```

```
PAGEY=30
WIDTH=400
BGCOLOR= "gray">
<P> Default Content </P>
</LAYER>
</BODY>
</HTML>
```

There are other methods that can be used to change the content in layers. The `load` method can also be used to change the content in the `layer` object.

In this section, we discussed the positioning of elements by using layers. In the next section, we will look at how you can dynamically change the content of the Web page by creating sections in an HTML document.

Working with Divisions

The `<division>` tag is a block formatting tag used in HTML documents. The `<division>` tag supports the creation of sections in an HTML document. Both Netscape and Internet Explorer support this tag, unlike the `<layer>` tag. Netscape and Internet Explorer also provide dynamic support for the `<division>` tag. A unique `div` object is made available for each division that occurs in an HTML document. You can use the properties and methods of the `div` object. The `div` object has a `style` property, which can be used to provide style information to the `<div>` tag.

Using the `<division>` tag, content can be dynamically changed on a Web page. The following example works with `<division>` tags and creates a division on a Web page. The content of the `<division>` tag is changed when the user clicks the different links on the page. The implementation of this example will be slightly different depending on the browser being used. In Internet Explorer 5 and Netscape 6, the `innerHTML()` property can be used to replace the content of the layer. In the case of Netscape 4, the `document.write()` method will be used. In this example, we will also examine how different browsers are detected and how the right method for changing the content is used.

```
<HTML>
<HEAD>
<SCRIPT LANGUAGE="javascript">
function forContentChange(num){
changedContent="<P><B>You just clicked on link "+num+"</B></P>";
  if(document.all){
      //This code is for Internet Explorer 5
      varlayer = document.all["myDiv"];
      varlayer.innerHTML=changedContent;
}
if(!document.all && document.getElementById()){
      //This code is for Netscape Navigator 6
      varlayer = document.getElementById("myDiv");
      varlayer.innerHTML =changedContent;
}
```

```
}
</SCRIPT>
</HEAD>
<BODY>
<a href="javascript:forContentChange(1)">Click this Link to change the
content: Link 1</a>
<BR>
<a href="javascript:forContentChange(2)">Click this Link to change the
content: Link 2</a>
<BR><BR>
<div id="myDiv" style="position:absolute;background-
color:lightblue;width:300;height:50">This is an example of changing
Content Dynamically.</div>
</BODY>
</HTML>
```

In the preceding code, a division section identified by myDiv is defined in the HTML document. There are two links defined in the document. The links are numbered as Link 1 and Link 2. When the user clicks any of the links, the content in div section myDiv changes accordingly. When the links are clicked, they call a JavaScript function forContentChange with an argument, which is the number of the link. In JavaScript, the browser is first detected. Accordingly, either the document.write method is used with the <division> tag or the innerHTML method is used. Using this method, the content of the division myDiv is changed.

Creating Animation Effects

You just learned about the use of the <division> tag to create sections on a Web page. You can also use the <division> tag to create simple animation. Moving the <division> tag in a controlled and logical manner will create an animation effect.

Let's now look at creating an animation in a Web page. To create an animation, you first define a division that has the id animationDiv. This division should be absolutely positioned, and the background color should be blue.

```
<div id="animationDiv" style="position:absolute;left:0;top:0;background-
color: blue;">sample animation</div>
```

To control the position of the division section, set the position property to absolute. The left and top properties will be read and set accordingly. The syntax to read and set the values in these properties varies from one browser to another. This example will work with Internet Explorer 5 or later and Netscape Navigator 6 or later.

The syntax to read the value of left or top property in Internet Explorer is:

```
document.all.animationDiv.style.top =  120 + "px";
```

For Netscape Navigator, the syntax would be:

```
document.getElementById("animationDiv").style.top=120+"px";
```

To make the division section move, a timer loop is required and the left position is continuously changed each time the function is called. Examine the following code:

```
function createAnimation(){
xposition=xposition++;
if(document.all){
document.all.animationDiv.style.left=xposition;
}
if(!document.all && document.getElementById()){
document.getElementById("animationDiv").style.left=xposition+"px";
}
if (xposition>=-screen.width){
window.clearTimeout(varIdentifier); varIdentifier =0;
}else{
varIdentifier = window.setTimeout("createAnimation()",100);
}
}
```

The setTimeout method of the window object sets a timeout to invoke the function that is passed to this method. The function will be invoked after the time interval set in milliseconds. To clear setTimeout, another function of the window object, clearTimeout(), is used. This method clears the timeout passed to the method. The setTimeout method returns an identifier for the timeout set. In the function createAnimation, the division animationDiv is moved to the right and the animation effect is created. In the preceding code, the statement if (document.all) is used to check if the browser is Internet Explorer 5 or later versions. The statement if(!document.all && document.getElementById) is used to detect the presence of Netscape Navigator 6 because it supports the getElementById method. This type of browser detection is necessary to produce desired effects in both Netscape Navigator 6 and Internet Explorer.

In the HTML document, create a link. By clicking the link, the animation effect should start.

```
<a href="javascript: createAnimation()">Click this Link to start
Animation effect</a>
```

Combine all these parts of the HTML document code, and you will obtain the following complete code:

```
<HTML>
<HEAD>
<TITLE> Animation Effects by using Divisions </TITLE>
<SCRIPT LANGUAGE = "javascript">
var xposition=0;
var varIdentifier=0;
function createAnimation(){
xposition++;
if(document.all){
document.all.animationDiv.style.left=xposition;
```

```
}
if(!document.all && document.getElementById){
document.getElementById("animationDiv").style.left=xposition+"px";
}
if (xposition>=200){
window.clearTimeout(varIdentifier); varIdentifier =0;
}else{
varIdentifier = window.setTimeout("createAnimation();",100);
}
}
</SCRIPT>
</HEAD>
<BODY>
    <DIV id="animationDiv"
style="position:absolute;left:0;top:0;background-color: blue;">sample
animation</DIV>
    <BR><BR>
    <A HREF="javascript: createAnimation()">Click this Link to start
Animation effect</A>

</BODY>
</HTML>
```

Creating Multimedia Effects

In the topics that we have covered so far in this chapter, we discussed how to work with DHTML by using JavaScript. The `layer` object can be used with Netscape Navigator 4.x to create an animation effect and to dynamically change content. Internet Explorer and Netscape 6 provide the same functionality by using the `<division>` tag. In the previous section, we showed you how to create an animation effect by using the `<division>` tag. A combination of all these methods with audio and video files can be used to create a multimedia effect. The `<division>` tag can be used on a Web page to highlight important points. An audio narration of these points can be played in the background. In the same scheme, you can display a video clip to create a multimedia experience for the user.

A Web page can be made more effective and appealing by adding audio and video effects to it. The audio files can be included on a Web page by using the `<embed>` tag. The `<embed>` tag has an attribute, HIDDEN, which can be used to keep the plug-in toolbar hidden. The AUTOSTART attribute of the `<embed>` tag can also be set to false for all the audio files embedded on the page. The `play()` method can be used to play the audio files when the corresponding slide is made visible on the Web page. The `stop()` method can be used to stop the audio files. Video files can also be included on the Web pages to increase the interactivity in the presentation.

The following example demonstrates the application of audio and video files with `<division>` tags. The user can select the section to be viewed. The selected section will be displayed, and an audio file will be played in the background. One of the sections also displays a video file with the audio file.

```
<HTML>
<HEAD>
<TITLE> Creating Multimedia Effects </TITLE>
<SCRIPT LANGUAGE = "javascript">
function createMultimedia(num){

      if(document.all){
             if (num==1) {

document.all.multimediaDiv1.style.visibility="visible";

document.all.multimediaDiv2.style.visibility="hidden";

document.all.multimediaDiv3.style.visibility="hidden";
             }
             else if (num==2)
             {

document.all.multimediaDiv1.style.visibility="hidden";

document.all.multimediaDiv2.style.visibility="visible";

document.all.multimediaDiv3.style.visibility="hidden";
             }
             else
             {

document.all.multimediaDiv1.style.visibility="hidden";

document.all.multimediaDiv2.style.visibility="hidden";

document.all.multimediaDiv3.style.visibility="visible";
             }
       }
      if(!document.all && document.getElementById){
             if (num==1) {

document.getElementById("multimediaDiv1").style.visibility="visible";

document.getElementById("multimediaDiv2").style.visibility="hidden";

document.getElementById("multimediaDiv3").style.visibility="hidden";
             }
             else if (num==2)
             {

document.getElementById("multimediaDiv1").style.visibility="hidden";

document.getElementById("multimediaDiv2").style.visibility="visible";

document.getElementById("multimediaDiv3").style.visibility="hidden";
```

```
                        }
                        else
                        {

document.getElementById("multimediaDiv1").style.visibility="hidden";

document.getElementById("multimediaDiv2").style.visibility="hidden";

document.getElementById("multimediaDiv3").style.visibility="visible";
                        }
                }
                if (num==1) {
                        document.embeds[1].play();
                }
                else if (num==2)
                {
                        document.embeds[2].play();
                }

}
</SCRIPT>
</HEAD>
<BODY>
        <DIV id="multimediaDiv1"
style="position:absolute;left:10;top:10;background-
color:lightblue;visibility: hidden;width:200;height:100;">
        Section One Details
        <P> Point 1</P>
        <P> Point 2 </P>
        </DIV>
        <DIV id="multimediaDiv2"
style="position:absolute;left:10;top:10;background-color:
lightblue;visibility: hidden;width:200;height:100;">
        Section Two Details
        <P> Point 1</P>
        <P> Point 2 </P>
        </DIV>
        <DIV id="multimediaDiv3"
style="position:absolute;left:10;top:10;background-color:
lightblue;visibility: hidden;width:200;height:100;">
         Section Three
        <EMBED SRC = "SectionThree.mpeg" HIDDEN = "false" AUTOSTART =
"true" WIDTH = 150 HEIGHT = 80>
        </DIV>
        <BR><BR><BR><BR><BR><BR>
        <A HREF="javascript: createMultimedia(1)">Show Section One with
background Audio</A><BR>
        <A HREF="javascript: createMultimedia(2)">Show Section Two with
background Audio</A><BR>
        <A HREF="javascript: createMultimedia(3)">Show Section Three with
Video</A>
```

```
<EMBED SRC = "SectionOne.asf" HIDDEN = "true" AUTOSTART = "false">
<EMBED SRC = "SectionTwo.asf" HIDDEN = "true" AUTOSTART = "false">

</BODY>
</HTML>
```

When the HTML document described by the code above is loaded in Internet Explorer 5+ or Netscape Navigator 6+, it will display three links. The names of the links are self-descriptive. When the link for section one is clicked, it calls the create-Multimedia() function with the argument as 1. In the createMultimedia() function based on the value passed to num, the function forks into the appropriate branch and displays the related division and plays the audio track associated with section one. Section two is selected the same as for section one. In section three, when selected, a video file is displayed with the division section defined for it. The audio and video files are embedded in the Web page by using the <embed> tag and changing the attributes as required.

Result

Based on the discussion, the style and Dynamic HTML methods that you'll use to add the functionality stated in the problem statement are as follows:

■ According to the specifications for the first functionality, when a customer visits the Home page of the Web site, options should be available to select a style for the Web site. The selected style should be applied to all the pages. When the Home page is loaded in a browser, the customer will see two buttons in the lower-left corner. The labels for the buttons are Corporate and Informal. User can either select a formal, corporate style for the Web site or choose an informal, fancy style. When the user clicks either of the two buttons, a JavaScript function, setStyle, is called. This function makes use of the disabled property of the styleSheets object as provided by the standard document object model. The styleSheets object contains information about all the style sheets defined on a Web page. You can access a style sheet by providing the index number in the styleSheets object array. To access the first style sheet, type the index value as 0. The disabled property can have the value true or false. A true value indicates that the specified style is not active and is disabled. A false value makes the specified style sheet active. This style sheet will be applied to the Web page. In the setStyle function based on the name passed to it as a parameter, the style sheets are enabled or disabled. In the <HEAD> section, two style sheets are defined. The first style sheet is named Corporate. The other style sheet is named Fancy. There are different elements defined on the Web page. In the style sheets, these elements have been assigned a style.

■ According to the specifications for the second functionality, when the pages for the Web site are loaded in a browser, the customer should see a consistent style throughout the Web site. The specific sections can have different styles. Inline styles are to be used to produce localized effects. To achieve this, you will have to first define the company-level style sheet. In the code given here, the style sheet is defined as **csssample2.css**. This style sheet is an external file that is included in the main HTML document by using the LINK method. Using embedded style tags in the same HTML document, you can provide the style information for the links and the table containing those links. At places such as the <H1> tag, some inline styling is also used. The style for <BODY> of the HTML document is taken from the external css file. Using the inline style attribute on the page, changes are made to some of the attributes of the elements.

- According to the specifications for the third functionality, when the customer loads the information page in the browser, a navigation toolbar is displayed on the left-hand side and at the bottom of the page. When the customer clicks any of the links, the information related to that link is displayed in a <division> tag. A <division> tag is created and content is changed in that <division> tag by using the innerHTML property. When a link is clicked, the function setStyle is called with a parameter. Based on this parameter, the function setStyle executes the required portion of the code and sets the content in the <division> tag dynamically. This code also uses an external style sheet for style information.

- According to the specifications for the fourth functionality, when the customer points to the product image, the description of the product should be displayed dynamically as a slide-out layer. This could be achieved using divisions on the specified Web pages. The product images will be placed on individual division sections. Behind each product image division, one product description division will be placed. The z-index of the divisions should be set so that the divisions carrying the descriptions are stacked below the divisions carrying the product image. When the customer points to the image, the description division, which is initially hidden behind the image division, is made visible by moving it from its initial position to a position 200 pixels to the right. When it reaches that position, the image becomes static. When the customer points away from the image, the left property of the description division is again set to 0. In this way, the description division is again hidden behind the image division. Using two JavaScript functions, you can complete this functionality. There are four division sections involved in this functionality for two sample products in the code for this functionality. The appearance of the division sections is defined using the style attribute of the <div> tag.

Write the Code

Functionality 1.   Create a feature on the Home Web page where the styles applied to the various elements on the page can be changed as per the option selected by the user. There should be two options available. One option should display the Web site in corporate style in gray and black fonts. The other option should use different colors and styles to provide a colorful Web site. Use two different CSS definitions on the Web site.

Code for **different_css.html:**

```html
<HTML>
  <HEAD>
  <TITLE></TITLE>
  <SCRIPT language="javascript">
  function setStyle(styleName)
  {
  var sheet;
    if (styleName=='Corporate')
      {
      document.styleSheets[0].disabled = false;
      document.styleSheets[1].disabled = true;
      }
    if (styleName=='Fancy')
      {
      document.styleSheets[1].disabled = false;
      document.styleSheets[0].disabled = true;
      }
  }
  </SCRIPT>
  <style type="text/css" id="Corporate" name="corporate"
  disabled="true">
  body{
      BACKGROUND-COLOR: gray;
      COLOR: navy;
      FONT-FAMILY: Arial;
      FONT-STYLE: normal;
      TEXT-DECORATION: underline;
      TEXT-TRANSFORM: uppercase
  }
  H1
  {
      COLOR: black;
      FONT-FAMILY: Verdana;
      FONT-STYLE: italic;
      FONT-VARIANT: small-caps;
      FONT-WEIGHT: bold
  }
  H3
  {
      COLOR: Dark Blue;
      FONT-FAMILY: Tahoma;
      FONT-STYLE: italic;
      FONT-VARIANT: small-caps;
      FONT-WEIGHT: bold
  }
  </style>
  <style type="text/css" id="Fancy" disabled="true">
  body{
      BACKGROUND-COLOR: lightpink;
      COLOR: magenta;
```

```
        FONT-FAMILY: Verdana;
        FONT-STYLE: italic;
        FONT-VARIANT: small-caps
}
H1
{

        COLOR: blue;
        FONT-FAMILY: sans-serif;
        FONT-STYLE: italic;
        FONT-VARIANT: small-caps;
        FONT-WEIGHT: bold
}
H3
{

        COLOR: brown;
        FONT-FAMILY: sans-serif;
        FONT-STYLE: italic;
        FONT-VARIANT: small-caps;
        FONT-WEIGHT: bold
}
TD
{

        COLOR: green;
        FONT-WEIGHT: bold;
        FONT-FAMILY: Arial;


}
</style>
</HEAD>
<BODY>
<script language="JavaScript">
if (!document.all && document.getElementById)
document.write('<DIV style="HEIGHT: 74px; LEFT: 20px; POSITION:
absolute; TOP: 20px; WIDTH: 576px"><h1>Welcome to Web
Shoppe<h1></DIV><BR><BR><BR>')
if (document.layers)
document.write('<Layer style="HEIGHT: 74px; LEFT: 100px; POSITION:
absolute; TOP: 20px; WIDTH: 376px"><h1>Welcome to Web
Shoppe<h1></Layer>')
if (document.all)
document.write('<DIV style="HEIGHT: 74px; LEFT: 20px; POSITION:
absolute; TOP: 20px; WIDTH: 576px"><h1>Welcome to Web
Shoppe<h1></DIV><BR>')
</script>
<BR>
<H3>Visit our wide range of products available</H3>
<TABLE align=center border=1 cellPadding=1 cellSpacing=1
style="HEIGHT: 145px; WIDTH: 545px" width="75%">

  <TR>
    <TD><A HREF="#" onClick="setStyle('Corporate');">Flowers</A></TD>
```

```
      <TD>Confectionery</TD>
      <TD><P>Books</P></TD>
   </TR>
</TABLE>
<BR>
Choose a Style:
   <FORM>
   <INPUT id=button1 name=button1 style="HEIGHT: 24px; WIDTH: 126px"
type=button value=Corporate onClick="setStyle('Corporate');">
<INPUT id=button2 name=button2 style="HEIGHT: 24px; WIDTH: 147px"
type=button value=Informal onClick="setStyle('Fancy');">

</Form>
</BODY>
</HTML>
```

Functionality 2.   The top management of Web Shoppe has decided on a standard style to be applied throughout the Web site. Create a style sheet according to the style specifications provided in the style definition document. Link this style sheet to all the Web pages on the site. There will be some differences in style from section to section. This should be achieved using embedded style statements. In one section also, there could be instances where some inline style might be required. Use an inline style attribute or <SPAN> tag to produce these styles. The inline changes can be done but keep them to a minimum.

The **cssSample2.css** style sheet:

```
BODY
{
     BACKGROUND-COLOR: lightgreen;
     CURSOR: default;
     MARGIN-LEFT: 10%;
     MARGIN-RIGHT: 8%;
     PADDING-BOTTOM: 0px;
     PADDING-LEFT: 0px;
     PADDING-RIGHT: 0px;
     PADDING-TOP: 0px
}
H1
{
     FONT-FAMILY: sans-serif;
     FONT-WEIGHT: bold
     FONT-SIZE: 28px
}
H2
{
     FONT-FAMILY: sans-serif;
     FONT-WEIGHT: bold;
     FONT-SIZE: 26px;
     COLOR: maroon;
}
```

```
H3
{
    FONT-FAMILY: sans-serif;
    FONT-WEIGHT: bold
    FONT-SIZE: 24px
}
H4
{
    FONT-FAMILY: sans-serif;
    FONT-WEIGHT: bold
    FONT-SIZE: 22px
}
H5
{
    FONT-FAMILY: sans-serif;
    FONT-WEIGHT: bold
    FONT-SIZE: 20px
}
H6
{
    FONT-FAMILY: sans-serif;
    FONT-WEIGHT: bold
    FONT-SIZE: 18px
}
TD
{
    MARGIN-LEFT: 0px
}
H1#Heading1
{
    COLOR: blue;
    FONT-FAMILY: Arial, 'Abadi MT Condensed Light', 'Arial Black';
    FONT-SIZE: 32px
}
A.toolbar
{
    COLOR: green;
    FONT-FAMILY: Verdana;
    FONT-SIZE: 12pt;
    FONT-WEIGHT: bold;
    TEXT-TRANSFORM: capitalize
}
```

Code for the **AssignCSS.html:**

```
<HTML>
<HEAD>
<TITLE></TITLE>
<Style>
A.menuItems
{
```

```
        COLOR: yellow;
        FONT-FAMILY: Tahoma;
        FONT-SIZE: 10pt;
        FONT-WEIGHT: bold;
        TEXT-TRANSFORM: capitalize
}
</Style>
<link rel="stylesheet" type="text/css" href="cssSample2.css" />
</HEAD>
<BODY>
<H1 style="FONT-FAMILY: Tahoma;color:darkgreen">Welcome to Our
<i>online</i> Web Shoppe</H1>
<H2> The best place to shop in the comfort of your home</H2>
<BR><BR>
<script language="JavaScript1.2">
if (document.all){
document.write('<DIV style="HEIGHT: 257px; LEFT: 0px; POSITION:
absolute; TOP: 120px; WIDTH: 105px">');
}
if (!document.all && document.getElementById)
{
document.write('<DIV style="HEIGHT: 257px; LEFT: 0px; POSITION:
absolute; TOP: 120px; WIDTH: 105px">');
}
if (document.layers){
document.write('<Layer style="HEIGHT: 257px; LEFT: 0px; POSITION:
absolute; TOP: 120px; WIDTH: 105px">')
}
</script>
<TABLE border=0 cellPadding=1 cellSpacing=1 style="BACKGROUND-COLOR:
maroon; HEIGHT: 238px; WIDTH: 100px" >

<TR>
    <TD><A href="#" class="menuItems" >Home</A></TD>
</TR>
<TR>
    <TD><A href="#" class="menuItems" >About Us</A></TD>
</TR>
<TR>
    <TD><A href="#" class="menuItems" >Contact Us</A></TD>
</TR>
<TR>
    <TD><A href="#" class="menuItems" >Login</A></TD>
</TR>
<TR>
    <TD><A href="#" class="menuItems" >Administrator</A></TD>
  </TR>
 </TABLE>
 </P>
<P>
```

```
 <script language="JavaScript1.2">
if (document.all){
document.write('</DIV>');
}
if (document.layers){
document.write('</Layer>')
}
if (!document.all && document.getElementById){
document.write('</DIV>')
}
</script>
 <script language="JavaScript1.2">
if (document.all){
document.write('<DIV id=content style="HEIGHT: 74px; LEFT: 150px;
POSITION: absolute; TOP: 100px; WIDTH: 376px"></DIV>')
}
if (!document.all && document.getElementById){
document.write('<DIV id=content style="HEIGHT: 74px; LEFT: 150px;
POSITION: absolute; TOP: 100px; WIDTH: 376px"></DIV>')
}
if (document.layers){
document.write('<Layer id="content" style="HEIGHT: 74px; LEFT: 150px;
POSITION: absolute; TOP: 100px; WIDTH: 376px"><h1>I am a
Layer<h1></Layer>')
}
</script>
<P> </P>
<script language="JavaScript1.2">
if (document.all){
document.write('<DIV style="HEIGHT: 32px; LEFT: 80px; POSITION:
absolute; TOP: 412px; WIDTH: 542px">')
}
if (!document.all && document.getElementById){
document.write('<DIV style="HEIGHT: 32px; LEFT: 80px; POSITION:
absolute; TOP: 412px; WIDTH: 542px">')
}
if (document.layers){
document.write('<Layer style="HEIGHT: 32px; LEFT: 80px; POSITION:
absolute; TOP: 412px; WIDTH: 542px">')
}
</script>
<P>
<TABLE border=1 cellPadding=1 cellSpacing=1 style="BACKGROUND-COLOR:
lightcyan; HEIGHT: 27px; WIDTH: 490px" width="75%">

  <TR>
    <TD><A href="http://www.mysite.com" class="toolbar">Home</A></TD>
    <TD><A href="http://www.mysite.com" class="toolbar">About
Us</A></TD>
    <TD><A href="http://www.mysite.com" class="toolbar">Contact
```

```
Us</A></TD>
    <TD><A href="http://www.mysite.com" class="toolbar">Login</A></TD>
    <TD><A href="http://www.mysite.com"
class="toolbar">Administrator</A></TD>
  </TR>
 </TABLE>
 </P>
<script language="JavaScript1.2">
if (document.all){
document.write('</DIV>');
}
if (!document.all && document.getElementById){
document.write('</DIV>');
}
if (document.layers){
document.write('</Layer>')
}
</script>
</BODY>
</HTML>
```

Functionality 3.   The Web pages in the products section display the images of the products sold in that section. Currently, there is a static display of product descriptions on these pages. These Web pages should be changed to display the description of products dynamically. When the customer points to a product image, an animated slide-out layer should be displayed. The description should be hidden when the customer points away from the image. This process should occur for all images.

Code for the **cssSample4.css**:

```
BODY
{
    BACKGROUND-COLOR: lightyellow;
    CURSOR: default;
    MARGIN-LEFT: 10%;
    MARGIN-RIGHT: 8%;
    PADDING-BOTTOM: 0px;
    PADDING-LEFT: 0px;
    PADDING-RIGHT: 0px;
    PADDING-TOP: 0px
}
H1
{
    FONT-FAMILY: sans-serif;
    FONT-WEIGHT: bold;
    FONT-SIZE: 24px
}
H2
{
    FONT-FAMILY: sans-serif;
    FONT-WEIGHT: bold;
```

```
        FONT-SIZE: 22px
    }
    TD
    {
        MARGIN-LEFT: 0px
    }
    H1#Heading1
    {
        COLOR: blue;
        FONT-FAMILY: Arial, 'Abadi MT Condensed Light', 'Arial Black';
        FONT-SIZE: 32px
    }
    A.toolbar
    {
        COLOR: brown;
        FONT-FAMILY: Verdana;
        FONT-SIZE: 12pt;
        FONT-WEIGHT: bold;
        TEXT-TRANSFORM: capitalize
    }
```

Code for the **content_change.html**:

```
<HTML>
<HEAD>
<TITLE></TITLE>
<script Language="javascript">
function setStyle(name)
{
 if(document.all)
{
//This code is for Internet Explorer 5
if (name=='Home')
content.innerHTML="<A class=menuItems style=BACKGROUND-
COLOR:Blue;>This web page gives us details about the home page</A>";
if (name=='About')
content.innerHTML="<A class=menuItems style=BACKGROUND-
COLOR:Blue;>This web page gives us details about the Company and its
profiles</A>";
if (name=='Contact')
content.innerHTML="<A class=menuItems style=BACKGROUND-
COLOR:Blue;>This web page gives us contact information of the
company</A>";
if (name=='Login')
content.innerHTML="<A class=menuItems style=BACKGROUND-
COLOR:Blue;>This web page gives us details about logging on to the
site</A>";
if (name=='Admin')
content.innerHTML="<A class=menuItems style=BACKGROUND-
COLOR:Blue;>This web page allows you to get in touch with the website
administrator</A>";
}
if(!document.all && document.getElementById)
```

```
{
varlayer = document.getElementById("content");
if (name=='Home')
varlayer.innerHTML="<A class=menuItems style=BACKGROUND-
COLOR:Blue;>This web page gives us details about the home page</A>";
if (name=='About')
varlayer.innerHTML="<A class=menuItems style=BACKGROUND-
COLOR:Blue;>This web page gives us details about the Company and its
profiles</A>";
if (name=='Contact')
varlayer.innerHTML="<A class=menuItems style=BACKGROUND-
COLOR:Blue;>This web page gives us contact information of the
company</A>";
if (name=='Login')
varlayer.innerHTML="<A class=menuItems style=BACKGROUND-
COLOR:Blue;>This web page gives us details about logging on to the
site</A>";
if (name=='Admin')
varlayer.innerHTML="<A class=menuItems style=BACKGROUND-
COLOR:Blue;>This web page allows you to get in touch with the website
administrator</A>";
}
}
</script>
<Style>
A.menuItems
{
    COLOR: yellow;
    FONT-FAMILY: Tahoma;
    FONT-SIZE: 16pt;
    FONT-WEIGHT: bold;
    TEXT-TRANSFORM: capitalize
}
</Style>
<link rel="stylesheet" type="text/css" href="cssSample4.css" />
</HEAD>
<BODY>
<H1 style="FONT-FAMILY: Tahoma;FONT-SIZE:
18pt;color:darkgreen">Welcome to Information Page for the
<i>online</i> Web Shoppe</H1>
<P>
<script language="JavaScript">
if (document.getElementById){
document.write('<DIV style="HEIGHT: 257px; LEFT: 0px; POSITION:
absolute; TOP: 100px; WIDTH: 105px">');
}
if (document.layers){
document.write('<Layer style="HEIGHT: 257px; LEFT: 0px; POSITION:
absolute; TOP: 100px; WIDTH: 105px">')
}
</script>
```

```
<TABLE border=0 cellPadding=1 cellSpacing=1 style="BACKGROUND-COLOR:
brown; HEIGHT: 238px; WIDTH: 100px" >

  <TR>
    <TD><A href="#" class="menuItems"
onclick="setStyle('Home');">Home</A></TD>
</TR>
<TR>
    <TD><A href="#" class="menuItems"
onclick="setStyle('About');">About Us</A></TD>
</TR>
<TR>
    <TD><A href="#" class="menuItems"
onclick="setStyle('Contact');">Contact Us</A></TD>
</TR>
<TR>
    <TD><A href="#" class="menuItems"
onclick="setStyle('Login');">Login</A></TD>
</TR>
<TR>
    <TD><A href="#" class="menuItems"
onclick="setStyle('Admin');">Administrator</A></TD>
  </TR>
 </TABLE>
 </P>
<P>
 <script language="JavaScript">
if (document.getElementById){
document.write('</DIV>');
}
if (document.layers){
document.write('</Layer>')
}
</script>
 <script language="JavaScript">
if (document.getElementById){
document.write('<DIV id=content style="HEIGHT: 74px; LEFT: 150px;
POSITION: absolute; TOP: 100px; WIDTH: 376px"></DIV>')
}
if (document.layers){
document.write('<Layer id="content" style="HEIGHT: 74px; LEFT: 150px;
POSITION: absolute; TOP: 100px; WIDTH: 376px"><h1>I am a
Layer<h1></Layer>')
}
</script>
<P> </P>
 <script language="JavaScript">
if (document.getElementById){
document.write('<DIV style="HEIGHT: 32px; LEFT: 80px; POSITION:
absolute; TOP: 412px; WIDTH: 542px">')
}
```

```
if (document.layers){
document.write('<Layer style="HEIGHT: 32px; LEFT: 80px; POSITION:
absolute; TOP: 412px; WIDTH: 542px">')
}
</script>
<P>
<TABLE border=1 cellPadding=1 cellSpacing=1 style="BACKGROUND-COLOR:
lightcyan; HEIGHT: 27px; WIDTH: 490px" width="75%">

  <TR>
    <TD><A href="http://www.mysite.com" class="toolbar">Home</A></TD>
    <TD><A href="http://www.mysite.com" class="toolbar">About
Us</A></TD>
    <TD><A href="http://www.mysite.com" class="toolbar">Contact
Us</A></TD>
    <TD><A href="http://www.mysite.com" class="toolbar">Login</A></TD>
    <TD><A href="http://www.mysite.com"
class="toolbar">Administrator</A></TD>
  </TR>
 </TABLE>
 </P>
 <script language="JavaScript">
if (document.getElementById){
document.write('</DIV>');
}
if (document.layers){
document.write('</Layer>')
}
</script>
</BODY>
</HTML>
```

Functionality 4.   In the products section there are Web pages that display the images of products sold in that section. There is currently a static display of product descriptions on these pages. These Web pages should be changed to display the description of products dynamically. When the customer points the mouse over a product image, the image should be displayed as an animated slide-out layer. The description should be hidden once the mouse is moved away from the image. This should happen for all images.

Code for file **animation_sample**.html:

```
<HTML>
<HEAD>
<TITLE> Animation Effects by using Divisions </TITLE>
<SCRIPT LANGUAGE = "javascript">
var xposition=0;
var varIdentifier=0;
var divId='';
function createAnimation(animationDiv){
divId=animationDiv;
xposition=xposition+10;
```

```
if(document.all){
document.all.item(divId).style.left=xposition;
}
if(!document.all && document.getElementById){
document.getElementById(divId).style.left=xposition;
}
if (xposition>=200){
window.clearTimeout(varIdentifier); varIdentifier=0;
}else{
varIdentifier = window.setTimeout("createAnimation(divId);",100);
}
}
var divId;
function stopAnimation(animationDiv)
{
divId=animationDiv;
xposition-;
if(document.all)
{

    document.all[divId].style.left=0;
    xposition=0;
}
    if(!document.all && document.getElementById)
    {
    document.getElementById(divId).style.left=0;
    xposition=0;
    }
}
</SCRIPT>
<STYLE>
H1
{
  COLOR: BLUE;
}
</STYLE>
</HEAD>
<BODY>
<H1> On-line Web <i>Shoppe</i></H1>
<B>Listed below are products currently available. Place the mouse
cursor over the images to see their descriptions:</B>
<DIV id="Div1" style="BACKGROUND-COLOR: lightgoldenrodyellow; HEIGHT:
87px; LEFT: 0px; POSITION: absolute; TOP: 100px; WIDTH: 129px; Z-
INDEX: 100; z-zndex: 1">
<IMG alt="" src="Cake.jpg"
onMouseOver="javascript:createAnimation('animationDiv1')"
onMouseOut="javascript:stopAnimation('animationDiv1')" style="HEIGHT:
150px; WIDTH: 143px; Z-INDEX: 2" align=top>
<B> Product One </B>
</DIV>
```

```
<DIV id="animationDiv1" style="BACKGROUND-COLOR: lightgoldenrodyellow;
BORDER-BOTTOM: black 2px solid; BORDER-LEFT: black 2px solid; BORDER-
RIGHT: black 2px solid; BORDER-TOP: black 2px solid; HEIGHT: 87px;
LEFT: 0px; PADDING-BOTTOM: 0px; PADDING-LEFT: 0px; PADDING-RIGHT: 0px;
PADDING-TOP: 0px; POSITION: absolute; TOP: 100px; WIDTH: 129px;HEIGHT:
140px; Z-INDEX: 99">
Your Mouse is currently over <B>Product One</B>. This Product was
launched last week. It is still exclusive.
</DIV>
<BR><BR>
<DIV id="Div2" style="BACKGROUND-COLOR: lightgoldenrodyellow; BORDER-
BOTTOM-COLOR: black; BORDER-LEFT-COLOR: black; BORDER-RIGHT-COLOR:
black; BORDER-TOP-COLOR: black; HEIGHT: 147px; LEFT: 0px; POSITION:
absolute; TOP: 275px; WIDTH: 139px; Z-INDEX: 100; z-zndex: 1">
<IMG alt="" src="Rose.jpg"
onMouseOver="javascript:createAnimation('animationDiv2')"
onMouseOut="javascript:stopAnimation('animationDiv2')" style="HEIGHT:
147px; WIDTH: 138px; Z-INDEX: 2" align=top>
<B> Product Two </B>
</DIV>
<DIV id="animationDiv2" style="BACKGROUND-COLOR: lightgoldenrodyellow;
BORDER-BOTTOM: black 2px solid; BORDER-LEFT: black 2px solid; BORDER-
RIGHT: black 2px solid; BORDER-TOP: black 2px solid; HEIGHT: 87px;
LEFT: 0px; PADDING-BOTTOM: 0px; PADDING-LEFT: 0px; PADDING-RIGHT: 0px;
PADDING-TOP: 0px; POSITION: absolute; TOP: 275px; WIDTH: 129px;HEIGHT:
140px; Z-INDEX: 99">
Your Mouse is currently over <B>Product Two</B>. This Product is very
cost effective and easily available.
</DIV>
<BR><BR>
</BODY>
</HTML>
```

Execute and Verify the Code

Execute the code and verify the successful running of the preceding HTML files with the `Style` statements and DHTML, enabled through JavaScript code. Different functionality is performed on each HTML file. Open the HTML files and perform the steps as specified to verify the functionality.

1. Open HTML file **different_css.html** in Internet Explorer 5.x or Netscape browser 6.x. When this file is loaded in Internet Explorer 5.x, the customer will see a default style on the Web page. There are two buttons at the bottom of the page. One of the buttons is labeled `Corporate`, and the other button is labeled `Informal`. When the customer clicks `Corporate`, the style on the page should change. This style consists of more gray shades. When the customer

clicks `Informal`, the style of the Web page should change again. This time, it should have a style with multiple colors and the Web page should look more decorated. When the same HTML file is loaded in Netscape Navigator 6.x, the first style sheet is applied on the Web page. The remaining functions remain the same with Netscape Navigator 6.x.

2. Open the HTML file Assign Css.html in Internet Explorer 5.x or Netscape Navigator 6.x. After the file is loaded in the browser, the customer should see the styles applied by using style sheets at different levels.

3. Open the Content_change.html file in Internet Explorer 5.x or Netscape Navigator 6.x. When this file is loaded in the browser, the customer will see a navigation bar on the left-hand side. When the customer clicks any of the links on the navigation bar, the description for that link is made visible in a `<division>` tag in the center of the page. This description changes as the customer clicks different links. This demonstrates dynamic content on a loaded Web page.

4. Open the animation_sample.html file in Internet Explorer 5.x or Netscape Navigator 6.x. When this file is loaded in the browser, the customer will see a page from the Web site of Web Shoppe. On this page, the customer will see images for different products that have been sold online. When the cursor points to one of the product images, a description of the product slides out from behind the product image. When the customer points away from the image, the description should be hidden. This process should occur for all the product images.

Summary

In this chapter, you learned about style sheets and the methods used in JavaScript to interact with style sheets. Style sheets are used to separate formatting information from content in HTML documents. Using style sheets, the task of changing styles has become very easy. The Cascading Style Sheets helps Web developers create style sheets at different levels and then use them together because the style sheets can be cascaded. You also learned how to use Dynamic HTML, a combination of document object model, style sheets, and JavaScript. DHTML can provide a great deal of interactivity to the Web pages without interacting with the Web server. The ability to change content on a loaded Web page has changed the way in which Web pages are designed. By using dynamic positioning of HTML elements in a document, animation effects can be created. This also helps in making Web pages more interactive and interesting for the users. There are many possibilities to combine audio and video files with dynamic content changing and dynamic style changing to create multimedia effects. Cascading style sheets and DHTML have surely changed Web design concepts and have made Web pages more user-friendly and interactive.

CHAPTER 12

Server-Side JavaScript Using Active Server Pages

Getting Started

In the preceding chapters, we considered the use of JavaScript for the development of client-side applications in detail. At this juncture, we need to remember that a typical Web scenario consists of the client/server environment. We have already delved into the details of JavaScript for client-side scripting. Interestingly, JavaScript can also be used as a server-side scripting language.

In this chapter we discuss how you can develop server-side scripts with the Microsoft servers. The chapter is divided into three sections: introduction to Active Server Pages (ASPs), creating server-side applications by using ASPs, and creating database connectivity and interaction by using ASP.

It should be noted that before beginning this chapter, you should have a good understanding of server-side scripting basics and LiveWire basics. Appendix A, "Using LiveWire for Server-Side Scripting and Database Connectivity," provides detailed information about both server-side scripting and LiveWire. To understand this chapter, you also need to read Appendix A.

Active Server Pages

Active Server Pages (ASP) is a Microsoft technology that enables us to implement server-side scripting. Active Server Pages, popularly known as ASP, is a built-in feature of Microsoft Web servers. ASP is a parallel technology to Netscape's LiveWire. Like LiveWire, ASP also exists at the middle tier of the three-tier architecture of the Internet. Although the two technologies, LiveWire and ASP, are different from each other, you'll notice that there are many similarities between these two technologies with respect to their core objects.

Before we delve into the details of Active Server Pages, it is important for us to explore the differences between ASP and LiveWire. This information will help you identify when to choose ASP and when to choose LiveWire. There are two significant differences. ASP allows you to use several scripting languages, such as JavaScript, VBScript, and PerlScript, for server-side scripting. However, LiveWire allows you to use only JavaScript for server-side scripting. ASP allows you to use a combination of different languages within your scripts. This helps you use the best features of all the languages supported by ASP to your advantage. However, LiveWire is at a disadvantage since it can use only JavaScript for scripting.

> **NOTE** This book focuses on JavaScript. Therefore, you'll notice that we have limited the discussion to server-side scripting in ASP using JavaScript only.

As with LiveWire, ASP does not require any special development environment components. ASP components include script engines that interpret ASP code. JavaScript and VBScript engines are integrated with Microsoft Web servers only.

To execute a LiveWire application, you need to install, start, and stop the application. However, ASP applications need not be compiled in this manner. To install an ASP application, you need to put the files in one of the server directories. (The details of this will be dealt with in the section *Creating an ASP Application.*) Then the ASP application executes automatically when a Web server receives a request for one of the application's pages. If you make any changes in an ASP application, you need not reinstall the application as you must with LiveWire.

In the preceding discussion, we stated that components of ASP include script engines that interpret the ASP code. ASP provides better communication between a browser and a server with the release of Internet Information Server 4.0 (IIS 4.0) and Personal Web Server 4.0 (PWS 4.0). The following are the Web servers that can be used with ASP:

- Microsoft Internet Information Server version 4.0 on Windows NT Server 4.0
- Microsoft Peer Web Services version 3.0 on Windows NT Workstation 4.0
- Microsoft Personal Web Server on Windows 95/98

Having looked at the key servers that can be used with ASP, let us now discuss how Active Server Pages are processed on the server. The following steps briefly describe how ASP files are processed on the server:

1. A client or the browser sends a request for an ASP page to the Web server, either by a URL or a form.
2. The Web server receives the request and retrieves the appropriate ASP file from the disk or memory.
3. The Web server forwards the ASP file to the ASP script engine for processing.
4. The ASP engine reads the file from top to bottom and executes any server-side script it encounters.
5. The processed ASP file is generated as an HTML document and the ASP engine sends the HTML page to the server.
6. The Web server then sends the HTML page to the client.
7. The client or the browser interprets the output and displays it.

The Web server generates and sends only the HTML output to the client. As a result, this mechanism helps in hiding the script commands of the ASP file.

Figure 12.1 displays how ASP files are processed on the server.

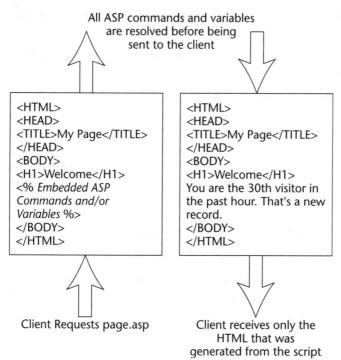

Figure 12.1   Processing the request for an ASP file by the Web server.

Let us now take up the scenario of Web Shoppe where Web Shoppe wants to display a personalized message and the hit count by using server-side scripting. At the end of this scenario, you will have created a server-side application in JavaScript.

Creating an ASP Application

Problem Statement

The current trend for most Web sites is to display personalized messages and the number of hits on the site. You may also find messages displayed in a personalized format, which contain the date of the user's last visit.

Web Shoppe has also decided to display personalized messages to the customer by using the customer's first name as a greeting. Web Shoppe has also decided that it will display the number of visits that a customer has made to its sites.

The development team has been assigned the task of displaying on the Home page the personalized message along with the number of times a customer has visited the site.

Task List

Based on the requirements specified in the preceding scenario, the development team has identified the following tasks:

- ✔ **Identify the ASP objects to add the personalized message and the hit count in the Home page.**
- ✔ **Write the code for the HTML page that will accept the customer's name and take the customer to the Home page.**
- ✔ **Write the ASP code for the Home page that will display the personalized message and the hit count.**
- ✔ **Execute and verify the successful running of the code.**

After having identified the tasks, let us consider each task in isolation to understand how the development team adds the personalized message and the hit count information in Web Shoppe's Home page by using Active Server Pages.

Identify the ASP Objects to Add the Personalized Message and the Hit Count in the Home Page

Before identifying the ASP objects to add the personalized message and the hit count in the Home page, let's first introduce you to some basic concepts of ASP. To create an application in ASP, you need to perform the following steps:

- Create an ASP file.
- Create a virtual directory on the IIS server.
- Browse the .asp file.

Creating an Active Server Pages (ASP) File

Unlike LiveWire, where you create a server-side JavaScript application by creating the `.js` source files, you create an ASP application by creating files that have an `.asp` extension. An ASP file can contain:

- HTML tags
- ASP scripts
- Client scripts
- Text

To create an ASP file, create an HTML document; embed it with the client-side JavaScript script and ASP scripts, and save it as an `.asp` file. A simple HTML file with a renamed extension as `.asp` also qualifies as an ASP file. However, renaming a simple HTML file to an `.asp` file can add extra expense to the processing of a Web page. As stated earlier, when a client sends a request for an ASP file, the script engine in the server reads the file and executes any server-side script it encounters before returning the file to the client. Because the execution process is going on in the server, the server compiles the complete file regardless of whether the file contains the server-side JavaScript code. This means that you should not use the `.asp` extension with HTML files that do not contain the server-side JavaScript code because each ASP file takes extra compilation time on the server.

To create an ASP file, you'll first need to learn about the server-side objects supported by ASP and the syntax for combining ASP scripts in HTML code.

ASP Delimiters

An ASP file needs to be processed by the Web server. Therefore, to signify that the server and not the client should evaluate a section of the ASP file, you can enclose the ASP scripts in the <% and %> delimiters, or the <SCRIPT> and </SCRIPT> tags with the RUNAT attribute set to SERVER. The following sections cover the situations where you should use the <% and %> delimiters and the <SCRIPT> and </SCRIPT> tags:

Using the <%...%> Delimiters to Enclose the ASP Script. The lines enclosed between the <% and %> markers are considered as ASP script. You can include any valid scripting language command within the script delimiters. For example, the following code includes the statement `Response.Write("An example of script delimiters.")` in the script delimiters.

```
<% Response.Write("An example of script delimiters.") %>
```

This statement displays the message "An example of script delimiters." on the client browser.

You can also include the script delimiters inside an HTML tag. Consider the following statement:

```
<A HREF="mailto: " + <% Response.Write(Session.Contents("email"))
%> Click here to send an e-mail</A>
```

For the preceding code, we assume that an ASP Session object has been used to create a client property, email. Now the preceding code uses the email property of the session object in a link.

> **NOTE** In the preceding code, the email **property of the** Session **object has been used as a parameter of the** Contents **collection. The details of** collections **and the** Session **object will be dealt with a little later in the chapter.**

Using <SCRIPT>...</SCRIPT> Tags to Enclose the ASP Script.

<SCRIPT>...</SCRIPT> tags are normally used in client-side scripting to enclose JavaScript. These tags, <SCRIPT>...</SCRIPT>, can also be used to enclose an ASP script. When should you use <SCRIPT>...</SCRIPT> tags in the server-side scripting? When your client-side JavaScript requires heavy processing that may be too taxing for the client's system, you may assign <SCRIPT>...</SCRIPT> tags to run on the server. You can include any server-side objects and methods in <SCRIPT>...</SCRIPT> tags. Consider the following example that uses <SCRIPT>...</SCRIPT> tags:

```
<HTML>
<HEAD>
<TITLE>Welcome</TITLE>
<H2>First example of an ASP page </H2>
<SCRIPT LANGUAGE=JavaScript RUNAT=SERVER>
var currDate = new Date();
function dispDate(){
    Response.Write(currDate.toLocaleString());
}
</SCRIPT>
</HEAD>
<BODY>
<SCRIPT LANGUAGE=JavaScript RUNAT=SERVER>
Response.Write("<HR>");
Response.Write("The current date and time is: ");
dispDate();
Response.Write("<HR>");
</SCRIPT>
</BODY>
</HTML>
```

Figure 12.2 displays the current date and time on the client's computer.

> **NOTE** To execute and view the output of the code used in this section, you'll first need to read through the next section.

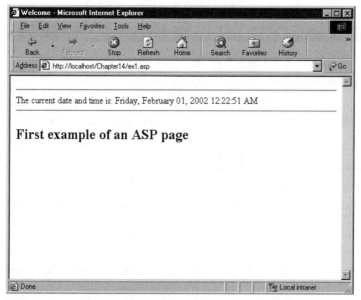

Figure 12.2 Current date and time on the client's computer.

ASP Directives

You can use ASP directives to indicate the scripting language used in an ASP file and to send the output to the browser. There are two types of ASP directives: processing and output.

Processing Directive. The ASP processing directive notifies a server with information about how to process the scripts in an ASP document. The following is the syntax for writing a processing directive:

```
<%@ LANGUAGE=ScriptLanguage %>
```

In the preceding syntax, the LANGUAGE=ScriptLanguage attribute sets the default scripting language used in an ASP application. If you are using JavaScript as the scripting language, you need to write the following statement:

```
<%@ LANGUAGE=JavaScript %>
```

In the preceding syntax and the example, only the LANGUAGE attribute is included in the processing directive. However, there are several other attributes of a processing directive. Table 12.1 lists all the attributes of the processing directive:

Table 12.1   Attributes of Processing Directive

ATTRIBUTES	DESCRIPTION
LANGUAGE	Indicates the default scripting language to be used in the document.
CODEPAGE	Indicates character set of an ASP document.
ENABLESESSIONSTATE	Indicates whether the ASP document maintains the state information.
LCID	Indicates the local identifier of a script.
TRANSACTION	Indicates whether a script has to be considered as a transaction.

It is not necessary to include a processing directive in an ASP document. However, as ASP supports a range of scripting languages, it is preferable to indicate what scripting language you will use in a particular server-side ASP application. In addition, you must place the processing directive on the first line of the HTML file, that is, even before the <HTML> tag.

Output Directive.   The output directive sends the result of an expression to a client's computer (browser). The following is the syntax for writing an output directive:

```
<% = expression %>
```

The following code makes use of both the processing and output directives:

```
<%@ LANGUAGE=JavaScript %>
<HTML>
<% var numOne = 10
var numTwo = 20;
Response.Write("The result of " + numTwo + " minus " + numOne + "
is "); %>
<%= numTwo - numOne %>
</HTML>
```

The preceding code displays the statement "The result of 20 minus 10 is 10" on the user's browser.

Figure 12.3 displays the output of using ASP directives example in a Web browser.

NOTE To execute and view the output of the code used in this section, you'll first need to read through the next two sections.

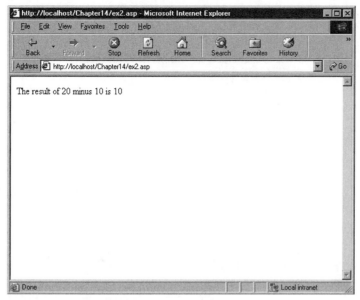

Figure 12.3 ASP directives example in a Web browser.

Creating the Virtual Directory on the Internet Information Server

The second step in creating an ASP application is to set up the virtual directory in the Internet Information Server (IIS) to host the ASP file. Although the IIS provides a default virtual directory in the default site, you can store the files in different directories and map them to a virtual directory that will be used to host the Web pages. The path of the default directory is C:\Inetpub\wwwroot. This default virtual directory is mapped to the Default Web Site in the Internet Service Manager. To view the Default Web Site, click **Start**, **Programs**, **Windows NT 4.0 Option Pack**, **Microsoft Internet Information Server**, **Internet Service Manager**. The Microsoft Management Console Window is displayed.

Figure 12.4 displays the Microsoft Management Console Window.

In the Microsoft Management Console Window, in the left panel, double-click **Internet Information Server** and then double-click **app_server**. Here, **app_server** is the name of the machine on which IIS is installed. In your case, it will be the name of the machine on which IIS is installed.

Figure 12.5 displays the Microsoft Management Console Window after you double-click **app-server**.

Figure 12.6 displays the Default Web Site in the Microsoft Console Window with the Default Web Site highlighted.

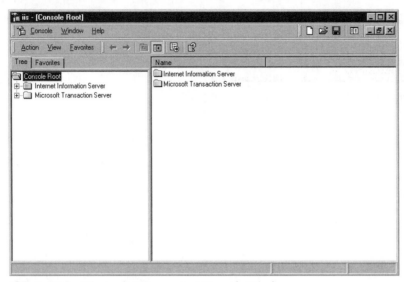

Figure 12.4 Microsoft Management Console Window.

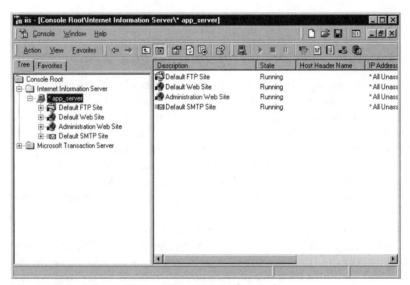

Figure 12.5 Microsoft Management Console Window.

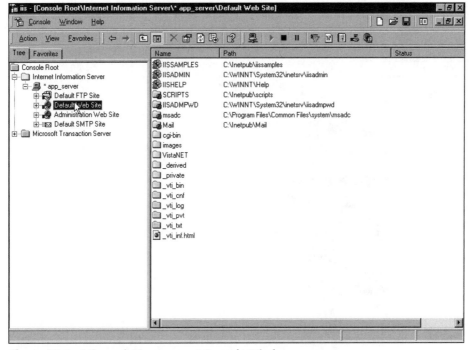

Figure 12.6 Microsoft Management Console Window.

Let us now create a virtual directory in the Default Web Site. You need to perform the following steps to set up a virtual directory:

1. Right-click **Default Web Site** and select **New, Virtual Directory** to start the New Virtual Directory Wizard. Figure 12.7 displays the Microsoft Management Console Window with the cursor pointing to the **New, Virtual Directory** option.

2. Provide a name for the virtual directory and click the **Next** button (Figure 12.8).

3. Type the path of the directory in which the ASP files are located on the hard disk or click the **Browse** button to select the path (Figure 12.9). Then, click the **Next** button.

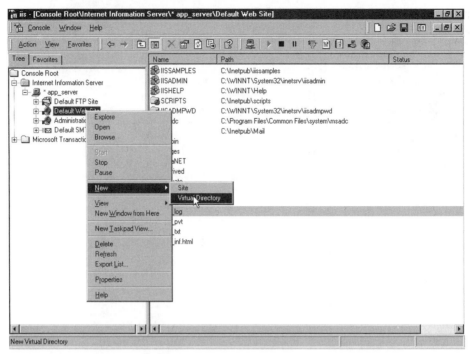

Figure 12.7 Microsoft Management Console Window.

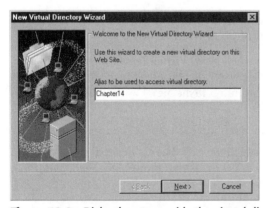

Figure 12.8 Dialog box to provide the virtual directory name.

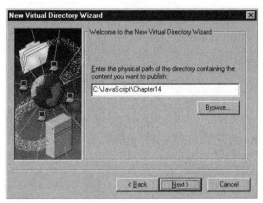

Figure 12.9   Dialog box to provide the physical path name.

4. Ensure that the **Read** and **Script** permissions are selected for this directory. Then, click the **Finish** button. Figure 12.10 displays the dialog box in which you'll set access permissions for the virtual directory.

NOTE If you are using Peer Web Services for Windows NT Workstation or Personal Web Server for Windows 95, the virtual directories should be added using their respective Web server management tool.

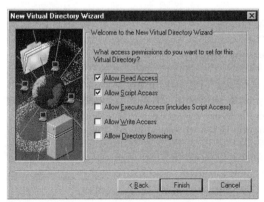

Figure 12.10   Dialog box to set access permissions for the virtual directory.

Browsing an ASP File

To browse the .asp file, open Internet Explorer. In the address box, type the URL in the following format:

```
http://servername/virtual directory name/ASP file name
```

In the preceding syntax, `servername` is usually the machine name if no other Web site is created on the machine. Therefore, you need to type the following address in the address bar:

```
http://localhost/Chapter12/ex1.asp
```

In the preceding URL, `ex1.asp` is the `.asp` file for which the browser has sent a request.

Until now, we have looked at some basic necessary concepts to create and execute a simple ASP file. To create an advance ASP application, you need to know about ASP core objects. The following section discusses in brief a few of the core ASP objects.

ASP Core Objects

ASP provides some built-in objects, which have methods, properties, and collections. The methods of an object are used to perform some tasks with the object. A property of an object can be set to a value, specifying the state of the object that can be used later. The collections of an object consist of different sets of key and value pairs related to the object.

Table 12.2 lists some commonly used ASP objects.

Table 12.3 lists LiveWire objects with functionality corresponding to ASP objects.

Table 12.2   Commonly Used ASP Objects

OBJECTS	DESCRIPTION
Request	Determines the information about a specific client request such as the type of method used and the details of cookies passed in the header with information in the form of Get and Post.
Response	Customizes the response sent from the server to the client.
Session	Stores user information that is needed for a particular client session. The variables stored in the `Session` object are retained for the entire session during which a user browses the pages of the Web application.
Application	Used for the processes of a Web application that are shared by all users of the application.

Table 12.3   ASP Objects versus LiveWire Objects

ASP OBJECTS	LIVEWIRE OBJECTS
Request	request
Session	client
Application	project

The following sections discuss the use of these objects.

The Request Object

As stated earlier, the `Request` object of ASP is analogous to the `request` object of LiveWire. The ASP `Request` object contains all information related to a browser's request. This information is passed to the `Request` object through the URL sent to the server. A `Request` object is created each time a client sends a request to the server. This object has the shortest life of all the ASP core objects. A `Request` object is created when a user clicks a link or selects a new URL in the browser or when a client-side JavaScript includes the `document.location` or `history.go()` methods.

The Request object consists of various properties, methods, and collections that help you retrieve values sent by a browser to a Web server during an HTTP request. The syntax for retrieving values from a `Request` object is as follows:

```
Request.[collection|property|method](variable)
```

Table 12.4 lists the property of the `Request` object.
Table 12.5 lists the collections of the `Request` object.
Table 12.6 lists the method of the `Request` object.

Table 12.4   Property of the `Request` Object

PROPERTY	DESCRIPTION	SYNTAX
TotalBytes	This is a read-only property. It specifies the total number of bytes a client browser is sending in the body of the request. For example, the following code sets a variable equal to the total number of bytes included in a `Request` object. `<% var count; count=Request.TotalBytes %>`	Counter = Request.TotalBytes Here, Counter specifies a variable to store the total number of bytes that the client sends in the request.

Table 12.5 Collections of the Request Object

COLLECTION	DESCRIPTION	SYNTAX
ClientCertificate	Retrieves values of the fields stored in the client certificate from a request issued by the client browser. For example, the expiration date of the client certificate can be displayed as follows: <%= Request.ClientCertificate ("ValidUntil") %>	Request.ClientCertificate(key[subfield]) Here, key specifies the name of the certification field to be retrieved.
Cookies	Retrieve values in the cookies sent in an HTTP request.	Request.Cookies(cookie)[(key)].attribute] Here, cookie specifies the cookie whose value should be retrieved, key specifies a parameter used to retrieve subkey values from cookie dictionaries, and attribute specifies information about the cookie.
Form	Retrieves values of the form elements in the HTTP request body. The value Request.Form(element) is an array of all values of an element that occur in the request body. The number of values of a parameter can be determined by calling Request.Form.(element).Count. Request.Form cannot be used when posting data with size more than 100 KB.	Request.Form(element)[(index)].Count] Here, element specifies the name of the Form element from which the collection is to retrieve values, index is a parameter that enables you to access one of the multiple values for a parameter and can be any integer in the range, 1, to Request.Form(parameter).Count

COLLECTION	DESCRIPTION	SYNTAX
QueryString	Retrieves values of variables in the HTTP query string. For example, if the following request is sent: http://localhost/scripts/list.asp?x=Sugar&x=Spice and list.asp contained the following script: <% For each item in Request.QueryString("x") Response.Write Request.QueryString("x") (item) & " " Next %> Output would be: Sugar Spice	Request.QueryString(variable)[(index)].Count] Here, variable specifies the name of the variable in the HTTP query string to be retrieved, index enables you to retrieve one of the multiple values for variable and is any integer value between the range, 1, to Request.QueryString(variable).Count
ServerVariables	Retrieves values of predetermined environmental variables.	Request.ServerVariables(server environment variable) Here, server environment variable specifies the name of the server environment variable to be retrieved.

Table 12.6 Method of the `Request` Object

PROPERTY	DESCRIPTION	SYNTAX
BinaryRead	To retrieve the data sent to the server from the client as part of a POST request. This method is typically used when the size of the data to be sent is more than 100 KB. This method retrieves data from client and stores it in an array.	Variant = Request. BinaryRead(count) Here, `Variant` contains an array of unsigned bytes returned by this method and before execution, and `count` specifies how many bytes to read from the client. After this method is executed, `count` contains the number of bytes successfully read from the client.

The code given below is used for displaying a form on the Web. It involves accepting the customer name and passing it to the `.asp` file that performs an action on the basis of the input given by **username.html**.

```
<HTML>
<HEAD> <TITLE>Query String Example</TITLE> </HEAD>
<BODY>
<H1> An example of Form collection </H1>
<FORM METHOD="POST" ACTION="result.asp">
<BR>Name:<INPUT TYPE=Text NAME="custname"><Br>
<INPUT TYPE="Submit" VALUE="Submit">
</FORM>
</BODY>
</HTML>
```

Figure 12.11 displays the interface of **username.html** file.
The following is the code for `result.asp` file:

```
<HTML>
<HEAD>
<Title> Query String Example</Title>
</HEAD>
<BODY>
<%
custname=Request.Form("custname")
%>
You have selected <%=custname%> as the customer name.
</BODY>
</HTML>
```

Figure 12.12 displays the output of the **result.asp** file.

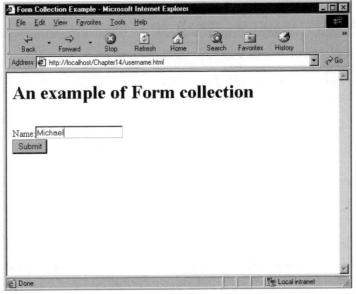

Figure 12.11 Interface of the **username.html** file.

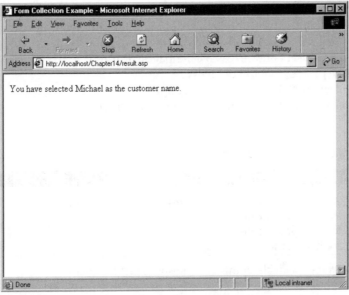

Figure 12.12 Output of the **result.asp** file.

Table 12.7   Collection of the Response Object

PROPERTY	DESCRIPTION	SYNTAX
Cookies	Used to set the cookie values. If the specified cookie does not exist, a cookie is created. If it exists, it takes the new value.	Response.Cookies (cookie)[(key) |.attribute] = value Here, cookie is the name of the cookie, (When key is specified, cookie is a dictionary and key is set to value) and attribute specifies information about the cookie.

The Response Object

A user communicates with a Web server through a browser, which sends a request to the Web server. When the Web server receives a request, it returns an HTTP response. The Response object sends the HTTP response information to the browser to display it to the user. The information can be sent directly to the browser, redirecting the browser to another URL or setting cookie values. A Response object does not have an analogous object in LiveWire.

A Response object also has several collections, properties, and methods.

Table 12.7 lists a collection of the Response object.

Table 12.8 lists some of the properties of the Response object.

Table 12.9 lists some of the methods of the Response object.

The Application Object

An Application object is used to initialize an application, automatically start processes that are required for an application, and allow the declaration of variables that can be used by all the users and across all the pages. The ASP Application object is analogous to the project object of LiveWire.

Table 12.10 lists a collection of the Application object.

Table 12.11 lists some of the methods of the Application object.

Table 12.9   Methods of the Response Object

COLLECTION	DESCRIPTION	SYNTAX
Redirect	Sends a redirect message to the browser causing it to attempt to connect to a different URL.	Response.Redirect URL
Write	Writes a variable or the specified string to the current HTTP output.	Response.Write variant

Table 12.8 Properties of the Response Object

COLLECTION	DESCRIPTION	SYNTAX
Buffer	Indicates whether the page output is buffered. When the page output is buffered, the server does not send a response to the client until all the server scripts on the current page have been processed. The Buffer property cannot be set after the server has sent output to the client. Therefore, the call to the Response.Buffer should be the second line, after <% @ LANGUAGE= %> statement, of the .asp file.	Response.Buffer [= flag] Where flag takes TRUE or FALSE to specify whether to buffer page output
CacheControl	Determines whether the proxy servers are able to cache the output generated by ASP.	Response.CacheControl [= Cache Control Header] Here, the Cache Control Header will be either public or private.
Charset	Appends the name of the character set to the content-type header.	Response.Charset(CharsetName) Here, CharsetName is a string that specifies a character set for the page.
ContentType	Specifies the HTTP content type for the response. The default content type is HTML.	Response.ContentType [= ContentType]
Expires	Specifies the length of time before a page cached on a browser expires.	Response.Expires [= number] Where number refers to the time in minutes before the page expires.

Table 12.10 Collection of the `Application` Object

COLLECTION	DESCRIPTION	SYNTAX
Contents	Contains all the items that have been added to the application. The Contents collection can be used to obtain a list of items that have application-level scope.	Application.Contents(Key) Here, `Key` specifies the name of the item to be retrieved.

The Session Object

The `Session` object is used to store the information needed for a particular session by a specific user. The variables stored in the `Session` object are available to the user even when the user navigates between pages in an application. The variables persist until the user is accessing pages in the application.

The Web server automatically creates a `Session` object for a user who requests a page of an application if the user does not already have a session. The Web server destroys the `Session` object when the session is terminated or timed out. The `Session` object is usually used to store user preferences.

An ASP `Session` object is analogous to the `client` object of LiveWire.

Table 12.12 lists a collection of the `Session` object.

Table 12.13 lists some of the methods of the `Session` object.

Table 12.14 lists some of the properties of the `Session` object.

Table 12.11 Methods of the `Application` Object

COLLECTION	DESCRIPTION	SYNTAX
Lock	Prevents other clients from modifying the properties of the Application object.	Application.Lock
Unlock	Allows the clients to modify the properties of the Application object.	Application.Unlock

Table 12.12 Collection of the `Session` Object

COLLECTION	DESCRIPTION	SYNTAX
Contents	Contains all the items that have been added to the session. The collection can be used to determine the value of a specific session item.	Session.Contents(key)

Table 12.13   Methods of the `Session` Object

METHODS	DESCRIPTION	SYNTAX
Abandon	Prevents other clients from modifying the Application object properties	Session.Abandon
Contents.Remove	Deletes a specific item from the Session object's Contents collection.	Sessions.Contents.Remove (Item|Index)

Result

Based on the previous discussion, the development team of Web Shoppe has decided that two files, **ShoppeStartPage.html** and **ShoppeHomePage.asp**, will be used for displaying the personalized message and the hit count. The **ShoppeStartPage.html** will accept the customer's name and contain the `Continue` button. When a customer clicks the `Continue` button, the customer is taken to the **ShoppeHomePage.asp** file. To enable this, the `<FORM>` tag in the **ShoppeStartPage.html** file is written in the following manner:

```
<FORM METHOD="post" ACTION="ShoppeHomePage.asp">
```

Table 12.14   Properties of the `Session` Object

COLLECTION	DESCRIPTION	SYNTAX
TimeOut	Has the timeout period for the session state for the current application in minutes. If the user does not refresh or request a page within the timeout period, the session ends.	Session.Timeout [= nMinutes]
SessionID	Returns the session ID, a unique identifier generated by the server when the session is created for the user of the current session.	Session.SessionID

The **ShoppeHomePage.asp** file, as the name suggests, displays the Home page of Web Shoppe with the personalized message and the hit count. The core content of the **ShoppeHomePage.asp** file is the same code as the **ShoppeHomePage.html** file used in Chapter 9, "Creating Cookies in JavaScript." However, the file also contains the code that will be processed on the server. The following is the additional code for displaying the personalized message and the hit count:

■ The beginning of the file will contain the statement:

```
<%@ LANGAUGE=JavaScript %>
```

■ The preceding statement sets the default scripting language used in an ASP application as JavaScript.

■ The <HEAD> tag of the HTML code will contain the following code:

```
<%
if (!Session.Contents("sameClient")) {
  Application.Lock();
  if (!Application.Contents("counter"))
    Application.Contents("counter") = 1;
  else {
    var curNumber = Application.Contents("counter");
    curNumber = ++curNumber;
    Application.Contents("counter") = curNumber;
  }
  Application.Unlock();
  Session.Contents("sameClient") = "true";
}
%>
```

■ The preceding code contains the if statement that uses the logical not (!) operator to verify that the sameClient variable exists in the Session object. If the sameClient variable does not exist, the variable is created and set to value true. The statement Application.Lock() is used to lock the application. The logical not (!) operator is used to verify that the counter variable of the Application object exists. The counter variable stores the number of times the page is visited. If the counter variable does not exist, its value is assigned to the variable curNumber. The curNumber variable is incremented by 1, and the updated value of the variable is assigned to the counter variable. Finally, the application is locked.

■ The following code uses the Request object with the output directive to insert the value of the first name text field from the **ShoppeStartPage.html**:

```
Hello <%= Request.Form("first") %> ! You've been on our site <%=
Application.Contents("counter")%> time(s).
```

Write the Code for the HTML Page that will Accept the Customer's Name and Take the Customer to the Home Page

The following is the code for the start page interface (**ShoppeStartUp.html**) that will accept the customer's name and take the customer to the Home page:

```
<HTML>
<HEAD>
<TITLE>Welcome to Web Shoppe !</TITLE>
</HEAD>
<BODY BGCOLOR="#CCCCFF">
<P><FONT FACE="Arial" COLOR="#5E00BB" SIZE="6"><STRONG>Welcome to
Web Shoppe !</STRONG></FONT></p>
<P> </P>
<P><FONT COLOR="#5E00BB" SIZE="3" FACE="Arial">Please enter your
first name and click Continue to proceed to our home page.</FONT></P>
<P> </P>
<FORM METHOD="post" ACTION="ShoppeHomePage.asp">
<FONT COLOR="#5E00BB" SIZE="3" FACE="Arial">
First Name:</font> <INPUT TYPE="text" NAME="first">
<INPUT TYPE="submit" VALUE=" Continue ">
</FORM>
</BODY>
</HTML>
```

In the preceding code, notice that the METHOD attribute is assigned the value POST and the ACTION attribute contains the name of the **ShoppeHomePage.asp** file. This means that when the user clicks the Continue button, the user is forwarded to the ShoppeHomePage.asp page.

Write the ASP Code for the Home Page that will Display the Personalized Message and the Hit Count

The following is the code for **ShoppeHomePage.asp** file:

```
<%@ LANGUAGE=JavaScript %>
<HTML>
<HEAD>
<TITLE>Web Shoppe Home Page</TITLE>
<%
if (!Session.Contents("sameClient")) {
  Application.Lock();
```

```
        if (!Application.Contents("counter"))
           Application.Contents("counter") = 1;
        else {
           var curNumber = Application.Contents("counter");
           curNumber = ++curNumber;
           Application.Contents("counter") = curNumber;
         }
     Application.Unlock();
     Session.Contents("sameClient") = "true";
    }
    %>
    </HEAD>
    <BODY>
    <TABLE BORDER="1" WIDTH="101%" HEIGHT="234" BORDERCOLOR="#FFFFFF">
    <TR>
    <TD WIDTH="26%" BGCOLOR="#CCCCFF" HEIGHT="56"> </TD>
    <TD WIDTH="73%" BGCOLOR="#9F81C0" HEIGHT="56"><STRONG><U><FONT
FACE="Arial" COLOR="#CCCCFF" size="6">Web
    Shoppe</FONT></U></STRONG></TD>
    <TD WIDTH="26%" HEIGHT="56" BGCOLOR="#9F81C0"> </TD>
    </TR>
    <TR>
    <TD WIDTH="26%" BGCOLOR="#CCCCFF" HEIGHT="166"> </TD>
    <TD WIDTH="73%" HEIGHT="166"><FONT COLOR="#5E00BB" SIZE="3"
FACE="Arial">Experience the world's largest shopping and entertainment
center at the mall of Web Shoppe Inc. Web Shoppe has over 350 stores and
services, over 110 eatery joints, plus seven Superb Attractions. It's
the only Web shopping mall of its kind - both a shopper's dream and a
world of excitement and adventure. Open round the clock, millions of
visitors from around the world visit this outstanding mall, which
features sale of flowers, books, confectionery, cards, computers, and
much more.
     </FONT></TD>
    <TD WIDTH="26%" HEIGHT="166"><IMG BORDER="0" SRC="Product.png"
WIDTH="217" HEIGHT="230"></TD>
     </TR>
    </TABLE>
    <HR color="#9F81C0" style="border-style: dotted">
    <font color="#5E00BB" size="3" face="Arial">
    Hello <%= Request.Form("first") %> ! You've been on our site <%=
Application.Contents("counter")%> time(s).</font>
    <HR STYLE="border-style: dotted" COLOR="#9F81C0">
    </BODY>
    </HTML>
```

Execute and Verify the Successful Running of the Code

To open the **ShoppeStartPage.html**: file, in Internet Explorer, type the URL http://localhost/Chapter12/ShoppeStartPage.html. The page as illustrated in Figure 12.13 is displayed.

Figure 12.13 displays the start-up page of Web Shoppe that accepts the customer name.

In the start-up page of Web Shoppe, enter the customer name as Michael and click the Submit button. The Home page of Web Shoppe is displayed with the personalized message and the hit count.

Figure 12.14 displays the Home page of Web Shoppe with the personalized message and the hit count.

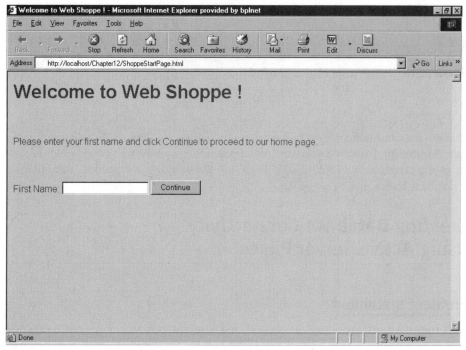

Figure 12.13   Start-up page of Web Shoppe.

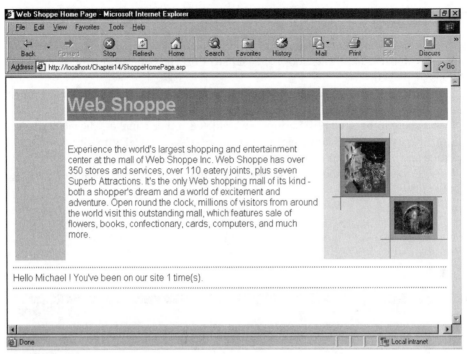

Figure 12.14 Home page of Web Shoppe.

In the previous scenario, we looked at creating a simple server-side ASP application using JavaScript. However, you can only appreciate the relevance of server-side scripting if you can store and retrieve data from databases. In the next section, we will look at database interaction by using ASP.

Creating Database Connectivity Using Active Server Pages

Problem Statement

On a shopping site, customers are usually asked to provide their personal and credit card details when making a purchase. However, for regular customers, it is inconvenient to provide these details each time they make a purchase. For customer convenience, Web Shoppe wants to create a customer registration form that provides an ID and password to the customer.

The development team of Web Shoppe has been assigned the task of creating the customer registration form.

Task List

Based on the requirements specified in the preceding scenario, the development team has identified the following tasks:

- ✔ **Identify a mechanism to store customer information and provide customer ID and password.**
- ✔ **Write the code.**
- ✔ **Execute and verify the successful running of the code.**

Having identified the tasks, let's now discuss the next step for the development team of Web Shoppe

Identify a Mechanism to Store Customer Information and Provide Customer ID and Password

Before we identify the mechanism to store customer information and provide customer IDs and passwords, let us first understand the basics of interaction between a database and a Web server. After that, we will also look at how Web Shoppe interacts with the server and thus provides a customer ID to the customer. However, we will begin with an introduction to ActiveX Data Objects (ADO), a Microsoft technology for accessing databases.

ActiveX Data Objects allow ASP and other Web development tools to access ODBC-compliant and OLE-DB-compliant databases, where ODBC stands for Open Data Base Connectivity and OLE stands for Object Linking and Embedding. ODBC- and OLE-DB are data source connectivity standards designed by Microsoft. The main difference between ODBC- and OLE-DB is that ODBC allows access to relational databases while OLE-DB provides access to relational as well as nonrelational databases. In this chapter, we will focus on how ADO can access ODBC-compliant databases.

ADO and OLE-DB are elements of Universal Data Access Architecture (UDA architecture). UDA architecture is a platform for developing enterprise wide applications that need access to various relational and nonrelational data sources across a network. The components of UDA architecture are Microsoft Data Access Components (MDAC). You can install MDAC from several Microsoft products, such as Windows NT option pack, Internet Explorer 4.0, Internet Information Server 4.0, and Microsoft Visual Studio 6.0. Most of these products automatically install MDAC. MDAC contains all software components of Microsoft for data access. In other words, MDAC installs several files on your system that are necessary in order to use ADO with certain programming languages. The ADO file that is essential to access databases with ASP is the **adojavas.inc** file. By default, all the ADO files are automatically installed in the C:\Program Files\Common\System\ado directory.

If you want ASP applications to access databases, you must copy the **adojavas.inc** file into the directory in which ASP files are placed. In addition, you also need to use the #include directive to insert the file into your program. The #include directive indicates that a file needs to be included before the ASP file is processed on the server. The following is the syntax for including the file in an ASP document:

```
<!--#include file="filename"-->
```

To include the **adojavas.inc** file into an ASP document, you must write the following statement:

```
<!--#include file="@adojavas.inc"-->
```

The preceding statement is placed after the processing directive of the ASP file but before any script delimiter.

Before we delve into the details of ADO objects and collections, you need to know how to connect to the Microsoft SQL Server by using ODBC.

Connecting to Microsoft Access by Using a Data Source Name

A Data Source Name (DSN) is a nickname given to a database so that it can be moved without changing the code. For example, if you register a database with any DSN, you can write the code to access it. Later, if you move or rename the database, you need not rewrite the code. You need only reconfigure the DSN.

There are three types of DSNs:

- User DSN is accessible only to the specific user who created it.

- System DSN is accessible to anyone who can access the machine, including programs such as services that have access to run on the machine.

- File DSN creates a file that acts as a shortcut to the database. A File DSN can be accessed anywhere throughout a LAN, as long as the file is in an all-accessible directory and the user trying to connect to the file has the proper database drivers installed on the machine.

Creating a file DSN for Microsoft Access

You need to perform the following steps to create a file DSN:

1. Click **Start**, **Setting**, **Control Panel** to open the window. In the window, double-click **Data Sources (ODBC)** to open the ODBC Data Source Administrator window.

2. Click the File DSN tab. Figure 12.15 displays the ODBC Data Source Administrator window with the File DSN tab activated.

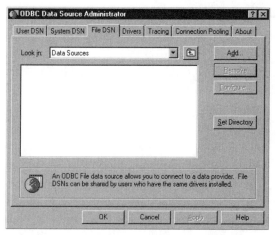

Figure 12.15   ODBC Data Source Administrator window.

3. In the ODBC Data Source Administrator window, click the **Add** button to create a new File DSN. A Create New Data Source window is displayed. From the list, select **Microsoft Access Driver (*.mdb)**. Figure 12.16 displays the Create New Data Source window with Microsoft Access Driver (*.mdb) selected.

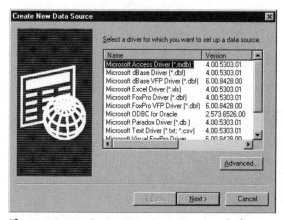

Figure 12.16   Create New Data Source window.

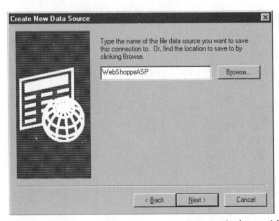

Figure 12.17   Create New Data Source window with DSN specified.

4. Click the **Next** button.

5. In the box, enter **WebShoppeASP**. WebShoppeASP is the data source name for the File DSN. Figure 12.17 displays the Create New Data Source window with data source name specified.

6. Click the **Next** button.

7. Click the **Finish** button. See Figure 12.18. The ODBC Microsoft Access Setup screen is displayed as shown in Figure 12.19.

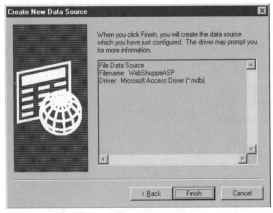

Figure 12.18   Create New Data Source window with details of the File DSN.

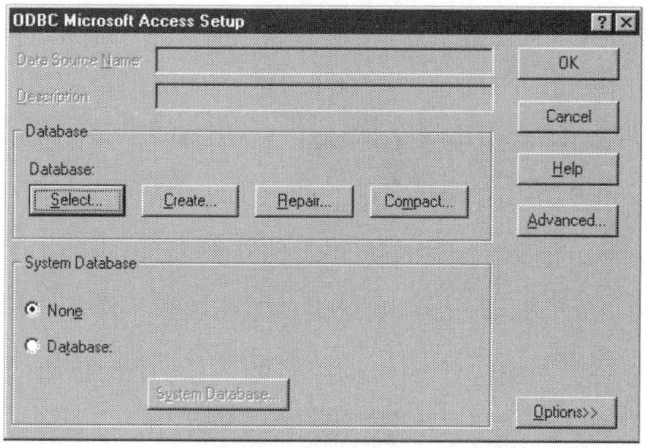

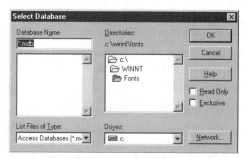

Figure 12.19 ODBC Microsoft Access Setup screen.

8. Click **Select**. The Select Database dialog box appears. See Figure 12.20.

9. Select the **WebShoppeDB.mdb** from the C:\JavaScript folder.

10. Click **OK**.

11. Click **OK** to close the ODBC Microsoft Access Setup screen.

12. Click **OK** to close the ODBC Data Source Administrator window.

We have created a basic setup to create a connection with the database. Let us now discuss how ADO objects help in writing the code for database connection. To understand ADO objects, it is important to know about the ActiveX Data Objects Model because this model lays the foundation for ADO.

ActiveX Data Objects Model

The ADO technology is based on ActiveX Data Objects Model that consists of objects and collections for accessing and manipulating data sources. Figure 12.21 illustrates the ADO2.0 object model.

Figure 12.20 Select Database dialog box.

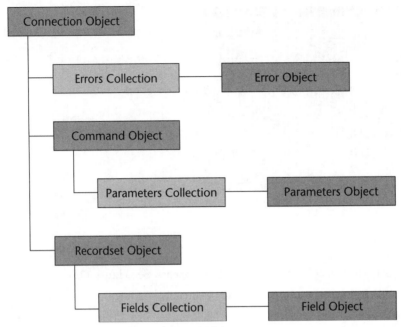

Figure 12.21 The ADO2.0 Object Model.

In Figure 12.21, the three main ADO objects are the Connection, Command, and Recordset objects. Errors, Parameters, and Fields are the collections that, in turn, contain the Error, Parameter, and Field objects, respectively. In the ADO object model, many of the objects are independent of one another. For example, you can create the Recordset object without first creating a Connection object. ADO creates a Connection object implicitly when you create a Recordset object. Table 12. 15 lists the objects of the ADO object model with their descriptions.

Table 12. 16 lists the collections supported by the ADO object model.

Table 12.15 Objects of the ADO Object Model

OBJECTS	DESCRIPTION
Connection	Makes a connection between an application and an external data source, such as Microsoft SQL Server, Microsoft Access, or a text file.
Command	Builds queries and accesses records from a data source.
Recordset	Accesses records returned by an SQL query. Using this object, you can navigate through records returned, add new records, modify existing records, and delete specific records.

Table 12.16 Collections of the ADO object model

OBJECTS	DESCRIPTION
Error	Returns detailed information about runtime errors or other messages returned from a data source.
Parameters	Passes specific data to a parameterized query or the stored procedures in an SQL database.
Fields	Accesses specific fields in an existing `Recordset` objects.

Let us now take each of these objects and see how these help in creating a connection and interaction with the server.

The `Connection` **Object**

To access a data source in Active Server Pages, use ADO. To communicate with the data source, you must first establish a connection. Use the `Connection` object to open a connection. The data sources with which you can establish a connection are databases such as Microsoft SQL Server and Microsoft Access.

The `Connection` object contains various properties and methods for accessing and manipulating databases. Before you use the `Connection` object, let us look at some of its properties and methods.

Table 12.17 lists some of the properties of the `Connection` object.

Table 12.18 lists some of the methods of the `Connection` object.

Table 12.17 Properties of the `Connection` Object

OBJECTS	DESCRIPTION
ConnectionString	Contains the information needed to establish a connection to a data store.
ConnectionTimeOut	Indicates how long to wait while establishing a connection before the attempt to connect is terminated or an error is generated.
CommandTimeOut	Indicates how long to wait while executing a command before the command is terminated or an error is generated.
Provider	Indicates the name of the provider for a `Connection` object.
Version	Indicates the ADO version number.
CursorLocation	Sets or returns the value of a cursor engine.
State	Indicates whether a connection is open, closed, or connecting.

Table 12.18 Methods of the `Connection` Object

OBJECTS	DESCRIPTION
Open()	Opens a connection to a data source.
Close()	Closes a connection and any dependent objects.
Execute()	Executes the specified query, stored procedure, or provider-specific text.
BeginTrans()	Begins a new transaction.
CommitTrans()	Saves any change and ends the current transaction, may also start a new transaction.
RollbackTrans()	Cancels any changes made to the transaction and ends the current transaction, may also start a new transaction.

Having discussed the properties and methods of the `Connection` object, let us look at how these methods are implemented to create a connection with the database.

To communicate with databases in ASP, you need to first create an instance of the `Connection` object. The `CreateObject()` method of the `Server` object creates an instance of the `Connection` object. The `CreateObject()` method takes a programmatic identifier or `progID` of the component on your computer. Here, component refers to the `Connection` object. The programmatic identifier is written in the following syntax:

```
vendor.component.version
```

The programmatic identifier to an ADO database is `ADODB.Connection`, where `ADODB` is the vendor and `Connection` is the component to be created. Therefore, the complete statement that will create an instance of the `Connection` object is as follows:

```
var MyConnection=Server.CreateObject("ADODB.Connection)";
```

In the preceding statement, `MyConnection` is the variable name that will be used to refer to the connection in the ASP code. You can create a variable with any name.

After the `Connection` object has been created, the next step is to open a connection with a data source. The `Open()` method is used to open a connection with the data source. The `Open()` method is passed to the connection string that contains the information about the data source. Based on the type of DSN used to make a connection with the data source, the connection string can contain different arguments. For example, if you are using System DSN, the connection string contains the following five arguments:

- **Provider.** This indicates the name of the data provider that exposes the data from the data source.
- **Data Source.** This indicates the data source name that you provide while creating a DSN.

- **Database.** This indicates the name of the database.
- **UID (User ID).** This indicates the login name of the user.
- **PWD (Password).** This indicates the password for user login.

If you are using File DSN, the connection string contains the statement:

```
FILEDSN=filename.dsn
```

This means that if you have created a DSN with the name WebShoppe, then the connection string will contain the statement:

```
FILEDSN=WebShoppe.dsn
```

When you are finished interacting with the database, you should end the connection. The Close() method is used to close the connection with the database.

The following statements are examples of how you can connect and disconnect to a File DSN that is named WebShoppe:

```
var MyConnection = Server.CreateObject("ADODB.Connection");
MyConnection.Open("FILEDSN=WebShoppe.dsn");
.
.
Additional Statements;
.
.
MyConnection.Close();
```

You have learned to open a connection with the data source. However, there may be situations where the connection with the data source may not be successful for some reason. In that case, the user may see an error message on the screen. Therefore, it is good programming practice to make sure that you have successfully connected to the database before you attempt reading, writing, adding, or modifying the records in the database. The State property of the Connection object can be used to determine the state of the connection, that is, if the connection is open, closed, or is still connecting. The State property returns the value adStateOpen if the connection with the database is successful and the value adStateClosed if the connection is unsuccessful. The following statements check the state of connection with the database and display a message in the case of an unsuccessful connection:

```
var MyConnection = Server.CreateObject("ADODB.Connection");
MyConnection.Open("FILEDSN=WebShoppe.dsn");
if(MyConnection.State == "adStateClosed")
    Response.Write("The connection with database was not
successful.");
.
.
Additional Statements;
.
.
MyConnection.Close();
```

There is a constraint with ASP programming in the context of a data source handling multiple requests at the same time. This means that if you are accessing a data source, another user cannot access that data source at the same time. However, the `Connec-tionTimeout` property of the `Connection` object helps to override this constraint to some extent. The `ConnectionTimeout` property enables you to abandon a client's database connection attempt if the client is not successfully connected after a particular period of time has elapsed. It is beneficial to use this property if your site is accessed frequently.

The `ConnectionTimeout` property takes an integer value to indicate the number of seconds before a client connection is dropped. After the number of seconds assigned to the `ConnectionTimeout` property has elapsed, the connection attempt is abandoned and an error message is returned to the client. By default, ADO waits for 15 seconds before abandoning a connection attempt. The following code displays the preceding example with a `ConnectionTimeout` property of 30 seconds:

```
var MyConnection = Server.CreateObject("ADOB.Connection");
MyConnection.ConnectionTimeout = 30;
MyConnection.Open("FILEDSN=WebShoppe.dsn");
If(MyConnection.State == "adStateClosed")
    Response.Write("The connection with database was not
successful.");
    .
    .
Additional Statements;
    .
    .
MyConnection.Close();
```

The obvious reason for accessing a database is that you want to view, retrieve, or update records. You have learned to open and close a data source connection. In the next section, we will discuss how you can execute SQL queries to access an ADO database.

Executing SQL Queries to Access ADO Database

ASP provides three methods by which you can execute SQL statements in an ADO database: the `Execute()` method of `Connection` object, the `Command` object, and the `Recordset` object. We have limited our discussion to the `Execute()` method of the `Connection` object and the `Recordset` object. Let us begin by exploring how the `Execute()` method executes SQL statements in ADO databases.

The `Execute()` method of the `Connection` object is analogous to the `execute()` of the `cursor` object. This method executes the specified query, stored procedure, or provider-specific text for updating or modifying a database table. The following is the syntax for the `Execute()` method:

```
connection.Execute(SQL statements);
```

There are two points that need to be considered when using the `Execute()` method. The `Execute()` method uses the native SQL language. Native SQL language means that the SQL statements are vendor-specific, which, in this case, is SQL language supported by ADO. The `Execute()` method returns the result of a query to the `Recordset` object. The `Recordset` object returned from the `Execute()` method is a forward-only and read-only cursor. A forward-only cursor allows only forward movement in the records in a record set. This means that you cannot make a backward movement or movement to specific records in a record set.

NOTE We have just touched on the concept of the `Recordset` object. The details of the `Recordset` object will be discussed later in this chapter. After you read about the `Recordset` object, it will be easier for you to understand this discussion about the `Execute()` method.

The `Execute()` method is most appropriate for inserting, deleting, and updating records in a database. Consider the following example where the `SQL INSERT` statement is used to add a new suppliers record to the Suppliers table. The SQL statement that will insert the record is assigned to the variable `SQLStatement` and is then executed using the `Execute()` method.

```
        var MyConnection=Server.CreateObject("ADODB.Connection");
        MyConnection.ConnectionTimeout=30;
        MyConnection.Open("FILEDSN=WebShoppe.dsn");
        if(MyConnection.State =="adStateClosed")
           Response.Write("The database is not available.");
        var SQLStatement = "INSERT INTO Suppliers VALUES('Carl', 'Lee',
'168 Spencer MA', '12890')";
        MyConnection.Execute(SQLStatement);
        MyConnection.Close();
```

We have looked at one of the methods for executing SQL statements in ADO databases. Let us now look at how the `Recordset` object executes the SQL statements.

The `Recordset` Object

As stated earlier, the `Recordset` object is used for executing SQL statements in ADO databases. The word Recordset means that the `Recordset` object creates a virtual table of values from a database. This virtual table is used to retrieve, add, delete, or modify records. After all retrievals, updates, and deletions are made in the virtual table and before the connection with the database is closed, the modified values are written back to the actual table.

Like the `Connection` object, you need to create an instance of the `Recordset` object by using the `CreateObject()` method of the `Server` object. However, instead of using the `ADODB.Connection` as the programmatic identifier, in the case of `Recordset` object, you use `ADODB.Recordset`. The following statement creates a new `Recordset` object:

```
        var MyConnection = Server.CreateObject("ADODB.Recordset");
```

After you have created the instance of the Recordset object, you need to use the Open() method of the Connection object to create a virtual record set table. Before you use the Open() method of the Recordset object, you need to assign values to the properties of the Recordset object. Assigning values to the Recordset object properties provides connection-related information. Let us now explore some properties and some more methods of the Recordset object.

Table 12.19 lists some of the properties of the Recordset object.

Table 12.20 lists some of the methods of the Recordset object.

After listing the properties and methods of the Recordset object, we'll now look at some examples so that you will have an understanding of how you can implement them.

The following example uses the Source and ActiveConnection properties of the Recordset object. Both these properties are assigned values before the Open() method is used for creating an instance of the Recordset object. The example first creates an instance of the Connection object and then by using the State property of the MyConnection object confirms that the database connection is live. Then, by

Table 12.19 Properties of the Recordset Object

OBJECTS	DESCRIPTION
Source	Indicates the source of data in a Recordset object
ActiveConnection	Indicates the database connection used to open the Recordset object
BOF	Returns the value true if the cursor is located at the beginning of the file, else returns false
EOF	Returns the value true if the cursor is located at the end of the file, else returns false
CursorLocation	Indicates the status of the location of the cursor, on a client or on a server. This property can contain three values: adUseNone, adUseClient, and adUseServer. The adUseClient value indicates that a client manages the cursor. The adUseServer value indicates that the server manages the cursor. The adUseNone indicates that the cursor is not managed.
CursorType	Indicates the type of cursor used in the recordset: adOpenForwardOnly, adOpenKeyset, adOpenDynamic, or adOpenStatic.
MaxRecords	Indicates the maximum number of records returned from a query.
RecordCount	Indicates the number of records in the recordset.

Table 12.20   Methods of the `Recordset` Object

OBJECTS	DESCRIPTION
AddNew	Creates a new record for an updateable Recordset object.
CancelBatch	Cancels a pending batch update.
CancelUpdate	Cancels any changes made to the current record or to a new record prior to calling the Update method.
Move	Moves the cursor to the specified record in a Recordset object.
MoveFirst	Moves to the first record in a specified Recordset object.
MoveLast	Moves to the last record in a specified Recordset object.
MoveNext	Moves to the next record in a specified Recordset object.
MovePrevious	Moves to the previous record in a specified Recordset object.
Open	Opens a recordset.
Requery	Updates the data in a Recordset object by re-executing the query on which the object is based.
Resync	Refreshes the data in the current Recordset object retrieved from the database.
Supports	Determines that a specified Recordset object supports a particular type of functionality.
Update	Saves any changes you have made to the current record of a Recordset object.
Close	Closes an open object and dependent objects, if any.

using the `CreateObject()` method with the programmatic identifier as `ADODB.Recordset`, the code creates an instance of the `Recordset` object. Next, the `INSERT` SQL statement is assigned to the `Source` property of the `Recordset` object and the `ActiveConnection` property is assigned the value `MyConnection` object. By assigning the `MyConnection` object to the `ActiveConnection` property, you are actually assigning connection information to the `Recordset` object and therefore opening the instance of the `Recordset` object. The `Open()` method ultimately makes the virtual table that contains the values inserted using the INSERT SQL statement and contained in the `Source` property. The code also includes a statement `rsCustomer.Close()`. This statement closes the `Recordset` object. Before the `Recordset` object is closed, the values inserted in the virtual table are copied to the original table in the database. Finally, the connection with the database is closed using the

`Close()` method of the `Connection` object. You cannot close a database connection using the `Close()` method until all the `Recordset()` objects are closed.

```
var MyConnection = Server.CreateObject("ADODB.Connection");
MyConnection.ConnectionTimeout = 30;
MyConnection.Open("FILEDSN=WebShoppe.dsn");
if(MyConnection.State == "adStateClosed")
    Response.Write("The database is not available.");
var rsCustomer = Server.CreateObject("ADODB.Recordset");
rsCustomer.Source="SELECT * FROM Customer ORDER BY First_Name,
Last_Name";
rsCustomer.ActiveConnection = MyConnection;
Additional Statements;
rsCustomer.Close();
MyConnection.Close();
```

We have looked at how you can select records from a table by using the `Recordset` object. The `SELECT` statement in the preceding example was based on the ORDER BY clause. This means that selection of records is based on a condition and to select the records from a table; navigation through the records in the table is necessary. To navigate through records in a table, the `Recordset` object provides the `MoveNext()` method.

Before we delve into details of the `MoveNext()` method, you need to know about cursors. When you navigate in a virtual record set table, your current position in the record set is marked by a pointer, which is called a cursor. The cursor is always placed in the first record of the record set when an instance of a `Recordset` object is created. (There are several types of cursors; details about cursors will be discussed later in the chapter.) The `MoveNext()` method moves the cursor to the next record in the `Recordset` object. The following example creates a new `Recordset` object and then moves the cursor forward by one row:

```
var rsCustomer = Server.CreateObject("ADODB.Recordset");
rsCustomer.Source="SELECT * FROM Customer ORDER BY First_Name,
Last_Name";
rsCustomer.ActiveConnection = MyConnection;
rsCustomer.Open();
rsCustomer.MoveNext();
Additional Statements;
rsCustomer.Close();
MyConnection.Close();
```

Like the `MoveNext()` method, the `Recordset` object contains several other methods. Some of these methods are: `Move()`, `MoveFirst()`, `MoveLast()`, and `MovePrevious()`. Before you use the `Open()` method, to use the `Move()`, `MoveFirst()`, `MoveLast()`, and `MovePrevious()` methods, you need to set the `CursorType` property of the `Recordset` object. The `CursorType` property of the `Recordset` object indicates the type of cursor that will be used in the result set. You can assign one of the four cursor type values to the `CursorType` property.

Table 12.21 lists valid cursor type values of the `CursorType` property.

Table 12.21   Values of the `CursorType` Property

OBJECTS	DESCRIPTION
adOpenForwardOnly	Indicates that the cursor can only move forward in a `Recordset` object by using the MoveNext(º) method.
adOpenKeyset	Indicates that the cursor is a keyset cursor and allows you to move forward and backward in a recordset. This cursor does not allow you to view new records added or access any records deleted by other users in a table. However, it allows you to view existing records updated by other users.
adOpenDynamic	Indicates that the cursor is a dynamic cursor that allows you to move forward and backward in a recordset. It also allows you to view any changes made in the records by other users.
adOpenStatic	Indicates that the cursor is static and allows you to move forward and backward in a recordset. However, this cursor does not allow you to view any changes made in the records by other users.

Of all the cursor values listed in Table 12.21, the `adOpenForwardOnly` cursor is the default cursor type value. It is the fastest and the most preferred cursor value because the cursor value enables you to move through a record set only once and does not allow you to view any modifications made by other users. If you want to navigate forward and backward in a record, you can use other cursor type values.

The following example illustrates how you can use the `adOpenStatic` cursor type:

```
     var rsCustomer = Server.CreateObject("ADODB.Recordset");
     rsCustomer.Source="SELECT * FROM Customer ORDER BY First_Name,
Last_Name";
     rsCustomer.ActiveConnection = MyConnection;
     rsCustomer.CursorType = adOpenStatic;
     rsCustomer.Open();
     rsCustomer.MoveNext();
     Response.Write(rsCustomer("First_Name") + " " +
rsCustomer("Last_Name"));
     rsCustomer.MovePrevious();
     Response.Write(rsCustomer("First_Name") + " " +
rsCustomer("Last_Name"));
     rsCustomer.Close();
```

The preceding example allows you to navigate forward and backward in a record set. The example uses the `MoveNext()` method to move to the second record in the recordset. You'll also notice that it uses the `rsCustomer("First_Name")` statement. The field names of a database table are assigned as variables in the `Fields` Collection of the `Recordset` object. Therefore, the statement `rsCustomer("First_Name")` refers to the field name `First_Name` of the database table.

When you work with `Recordset` objects methods, you can never be certain that there is another record before or after the current position of the cursor. In addition, you can never be certain that any records were returned at all from your `SQL SELECT` statement. For example, the preceding code assumes that records exist in the Employees table. However, your SQL query may not have returned any records at all. To ensure that the next or the previous record is available, you use the `Recordset` object's BOF and EOF properties. The BOF (beginning of file) property returns a value of true if the cursor is located before the first record in a record set and a value of false if the cursor is located on or after the first record. Similarly, the EOF (end of file) property returns a value of true if the cursor is located after the last record in a record set and a value of false if the cursor is located on or before the last record. The following code shows how to use a while loop to check the value of the EOF property before moving the cursor. The while loop continues as long as the EOF property is not equal to true.

```
var rsCustomer = Server.CreateObject("ADODB.Recordset");
rsCustomer.Source="SELECT * FROM Customer ORDER BY First_Name,
Last_Name";
rsCustomer.ActiveConnection = MyConnection;
rsCustomer.CursorType = adOpenStatic;
rsCustomer.Open();
while(rsCustomer.EOF != true) {
    Response.Write(rsCustomer("First_Name") + " " +
rsCustomer("Last_Name") + "lives in " + rsCustomer("Address") + "<BR>");
    rsCustomer.MoveNext();
}
rsCustomer.Close();
```

Result

Based on the previous discussion, the development team of Web Shoppe has decided that two files, **CustomerDetails.html** and **GetCustomerID.asp**, will be used for assigning an ID to the customer. The **CustomerDetails.html** will accept the customer details from the customer and will contain the `Get Customer ID` button. When a customer clicks the `Get Customer ID` button, a page containing the message with the ID of the customer is displayed. To enable this, the `<FORM>` tag in the **CustomerDetails.html** file is written in the following manner:

```
<FORM NAME="customerDetailsForm" METHOD="post"
ACTION="GetCustomerID.asp">
```

The **GetCustomerID.asp** file contains the following server-side code that generates the Customer ID. The code stores the details of the customer along with the Customer ID in the Customers table in the WebShoppe.mdb database:

- The code will contain the # include directive that directs to insert the ado-javas.inc file into the ASP file to access a database

  ```
  <!-- #include file="adojavas.inc" -->
  ```

- The Session object will be used to generate the Customer ID.

- The Connection object will be used to create the connection with the database.

- The Execute() method will be used to insert records into the Customers table.

Write the code

Following is the code for the **CustomerDetails.html** file:

```
<HTML>
<HEAD>
<TITLE>Web Shoppe </TITLE>
</HEAD>
<BODY BGCOLOR="#CCCCFF">
<P ALIGN="center"><FONT COLOR="#5E00BB" SIZE="6"><b>Web
Shoppe</B></FONT></P>
<P ALIGN="center"><B><FONT SIZE="6" COLOR="#5E00BB">Customer
Registration Form</FONT></B></P>
<p align="left">Welcome to customer registration form of Web
Shoppe ! This
page provides you with a customer ID . To obtain a new customer ID
and password, please fill out the
Customer Registration form and click the
<B>Get Customer ID</B>
button.
<FORM NAME="customerDetailsForm" METHOD="post"
ACTION="GetCustomerID.asp">
<P ALIGN="left"><FONT SIZE="3"><B>Title:
(Optional):</b>::::::::::::::::::::::::::::::::::::::::::::<b>Mr.
<INPUT TYPE="radio" VALUE="Mr." CHECKED NAME="Title">  Mrs.
<INPUT TYPE="radio" VALUE="Mrs." NAME="Title">  Ms. <INPUT
TYPE="radio" VALUE="Ms." NAME="Title">
  Dr. <INPUT TYPE="radio" VALUE="Dr." NAME="Title"></B></FONT></P>
<P ALIGN="left"><FONT SIZE="3"><B>First Name</B></FONT><FONT
SIZE="3"><B>:</B>::::::::::::::::::::::::::::::::::::::::::::::::::::::</
```

```
FONT><INPUT TYPE="text" NAME="First_Name" SIZE="20"></P>
      <p align="left"><font size="3"><b>Last Name</b></font><font
size="3"><b>:</b>:::::::::::::::::::::::::::::::::::::::::::::::::::::</
font><input type="text" name="Last_Name" size="20"></p>
      <p align="left"><font size="3"><b>Home
Address:</b>:::::::::::::::::::::::::::::::::::::::::::::::</font><input
type="text" name="Address" size="20"></p>
      <p align="left"><font
size="3"><b>Region:</b></font>:::::::::::::::::::::::::::::::::::::::::::
:::::::::::::::::::<select name="Region">
      <option value="Appalachia">Appalachia</option>
      <option value="Atlantic Coast">Atlantic Coast</option>
      <option value="Great Plains">Great Plains</option>
      <option value="Midwest">Midwest</option>
      <option value="New England">New England</option>
      <option value="Pacific">Pacific</option>
      <option selected value="Northwest">Northwest</option>
      <option value="Rocky Mountains">Rocky Mountains</option>
      <option value="South">South </option>
      <option value="Southwest">Southwest</option>
      <option value="Western States">Western States</option>
      </select></p>
      <p align="left"><font size="3"><b>Home
Phone:</b>:::::::::::::::::::::::::::::::::::::::::::::::::::::::</font><input
type="text" name="Phone" size="20"></p>
      <p align="left"><font size="3"><b>E-
mail:</b>:::::::::::::::::::::::::::::::::::::::::::::::::::::::::::::
<b><input type="text" name="Email" size="20"></b></font></p>
      <p align="left"><font size="3"><b>Preferred mode of
payment:</b>:::::::::::::::::::<b>Credit
      Card</b></font> <input type="radio" value="Credit Card" checked
name="ModeOfPayment"> 
      <font size="3"><b>Payment on Delivery</b></font> <input
type="radio" value="Payment on Delivery" name="ModeOfPayment"> </p>
      <p align="left"><font color="#5E00BB" size="3"><b>If mode of
payment
      selected is Credit Card, please also provide us with the credit
card
      details that you usually like to use:</b></font></p>
      <p align="left"><b><font size="3">Card
Type</font>:</b>:::::::::::::::::::::::::::::::::::::::::::::::::::::::::::
:<font size="3"><b>Master
      Card</b></font> <input type="radio" value="Master Card"
name="CardType"> <font size="3"><b>Visa
      Card</b></font>  <input type="radio" value="Visa Card"
name="CardType"></p>
      <p align="left"><input type="submit" value="Get Customer ID"
name="Submit" onClick="dispV()">    
      <input type="reset" value="Reset"
name="Reset">    </p>
      </FORM>
```

```
    </BODY>
    </HTML>
```

Following is the code for **GetCustomerID.asp** file:

```
<%@ LANGUAGE=JavaScript %>
<! -- #include file="adojavas.inc" -->
<%
Application.Lock();
if(!Application.Contents("custId")){
    Application.Contents("custId") =100;
    var customerID = Application.Contents ("custID");
    Session.Contents("ID")=customerID;
}
else{
    var customerID=Application.Contents("custID");
    ++customerID;
    Session.Contents("ID") = customerID;
    Application.Contents("custId") = customerID;
}
Application.Unlock();
    var dbConnection=Server.CreateObject("ADODB.Connection");
    dbConnection.ConnectionTimeout = 30;
    dbConnection.Open("FILEDSN=WebShoppeASP.dsn");
    if(dbConnection.State == "adStateClosed")
    Response.Write("The database is not available.");
    else {
        var SQLString = "INSERT INTO Customer VALUES('"+ customerID +
"', '"+ Request.Form("Title") + "', '"+ Request.Form("First_Name") + "',
'"+ Request.Form("Last_Name") + "', '" + Request.Form("Address") + "',
'"+ Request.Form("Region") + "', '"+ Request.Form("Phone") + "', '" +
Request.Form("Email") + "', '"+ Request.Form("ModeOfPayment")  +"',  '"+
Request.Form("CardType") + "')";       dbConnection.Execute(SQLString);
        Response.Write("<body bgcolor='#CCCCFF'>");
        Response.Write(" <p align='center'><font color='#5E00BB'
size='6'><b>Web Shoppe Customer ID Confirmation Page</b></font></p>");
        Response.Write("<P>");
        Response.Write("<p ><font size='4'><b>Thanks " +
Request.Form("Title") + Request.Form("First_Name") + "! Your customer ID
is <B>" + customerID + "</B></b></font></p>");
        dbConnection.Close();
    }
    %>
```

Execute and Verify the Successful Running of the Code

In Internet Explorer, type the URL http://localhost/Chapter12/CustomerDetails.html file. An interface, as shown in Figure 12.22, is displayed.

Figure 12.22 illustrates the Customer Registration Form.

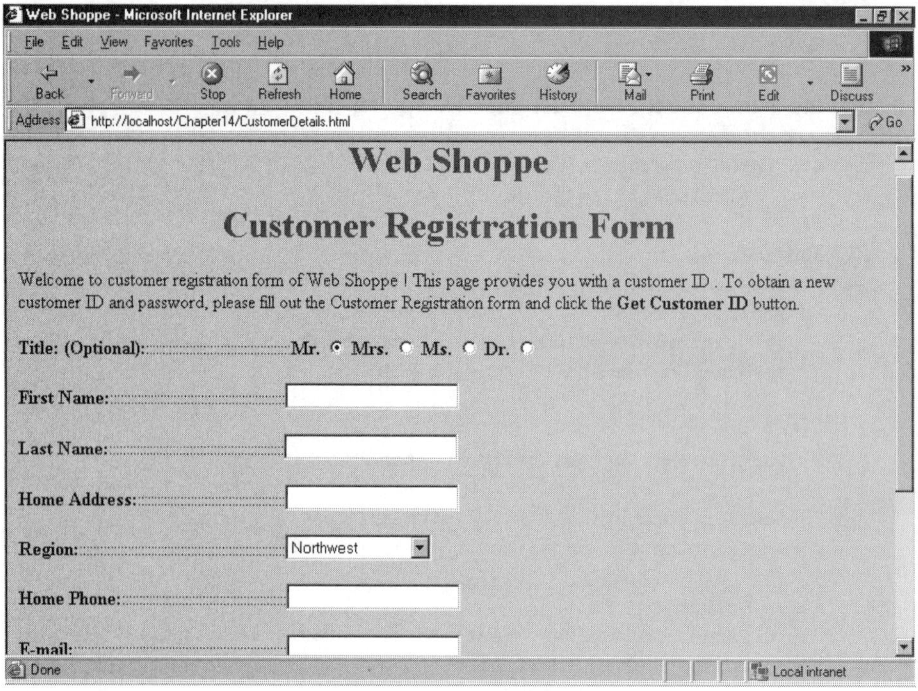

Figure 12.22 The Customer Registration Form.

In the Customer Registration Form, enter the following details:

```
Title: Mr.
First Name: Blake
Last Name: Stevenson
Home Address: 9966, 211th Street, Kingston Washington 98346
Region: Northwest
Home Phone: 2123273423
E mail: blakesteve@xyz.com
Mode of Payment: Credit Card
Card Type: Visa Card
```

Then, click the Get Customer ID button.

Figure 12.23 illustrates the Web Shoppe Customer ID Confirmation Page.

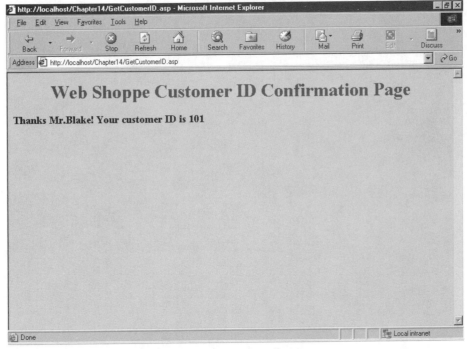

Figure 12.23 Web Shoppe Customer ID Confirmation Page.

Summary

In this chapter, you learned to develop server-side scripts with the Microsoft IIS server. The chapter began by comparing two technologies, ASP and JavaScript. We explained the differences between the two technologies and gave you some insight into which technology should be chosen when. The chapter also introduced you to various server-side objects of ASP, such as `Request`, `Response`, `Application`, and `Session`. Various properties, collections, and methods of each of these objects were discussed in detail. You also learned about the concept of database interaction by using ADO objects.

Using LiveWire for Server-Side Database Connectivity

All the other chapters of this book have focused on the use of JavaScript for the development of client-side applications. However, a typical Web scenario consists of both the client and server environment. JavaScript can also be used as a server-side scripting language.

JavaScript as a server-side scripting language facilitates the retrieval and manipulation of data from a database. Before using JavaScript as a server-side language, let's briefly discuss the fundamentals of the client/server environment. The discussion centers around the importance of measuring the amount of processing required at client and server ends before deciding on whether to use JavaScript as a client- or server-side scripting language. A major part of server-side processing involves a database interaction. In the case of JavaScript, database interaction is achieved by using a Netscape product called LiveWire. LiveWire uses various objects to connect to a database to help retrieve and manipulate the records of a table.

Client/Server Architecture

In a traditional client/server system, the server side consists of an information pool known as a database. A Web interaction is defined by the request-response cycle that is initiated with a client request and concluded with the server response from the other end. This led to the emergence of a two-tier system composed of a client at one end and the server at the other. The functions of the two sides in such a system are explicitly demarcated. The client side is responsible for the presentation of an interface to accept user or customer input. The gathered user input is submitted to the server side for further processing. The server side is responsible for business logic-based calculations, data storage, and data management. Consider the following example to further clarify a typical interaction between a client and a server. An online banking site provides facilities for accessing the current status of an account at all times. What type of interaction transpires between a client and a server during such a transaction? Each user is provided with an account number and a password to access the details of the particular account. The interaction begins at the client side where an interface is used to accept an account number and a password from a user. The account number and the password are then submitted to the server side for validation and calculations. The validation process involves mapping and authenticating the user input with the stored details held in a server database. As a result of this validation, only authentic account holders are allowed access to account details. The logic behind such a validation is obvious; after all you do not want user A to be able to access the details of the account of user B, or vice versa. Once a user has access to an account, the user can perform monetary transactions, such as credit, debit, and transfer of money. Figure A.1 illustrates the design of a typical two-tier client/server system.

With technological developments and advancements, the two-tier client/server system was further split into the client tier, the processing tier, and the database tier. The presence of three distinct tiers resulted in the emergence of the three-tier architecture. Although the client side still consisted of a user interface, the server side was split to handle the processes of database interaction and data storage separately. It is important to remember that the processing and database tier of the three-tier system is largely a conceptual demarcation. This is because most of the time, the second and third tiers are located on the same server. The processing tier receives a request from the client and performs the necessary calculations for the generation of the response. The database tier acts as the information backup for the processing tier by providing access to the information necessary for calculations. The generated response is then transmitted from the processing tier to the client end. Figure A.2 illustrates the design of the three-tier client/server system.

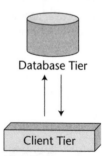

Database Tier

Client Tier

Figure A.1   Two-tier client/server system.

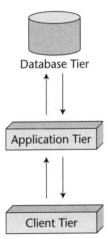

Figure A.2 Three-tier client/server system.

When designing a client/server system, an important decision must be made regarding the amount of processing to be performed at each end of the system. Since JavaScript is a multifunctional language, it can be used to create applications for both the client side and the server side. However, the choice of whether to use client-side or server-side JavaScript depends on whether the bulk of the processing is performed at the client or server side. Conceptually, this may sound confusing since both client-side JavaScript and server-side JavaScript share the same core language. Functionally, as a rule of thumb, JavaScript can be used at the client side to handle user interface processing and validations for input formats. And at the server side, JavaScript can be used to perform more intensive calculations and data storage. Such a clear-cut division of functionality at the client side and server side is important for Web applications. This is because the Internet consists of a vast network, which is accessed by many clients. As a result, there is no guarantee that a client browser accessing a particular application has the capabilities of performing processing according to the design of the application. Good programming practice, therefore, is to limit the amount of processing on the client side and place all intensive processing that is universal and not client-specific on the server side.

The object-based control structure and syntax of JavaScript are easily adapted for server-side scripting. The only additional knowledge required consists of a handful of new language elements and the basics of SQL. Simultaneously, you also need to have the backup of Netscape's LiveWire Web development environment complete with all its components. Beginning with the new language elements, we'll discuss each of these additional concepts separately.

Server-Side Scripting and JavaScript

We have already used JavaScript on the client side with HTML forms for validating data before submitting it to the processing tier on the server side. Typically, after receiving data, the processing tier uses Common Gateway Interface (CGI), along with a scripting language, such as Perl, to process the data before submitting it to the data storage tier for further manipulations. However, CGI is a protocol and not a programming language. It is often used with a scripting language, such as Perl, to handle the communication between the client tier and the data storage tier.

In contrast, server-side JavaScript is a programming language, which is based on the client side. Server-side JavaScript allows communication between the client tier and the data storage tier and can also interact with client-side JavaScript. This is because both client- and server-side JavaScript share the same basic programming features. As a result, some developers prefer to use server-side JavaScript for handling the processing tier of a three-tier client/server system.

Before drawing any conclusions, it is important to be aware of the drawbacks of JavaScript as a server-side programming language. JavaScript is a proprietary and vendor-specific programming language. As a result, you need to be acquainted with slightly different versions of server-side JavaScript for each vendor's Web server. Another point is that in contrast to ECMAScript, there is no exact server-side programming standard specified for JavaScript. In addition, because of the support from almost every type of server, CGI is still a popular technology for use in the processing tier. However, despite these drawbacks, to create applications for server-side JavaScript, you can use the same core language syntax as that of client-side JavaScript. You can, therefore, easily write server-side JavaScript programs by using the skills learned in client-side JavaScript, regardless of the version of server-side JavaScript that you are using.

Server-side JavaScript can also be used to create Web applications without a data storage tier. For example, you can create a server-side JavaScript program to dynamically generate a Web page for display at the client end. Similarly, you can create an application using a server-side JavaScript program to count the number of hits a Web site receives. Web applications that do not include a data storage tier are referred to as distributed applications.

Let's now look at how LiveWire can be used to create server-side JavaScript programs.

Using LiveWire for Server-Side Scripting

LiveWire provides the environment and the tools to develop and integrate all parts of a Web application. It works in conjunction with Netscape FastTrack and Enterprise servers. What LiveWire provides is a platform for the development of both client- and server-side applications using a common language. Server-side scripts are written and then integrated with client-side JavaScript and HTML to display results in a browser.

The browser elements of the client side and the server elements of the server side are compiled to generate *.web* files. The server uses these files to handle incoming requests. During compilation, client-side JavaScript and an HTML interface are bundled into a single file. As a result, there is no need to separately develop and manage the browser and server elements of the same Web application. LiveWire is compatible with a variety of operating systems including Windows NT. However, you need to have access to a FastTrack or Enterprise server to run LiveWire.

Before execution, each LiveWire program must be compiled and installed. The following steps are used to create a server-side JavaScript program by using LiveWire.

1. Create a server-side script.

2. Compile and deploy the program, by using the jsac compiler.

3. Install and start the program by using the LiveWire Application Manager.

Creating a Server-Side Script

As a matter of fact, server-side JavaScript is created in HTML documents or in .js source files. This is similar to the way client-side JavaScript is created. Therefore, it is obvious that an HTML document can contain both client-side and server-side JavaScript. On receiving a client request for an HTML document, the server executes a server-side JavaScript. On the other hand, client-side JavaScript is executed only after the Web browser receives the requested HTML document from the server.

Server-side JavaScript included in an HTML document is enclosed in a <SERVER>...</SERVER> tag. This syntax is very different from the <SCRIPT>... </SCRIPT> tag used for client-side JavaScript. As discussed earlier, the code for server-side JavaScript is a slight variant of client-side JavaScript. Recapitulating the concepts of client-side JavaScript that you have learned so far, how will you write the JavaScript code to display a message on the browser? The following code snippet is used to display the Hello World message on the browser.

```
<SCRIPT LANGUAGE="JavaScript">
document.write("Hello World");
</SCRIPT >
```

Let's write the same code for the server side. It is important to bear in mind that in the case of server-side JavaScript, the write() method designates that the specified message be returned to the client, instead of being output to the browser. The following code snippet uses the write() method to return the Hello World message to the client.

```
<SERVER>
write("Hello World");
</SERVER>
```

In the preceding code, notice that the write() method in the server script is written as write("Hello World") instead of the familiar document.write("Hello World") that is used in client-side JavaScript. This is because the write() method in server-side JavaScript is a global method and is, therefore, not associated with any particular object. As a result, server-side JavaScript does not contain any references to the document object, window object, or other browser-specific objects of client-side JavaScript.

Server-side JavaScript can also be placed in source files with.js extensions to maintain a library of functions accessible to all the server-side JavaScript code in an application. In this regard, there exists another miniscule difference between referencing client- and server-side .js files. You'll recollect that in client-side JavaScript, references to a server-side source file are made using the SRC attribute. However, in the case of server-side JavaScript, you do not reference the name of a server-side source file by using the SRC attribute but include the name of the .js source file when you compile the application. Then the compiler will ensure that the JavaScript code in the .js source file is available to other HTML documents of the application.

To include server-side JavaScript within an HTML tag, the code should be enclosed within back quotes (`) (the lowercase character to the left of the !-1 key on the keyboard) or used with the escape characters \ and Q. Consider the example of a shopping site that provides customers with a direct link to mail grievances to a specific executive. The grievance itself can be accepted using an HTML text area. However, how will you provide a mail link along with the HTML element <A HREF>? You can create a client object in server-side JavaScript programming containing a custom client property named email. The MAILTO attribute of <A HREF> can then use the custom property in a link. The following code snippet illustrates the use of a server-side JavaScript within an HTML tag using back quotes.

```
<A HREF="mailto:" + `client.email`> Click here to send your grievance to
our executive</A>
```

Alternatively, you can also use escape characters in the following manner:

```
<A HREF="mailto:" + \Qclient.email\Q> Click here to send your grievance
to our executive </A>
```

The contents within <SERVER>...</SERVER> tags are executed before the server delivers an HTML document containing server-side JavaScript to the client. On receiving the source document at the client side, neither the <SERVER>...</SERVER> tags nor the encapsulated server-side JavaScript code is visible in the HTML document. The client is able to view only the results that are returned by the code. Consider the following example of a code snippet containing client-side JavaScript and server-side JavaScript enclosed in <SERVER>...</SERVER> tags and escape characters.

```
<HTML>
<HEAD>
<TITLE>An example with both Client and Server-Side JavaScript</TITLE>
<SCRIPT LANGUAGE="JavaScript1.2">
document.write("<H3>This Is the line that is generated by client-side
JavaScript.</H3>");
</SCRIPT>
</HEAD>
<BODY>
<SERVER>
```

```
write("<H3>This Is the line that is generated by server-side
JavaScript.</H2>");
</SERVER>
<A HREF="mailto:" + \Qclient.email\Q>
Click here If you wish to send an e-mail to Anna Marie</A>
</BODY>
</HTML>
```

The code that is present in the document received at the client end is as follows:

```
<HTML>
<HEAD>
<TITLE> An example with both Client and Server-Side JavaScript </TITLE>
<SCRIPT LANGUAGE="JavaScript1.2">
document.write("This is the line that is generated by client-side
JavaScript.");
document.write("<BR>");
</SCRIPT>
</HEAD>
<BODY>
<H1>This is the line that is generated by server-side JavaScript.</H1>
<A HREF="mailto:annamarie@service.provider.com" >
Click here If you wish to send an e-mail to Anna Marie </A>
</BODY>
</HTML>
```

After creating a server-side script in JavaScript, you need to compile the code to eliminate errors. Let's look at how server-side JavaScript applications are compiled.

Compiling a Server-Side JavaScript Application

Server-side scripts in the form of HTML documents or .js source files are compiled before deployment. LiveWire applications are compiled using the jsac program. The jsac program is executed at the command prompt that compiles server-side JavaScript into a single file with an extension, .web. The syntax for using the command-line compiler jsac is as follows:

```
jsac (compiler options) name of file for compilation
```

Netscape servers identify all .web files as executable Web applications. A LiveWire application can be defined as a collection of related files that are compiled into a single .web file. After successful compilation, .web files need to be moved to the Web server. Despite being placed at the server side, .web files can also be accessed from the client end. All that you need to do is type the full name of a file with its .html extension in the client's Web browser. The jsac program can be executed with a number of different options. Table A.1 lists the various command-line options that can be used with the LiveWire compiler.

Table A.1 Command-Line Options of the LiveWire Compiler

COMMAND LINE OPTION	USED TO...
-c	Check the syntax of the script without generating the .web file.
-d	Display generated JavaScript statements.
-o name of output file (.web)	Identify the target .web file to which the output should be written. In case you are using multiple options during compilation, be sure to append this option at the end.
-v	Display a detailed list of error messages from the compiler.
-?	Request for a display of help information from the compiler.
-h	Display a list of the compiler options at the command line.

To include multiple programs in a LiveWire application, append the name of each file separated by spaces to the jsac command. For example, the following statement illustrates the use of the jsac command to add two files, **homepage.html** and **funclibrary.js,** to a single LiveWire application with **main.web**. In addition, the execution of the statement will also display a detailed description of the compilation process.

```
jsac -v -o main.web homepage.html funclibrary.js
```

Installing and Starting an Application

After compiling server-side JavaScript, the Application Manager is used to install and manage the LiveWire applications on the Web server. The Application Manager is a browser-based JavaScript application that opens in your browser. To open Application Manager, use the URL http://server.domain/appmgr/ and substitute the name of your server and domain for the words server.domain. The Application Manager interface consists of a form with a list of all installed applications and links to execute various commands. You can use the form and links to perform the following tasks:

- Add new LiveWire applications to the Web server
- Modify an existing LiveWire application
- Start, restart, and stop LiveWire applications
- Debug and run LiveWire applications
- Remotely manage a Netscape Web server
- Access the online help option through the Help link

Clicking a link in the Application Manager form displays an associated page in the adjacent frame. When adding or modifying a LiveWire application, you are prompted to fill out information that is presented in the form of fields. Table A.2 lists the fields in the Add Application form of Application Manager that is displayed after clicking the `Add Application` button.

An application is started automatically after it is added to the server using the Add Application form. The application can be executed by selecting it from the list of installed applications and clicking the Run button. Alternatively, the application can be executed by opening its URL in Netscape Navigator. If any changes are made to an application, you must restart the application in Application Manager for the changes to take effect.

We have already discussed the fact that the syntax for writing server-side JavaScript is the same as that for client-side JavaScript except for the addition of a few language elements. However, unlike client-side JavaScript, LiveWire does not recognize the `document` and `window` objects of a browser. On the contrary, it uses server objects for developing server-side applications. Let's look at the server-side objects of LiveWire.

Table A.2   The Fields of the Add Application Form

FIELD	USED TO FILL...
Name	The name of an application. It is important to remember that the name input for the Name field should not be the same as an existing directory on a Web server. In such a case, a client is not able to access the documents in the directory.
Web File Path	The full pathname to the application .web file that is created with the `jsac` command.
Default Page	The name of the default page to be delivered to a client when there is no request for a specific file. This field is optional.
Initial Page	The name of the first page to be executed when you first start the application. This page is used for performing any tasks required at the startup of an application, which performs tasks such as initializing counter values or establishing database connections. This field is optional.
Built-in Maximum Database Connections	The maximum number of database server connections allowed by a database server license. The default value for this field is zero.
External Libraries	The pathnames of external libraries to be used with the application. This field is optional.
Client Object Maintenance	The technique used for maintaining state information. You can select client-cookie, client-URL, server-IP, server-cookie, or server-URL.

Server-Side Objects of LiveWire

If LiveWire does not recognize the `document` and `window` objects of a browser, how is the client able to access information from the server side? Well, the following four built-in objects can be used to access information from the server side in any server-side JavaScript application.

- `request`
- `client`
- `project`
- `server`

Server objects are also called session management objects. Each of the session management objects has different lifetimes and availability. Server objects function at the processing tier between the client tier and the data storage tier. They are used to access specific information from the processing tier and store the state information on the server.

`request` Object

The `request` object represents the current URL request from a client. Each time a client requests a particular URL, a new `request` object is created. In addition, a `request` object is also created when client-side JavaScript uses the `document.location()`, `history.go()`, or the built-in `redirect()` method. The `redirect()` method is used to forward a client request to a different Web page, which is quite similar to the `href` property of the `location` object of client-side JavaScript.

The `request` object exists only until the current request is fulfilled and ceases to exist after the client is served the requested Web page. As a result, the `request` object has the shortest lifetime of all the session management objects. The `request` object uses a number of predefined properties to return information about a client request. Table A.3 lists some of the most used properties of the `request` object.

Table A.3   The Properties of the `request` Object

PROPERTY	USED TO ACCESS...
agent	The name and version of a client browser.
ip	The IP address of a client.
method	The HTTP method used for a request.
protocol	The HTTP protocol supported by a client browser.
imageX	The horizontal position of the cursor after the user clicks an image map.
imageY	The vertical position of the cursor after the user clicks an image map.

The `agent` property of the `request` object returns the name and version of the browser making a URL request. This property can be used to generate dynamic HTML pages and JavaScript code according to the browser specification. As a result, the `agent` property can be used as an alternative to support cross-browser compatibility issues.

User-defined properties can also be created for the `request` object by using the following syntax:

```
request.property = value of the property;
```

One of the most common uses of the `request` object is to retrieve the value of user input in the controls of an HTML form. The named elements of a form on a client browser are appended as properties of the `request` object. The following example of an HTML form will explain this use of the `request` object as a retriever of the values of a named element.

```
<HTML>
<HEAD>
<TITLE>Customer Information</TITLE>
</HEAD>
<BODY>
<H2>Customer Information</H2>
<FORM METHOD="post" ACTION="OrderProcess.html"
NAME="customer_information">
Name<BR>
<INPUT TYPE="text" NAME="name" SIZE=30><BR>
Address<BR>
<INPUT TYPE="text" NAME="address" SIZE=30><BR>
City, State, Zip<BR>
<INPUT TYPE="text" NAME="city" SIZE=28>
<INPUT TYPE="text" NAME="state" SIZE=2 MAXLENGTH=2>
<INPUT TYPE="text" NAME="zip" SIZE=5 MAXLENGTH=5><BR>
E-Mail<BR>
<INPUT TYPE="text" NAME="email" SIZE=30><P>
<INPUT TYPE="reset">
<INPUT TYPE="submit">
</BODY>
</HTML>
```

When the `Submit` button of the form is clicked, a `request` object with properties for each of the form elements is created and submitted to a LiveWire document called OrderProcess.html. Subsequently, the properties of the `request` object can be used to reference the name, address, city, and other elements of the HTML form.

- request.name
- request.address
- request.city
- request.state
- request.zip

client **Object**

We have already discussed the life of a new request object that begins with a client request and ends after the requested URL is delivered to the client. As a result, if a LiveWire application consists of multiple documents, the same request object cannot be used with all the pages of the application. In such situations, the client object can be used to retain information across multiple pages of a LiveWire application. A client object is instantiated the first time a client accesses a URL. The client object is used as a temporary storage location to allow specific client information to be available to all the pages in a LiveWire application.

Contrary to the request object, the client object uses only user-defined properties to store information about the client of a particular application. The syntax for creating a new property for a client object is:

```
client.property = value;
```

The user-defined properties of a client object can be used to store information regarding the items of a shopping cart or to preserve the field values of a form with multiple pages. For example, to create a personalized greeting for a customer logging on to a shopping site, you can begin by first creating a property containing the user's name. The name property can include the greeting to generate a customized display for each user. The following code snippet illustrates the use of the client property in a server script to retain form values between the multiple pages of a form.

```
<SERVER>
client.name = request.name; client.address = request.address;
client.city = request.city; client.state = request.state;
client.zip = request.zip; client.email = request.email;
</SERVER>
```

There is no mechanism in LiveWire to indicate the completion of a user transaction. A request for a document can be mapped to the initiation of a user transaction. However, after the user is served the requested document, there is no way to know whether the client is finished working with the application. A second request can be used to determine whether the client wants to continue to work with the application. As a result, a client object has a default life span of 10 minutes. The life span of a client object can be increased using the expiration() method in the following syntax.

```
client.expiration(time In seconds);
```

For example, to set the time for the life span of a client object to 20 minutes, convert 20 minutes to seconds (20 × 60) and use the following statement.

```
client.expiration(1200);
```

At the end of a transaction, the client object can be deleted using the destroy() method. In situations where you need to retain the client object but destroy its associated properties, all you need to do is set the value of the expiration() method to 0. The following statement can be used to destroy only the associated properties of the `client` object.

```
client.expiration(0);
```

`project` **Object**

Often, the information contained in an application needs to be available globally so that it can be shared by all the clients accessing the application. Server-side JavaScript uses a `project` object to globally store application-specific information. A `project` object is created when an application is started by using the `Start` button of the Application Manager. Thereafter, the `project` object for the application is available to all clients accessing the application until the application is stopped by using the `Stop` button of the Application Manager.

A `project` object does not contain predefined properties because it is created explicitly to contain application-specific information. The syntax to add user-defined properties to an application remains the same as that for the `request` property. The following statement illustrates the syntax for creating a user-defined property for the `project` object.

```
project.property = value;
```

The `project` object can be used to contain properties to uniquely identify a client, maintain a page hit count, or store variable values that can be used later for other manipulations. For example, in an application for an online toy shop, assigning a unique invoice number to the list of items in the shopping cart can be used to generate a bill for the items of a single transaction. A `project` object can be used to store the value of the last invoice number that can be subsequently incremented to generate a new invoice number. The new invoice number can then be assigned to a `client` object so that it is available when the client accesses the page. The following code snippet can be used to generate an incremented invoice number.

```
<SERVER>
Project.lastInvoiceNumber = ++Project.lastInvoiceNumber;
Client.invoiceNumber = Project.lastInvoiceNumber;
</SERVER>
```

During a Web interaction, there is no rule that prevents multiple clients from accessing the same page at the same time. As a result, it is quite possible that an application could receive a request from another client before the end of a transaction with the current client. It is therefore possible that two clients can be assigned the same identification in the form of an ID or an invoice number. A situation such as this can lead to data integrity problems. To avoid such a crisis, the properties of a particular `project` object can be secured using the `lock()` and `unlock()` methods. The `lock()` method prevents clients from accessing properties of the `project` object, and the `unlock()` method releases the property for access by other clients. The `lock()` and `unlock()`

methods can be added to the preceding code example to ensure that the last Invoice-Number property is accessed by a single client at a given time.

```
<SERVER>
project.lock();
project.lastInvoiceNumber = ++project.lastInvoiceNumber;
client.invoiceNumber = project.lastInvoiceNumber;
project.unlock();
</SERVER>
```

In the preceding code, notice the placement of the lock() and unlock() methods. The statement containing the lock() method is placed before the code that is used to access the project properties. On the other hand, the unlock() method is placed as the last statement.

server **Object**

Information related to running a Netscape server is stored in a server object. The server object is created at server startup and is destroyed at shutdown. In an environment containing multiple servers, each server is assigned an individual server object whose predefined properties can be accessed by all the applications on the server. Table A.4 lists the properties of a server object.

In addition to its predefined properties, a server object can also contain customized, user-defined properties. The following syntax is used to create a customized property for a server object.

```
server.property = value;
```

In situations where multiple applications are placed on a server, the server object also uses the lock() and unlock() methods of the project object to prevent data integrity problems. These methods ensure that two applications do not access the same server property at the same time.

In the preceding discussions we have explained the use of the four server-side objects that are used to maintain the state of the otherwise stateless HTTP protocol. Let's now move on to discuss the use of LiveWire in initiating database interactivity to enable the retrieval and manipulation of database records.

Table A.4 The Properties of a server Object

PROPERTY	USED TO SPECIFY ...
Hostname	The full name of the host.
Host	The name, subdomain, and domain name.
Protocol	The communications protocol of the server.
Port	The port number being used to run the server.
JsVersion	The version and platform used by the server.

Using LiveWire to Retrieve and Manipulate Database Records

All through the discussions on the client/server architecture in the preceding sections, we have used terms such as information pool, data storage, and database to define the functioning unit placed at the server side. It is evident that a database is responsible for providing information based on a user request that can be further processed to generate the required response. Since the word database is frequently used in conjunction with the client/server environment and server-side scripting, let's first understand databases before discussing JavaScript as a server-side scripting language.

It is quite obvious that with the increase in the popularity of the Internet, the two areas that have benefited the most are email services and online trading. Of course, you can list many more services that have profited due to the advent and advancement of the Internet. As a result, it should come as no surprise that many retail companies are using online shopping sites to promote their products and services. In response to this, more and more users are relying on Web sites to shop for items ranging from toys and flowers to gift items and computers. To understand the importance and functioning of a database, let's look at an example. A group of young adventure enthusiasts has launched a site for accepting registrations for an adventure camp. The site provides various details about the group, the campsite, the registration fee, and also day-to-day program details. In addition, a registration form is provided to accept the details from interested youngsters wishing to register for the camp. Figure A.3 illustrates the registration page of the site.

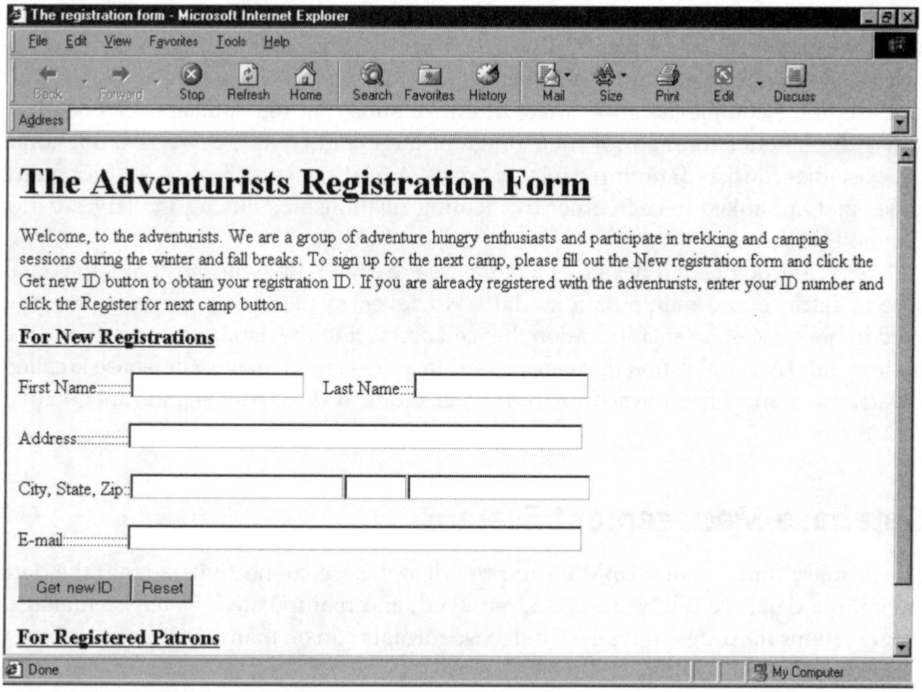

Figure A.3   Registration page.

In the preceding example, after a new user registers with the group, the individual's details are stored in an information pool, or database. In addition, the registered user's ID is validated by mapping it to the IDs stored in the database. As a result, for any future references to a particular ID, the database can be accessed to retrieve and manipulate the stored information.

Understanding Databases

Based on the preceding discussions, a *database* can be formally defined as an ordered collection of information that can be accessed for the retrieval and manipulation of data. The use of a database can be mapped to various examples from everyday life. For example, an address book or manila folders containing your mother's recipes are all databases or information repositories that can be referred to when required. Other examples of databases include an organization's employee directory, client information, or product details. In other words, information in any form that can be organized into ordered sets of data and placed at the server end is a database. At this juncture, we need to understand the importance of storing data in an organized and ordered form. For example, alphabetically organized employee details are easier to retrieve than details stored in a random manner. The objective of a database is to store data or information in a manner so that the data or information is easy to locate and retrieve.

The data in a computer database is stored in tables consisting of rows and columns. Each column of a table is a field consisting of a piece of information. Each row is a record that consists of a complete set of information. For example, a record in an employee database will consist of the details of an employee in the form of fields such as employee code, name, address, department, grade, and salary details. When a database consists of a single table, it is known as a flat-file database. However, with an increase in the complexity and variety of information, flat-file databases can be quite unwieldy. A better solution for the storage of large and complex data is a relational database that consists of multiple related tables. A relational database consists of many tables that are linked to each other by creating relationships among the tables using common fields.

After the structure and design of a database are drawn up, you can access the database to retrieve and manipulate its data. However, to perform manipulations, you need to have access to an application that can connect to the database and retrieve the desired data. An application that can be used to access and manage a database is called a Database Management System (DBMS). Let's look at the contents and function of a DBMS.

Database Management System

The primary function of a DBMS is to provide database connectivity so that the data stored in a database can be accessed, retrieved, and manipulated. Database management systems for different types of database formats run on many different platforms, ranging from simple personal computers to complex and huge mainframes. A database management system that stores data in a flat-file format is called a flat-file database management system. A database management system that stores data in a relational format is called a relational database management system, or RDBMS. Some of the popular relational database management systems are Oracle, Sybase, Informix, and DB2 for mainframes, and Access, FoxPro, and Paradox for PCs.

Although different database management systems support a specific database format, each database management system is an individual application that creates its own proprietary file types. For example, Access and Paradox are both relational database management systems but Access creates its database files in a proprietary format with an extension of .mdb, whereas Paradox creates its database files in a proprietary format with an extension of .db. In addition, both Paradox and Access contain filters that facilitate the import of files in each other's formats. However, in the case of most database management systems, database files are not completely interchangeable between the two programs. Although files can be imported into each other's formats, they cannot be read directly. As a result, the proprietary nature of database management systems compels programmers to write an application that is DBMS-specific to access the file formats of a particular database management system.

Applications such as word-processing and spreadsheet programs provide an interface between a user and a computer and simplify tasks. Similarly, a database management system performs the following tasks:

- Database-related tasks, such as the creation of new database files. It also contains interfaces that can be used to enter and manipulate data.

- Structure and preserve database files.

- Ensure that data is stored in database tables in the correct format. For example, in a relational database, a database management system ensures that appropriate information is entered in database tables according to the structure of the relationship between the tables. As a result, if two tables are linked by a common field, say, employee code, the DBMS ensures that the format of the code in both tables is the same.

- Query a database and display the retrieved records in the form of a report. A query is a structured set of instructions that is used for retrieving, adding, modifying, and deleting data from a database. A report is the formatted output of a database table or the results of a query.

A Data Manipulation Language (DML) is used for creating queries to retrieve the resultant records from a database. Although different database management systems support different data manipulation languages, Structured Query Language (SQL) (pronounced sequel) is a standard data manipulation language used in many database management systems.

Queries can be designed to programmatically manipulate the data in a database by using an interface for end users. However, it is always good programming practice to be aware of the basics of a programming interaction or an application. Therefore, let's look at the structure of a SQL query.

Structured Query Language

In a client/server environment setup, it is often necessary for an application to access multiple databases created in different database management systems. For example, an organization may need a server-side JavaScript application to simultaneously access a large legacy database written in dBase and a new database written in Oracle. The process of converting the large dBase database to Oracle would be cost-prohibitive. On the other hand, the organization cannot continue to use the database created in dBase, owing to the increase in the quantity of organizational information. However, from the organization's point of view, it is imperative to have access to the data in both systems. Microsoft provided the first Open Database Connectivity (ODBC) standard to allow easy access to data in various database formats. ODBC uses SQL commands, known as ODBC SQL, to allow an ODBC-compliant application to access a database. Essentially, an ODBC application connects to a database by using an ODBC driver and then executes ODBC SQL commands. The ODBC driver then translates the SQL commands into a format that a database can understand. Data is subsequently retrieved and displayed in the report format. LiveWire and ASP are both ODBC-compliant applications, which allow access to any database for which an ODBC driver exists.

To facilitate easy access to an ODBC-compliant database in 32-bit Windows operating systems, such as Windows NT and Windows 98, you need to create a Data Source Name (DSN) to locate and identify a database. A Data Source Name contains the configuration information that Windows operating systems require to access a particular ODBC-compliant database. The three types of DSNs to which you can connect in a Windows environment are installed and managed using the ODBC Administrator utility in Control Panel. These DSNs are:

System DSN.   The system DSN enables all users logged on to a server to access a database.

User DSN.   A user DSN restricts database access to authorized users.

File DSN.   A file DSN creates a file-based data source with an extension of .dsn, which can be shared by users.

IBM invented SQL in the 1970s to provide a medium for querying databases based on specific criteria. Since then, SQL has been adopted by numerous database management systems running on PCs, minicomputers, and mainframes. The American National Standards Institute (ANSI) approved an official standard for the SQL language in 1986. Subsequently, in 1991, the X/Open and SQL Access Group created a standardized version of SQL known as the Common Applications Environment (CAE) SQL draft specification. Despite being accessible to two available major standards, most database management systems use their own version of the SQL language for querying a database. ODBC SQL corresponds to the X/Open and SQL Access Group's CAE SQL draft specification. It is, therefore, important that an ODBC driver for a specific database management system support ODBC SQL.

SQL uses fairly easy-to-understand statements to execute database commands. Let's look briefly at some basic SQL commands and their uses. Table A.5 tabulates each of these commands to demonstrate their uses.

Table A.5   Basic SQL Commands

SQL COMMAND	USED TO...
CREATE TABLE	Create a table in a database
SELECT	Select records from a table
INSERT INTO	Insert new records in a table
UPDATE	Modify the values in the records of a table
DELETE	Delete records from a table
DROP	Delete a table from a database

Let's now look briefly at the use of the SQL commands by using examples.

Creating a Table

The CREATE TABLE command is used to create a new table in a database. The following syntax illustrates the line of code used for creating a table:

```
CREATE TABLE tableName (columnName1 datatype, columnName2 datatype...);
```

Consider a task such as the creation of a table for a bank database. The table is used to validate the authenticity of user input in the form of the account ID and the pin number. Column fields for this table are cAccountId and cPin_no. The following code snippet shows the use of the CREATE TABLE command to create the Login table:

```
CREATE TABLE Login (cAccount_Id char(10), cPin_no char(10));
```

Viewing the Records of a Table

The SELECT command is used to view the records of a database. The following syntax illustrates the line of code used for viewing the records of a table:

```
SELECT * from tableName;
```

The use of an asterisk specifies the retrieval of all records from a particular table. The WHERE clause is used along with the selection criterion to specify the selective retrieval of records from a table. The syntax in such a case will be:

```
SELECT * from tableName WHERE selectionCriterion;
```

The following code snippet shows the use of the SELECT command for the retrieval of records for a customer named Garrett:

```
SELECT * from Registration WHERE firstName="Garrett";
```

Inserting Records in a Table

The INSERT INTO command is used to insert new records in a table. The following syntax illustrates the line of code for creating a table:

```
INSERT INTO tableName VALUES (columnValue1, columnValue2 ...);
```

It is important to maintain the sequence for the column values being inserted, which should be similar to the order of the column names specified during creation of the table. The following code snippet is used to insert the first name, last name, address, account type, and annual income of a customer in the registration table:

```
INSERT INTO Registration VALUES("Dunston", "Payne", "21, Sunley House,
Eastern Avenue", "Loan", 20000);
```

Modifying Records in a Table

The UPDATE command is used to modify the records in a table. The following syntax illustrates the line of code for creating a table:

```
UPDATE tableName SET columnName="newColumnValue";
```

The following code snippet is used to modify the last name of Betty from Smith to Charles in view of her recent marriage:

```
UPDATE Registration SET lastName="Charles";
```

Deleting Records from a Table

The DELETE command is used to delete records from a table. The following syntax illustrates the SQL statement used for deleting all the records of a table:

```
DELETE * from tableName;
```

As with the SELECT command, the use of an asterisk specifies the deletion of all records from a particular table. The WHERE clause is used along with the selection criterion to specify the selective deletion of records from a table. The syntax in such a case will be:

```
DELETE * from tableName WHERE selectionCriterion;
```

The following code snippet illustrates the use of the SELECT command used for the retrieval of records for a customer named Jonathan:

```
DELETE * from Registration WHERE firstName="Jonathan";
```

Deleting a Table

The DROP TABLE command is used to delete a table from a database. The following syntax illustrates the SQL statement used for deleting a table:

```
DROP TABLE tableName;
```

The following code snippet shows the use of the DROP TABLE command to delete the tempTransaction table:

```
DROP TABLE tempTransaction;
```

SQL statements also contain certain predefined keywords that perform specific actions on a database. Table A.6 lists several SQL keywords that are common to most versions of SQL.

The following code illustrates the use of a more complex SQL statement containing some keywords.

```
SELECT Last_Name, First_Name FROM Registration
WHERE City = "Spencer" ORDER BY Last_Name, First_Name
```

The preceding code uses a SQL statement to select Last_Name and First_Name fields from the Registration table only if the value of the field City is equal to Spencer. The ORDER BY keyword is used to sort the results using the Last_Name and First_Name fields.

Table A.6 Common SQL Keywords

KEYWORD	DESCRIPTION
FROM	Specifies the tables from which records are to be retrieved or deleted.
SELECT	Returns information from a database.
WHERE	Specifies the conditions that must be met for records to be returned from a query.
ORDER BY	Sorts the records returned from a database.
INSERT	Inserts a new row into a database.
INTO	Determines the table into which records should be inserted.
DELETE	Deletes a row from a database.
UPDATE	Saves changes to the fields in a record.

From the preceding discussions, we can see that a database can be a large repository of data that can be maintained and manipulated by applications. In addition, the tabulated format of relational database management systems has gained immense popularity over the years. The success of RDBMS lies in the fact that, to a certain extent, databases have been able to retain consistency and avoid redundancy by using the RDBMS approach. As a result, it is not surprising that JavaScript has incorporated the capability of working with databases by using LiveWire database objects.

Using LiveWire to Access a Database

Before initiating a database interaction, you need to have access to a database. In the next sections, we'll discuss database connectivity in JavaScript by using an ODBC-compliant Microsoft Access database. We have already discussed that before establishing a connection to a database, you need to create a DSN to identify and locate the database. The use of LiveWire database services involves the following steps:

1. Create a database on the server.
2. Add tables to the database.
3. Create a database object to connect to the database.
4. Use the methods of the database object to retrieve and manipulate the data in the database tables.

Assuming that you have already created a database with the relevant tables, let's proceed to examine the database object of JavaScript.

LiveWire database Object

LiveWire uses three objects for accessing databases: DbPool, connection, and database. The DbPool and connection objects are used for creating and managing pools of database connections. The database object, on the other hand, is used for creating and managing a single connection between a client and a database. Database connection using a connection pool is not within the scope of this book. Therefore, we will not discuss DbPool and connection objects. Instead, we'll concentrate on the database object.

The database object is a server-side JavaScript object that contains various methods for accessing and manipulating databases. Table A.7 lists the methods of the database object.

A database interaction begins by connecting to a database. The connect() method of the database object is used to establish a connection with a database. The syntax for using the connect() method is:

```
database.connect("database type", "server name", "user name",
"password", "database name");
```

Table A.7   Methods of the `database` Object

METHOD	USED TO...
beginTransaction()	Begin an SQL transaction.
commitTransaction()	Save the current SQL transaction.
connect()	Connect LiveWire to a database.
connected()	Return a value of true if a database connection was successful.
cursor()	Create a database cursor for specified SQL statements.
disconnect()	Close a database connection.
execute()	Send SQL statements to the database management system for processing.
majorErrorCode()	Return a major error code generated by ODBC or the database server.
majorErrorMessage()	Return a major error message generated by ODBC or the database server.
minorErrorCode()	Return a minor error code generated by ODBC or the database server.
minorErrorMessage()	Return a minor error message generated by ODBC or the database server.
rollbackTransaction()	Reverse the current SQL transaction.
SQLTable()	Execute SQL statements and return the results as an HTML table.

The parameter database type is used to specify the type of database you are accessing. The accepted and valid values for this parameter are DB2, ODBC, ORACLE, INFORMIX, and SYBASE. The parameter server name is used to specify the name of the server where the database is located. The ODBC connections on Windows platforms use the DSN to specify the name of the server. The username and password parameters are used to specify a username and a password on the server. The database name parameter is valid for only Informix and Sybase databases. For DB2, ODBC, and Oracle databases, the database name argument must be an empty string.

The end of a database interaction is marked using the `disconnect()` method. If the database being used does not support any of the parameters of the `connect()` method, include an empty string for each unsupported parameter. In the case of ODBC databases, you need to specify values for database type and the server name only. The following statement illustrates the use of the `connect()` method to establish a connection with a Microsoft Access database by using the DSN as WebShoppe.

```
database.connect("ODBC", "WebShoppe", "", "", "");
```

After establishing a connection with a database, it is advisable to verify the database connectivity before proceeding with data retrieval or manipulation. The `connected()` method of the `database` object returns a boolean value of true indicating that a connection to a database is successful. The following code snippet illustrates the use of the `connected()` method to verify a successful database connection by using the `write()` method.

```
database.connect("ODBC", "WebShoppe", "", "", "");
if (!database.connected())
write("The database is not available.");
additional statements;
database.disconnect();
```

Most database management systems include a license based on the number of current users anticipated to access a single database. As a result, it is important to estimate the maximum number of users that can connect to a database at one time. You can use two types of connections to access a database using a LiveWire application.

A *standard connection* allows multiple users to access a database at the same time. A standard connection usually performs better than a serial connection. This is because a standard connection processes requests from multiple users immediately without waiting for a user's request to finish. You can choose to have a standard connection if the estimated number of users connecting to a database simultaneously does not exceed the set limit for users permitted to access the database.

A *serial connection* allows only a single user to access a database at a time. A serial connection is preferred in cases where the maximum number of users may exceed the set limit for users permitted to access a database.

The `lock()` and `unlock()` methods of the `project` object are used to designate the type of connection to be used for establishing database connectivity. If the `lock()` and `unlock()` methods are not specified, the standard type of connection is used for database connectivity. The use of the `lock()` and `unlock()` methods establishes a serial connection to a database. The following lines can be added to the preceding code to establish a serial connection.

```
project.lock();
database.connect("ODBC", "WebShoppe", "", "", "");if
(!database.connected())
write("The database is not available.");
..............
..............
database.disconnect();
project.unlock();
```

After connecting to a database, you can retrieve records and manipulate data by executing specific SQL statements. Let's look at how SQL statements can be used to perform data retrieval and manipulation.

Executing SQL Commands

After connecting to a database, you can use either of the following three methods of the `database` object to execute SQL queries for a database.

- The `execute()` method
- The `cursor()` method
- The `SQLTable()` method

Each of these methods has different uses. Let's discuss each of these methods in detail.

The *execute()* Method

The `execute()` method is used to send SQL statements to a database management system for processing. All updates and deletions in a database table are performed using the `execute()` method. However, it is important to note that native SQL statements are used with the `execute()` method instead of the regular ODBC SQL statements. Since the SQL statements used with the `execute()` method are directly passed to the database management system, they are known as passthrough SQL statements. The following is the syntax for using the `execute()` method.

```
database.execute(SQL string);
```

It is important to limit the use of keywords in a SQL string when using the `execute()` method. Good programming practice is to restrict the use of SQL commands to common SQL keywords such as SELECT, INSERT, and DELETE.

The `execute()` method does not return query results to LiveWire. As a result, the `execute()` method can only be used for data updates, insertions, and deletions. The `execute()` method cannot be used to retrieve data from a database. The following code illustrates the use of the `execute()` method to insert values into the Customer table.

```
var SQLString = "INSERT INTO Customer VALUES('Mr',
 'Pierre', 'McKinnon''106 Gunthorpe Street', 'Pacific',
'01562', 'pierre@service.provider.com' 'Card', 'Master')";
database.execute(SQLString);
```

The following code illustrates the use of the `execute()` method to delete a row from the Customer table. The DELETE statement uses the FROM clause to designate the table from which a row should be deleted:

```
var SQLString = "DELETE FROM Customer
WHERE First_Name = Arnold";
database.execute(SQLString);
```

In the preceding code, the SQL string uses the WHERE clause to identify a row in the table with the value of the First_Name field as Arnold. Remember that the table may have multiple entries of the same first name. As a result, the preceding statement will actually delete all rows in the table where the First_Name field is equal to Arnold. Therefore, when using a DELETE statement, you need to be absolutely sure about the details of the record to be deleted before executing the SQL statement. In addition, when using the DELETE statement, it is very important to include a WHERE clause in the SQL statement to avoid deletion of all of the rows of a specified table.

The `cursor()` Method

We have already discussed how the `execute()` method allows addition, deletion, and modification of the records in a table but does not return any result except for error code. However, an equally important task performed during a database interaction is navigating through the records of a database while making changes or retrieving values. It is obvious that this task cannot be performed using the `execute()` method. The `cursor()` method of the `database` object is used to navigate and retrieve records from a database table. The `cursor()` method creates a `cursor` object that contains the records returned from a SELECT query executed using the `cursor()` method. Accordingly, you can use the `cursor` object to navigate through the records of a table and retrieve values or to add, delete, and modify records. The following is the syntax for using the `cursor` object:

```
variable name= database.cursor("SQL statement", updatable);
```

In the preceding syntax, the `cursor` object is assigned a name and a valid ODBC SQL SELECT statement. The parameter updatable is a boolean value that is used to specify whether the records in the `cursor` object can be modified. A true value for the updatable parameter indicates that the records in the `cursor` object can be modified while a value of false makes the `cursor` object read-only. Table A.8 lists the methods that can be used with the `cursor` object to perform operations on retrieved record sets.

Table A.8   Methods of the `cursor` Object

METHOD	USED TO...
close()	Close a Cursor object.
columnName(position)	Return the name of a column designated by the position argument.
columns()	Return the number of columns in a record set.
deleteRow()	Delete a row from a record set.
insertRow()	Insert a row into the record set.
next()	Move to the next record in the record set.
UpdateRow()	Save changes to the current row in the record set.

The close() method of the cursor object should always be added to the code to release the memory resources used by retrieved result sets. A database connection cannot be closed by merely using the disconnect() method of the database object. You need to explicitly close all cursor objects before disconnecting from a database. The following code illustrates the use of the close() method.

```
WebShoppeTable = database.cursor("SELECT * FROM Customers
ORDER BY Last_Name, First_Name", false);
. . . . . . . . . . . . . .
. . . . . . . . . . . . . .
WebShoppeTable.close();
```

The position of the current record set is marked by the cursor object and is called the cursor. When the cursor object is created the first time by using the cursor() method, the cursor is initially placed before the first row in the record set. The next() method is used to navigate through the records in a cursor object. The following code illustrates the use of the next() method.

```
WebShoppeTable = database.cursor("SELECT * FROM Customers
WHERE Last_Name = 'McKinnon'", false);
WebShoppeTable.next();
statements;
WebShoppeTable.close();
```

When working with record sets and the next() method, how can you ascertain that records exist after the current position of the cursor? Or how can you verify that the SELECT statement returned records? Well, the cursor object uses the next() method to ensure that there is a next record available. The next() method returns a boolean value of true if it finds a next row in the record set or a value of false if it does not find a next row in a record set. The following code illustrates the use of the if statement to check the value returned by the next() method before moving the cursor.

```
WebShoppeTable = database.cursor("SELECT * FROM Customers
WHERE Last_Name = 'McKinnon'", false);
if (WebShoppeTable.next()) {
. . . . . . . . . . . . . . . . .
. . . . . . . . . . . . . . . . .
}
WebShoppeTable.close();
```

The field names of a database table are assigned to an instantiated cursor object as properties. Therefore, for an instantiated cursor object named WebShoppeTable, a reference to the First_Name field can be made using the following statement:

```
WebShoppeTable.First_Name.
```

When the next() method is used after the instantiation of the cursor object, the contents of each field specified in the properties of the cursor object change. As a result, the contents of the record at the current location of the cursor are displayed. The following code illustrates the use of a `while` statement to navigate through the records and return the name and address of each customer of the WebShoppe site.

```
WebShoppeTable = database.cursor("SELECT * FROM Customers",
false);
while(WebShoppeTable.next()) {
    write(WebShoppeTable.First_Name + " " + WebShoppe Table.Last_Name + "
lives in " + WebShoppeTable.Address + "<BR>");
}
WebShoppeTable.close();
```

The cursor object can also create an `updatable` cursor that can be modified to complement an insertion, update, or deletion of a record in a table. An `updatable` cursor is created when the value of an updatable parameter of the `cursor` object is set to true. In other words, an `updatable` cursor is a `cursor` object record set that can be modified. However, when using an `updatable` cursor, you cannot specify the retrieval of data from multiple tables by using the SELECT statement. In addition, the select statement needs to include the key values of a table, such as its primary key. Another point to remember when using an `updatable` cursor is that the select statement cannot use the GROUP BY clause to sort the results returned from a query. The `updatable` cursor uses the following three `cursor` object methods to update, insert, or delete records from a table.

updateRow() method. The `updateRow()` method is used after changing the field values of a table. This method saves the changes made to a row in a record set. For example, the following code illustrates the use of the `updateRow()` method to update the last name of a customer.

```
WebShoppeTable = database.cursor("SELECT * FROM Customers
WHERE Last_Name = 'Smith'", true);
if (WebShoppeTable.next()) {
   if (WebShoppeTable.Last_Name == "Smith") {
     WebShoppeTable.Last_Name = "Brown";
     WebShoppeTable.updateRow("Customers");
}
WebShoppeTable.close();
```

insertRow() method. The `insertRow()` method is similar to the SQL INSERT statement. The only difference is that instead of adding a row to the end of a table, the `insertRow()` method inserts a new row at the position where the cursor is located in a record set. Before executing the `insertRow()` method, it is necessary to assign the new field names of the row to the properties of the `cursor` object. If this is not done, the current field values are assigned to the fields of the new record. For example, the following code illustrates the use of the `insertRow()` method to add a customer's spouse to the Customer table. The while loop is used to locate Edwin's record. After this his wife's name, Catherine, is added to the customer list. Since both Edwin and Catherine share the same address and last name, the values for the other fields are inserted in the table.

```
WebShoppeTable = database.cursor("SELECT * FROM Customers", true);
while(WebShoppeTable.Last_Name != "Edwin") {
     WebShoppeTable.next();
}
WebShoppeTable. Title = "Ms";
WebShoppeTable. First_Name = "Catherine";
WebShoppeTable.email = "catherine@service.provider.com";
WebShoppeTable.insertRow("Customers");
WebShoppeTable.close();
```

deleteRow() method.   The deleteRow() method is similar to the SQL DELETE
statement. The difference between the two is that instead of deleting all rows
that match the results of the SELECT statement, the deleteRow() method
deletes the record marked by the cursor. For example, the following code illustrates the use of the deleteRow() method to delete the record of a particular
customer from a table.

```
WebShoppeTable = database.cursor("SELECT * FROM Customers", true);
while(WebShoppeTable.Last_Name != "Hall") {
 WebShoppeTable.next();
}
WebShoppeTable.deleteRow("Customers");
WebShoppeTable.close();
```

All three methods of the updatable cursor accept a single string argument that
contains the name of the table in the database where the row is to be updated, inserted,
or deleted. It is important to include the name of the table of the database in the statement instead of the name assigned to the cursor object.

SQLTable() Method

One of the modes that works the fastest to return database information to the client is
the use of the SQLTable() method. The SQLTable() method returns the results of a
SELECT statement to the client in the form of an HTML table. The HTML table consists
of rows and columns that correspond to a database table's records and fields. In addition, a header row containing the name or caption of each field is added in the HTML
table. However, it is interesting to note that the formatting of the table returned to the
client cannot be changed. The following example illustrates the use of the
SQLTable() method to return an HTML table to the client.

```
write("<H2>Welcome to Web Shoppe</H2>");
database.SQLTable("SELECT * FROM Customers ORDER BY
Last_Name, First_Name");
```

Transaction Processing with LiveWire

A transaction can be defined as a group of one or more database operations. Almost all
databases perform transactions during updates. As a result, sets of database operations

are performed as a single unit. During transaction processing, a lock is obtained that prevents other scripts from interfering with the progress of the transaction. The database object of LiveWire supports transaction processing.

A transaction is initiated by invoking the `beginTransaction()` method. The changes and proceedings of a transaction are saved and closed using the `commitTransaction()` method. In addition, you can use the `rollBackTransaction()` method to undo a transaction before it is committed. The following code illustrates the use of transaction processing to add a new customer record to the Customer table:

```
WebShoppeTable = database.cursor("SELECT * FROM Customers",
true);
database.beginTransaction();
while(WebShoppeTable.Last_Name != "Edwin") {
     WebShoppeTable.next();
}
WebShoppeTable. Title = "Ms";
WebShoppeTable. First_Name = "Catherine";
WebShoppeTable.email = "catherine@service.provider.com";
WebShoppeTable.insertRow("Customers");
WebShoppeTable.close();database.commitTransaction();
employeesTable.close();
```

Summary

In this chapter, you learned how LiveWire can be used to create server-side JavaScript and establish database connectivity. In the initial sections of the chapter, we discussed the client/server environment, which is a typical setup for Web applications. We discussed how the introduction of the Internet and the subsequent changes in the system setup led to the introduction of two- and three-tier system architecture.

Then we discussed the standards and syntax of server-side JavaScript. In the course of the discussions, it was reiterated that the language syntax of both client- and server-side JavaScript is the same. The only difference lies in the use of server-specific objects, methods, and properties. In this context, we discussed the four server-side objects: `request`, `client`, `server`, and `project`.

We then discussed the use of LiveWire to connect to a database in order to retrieve and manipulate data from a database table. We discussed the use of a database management system, which is an application or a collection of applications used to create, access, and manage a database. We also discussed Open Database Connectivity that allows written applications to access any data source by using an ODBC driver.

In the final sections, we discussed how the three `database` objects are used to connect to a database and retrieve and manipulate the data in a table. We discussed the use of the `execute()`, `cursor()`, and `SQLTable()` methods to send SQL statements to a database and fetch the retrieved records in a record set.

Index